SMALLVILLE

SEASON 4

THE OFFICIAL COMPANION

Superman created by Jerry Siegel and Joe Shuster

SMALLVILLE: THE OFFICIAL COMPANION SEASON 4
ISBN-10: 1 84023 957 3
ISBN-13: 9781840239577

Published by
Titan Books
A division of
Titan Publishing Group Ltd
144 Southwark St
London
SE1 0UP

First edition May 2007
10 9 8 7 6 5 4 3 2 1

Visit our websites:
www.titanbooks.com
www.dccomics.com

Did you enjoy this book? We love to hear from our readers.
Please e-mail us at: **readerfeedback@titanemail.com**
or write to Reader Feedback at the above address.

A CIP catalogue record for this title is available from the British Library.

Printed and bound in Canada.

SMALLVILLE

SEASON 4

THE OFFICIAL COMPANION

Craig Byrne

TITAN BOOKS

ACKNOWLEDGEMENTS

Special thanks go out to everyone who helped make this book a reality. Folks deserving a special shoutout are Susan Kesser and Kendra Voth, for getting the interviews rolling; Chris Cerasi at DC Comics for your constant support and answers to any questions I ever have; Danny Lee, Neil Sadhu, and Erin Fitzgerald for further interview coordination; the visitors of KryptonSite, without whom I would have never had the chance to do this book in the first place; Bryan, Jesse, Jennifer, Tabitha, Cheryl, Melanie, Kat, The Brat, Logan, Brian, Jayme, Andre and Jake who provided support both online and offline to help me get this all finished; my Mom, the best mother this side of Martha Kent; and Adam Newell, Cath Trechman and Victoria Nemeth, the editorial folks at Titan who made this all happen.

I'd also like to thank the following cast and crew members from *Smallville* who gave their time to be interviewed for this book: Alfred Gough, Miles Millar, Annette O'Toole, John Glover, John Schneider, Allison Mack, Erica Durance, Kyle Gallner, Christine O'Connor, Rick Faraci, Christopher Sayour, Caroline Cranstoun, Mike Walls, Steve DeKnight, Todd Slavkin, Darren Swimmer, Holly Harold, Mark Warshaw, Brian Peterson, Kelly Souders, and Greg Beeman.
— Craig Byrne

The publishers would like to thank the following people who contributed to the *Torch* and *Ledger* articles featured in this book: Mark Warshaw, Jake Black, Genevieve Sparling, Caroline Dires and Chris Freyer. Many thanks to the *Official Smallville Magazine* and interviewers Paul Simpson and Richard Matthews. Thanks also to John Glover for letting us use his photograph on page 153. We would also like to thank Chris Cerasi at DC Comics, and the cast and crew of *Smallville* for all their help with this project.

DEDICATION
This book is dedicated to the memory of my father, Clyde "Bud" Byrne.

CONTENTS

FOREWORD
BY ANNETTE O'TOOLE

Dear Smallvillians,

Welcome to my world, which is one of muffin-baking and hero-training, especially in season four.

As I write this, we are just finishing up season six, so the amazing walking encyclopedia of *Smallville* lore, Craig Byrne, reminded me of what took place in the fourth season episodes. Here's what I remember most from that year:

Clark FLYING in 'Crusade'. Greg Beeman directed the sequence beautifully and skillfully (as he always does), and I remember having to freeze in a very awkward position while Tom crouched into his take-off. Since I couldn't hold that sort of pose myself for very long, the grips (sort of movie stagehands) built a stand for me to lean on. Our visual effects supervisor, John Wash, somehow erased the stand from the film so all you are left with is Martha frozen in a fall as Clark zooms away. It was so much fun to film, and even more fun to watch. I was as amazed and excited as anyone to see it — it is actually my favorite moment of any season.

Margot Kidder as Bridgette Crosby in 'Crusade'. She was absolutely wonderful, and I had a very happy day working with her. She had a ton of really difficult dialogue to get out, and she nailed it every time.

Clark and Lionel switching bodies in 'Transference'. It was creepy and hilarious to do the scenes with each of them playing the other's part.

Martha being possessed in 'Spirit' and singing (very badly) that Ashlee Simpson song, 'La La'.

The teamwork on this show is the truly amazing thing about it. The crew are the most dedicated, lovely, hard-working people I have ever known. *Smallville* is such a technically difficult show to do, and the crew work miracles every day to bring it all to cinematic life. We have become a pretty close group.

I hope you enjoy this book; it will give you lots more insight into our fourth season. It's been my privilege to play Martha. I love her very much because she is the kind of hero we can all try to be. She is kind, honest (well, as much as she can be seeing that her son is an alien), works hard, and looks for the good in people.

With love,

Annette

P.S. Martha has a secret crush on Perry White. He came to Metropolis U and gave a journalism lecture, which she attended when she went to school there. She spoke to him briefly afterward, but had a date with Jonathan so didn't stick around.

INTO SEASON FOUR

EXT. KENT FARM — DAY

Martha steps forward, staring in disbelief at wisps of smoke rising from the grassy field. CAMERA CRANES UP TO REVEAL

A GIANT KRYPTONIAN SYMBOL

mysteriously scorched into the grass. OFF Martha, troubled by the ominous sign...

                                                 CUT BACK TO:

INT. PRISONER INTAKE AREA - FEDERAL DETENTION CENTER — DAY
The BUZZING clippers CLICK off. The Barber unsnaps the cape and whips it off to reveal

LIONEL IS COMPLETELY BALD,
looking eerily like Lex Luthor. As Lionel runs his hand over his pate...

                                              MATCH CUT TO:

INT. LIBRARY — LUTHOR MANSION — DAY
CLOSE ON: LEX'S HAIRLESS HEAD. REVEAL Lex standing before the fireplace, amber light dancing across his face as he twirls brandy in a snifter. Relieved after the day's events,

LEX DRINKS
his first sip. As he savors the taste, an odd look comes over his face, then he begins to gasp,

HIS HAND DROPPING THE SNIFTER,
crystal SHATTERING. Lex staggers back, clutching his chest, the color draining from his face as his lips turn blue. He collapses,

FALLING THROUGH THE COFFEE TABLE
in a shower of glass. As he convulses, OFF Lex, curling into a fetal position, his life ebbing away...

                                              MATCH CUT TO:

INT. VOID
Clark is curled into a fetal position, naked, suspended in blackness, his eyes open in a trance-like state.
                                 VOICE
                      Kal-El, my son. Now you shall be reborn.

Clark's eyes don't blink as a tide of Kryptonian symbols begins to slowly swirl around him. CAMERA SLOWLY PULLS BACK TO REVEAL Clark is surrounded by a never-ending ocean of rotating symbols. As Clark recedes further and further away into the enigmatic void, OFF the stunning image...

                                                 FADE OUT.

                      END OF SEASON THREE

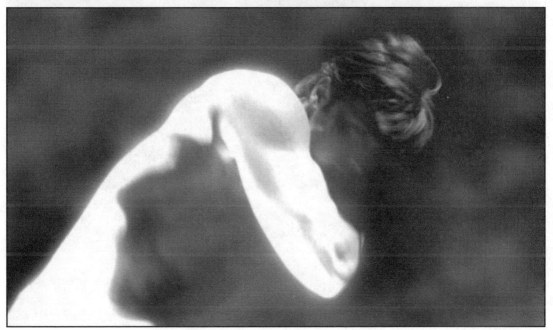

"The theme of this season is graduation." — Miles Millar

Below: Clark Kent, football hero.

Opposite above: Lois Lane meets Lana Lang... and Clark has got his work cut out for him.

Opposite below: Lois Lane enrols at Smallville High.

After three years of telling the story of young Clark Kent and his adventures as a teen, it seemed time for a shift. "As good as I think the third season was, I think it just got very dark and a little too adult," Alfred Gough said in an interview prior to the start of season four. "We got a little too sci-fi and it lost the core idea of Clark Kent before he's Superman, in high school dealing with his issues, and this year we try to get back to that." So, with the advent of the show's fourth season in September 2004, it was time to return to the show's lighter roots. It was announced that Clark would be joining the football team, as he had in John Byrne's classic comic book mini-series, *The Man of Steel*, and in Jeph Loeb's seminal young Clark Kent

story *Superman For All Seasons*.

Also promised for the new season was a respite from the angst-ridden relationship between Clark and his high school love interest Lana Lang. "We played the Clark and Lana relationship for sixty-odd episodes," Miles Millar said that summer in the *Official Smallville Magazine*. "Enough already —let's find something else. He's always going to love her, so that for us is still the core, and he can be the unrequited love for her."

New additions for the fourth year included Erica Durance, playing Superman's future lady love, Lois Lane. The character would be coming to Smallville to learn the truth about the apparent death of her cousin, Chloe Sullivan. Also joining *Smallville* in its fourth year would be Jensen Ackles as Jason Teague, a potential romantic connection for Lana who she would meet while in Paris. "Those two characters are really helping to reinvigorate the show and the storylines with some new dynamics and new triangles," Gough promised.

After the success of the season three episode 'Perry', more ties to the comic book mythology were planned. DC Comics' Impulse and Superman foe Mr. Mxyzptlk were included on the season four agenda. Also on deck were some changes for Lana. "I think the fans will be the most satisfied, the most intrigued, and the most surprised, by what's going to happen to Lana," *Smallville* director and executive producer Greg Beeman said prior to the season's launch.

The final promise for season four was that the year's story arc — beginning with 'Crusade' — would all come together in a "very big" final moment that would play a major role in the overall Superman mythology.

With WB promotions showing a flying Clark Kent and the iconic tagline 'Look Up', fans were anxious and excited to see what was in store for the new season. ∎

THE EPISODES

"Three relics hidden around the world by scientifically advanced ancient cultures. Legend has it that when united, they point the way to a treasury of knowledge that puts the Library of Alexandria to shame."

— Lex Luthor

SEASON 4 REGULAR CAST:

Tom Welling (Clark Kent)

Kristin Kreuk (Lana Lang)

Michael Rosenbaum (Lex Luthor)

Jensen Ackles (Jason Teague)

Allison Mack (Chloe Sullivan)

John Glover (Lionel Luthor)

John Schneider (Jonathan Kent)

Annette O'Toole (Martha Kent)

CRUSADE: IN DEPTH

WRITTEN BY: Alfred Gough & Miles Millar
DIRECTED BY: Greg Beeman

GUEST STARS: Erica Durance (Lois Lane), Rekha Sharma (Dr. Harden), Margot Kidder (Bridgette Crosby), Ona Grauer (Dr. Gabrielle Vaughn), Dan Joffre (Hospital Receptionist), Helena Yea (Old Lady in Hospital)

Three months have passed since anyone has seen Clark Kent. A young woman comes to Smallville searching for answers about her cousin Chloe Sullivan, who was killed in a safe house explosion just days before she was to testify against Lionel Luthor in court. Her journey leads her directly into the path of an amnesiac, naked Clark. She introduces herself to the naked stranger as "Lois. Lois Lane."

On the other side of the world, deep in an Egyptian pyramid, researchers find a statuette containing a sacred artifact. A sickly Lex Luthor arrives to collect the prize, which features a Kryptonian inscription on its obverse.

Still studying art in Paris, Lana has become romantically involved with a young man named Jason Teague. Smallville seems to be part of her past until a carving of the French Countess Margaret Isobel Thoreaux creates a new mystery — a mystery that is somehow tied to a strange symbol now permanently tattooed on Lana's back.

Clark is reunited with his mother, but fails to recognize the people in the family photos she shows him. Summoned by an ultrasonic sound, Clark takes off into the sky, intent on procuring Lex's recently obtained fire element. Dr. Swann sends his emissary, Bridgette Crosby, to provide Martha with a special form of kryptonite — her "only hope" for restoring the real Clark. When exposed to the black kryptonite, the two sides of Clark battle, and his human side emerges victorious. Later, he meets up with Lois by Chloe's grave. Using his X-ray vision, Clark discovers that no one is buried in the coffin...

CLARK: I am Kal-El of Krypton. It is time to fulfill my destiny.

After the incredibly exciting finale to the show's third season, the creators of *Smallville* knew that they had to produce a season première that would maintain that momentum. It was a challenge that the show's creators rose to by bringing in two famous elements of Superman lore — the power of flight... and the introduction of Lois Lane.

"Writing the season four opener was like writing a new pilot, with the introduction of Lois and Jason," Al Gough said. "All of the relationship dynamics had changed. I think we embraced the fact that in many ways the series was approaching middle age, and we had to shake things up and add new characters, new dynamics, and bring in new ideas."

When we meet Lois Lane she is headed to Smallville with hopes of learning the truth behind her cousin Chloe's death. "Chloe is one of those best friends that maybe you don't see for a while, but when you get back together, it's like no time has passed at all, and you feel safe," Erica Durance said about the relationship between Lois and Chloe. "She's the one person that I think Lois really does feel safe with. It's the one relationship

Opposite: WB Network promotions advised viewers to 'Look Up' for the season première.

Smallville ⬤ Ledger

ONE WITNESS GONE!

With only two weeks left before Lionel Luthor stands trial for murder, stunning new developments once again place the former CEO of LuthorCorp in the center of speculation. Clark Kent, a witness for the prosecution conspicuously absent for the past several months, has returned.

Kent's return may prove consequential in a case that Luthor's attorneys argue is largely built on circumstantial evidence. When asked about Kent's mysterious absence and then sudden return, Gwendolyn Reed, counsel for Luthor, seemed unconcerned about the possible ramifications the teenager could have on the trial.

"Mr. Kent's recent absence and, likewise, his sudden return do not surprise us in the least. He is, after all, only a teenager," Reed said in a public statement yesterday. "Such impulsive and irresponsible behavior is common with people his age, a fact I am confident the jury will also recognize when considering Mr. Kent's testimony." Kent was unavailable for comment.

Kent's renewed participation in the trial seems to be a twist of fate for Lionel Luthor. But twists of fate seem standard these days. Chloe Sullivan, another student at Smallville High and primary witness for the prosecution, is presumed dead after a house she entered exploded three months ago.

As a key witness in a federally prosecuted trial, Sullivan's death was under investigation until recently. Details of the explosion were kept secret during that time, but her death is now attributed to an accidental gas explosion.

Without Sullivan's testimony, the outcome of Luthor's trial is unclear. "Miss Sullivan's untimely death was, of course, tragic and regretful," Reed said, when asked about the investigation. "I offer my deepest sympathies to those she left behind," she added.

One of those people is Lois Lane, a cousin of Sullivan's. "I just can't believe Chloe's actually gone," Lane said in a phone interview. "I keep thinking that, if I just look a little deeper, I'll find her."

With such tragedy and mystery already surrounding Luthor's trial, one can only hope that it will be a matter of time before the truth is unearthed from the labyrinthine tunnels of death and destruction winding around this case.

By Paige Montgomery

she had growing up that was true, with no pressure, and with unconditional love. That is what drives her to try to solve Chloe's murder.

"I do remember a point where I got quite nervous, when we were about to start," Erica Durance remembered of her first days on set. "I looked at the slate and it said 'Smallville, Lois Lane' under it. I kind of looked over my shoulder, thinking 'Oh, who is going to be doing that?' And then I realized 'Oh, that's me!' There were definitely the nerves that accompany that sort of thing, but everybody was lovely and gracious. All in

all, it was really great, it was just nerve-wracking at first!"

Above: A new side of Clark Kent awakens.

LOIS: You've just been hit by lightning, you're stark naked, and, uh, you don't even remember your own name. You have a fairly loose definition of "fine".

One of Durance's first scenes in the episode involved Lois coming across a naked Clark in a corn field, and Erica often gets asked exactly what Tom Welling wore when that sequence was being filmed. "Everybody wants me to say that he was wearing nothing," she laughed, "but we're a purely professional set. I can tell you this much — it was strange enough to film after having barely met him. I was actually blushing a little bit. Not because there was anything to see, but because the whole scenario was so ridiculous. I barely knew this person, and I knew everybody was watching to see 'Is she going to react properly?'" she recalled. "Tom is a really, really nice guy and he is very easygoing, and you just have to laugh a lot. I think it was such a great story point, anyway, for Lois to have that in her back pocket, that no matter how tough and awesome he thinks he gets, she has seen him naked; that was really clever on the part of the writers."

Erica very quickly impressed her fellow cast members. "She was grand," Annette O'Toole said of Durance's work in 'Crusade'. "She has always been there 110 percent in wanting to learn, and she was great. I remember being really pleasantly surprised that

Above: Lois Lane makes her début.

they cast someone like her."

"Erica Durance plays her very well," writer Holly Harold commented. "Lois is so honest and from the heart, and will say things just because they need to be said, whether or not she knows how she's going to affect somebody else. She's the girl that blurts that out. She's also the girl that would rush into trouble to save anybody, no matter what the risk to herself, which actually makes her, in her own way, as heroic as Clark Kent. To go into a situation knowing you could be killed is, to me, amazing and brave, and Lois would never hesitate."

Also making his *Smallville* début was Jensen Ackles as Jason Teague. The veteran of such TV series as *Days Of Our Lives*, *Dark Angel*, and *Dawson's Creek* was quickly assimilated into the cast, and had an immediate on-screen chemistry with Kristin Kreuk, who plays Lana. The two characters met during Lana's sojourn in France — a location that was realized by the simple creation of a matte painting of a Paris background inserted into the Vancouver skyline by a computer in post-production.

Beyond the introductions of Lois Lane and Jason Teague, the other much-anticipated event 'Crusade' was famous for was the very first sequence where Clark Kent flew. Correction — it was not Clark, but his all-Kryptonian alter-ego Kal-El that took flight. "It's a little like Dumbo," Al Gough mused. "Clark has it within him, it's just a level of maturity that he hasn't reached yet in order to do it."

"I loved it when he flew," Annette O'Toole said. "It was thrilling. Tom was just standing there crouched, and then when you see it, it's like, wow! He takes off. Things

that are Superman-related, like flying for the first time, are huge."

JASON: I'm supposed to meet my girlfriend here. Well, she's not really my girlfriend, even though we spend every waking moment together. See, we met two months ago today on this exact street corner, and I bought her something to mark the occasion. I wanted to get your opinion.

"Clark flying was a lot of fun," the episode's director, Greg Beeman, said. "It was very hard on Tom. We built a special rig for him to lay in, and then we hung him on this gigantic, five-sided green screen stage, and we swooped the camera around him. Mat Beck [visual effects supervisor] filmed some of those key shots. Also, the sequence where he takes off, and the way Annette freezes and the ground distorts, and the way he rippled and flew through the air and everything starts swirling around; filmically, that was all satisfying."

"We did a bunch of green screen work with Tom," stunt coordinator Chris Sayour shared, "and he did, as usual, fantastically. He's one of the better actors with wires. He just took to it naturally. He learned to keep his body in good positions and look as real as possible to give the effect that the audience loves."

Despite the favorable reaction to Clark's flight on the show, it is not something that special effects supervisor Mike Walls would like to see all that often. "We're pretty true

Above: New year, new love. Lana Lang meets Jason Teague in Paris.

to form when it's 'No flights, no tights' on this show," he said. "At times, it's like 'Oh, it'd be really great to be able to have that power,' but it forces us to be able to think of other ways of handling a problem."

Another intricate effects sequence in 'Crusade' came by Isobel's tomb, as Lana is filled with a bright light after rubbing a carving of the Countess. "That was mostly in the computer with a lighting crew helping out," Walls revealed. "They actually cut away when you see the light hitting her face, it's just a lighting effect at that point. Only when you are looking at the actual crypt and you see the shafts of light coming out, do you see where the computer took over."

Since Jonathan Kent was hospitalized, Annette O'Toole's Martha Kent was given a rare chance to be the one to bring her son back to "normal". "I was really glad when it happened because up until then it had always been Jonathan going after him. It was nice to be the one to be really active and save the day," she noted. To rescue Clark, Martha Kent summoned help from a famous face from Superman lore.

"Originally, we had talked to Christopher Reeve about being in the season four première," Al Gough revealed. "We wanted a scene with Martha and Swann, where Swann gives her the black kryptonite to change Clark back from Kal.

"We talked to Chris three months before his death about returning. He was directing a movie at the time. He was interested, but he didn't want Swann to come to Smallville; he felt they would come to him," Gough continued. When it became clear that Reeve would be unable to reprise his role, the producers got the idea of bringing in the woman who famously played Lois Lane in the four *Superman* movies from decades past.

MARTHA KENT: You don't know anything about my son!
DR. CROSBY: You're right, I don't. But I do know what it's like to love someone whose calling is greater than your own.

Margot Kidder was recruited to play Dr. Bridgette Crosby, an emissary for Dr. Swann. Her scene in the barn with Annette O'Toole reunited the two actresses who appeared together as Lois Lane and Lana Lang in the film *Superman III*.

"It was fabulous," Annette said. "It was just her and me for the most part, and we had a lovely time. We talked about our kids. She has a grandchild, and we talked about that, and it was just really fun to be with her again. She was so kind to me when we did *Superman III*, though I was pretty much her replacement. She was absolutely generous about all that."

Below: Lois Lane tells her strange new friend that Smallville Medical Center is where he needs to be.

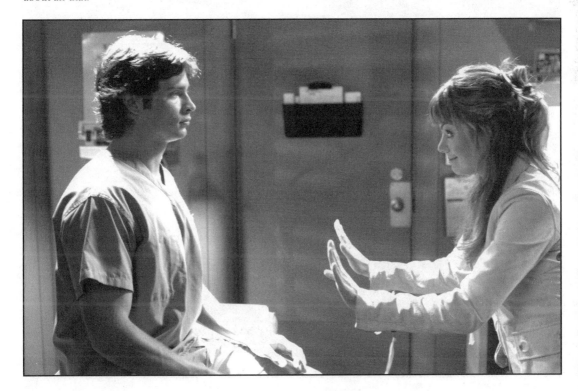

"There was a real camaraderie between Margot and Annette," Greg Beeman recalled. "They kind of came out of the same era, and they had a lot of respect for each other, and so that scene was very enjoyable."

Once Martha had obtained the black kryptonite, it was up to her to bring her son back home safely. The exposure to this newly discovered form of kryptonite temporarily split Clark into two beings — his human side, and his Kryptonian side. "We had to be really careful as to how it was staged," Mike Walls revealed. "Whenever you see Clark interacting with himself, there was always a body double there. We had to be really precise in terms of where the face was and in terms of hand positioning, so that we could always change the face out if we had to. It was a little difficult, but not overly so. I thought it went very smoothly."

Ultimately, Clark's Kryptonian half is defeated by his human side. Just as the two halves of Clark are fused, Jonathan simultaneously and miraculously awakens in his hospital bed.

One long-standing mystery among fans concerns a group known as 'The Seers'. News of these robed characters arriving leaked onto the Internet in the summer of 2004, but when 'Crusade' finally aired, these enigmatic characters were nowhere to be found. "It was to be a version of the Illuminati," writer Todd Slavkin explained. "At one point we felt the stones might be part of a secret, global organization that possibly involved Virgil Swann and Lionel Luthor. That idea was nixed in favor of making the plot smaller and more contained."

Opposite above and below: *Smallville's* special effects wizards create one of their most exciting sequences to date.

Above: Black kryptonite unleashes the two sides of Clark.

SMALLVILLE TORCH

TORCH EDITOR PRESUMED DEAD, FUTURE OF NEWSPAPER UNKNOWN

Below: Lana finds a mysterious new tattoo on her back...

Opposite above: Lois vs. Lionel.

Opposite below: Lois pays her respects to her departed cousin.

If you're reading this you probably know of Chloe Sullivan. She was a friend, an honors student, and a charge of verbal energy. To us at the *Torch*, she was our pioneering editor-in-chief known for keeping tabs on Smallville's "weirdar" and exposing the truth with daily injections of wit and braininess.

The sudden and mysterious death of the SHS student is, ironically, the type of story Chloe loved to chase.

By Caroline Dries

An intricate prison set was created for John Glover's Lionel Luthor, and the episode gave Lionel some great scenes opposite both his son and Lois Lane. "We had a great time together," Glover said of the scene he shared with Erica Durance. "We both thought that we would continue working together, but then they dropped that part of the story." Their brief time together still gave Lionel a chance to observe and figure out this smart young woman who could potentially become an enemy down the line. "She bites her nails," Glover said. "Lionel's so smart, he looks for those weaknesses; the Achilles heel. I remember looking down and seeing that and I added it into a scene, saying, 'Oh, you bite your nails?' That was a big clue to who she really was, for all the external beauty."

Most everyone involved was pleased with the final result of the season four première. "'Crusade' was fantastic," Greg Beeman concluded. "Both in terms of the direction and the production, I had some of the most amazing experiences, beyond what you get to do normally in television. I was very happy with 'Crusade'. I thought that Tom did a great job playing Kal-El and having no memory, and I thought Lois was introduced to the show very well." ∎

GONE

WRITTEN BY: Kelly Souders & Brian Peterson

DIRECTED BY: James Marshall

GUEST STARS: Erica Durance (Lois Lane), Robert Wisden (Gabe Sullivan), Colin Lawrence (Agent Stockard), Michael Ironside (General Sam Lane), James Bell (Trent MacGowan), James Michalopolous (Prisoner)

Suspecting that Chloe might still be alive, Clark and Lois investigate the remains of the safe house. They are interrupted by the sound of a helicopter, as operatives in black approach them with stun rifles. Clark's heat vision downs the chopper and they escape.

Lana discovers that her tattoo is identical to a symbol in the Kawatche caves and she decides to return to Smallville.

Lois finds her cousin's grave empty, but is attacked by a man who can turn his arms into razor-sharp metal blades. After a timely save by Lana, Lois returns to the Kent farm. Lois's father, General Sam Lane, arrives to take her back to Fort Ryan. Lois seizes this opportunity to look through the files in his office back at the base. There she finds herself face to face with Clark, who is performing his own investigation. Together they find Chloe's new safe house, but inside Clark discovers two dead men — and Lex. Clark speeds off to find Chloe at the Smallville Foundry.

The man who attacked Lois at the cemetery, Trent, has taken Chloe to the foundry. Lois and Clark take down Trent, and Chloe is finally safe and able to testify against Lionel. Lionel is officially locked behind bars. Lex, now in full control of LuthorCorp, watches smugly as his father is taken to his new 'home'.

Meanwhile, Jason Teague turns up at Lana's apartment, having relocated to Smallville to be with her.

CLARK: Uh... we usually take turns in the bathroom.

LOIS: Oh, don't start with me, Smallville. You're the one taking the marathon shower. Besides, my delicate feminine sensibilities weren't offended the first time I got a glimpse of Clark Junior.

Veteran character actor Michael Ironside was cast in this episode and in 'Facade' as Lois's no-nonsense father, General Sam Lane. "We always knew that Lois had this very tough, sort of gruff side to her," writer Kelly Souders explained. "It made sense that her father should be really gruff, to show that's where that part of her personality came from. Introducing him gave us a chance to show a part of her past, to explain the psychology of Lois Lane."

The backstory for the General was tied heavily to the background of his comic book incarnation. "We actually worked quite a bit with Jeph Loeb, along with Al [Gough] and

Opposite: A new face in Smallville: Lois Lane!

'A Long Way' by Dara Shindler
'She Will Be Loved' (Acoustic
Version) by Maroon 5

Miles [Millar], to come up with that backstory," Brian Peterson revealed. "I know Jeph had a lot of references in the comic books that it sprang from, and then we molded the story, as far as how it actually played into our show."

CLARK: The truth is, he's been lying to me from day one. The legend on the cave wall says I'm destined to have an enemy. All this time, I've been worried about Lionel. But I'm beginning to think that the real threat was right in front of me. I think it's Lex.

Although reaction to Ironside's performance as the General was favorable, the *Smallville* writers are in no hurry to bring him back, unless he could be serviced in the right kind of story. "I think what we find is, a lot of times when we veer too far off from our main cast, the episodes aren't as compelling," Peterson lamented. "If we center stories around people that are too far removed from our cast, even though he is Lois's father, unless we were to actually go completely into his world with the military... it

Below: Martha discovers that Clark and Lois seem to be bonding already.

Daily Planet

METROPOLIS' GREATEST NEWSPAPER

GUILTY!

After Chloe Sullivan's damning testimony yesterday, Metropolis titan Lionel Luthor was found guilty of murdering his parents in a tenement fire. Luthor's attorney Gwendolyn Reed's case was shattered by the surprising return of Sullivan, who was presumed dead just forty-eight hours ago. Reed rushed out of the courthouse without her confident swagger. She promised to appeal the jury's "idiotic decision".

The key evidence existed in a ten-second sound bite obtained by Sullivan in which Luthor admitted to the murder.

"Did you order Morgan Edge to kill your parents?" Sullivan asked after activating the voicemail on her hidden Verizon cell phone.

"Of course," said Luthor. "Their life insurance provided the seed money I needed to start my company."

The confession was enough to get the jury's unanimous guilty verdict.

Luthor's son Lex was among the many attendees crammed into the at-capacity courtroom. Witnesses claim to have seen the emotionally reserved Lex breathe a sigh of relief after the jury announced its decision. "It's over, and we can all move on with our lives," he said, before he slid into his Carrera. With his father now behind bars, Lex will now officially assume Lionel Luthor's former role as CEO of LuthorCorp.

Sullivan fielded questions on the courthouse steps. "It took a lot of stars to line up just right in order for us to get Lionel Luthor behind bars," Sullivan said. "Oh, and p.s., those of you who bounced early at my wake — ya missed a stellar cheese tray."

By Caroline Dries

wouldn't have the emotional resonance that it does if our stories stay centered around Chloe, Clark, Lana, and Lex."

Near the episode's climax, Chloe Sullivan was finally found and rescued by Clark and Lois. "It was never a consideration to keep Chloe dead," executive producer Al Gough confirmed.

With Chloe's testimony, Lionel Luthor was convicted and sentenced during his trial. A scene where Chloe prepares for the trial was originally shot for the episode and is included on the fourth season DVD set, but it did not make it to the final aired cut of the show. "Our show isn't really a trial show," Brian Peterson explained. "It was much more interesting just to see what happened before and after, rather than the whole trial."

The final moments of 'Gone' brought Jason Teague from Paris into the world of Smallville and reunited him with Lana. "I think after Clark Kent, Jason Teague was such a wonderful reprieve," writer Todd Slavkin commented. "He was warmhearted, seemingly had no secrets whatsoever, cared about Lana, and treated her like a princess. His whole life revolved around her. So, for Lana, he was a nice, comforting guy after a very troublesome season three." ■

DID YOU KNOW?

An early draft of the script for 'Gone' had a scene between Clark and Dr. Virgil Swann, where Clark accused Dr. Swann of sending the helicopter after him and Lois. The scene was cut when Christopher Reeve's schedule limited his availability.

FACADE

WRITTEN BY: Holly Harold
DIRECTED BY: Pat Williams

GUEST STARS: Erica Durance (Lois Lane), Jared Keeso (Nate), Michael Ironside (General Sam Lane), Lee Rumohr (Brett Anderson), Rob Freeman (Coach Quigley), Brianna Lynn Brown (Abigail Fine), Julianne Christie (Dr. Elise Fine), Eric Johnson (Whitney Fordman)

DID YOU KNOW?

One of Brianna Lynn Brown's early roles was as a train passenger in the movie *Spider-Man 2.*

A girl named Abby who used to be mercilessly teased, comes back to Smallville High with a new look, thanks to a special treatment from her mother involving serotonin and meteor rocks. An unfortunate side effect of this treatment is that anyone whom Abby kisses hallucinates that they have become hideous.

Lois Lane grudgingly starts classes at Smallville High and joins the *Torch*. Chloe assigns her an article about the typical insecurities and shallowness of high school, where people hide who they really are for fear of rejection. Clark considers joining the football squad, despite Jonathan's protests. Dr. Fine, Abby's mother, tells Lana that her tattoo is not made of ink; instead, it may be some sort of a brand. Dr. Fine learns that Lana saw Abby with Brett (who after kissing Abby was convinced his face was decaying and ran out into traffic and was hit by Lois) and sends her daughter after Lana. Abby kisses Lana, causing her to become insecure about her relationship with Jason.

Lois also goes to visit Dr. Fine to uncover the truth about her methods. The doctor quickly realizes the ruse and confines Lois to the same apparatus used to 'treat' Abby. Clark rescues Lois, and Dr. Fine is jailed. Lois's first article is the hit of the school paper, and Clark and Jonathan come to an understanding about his playing football. Jason assures Lana that his attraction to her goes beyond the superficial.

LOIS: No hard feelings, cuz, but unlike you, the last thing I want to be is a reporter.

"Kids can be victimized by their parents," writer Holly Harold said of this episode about plastic surgery gone wrong. "Their parents try to live out their own dreams through their children. Plus, teenage plastic surgery is just a huge and very controversial subject. Is it the right thing to do? Is it the wrong thing to do? It was a really fun topic to embrace; to try to figure out the ins and outs and the morality of that."

The episode not only reestablished the high school elements of the series, it also gave Lois Lane her first shot at journalism. Lois takes on a spot at the *Torch* when she is a few credits short of finishing high school. "Lois is such a fun character, and she's such a rebel and a renegade that we wanted to do something that would bring her back down to earth, bring her a little bit more on a level playing field with our characters, because she's more worldly and had been out there," Harold noted. "So it was thrusting her back into everybody's nightmare: high school, which was very fun."

Opposite: Lana and Jason share a secret kiss.

FACADE

The writers of the show knew that this would be their last year to do high school stories, and they decided to start their first story of senior year with a flashback to the days of season one. Hair and make-up techniques from *Smallville*'s first season were purposely recreated for the flashback sequence. "We had a lot of hair issues and wardrobe issues in season one, especially for the first five or six episodes," frequent *Smallville* director and executive producer Greg Beeman shared. "About halfway through season one we got the right team and we started to be happier with the hair. So when we suddenly had a flashback [to that time], Miles and Al were in on the joke and were supportive of it, and we decided let's go to the bad hairstyles, let's go to the bad clothes, let's call that all back. It was a very conscious effort."

LOIS: Call me crazy, but I've always been a firm believer that beauty... it's on the inside.
DR. FINE: The only people that say that are the ones who already have it on the outside.

Also returning for the flashback sequence was Eric Johnson, who portrayed Whitney Fordman in *Smallville*'s first season, and in the season two episode 'Visage'. "I love Eric; he's a great guy," Beeman said. "It's always a little bittersweet for him to

Below: Chloe examines the facts.

come back to *Smallville*, but he has always been great about it, and he was great in 'Facade' playing Whitney."

In early drafts of the episode's script, Abby's doctor was not her mother. "We've had to do so many different kinds of shows on *Smallville*," Holly Harold said. "We've done road rage and steroid rage and crazy people and homicidal killers. But the one that really touched a nerve was plastic surgery. There was a lot of discussion and debate, and at one point the girl was getting revenge on the people who were mean to her in high school, but then that didn't seem very sympathetic." The "pusher parent" approach seemed to work better for the episode that was ultimately shot.

"Chloe has a line that I love about, 'The world is better to pretty people,' which is very true in a horrible, sad way," Harold reflected. "Reality shows right now [about makeovers] are huge, because people want to embrace that dream. We also made sure that there was nothing wrong with this girl in the first place, so it was a bit of a twist on that.

"Abby was a really sweet girl who was victimized by her mother. At least, that's the way it came out in the end." ∎

SMALLVILLE TORCH

SKIN DEEP

Thousands of teens every year decide they are unhappy with their self-image and want to get plastic surgery. But is it something that is truly needed, or is it something that is brought on by peer pressure?

The recent admission of Dr. Elise Fine, mother of Abby, revealed that the pressure sometimes might come from a source as unlikely as one's parents. "When I was your age, I wasn't exactly homecoming queen," she told this reporter. "I worked harder than all the pretty girls only to watch everything get handed to them. It took seven surgeries and two years, but all that changed."

Dr. Fine took her obsession with appearance to the next level by practically forcing a treatment upon her daughter. "I didn't want to see my daughter go through the pain I endured to have what other girls are lucky enough to be born with."

Young people today should be proud of who they are, and should let themselves grow naturally into their adult bodies. You never know... that awkward nerd in glasses in high school might be the unattainable object of desire once adulthood rolls around. Hopefully Abby Fine will make a full recovery, though the pain inflicted by her psycho mom might have given her scars deeper than anything you could have on your face.

So before you decide to get under the knife, give yourself some time, because true beauty comes from the inside.

By Lois Lane

DEVOTED

WRITTEN BY: Luke Schelhaas	GUEST STARS: Erica Durance (Lois Lane), Amanda Walsh
DIRECTED BY: David Carson	(Mandy), Moneca Delain (Mara), Chelan Simmons
	(Rhonda), Rob Freeman (Coach Quigley), Graham
	Kosakoski (Dan Cormay), Jared Keeso (Nate)

The football team's juice cooler is filled with a kryptonite-laced punch that causes imbibers to act incredibly devoted and obedient to their partners. Several cheerleaders use this drink to control and get attention from their boyfriends. But the effect is too strong, inducing jealous and violent rages; first from quarterback Dan, who thinks Jason has been checking out his girlfriend; and later from Jason himself, who attacks Clark in his barn, accusing him of checking out "his girl", not letting on that the girl in question is Lana. The meteor-laced drink even causes Chloe, who still has feelings for Clark, to do anything — including quitting the *Torch* and dressing as a cheerleader — to get his attention. Clark also ingests some krypto-ade, making him sick.

Dan's jealous rage boosts Clark to the spot of starting quarterback, which at first provokes negative feelings from his teammates. Clark learns that his father went through similar trials back when he was a starting sophomore on the team. Ultimately, Clark helps lead the Crows to victory, earning the respect of the other players who had doubted him.

CLARK: Chloe, are you feeling okay?
CHLOE: I've never felt happier. Clark, can't you see? I'm devoted to you.

'Devoted', like 'Facade' the week before, continued to establish the plotline of Clark joining the Smallville High football team, thereby defying his father's wishes. "After season three, which I think had been getting kind of dark, where we spent a lot of time in secret labs, we wanted to get back to the high school aspect of the show, figuring it's their last year of high school," executive producer Al Gough noted. "The idea being that in season one, Clark couldn't play football because Jonathan was concerned about his ability to control his powers, and now, we felt that Clark's a senior, let's let him play, and let him have some conflict with Jonathan about that. It went a little to the John Byrne reboot of Superman where he did play football in Smallville, so there was a precedent for it. We liked the idea of letting Clark have some popularity as a football star. If you had superpowers, wouldn't you do it?"

The krypto-ade plot device that inspired total infatuation and devotion gave some of the actors the opportunity to act out scenarios they wouldn't normally be able to. In Allison Mack's case, the usually determined workaholic Chloe suddenly took a shine to pom-poms and football jerseys.

Opposite: The football storyline allowed Smallville's producers to further enrich Clark's high school experience.

"It was so much fun!" Allison Mack said of her chance to portray Chloe as a devoted cheerleader with no desire other than pleasing Clark Kent. "I always say one of the

better things about being on the show is the fact that we have the opportunity to be so many different things. Because we are a sci-fi show, we have that element of fantasy, so we can push the limits in a lot of ways. We aren't just restricted to being the same thing all the time, and so that episode was a great example of how we get the chance to just be something really outrageous and totally different.

"In the scene where I dress up in the cheerleading outfit — the director just had me go for it," Allison recalled. "He put the camera on me and had me do whatever I wanted for ten minutes. It was so much fun. I love broad comedy, and it's such a rare occasion that I actually get to do that on this show, so I really, really enjoyed my time."

At episode's end, it appeared that, with the help of Lex, Clark (and the show) would not be seeing Lois Lane again for a little while. "In 'Devoted', when you see her leaving, that's because that's all we thought we had her for," executive producer Miles Millar revealed, as only four Lois Lane episodes were originally cleared by the Warner Bros. Feature division. Gough and Millar, working with Peter Roth at Warner Bros. Television, explained their intentions to the movie people as to how the Lois Lane character on

DEATH OF A SUPERMAN

The passing of actor Christopher Reeve on October 10, 2004 inspired tributes from fans and friends all across the world. Here are some thoughts from members of the Smallville cast and crew who were able to work with or meet this incredible individual, lifted directly from the headlines of that somber week in 2004:

"Everyone at Smallville was shocked and saddened to hear about Christopher Reeve's passing. We feel honored and grateful to have had him as part of our family. He not only made you believe a man could fly, but he showed that, with the power of perseverance, any adversity can be tackled, and that is what truly made him super. Our thoughts and prayers are with his wife and family, and we encourage everyone to remember that his legacy lives on through the Christopher Reeve Paralysis Foundation."
Miles Millar and Alfred Gough, Smallville Executive Producers

"Christopher Reeve played the role of one of the most memorable and heroic characters ever created... Superman. But it is obvious to me, as I'm sure it is to others, that he was far more of a Superman than he could have possibly imagined."
Michael Rosenbaum, Smallville's Lex Luthor

"What can you say about such a man as Christopher Reeve? He embodied all the best that a human being can hope to be. To continue life in the face of such adversity and to make things BETTER for other people and to continue to contribute so much is a miracle. He was so kind and generous and funny. He was a prince. His presence in our lifetime has given us all an example of how to live our lives. I am so grateful I knew him. And while I am so sorry for the loss his family must now endure, to me he will always be a constant source of comfort and hope, and will remain up in the stratosphere where he has always been in my eyes."
Annette O'Toole, Smallville's Martha Kent (Starred alongside Christopher Reeve in Superman III as Lana Lang.)

Smallville would work, and assured them that she and Clark would not have a romance and would be more like sparring partners. Ultimately, the movie division allowed them to use Lois for more episodes in season four, beginning with 'Spell', and then with her appearing more frequently as of 'Pariah' in the latter half of the season.

Above: Jason notices that Clark is not feeling well.

Lois: Don't worry, I'll visit.
Clark: Is that a promise or a threat?

"It was a really gradual process," Erica Durance said about the rumors of her character's return. "Around episode three, I was hearing little buzzings of maybe being in a couple more. Maybe I was going to be written into six and seven. It's kind of funny, because I look back on it now, and I go, 'That just seems to have turned into quite the wild ride,' and I really didn't expect it. It really was gradual, and then it totalled to thirteen episodes. I never count my chickens before they hatch, as it were. I was just really interested in each little bit that I was getting to do, because before this point, I didn't have the experience of having a steady job. It was just great to get to work."

'Devoted' was dedicated to the memory of Christopher Reeve. Reeve, who was paralyzed in an accident during an equestrian tournament in 1995, passed away on October 10, 2004. ■

SMALLVILLE MUSIC

'Meltdown' by Ash
'Revolution' by Authority Zero
'Our Mystery' by Bebo Norman
'Better Off By Myself' by Bosshouse
'California' by Hawk Nelson
'On The Run' by Sam Roberts
'Medicated' by Sub Space Radio
'Disco MF' by The Penfifteen Club

RUN

WRITTEN BY: Steven S. DeKnight, Carmine Infantino (former illustrator of the *Flash* comic book)
DIRECTED BY: David Barrett

GUEST STARS: Kyle Gallner (Bart Allen), Benjamin Ratner (Hanison)

While on a visit to Metropolis, Clark and Jonathan cross paths with Bart Allen — a boy who may be even faster than Clark. Bart uses his powers for petty thievery, and one of the items he steals is a fourteenth-century manuscript owned by Lex Luthor. Bart's swindling ways get him into trouble with both Lex Luthor and a thug named Hanison, who threatens Bart's life.

Lana and Martha have a heart-to-heart about Martha's avoidance of Jonathan and their problems at home. Martha confides that she is worried about her husband's health, and that is the true reason she is spending so much time at the Talon.

Clark struggles to convince Bart that stealing is immoral, and finally earns his respect. The manuscript is returned to Lex, who tells Clark that the page is actually not worth as much as he had paid for it. After Clark leaves, it is revealed that within the manuscript is a Kryptonian map that may offer clues to the location of one of the elements.

BART: Dude, we are two superpowered studs here. Why else do you think I came to Smelly-ville looking for you, man? Let's crank it up and go have some fun.

A year before Bart Allen sped through *Smallville*, the WB network had announced that they were developing a new live-action television series based on the DC Comics hero, the Flash. The project was eventually aborted; however, one of the potential writers they spoke to was Steve DeKnight. "Let's just say we had creative differences about what a Flash series should be," DeKnight said, referring to the proposed series' reinvention of the Flash as a time-traveling college student from Gotham City. Fortunately, this diluted take on the Flash mythos didn't materialize, and DeKnight instead landed a position on *Smallville*'s creative team.

"I grew up reading the classic *Flash* comics," DeKnight revealed, "and one of the things that I remember very fondly about my childhood back in the sixties was looking at the comics where the Flash and Superman would have these races. I knew going into this episode, that firstly, they had to have a race — that's just a classic thing. Secondly, the Flash is faster than Clark... than Superman, that's his one thing. And, thirdly, that he's a smart-ass, quite frankly. I also took a lot of inspiration from the *Justice League* animated show, with the amazing Michael Rosenbaum as the voice of the Flash. He's

Opposite: Bart Allen (Kyle Gallner) tries to win Chloe's affection with some quick charm.

just a wise-ass, and it brought a sense of fun to the show. This character was not somber or serious; he was quite the opposite. He enjoyed his powers."

BART: I'll be a thousand miles away before you can even blink.
CLARK: I don't know. I can blink pretty fast.

Playing with comic book legends was a serious job for Steve DeKnight. "It's always a little tricky, because you want to be as respectful to the source material as possible, but you can't be 100 percent married to it. You have to make it fit into the context of *Smallville* and the limitations of television. Originally we had talked about using Wally West or the classic Barry Allen, but Bart was the character that DC Comics would let us use, so we played with that."

Bart Allen made his first full appearance in issue #92 of DC Comics' *The Flash* comic book. He quickly took on the code name of Impulse and had his own comic book series, which ran from 1995 to 2002. In 2006, after a few years of using the Kid Flash moniker, the character of Bart Allen took on the mantle of the Flash in the current comic book series *The Flash: The Fastest Man Alive*. In the comics, Bart is actually the

Below: Catch him if you can!

grandson of the legendary Flash, Barry Allen, and was born in the thirtieth century. This element from Bart's comic book origins was referenced within the episode. "We wanted to tip our hats to the people that knew everything about the character with the funny line he gives to Chloe about, 'I came from the future. You know, we're still in love a hundred years from now.'" DeKnight recalled. "We had to play a little fast and loose with what exactly his backstory was."

In the episode itself, however, Bart's official story is that he somehow attained his powers from a bright flash of light. Though, considering Bart's history of tall tales, his true origins could very well be unknown. Bart's development is something that DeKnight would have enjoyed looking into. "We were talking at one point about a Metropolis spin-off with Green Arrow, Cyborg, Bart and a couple of other characters; some from the Teen Titans, some from just the DC Universe. I would've liked to have gotten into that at some point and explored Bart's real backstory." ∎

FLASH FACTS!

Bart Allen wasn't the first DC Comics superspeedster to go by the name of the Flash. Here's a look at some of the other heroes to take on that title:

JAY GARRICK

Jay Garrick first appeared in Flash Comics #1 in 1940. He obtained his powers during a lab accident involving hard water. The super-swift original Flash wears a Mercury helmet on his head. He is still active in comic books, most recently appearing with other classic heroes as a member of the Justice Society of America.

BARRY ALLEN

Editor Julius Schwartz had his staff create a new Flash character in 1956, only five years after Jay Garrick's last appearance. This Flash gained his powers from a lightning strike. Later it was revealed that Barry Allen existed in a different Earth from Jay Garrick, and the two characters eventually teamed up as the heroes of Earth-1 and Earth-2. Allen died in DC Comics' *Crisis on Infinite Earths* — that had all of the Earths merging together. Barry Allen was also the subject of a short-lived CBS TV series starring John Wesley Shipp.

WALLY WEST

Originally Barry's sidekick, Kid Flash, Wally West obtained his powers in a similar fashion to his predecessor. Wally was the first Flash to truly master the Speed Force — an energy that has given many fast characters their powers. The Wally West version of the character was seen in the Warner Bros. *Justice League* and *Justice League Unlimited* animated series, where he was voiced by *Smallville*'s Lex Luthor, Michael Rosenbaum.

TRANSFERENCE

WRITTEN BY: Todd Slavkin & Darren Swimmer DIRECTED BY: James Marshall	GUEST STARS: J.P. Manoux (Edgar Cole), Margot Kidder (Bridgette Crosby), Rick Faraci (Tattooed Inmate), Terence Kelly (Doctor)

Lionel Luthor's eccentric new cellmate, Edgar Cole, helps him master the water element, as Lionel intends on switching bodies with Lex. When Clark unexpectedly intervenes, the crystal's power instead causes Lionel to switch bodies with Clark. Within Clark's body, Lionel learns that he has power beyond his wildest imagination. He uses his new body to attack Lex and play mind games with Chloe. Clark/Lionel also impulsively quits the football team and puts inappropriate moves on Lana when she comes to talk to him about her relationship with Jason. Meanwhile, the real Clark — now inside Lionel's body — tries to convince Martha that it's really him stuck inside prison. Lionel learns that the transference only stays permanent if one of the two people dies, and so he returns to the prison to kill Clark in his own former body. However, Clark is secretly wielding the element, causing the transference to reverse.

Chloe and Lana are both incensed by 'Clark's' behavior, not knowing that it was really Lionel, and Chloe suggests that he should possibly get some psychiatric help.

Back at the prison, a baffled doctor informs Lionel that his liver disease has suddenly been cured. Clark arranges for Edgar Cole to be released from prison, and Bridgette Crosby greets Cole in a limo. She asks Cole if he has the element, and the water element is now in the possession of the Swann Foundation...

LIONEL (AS CLARK): I'm not surprised. A man would travel across the world to pluck your succulent fruit.

"We wanted to do a show with body transference involving a krypto-freak or an escaped prisoner from Belle Reve and Clark for a long time," episode co-writer Todd Slavkin revealed. With Lionel Luthor now in prison, the writers were faced with an irresistible opportunity. "We had this transference stone, and it all came together very organically."

John Glover found portraying Clark, rather than his own character, a real challenge: "[For Tom to play Lionel] I'd block out the scenes, and then Tom would take over. It was very interesting. I had a lot of trouble portraying Clark because I'm so used to playing neurotic men, psychotic men, villainous men — they're all complicated. And this kind of pureness that Tom does [as Clark] — I kept wanting to complicate it. I felt that by just standing there and being simple and heroic... it was a difficult task. I realized how wonderful Tom is in that part. I knew before he was wonderful, but I didn't realize *how* wonderful he was."

Opposite: Bridgette Crosby (Margot Kidder) arrives to retrieve the element from Edgar.

"John was here every day for Tom," Allison Mack recalled. "You could really see the two of them working together, and it was such a beautiful exchange between the two

TRANSFERENCE

SMALLVILLE MUSIC

'Pain' by Jimmy Eat World

actors. John was so helpful. That made it really fun."

CLARK (AS LIONEL): "Remember when I was six, and I was playing tag with Dad, and all of a sudden I started running faster than I'd ever run before, and I was in the middle of Palmer Woods, completely lost. And you and Dad had to call Sheriff Ethan, and when you saw me you started crying, and I thought something was wrong with me. And you said no there wasn't. And then you held me in your arms and told me I was just special. I'm your special boy."

The episode gave a new opportunity for Lionel Luthor to interact with Chloe Sullivan, albeit in Clark's body. "Chloe has a big attraction for Lionel, because of her brain," Glover said. He is not totally convinced that Chloe has no similar interest in Lionel. "She probably has dreams about Lionel," he joked.

"I thought Tom did an amazing job," Annette O'Toole said, proud of her TV son. "He really, really nailed it. There are just some wonderful moments where he's so much like

Below: As Clark, Lionel has the power to throw Jonathan around any way he pleases.

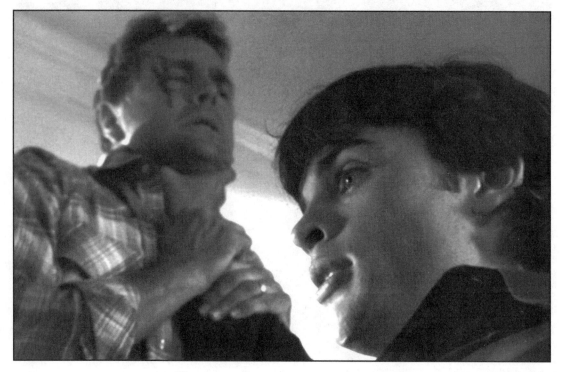

SMALLVILLE TORCH

OUT OF CHARACTER

I know that we live in a town where strange things and odd behavior are commonplace, but I admit that even after living here for a few years, it's still jarring when someone acts out of character.

This phenomena — whether it's tied to the meteor rocks or if there's some other explanation — may appear to an outsider like a thing of science fiction. However, it seems to happen around here at least ten times a school year. If I've been through it with my friends, chances are you have, too.

So, if your friend starts behaving completely different than usual, ask them about it; and if it's found out that they've fallen under this affliction, forgive them. But, if you happen to be the victim of a rock-spawned personality change, there's nothing to be ashamed of... just be honest and talk about it. Your real friends will understand. More secrecy and shame really don't help the matter at all.

by Chloe Sullivan

Lionel that he's scary. It was a little creepy when he looked at me, and it was like it was Lionel looking at me, but out of Tom's eyes. It was a little incestuous there."

Playing the tattooed thug who harassed 'Lionel' in prison and later fought him in a full-on prison riot was Rick Faraci. A ten-time martial arts champion, his skills have brought him to feature films such as *Timecop*, and jobs providing security for talent. For several years now, Faraci has been the head of security on the Vancouver set of *Smallville*. This was not the first time Faraci had appeared on the show, he was also in the season three finale, 'Commencement', shaving Lionel Luthor's hair as he entered prison.

For the riot sequence, Faraci and Glover performed many of their own stunts. "We both pulled skin, we were bleeding. We both went to the same chiropractor after," Faraci laughed. "John impresses me all the time. He's a consummate professional. He was so cool with the fight stuff. He's just amazing."

"John Glover is someone I know I can turn to and say, 'John, this is safe for you,' and he gets all excited," *Smallville* stunt coordinator Chris Sayour said of Glover's enthusiasm to perform his own stunts. "He doesn't go, 'Oh, darn.' He likes to do the physical stuff."

The episode ended with a brief return appearance by Margot Kidder as Bridgette Crosby. Edgar Cole, and the transference crystal, were now in the custody of the Swann Foundation. Todd Slavkin explained: "We wanted to keep the story of Virgil Swann alive. Even though Christopher Reeve wasn't around anymore, Swann would want one of those crystals, and he would be involved in the mythology and the building of the Fortress of Solitude. I think that was our intent." ∎

DID YOU KNOW?

Margot Kidder's scene for 'Transference' was filmed in the same block of time in which she filmed her 'Crusade' scene.

JINX

WRITTEN BY: Mark Warshaw
DIRECTED BY: Paul Shapiro

GUEST STARS: Trent Ford (Mikail Mxyzptlk), Kevan Kase (Danny Crozier), Rob Freeman (Coach Quigley)

Luthor-sponsored exchange student Mikail Mxyzptlk is Smallville High's resident underground bookie, with a mysterious ability to stack the odds. During a Crows game, Mxyzptlk wills Clark to trip. The impact from Clark's body results in a serious injury to an opposing player, causing Jason and Coach Quigley to suspect that Clark may be using performance-enhancing drugs. Jonathan reminds Clark that he was only allowed to join the football team because he understood his responsibility not to allow anyone to get hurt. With that promise broken, Jonathan feels it is Clark's duty to step down from the roster. Clark and Chloe discover that Mikail comes from a region of Eastern Europe that had been terrorized by a bloodline of people possessing the ability to control the hand of luck. Their only weakness was the locust plague, so Clark and Chloe replicate locust sound frequencies and successfully neutralize Mxyzptlk's ability. Mikail realizes his power is being scrambled and discovers Chloe at the source of the signal. Thanks to a jolt of superspeed, Clark manages to simultaneously play in the football game and rescue Chloe. Back at the LuthorCorp Plaza in Metropolis, Lex takes Mikail Mxyzptlk to his new home: a hidden facility labeled Level 33.1. In this new place, Mikail is not alone...

MARTHA: Something happened to you out there. And if you really want to play in the game on Saturday, you need to find out what it was.

'Jinx' was written by Mark Warshaw, who has spearheaded *Smallville*'s online and mass media content ever since the show's first season. Interestingly, the episode was originally meant to feature the return of Clark's best friend and former confidante, Pete Ross, in a championship football game against the Smallville Crows.

"We would have had Pete saying to Clark, 'Listen, dude, this is the first thing I did on my own. You're cheating. I know you're a cheater. I'm going to tell everyone you're cheating,'" Warshaw said, explaining that Clark would try to use kryptonite to power down and inhibit his abilities, in a sequence much like the one that appeared in the final cut of the show. Unfortunately, actor Sam Jones III was in the midst of shooting the film *Glory Road*, and was thus unable to return as Pete.

Gambling was an element in early outlines of the script, and the story quickly evolved into one featuring the probability-altering Mxyzptlk. As with other comic book characters brought to life on the show, *Smallville*'s Mxyzptlk had his own twist — that of being a foreign exchange student brought to Smallville by the Luthors.

The decision about Mxyzptlk's accent was made very much at the last minute. "Trent's a really talented actor," Warshaw enthused. "Al Gough had seen him on *The West Wing* doing a French accent, and we had heard he could do an Eastern European

Opposite: Mxyzptlk (Trent Ford) tries to use his magic powers to seduce Chloe.

accent, though he's actually British. He was written as Eastern European and it kind of fit with his backstory, and people were pretty confident that's what he could pull off, and he did."

Allison Mack had previously worked with Mark Warshaw on the *Chloe Chronicles* webisodes, and the two had formed a friendship during that time. "The episode was fun because I knew that Mark wrote it, and I knew that he did so with me in mind," she revealed. "That's always really great, and it's also fun to be a part of your friend's progression, knowing that this was something that Mark had wanted to do for a long time. Being such a big part of his script and his story and helping him execute his dreams was such a joy. It was really great."

Chloe: So, are you the guy?

Mikail: I guess that depends on what you're looking for.

Chloe: Uh, Mikail Mc... Mixyl... put... lik?

Mikail: Micks-ill-pittle-ick. Let me guess, you want to buy a vowel?

Warshaw had equally glowing words for Allison. "Allison is, to me, one of the most talented young actresses of her generation," he said. "She's definitely our go-to girl. I love working with Allison. When I was going to get to actually write a full episode, there was no way it was going to be Clark-centered."

'Jinx' also provided the opportunity to bring some elements from the online *Ledger* and *Torch* sites — such as B.B. Davenport's Auto Body — into the televised show canon. "It was

MXYZP-WHAT?!

While *Smallville*'s Mxyzptlk hailed from a foreign country, long-time fans of Superman comics know him better as a magical imp from a place known as the Fifth Dimension.

The original incarnation of Mxyzptlk (spelled "Mxztplk" back then) first plagued Superman and friends in issue #30 of DC Comics' *Superman* comic book, way back in 1944. Mxy's plan was to return to cause mayhem in Superman's life every ninety days.

Since then, the character of Mxyzptlk has evolved; appearing in his classic 'derby hat and bow tie' form in some places, and in an orange-and-purple motif in others. He has made appearances in several forms of *Superman* media, including the *Super Friends* cartoon and the 1990s *Superman* animated series. In live action, he showed up on both the *Superboy* syndicated TV series as well as *Lois & Clark: The New Adventures of Superman*. In his *Lois & Clark* appearance he was played by Howie Mandel of game show *Deal Or No Deal* fame!

Mxyzptlk is unique in every medium, because you never know where he'll show up next. It would not be surprising if *Smallville* hasn't seen the last of him...

Above: A hint of what's to come...
Level 33.1.

the synergy of everything we do," Warshaw noted. "I love the continuity and tying them all together."

In her interactions with Mikail Mxyzptlk, it seemed that, as with the previous seasons' episodes 'Crush' and 'Dichotic', Chloe had made another bad choice in men. "I don't know if it's so much the boys that choose her, I think it's her choice in boys," Allison reflected. "I think Chloe has an innate attraction to anything strange and abnormal, and so I think she subconsciously seeks them out."

Clark met his own challenges on the football field in this episode, seeing that he could easily hurt people. "'Jinx' was one of our best Superman moments in the whole series, because it's not just about him making a physical journey, it's about him taking a real emotional chance and putting a lot at stake in his personal life, and in the choices he made," series writer Brian Peterson said. "It's one of my favorite episodes of the series."

'Jinx' concluded with one of the most exciting moments of that season, as it was revealed that Lex was keeping and studying some 'meteor freaks', including Mxyzptlk, in a secret lab called Level 33.1. "That's an example of a storyline that has not paid off until season six, really. But I think it's given the show a lot of levels, that we plant things knowing that we're not just going to let them drop, which is why I think people keep watching. We absolutely knew that we were bringing it back," Peterson revealed. Level 33.1 returned in a big way with the later *Vengeance Chronicles* and season six plots... ■

SPELL

WRITTEN BY: Steven S. DeKnight DIRECTED BY: Jeannot Szwarc	GUEST STARS: Erica Durance (Lois Lane), Mark Acheson (Magistrate Wilkins), William Taylor (Mr. Jacobson), Lara Gilchrist (Madeleine), Melanie Papalia (Brianna)

Lana purchases a weather-worn spell book that once belonged to the Countess Margaret Isobel Thoreaux. When she touches a Kryptonian symbol on one of the book's pages, she becomes possessed by the spirit of Isobel. Lois returns to town to celebrate Chloe's eighteenth birthday and, thanks to one of Isobel's spells, the two girls end up hosting the spirits of Isobel's seventeenth-century entourage. The three witches then head to the Kent farm to make the wild party even wilder, and Isobel seems to be much more attracted to Clark than to Jason. With her magic powers, she encourages Clark to "release his inner animal", which doesn't score points with the visiting Princeton recruiter.

Isobel's reincarnation in the twenty-first century puts her back on her four-hundred-year-old quest — to collect the three Kryptonian elements of power. She uses her witchcraft to rid Clark of his abilities and force him to share the location of the stones. The witches' quest is foiled in the caves when a repowered Clark destroys the spell book, returning Lana, Lois, and Chloe to their normal states.

LANA: Clark, what happened?
CLARK: Well, let's just say that you haven't been yourself lately.

"The whole witch storyline is a tricky bit of business," writer Steve DeKnight says of *Smallville*'s first true foray into the world of magic. "You walk a fine line. We wanted to — again, this is basically from the comics — layer in more of the Superman myth, and one of my favorite parts of the myth is that he's vulnerable to magic. That's one of his few weaknesses. I always remember the great page in *Kingdom Come* where he has Wonder Woman's sword and he cuts his thumb on it, and she references that he was always susceptible to magic. We were interested in bringing up this part of the myth, that magic is one of his weaknesses besides kryptonite. Because Superman is so powerful, how do you weaken him? But in doing so, the tricky thing is that magic and *Smallville* is a very odd mix. It was very tricky to try to get it to mesh together correctly."

"The Isobel witch story was just going to be the one episode — 'Spell' — and then we ended up making Isobel a bigger part of the overall crystal story. The idea being that, several hundred years ago, she had been on this crystal hunt," creator Al Gough said, though he admitted that the story may have eventually gone too far. "I think that whole Lana witch element is the point where the crystal story went off the rails and we just got a little hokey. It's something that led to a great conclusion with the Fortress and the

Opposite: Lois Lane's bewitching new look.

SPELL

CLARK KENT VS. MAGIC

Superman's powers make him impervious to many things, but beyond kryptonite, there is one thing that can always stop him in his tracks — magic.

In Mark Waid and Alex Ross' seminal graphic novel *Kingdom Come*, Superman faced one of his greatest challenges as he battled Captain Marvel — a hero whose powers are based around magic. Captain Marvel took advantage of Kal-El's vulnerability by repeatedly summoning lightning from the sky to strike him.

The vulnerability to magic is what would allow a character like Mxyzptlk to be an actual threat to Superman, despite not being in his physical class or Kryptonian himself.

On *Smallville*, the powers of witchcraft coming from the Countess Isobel Thoreaux allowed the three witches to capture Clark, and even make him bleed. Unfortunately, Clark has to learn about this weakness the hard way...

season finale with the second meteor shower; but while it was interesting, after a while, we just felt like the tires were a bit stuck in the mud."

Allison Mack initially enjoyed the revealing outfits worn by Isobel and her crew, though the costumes quickly wore out their welcome. "It was fun for the first day," she remembered, "and then it got really tiresome, just because the clothes were really uncomfortable, and we were in them for such long, long periods of time. So the corsets got a little old, the spiked heels got a little old. But it was, again, a great, fun opportunity to do something different."

CLARK: It was Lana — well, it wasn't Lana exactly. She was possessed by a witch, who then cast a spell on us, and that's how that happened.
JONATHAN: Son, I realize that; after all, this is Smallville. But witches, and spells, and... magic?

Special effects supervisor Mike Walls explained that there were some effects in the series that were very difficult, even if they looked minor on the screen. "One of the toughest gags, actually, was the bloody claw mark down Clark's chest," Walls recalled. "We built a soft copper piece that fit Allison's hand, and it had little pipes coming out of it so that we could feed the blood through it from off-camera. We worked with her for two days on the timing of where her hand would go and when we would push the blood and everything. I thought it turned out really well, considering what we went through."

"I think 'Spell' succeeds on some levels and fails on others," Steve DeKnight concluded, "and of course the failure I blame completely on myself!" ∎

Opposite above: Isobel and her friends have their way with Clark.

Opposite below: Jason Teague to the rescue.

SMALLVILLE MUSIC

'Blame' by Black Toast Music
'What You Waiting For?' by Gwen Stefani
'We Might As Well Be Strangers' by Keane
'Impromptu No. 2 In E Flat' by Franz Schubert

BOUND

WRITTEN BY: Luke Schelhaas
DIRECTED BY: Terrance O'Hara

GUEST STARS: Jane Seymour (Genevieve Teague), Claudette Mink (Corinne Hartford), Cobie Smulders (Shannon Bell), Mark Acheson (Magistrate Wilkins), Patricia Mayan Salazar (Maid)

After sleeping with an alluring stranger, Lex wakes up next to her dead body, and quickly becomes a murder suspect. Clark accuses Lionel of framing Lex, but Lionel claims to have turned over a new leaf. Lionel informs Clark that Lex has had a series of one night stands after which he sent each woman a pair of conciliatory earrings. Chloe obtains video surveillance of the elevator showing Lex with a woman, and notices that she is missing an earring, and the dead girl, Eve Andrews, was not. Lionel suggests that the woman in the elevator was the true killer.

Lex finds his lawyer, Corinne Harper, dead in her office. Out of the shadows, with a pistol pointed in his direction, appears a woman Lex doesn't recognize: Corinne's assistant, Shannon. A spurned lover of Lex's from long ago, Shannon sought her revenge by finding Eve Andrews to lure in Lex before framing him for Eve's murder. Shannon ties up Lex and ignites a trail of alcohol to create a ring of fire, but Clark arrives, knocks out Shannon, and puts out the fire. Lex's questionable history leaves Clark wondering if he knew his onetime friend as well as he thought he did.

Lana has a dream about her ancestor, Isobel, including a vision of another woman. Later, when Lana meets Jason's mother, she recognizes Genevieve as the woman in her dream...

CLARK: There's a whole side of you that I don't know about, Lex. And what else don't I know about you?
LEX: You don't know that every day, I wonder why I keep going. Why I do the things I do. You know, Shannon might have been crazy, but she was right about me. I treated those women terribly, Clark. People died, and I could've stopped it. I see that now.

'Bound' gave the show's writers and producers, as well as actor Michael Rosenbaum, the opportunity to show a different, darker side of Lex Luthor. "It was something we'd done a little in season one with the episode 'Zero', but we hadn't really done since then, in terms of exploring Lex's lifestyle before he came to Smallville," executive producer Al Gough said. "Especially in terms of the lifestyle of a young billionaire playboy. That's where that story came from."

The vengeance of jilted lovers of Lex came not only as a surprise to Clark, but also

Opposite: Lionel Luthor turns over a new leaf?

to many fans of the show, who at this point were used to seeing Lex's more savory side on the series, when he appeared devoted to characters like Helen Bryce.

'Bound' also featured the first appearance of Jane Seymour as Jason's mother, Genevieve Teague. The mysterious Mrs. Teague was a descendant of one of the Countess Isobel's rivals for the stones, and her arrival signaled an immediate change in the Lana-Jason relationship.

"When we were looking for somebody to play this part, we wanted someone recognizable, but not necessarily from the Superman lore," Al Gough explained. "We found out that Jane was available. We liked the idea, after years and years of playing Dr. Quinn, of having her play a character who was much more of a villain. We approached her, and she jumped at the whole challenge of doing that. She liked the idea of

Below: Father and son meet.

Genevieve, and how she was kind of dark."

"I give her credit," Gough continued, "she just went for it. She had some great scenes with Lionel, and some fantastic scenes with Lex. She was a real delight to work with."

JASON: It's probably not that unusual to dream about someone you just met.
LANA: Jason, I dreamed about her before I met her.

"Genevieve was a user and would use everybody, and I think both Lionel and Lex saw her for exactly what she was," writer Holly Harold notes. "I enjoyed Genevieve because the Luthors were meeting a woman of their own ilk who had as much money and as much power and was just as cutthroat as the two of them were." ∎

SMALLVILLE MUSIC

'Daddy's Little Girl' by Amanda O'Connor
'I Want More: Part 2' by Faithless
'Chopin Etude, Opus 10'
'No. 3 in E Major: *Lento, ma non troppo*' by John Rusnak

LEX LUTHOR'S WOMEN

Shannon Bell is just one of the women we have seen Lex Luthor with on *Smallville*. Here's a look at some of the other ladies in Lex Luthor's past...

AMANDA ROTHMAN

Amanda was an engaged woman who had an affair with Lex before discovering that her fiancé, Jude Royce, had also been seeing other people. She shot Royce, and Lex and his team tried to pin the blame on someone else. When she was told she could no longer see Lex, she apparently killed herself, although the true events leading to Amanda Rothman's death have yet to be confirmed.

VICTORIA HARDWICK

The daughter of one of Lionel Luthor's business rivals and an old lover of Lex's, Victoria came to Smallville hoping to steal private information for her father. Lex was on to her ruse and intentionally planted false information. After Hardwick's blunder, Lex and his father took over the Hardwick earnings, absorbing them into LuthorCorp.

DR. HELEN BRYCE

Though they'd met several years before in Metropolis, Dr. Helen Bryce and Lex Luthor were reunited while she was on staff at the Smallville Medical Center. They became reacquainted while she was in an anger management class, and soon began dating. Lionel attempted to blackmail her in order to control the relationship, but Helen had devious plans of her own. After she and Lex got married, Helen staged a plane crash so it would appear she survived and Lex did not. In actuality, Lex survived and got his ultimate revenge. It is not known if she survived the fall from the plane or if she perished; either way, Helen has not been seen since.

DID YOU KNOW?

Jane Seymour (Genevieve Teague) was close friends with Christopher Reeve until the time of his death, and they appeared together in the romantic film *Somewhere In Time*. Her son Christopher is named after her one-time co-star.

SCARE

WRITTEN BY: Kelly Souders & Brian Peterson

DIRECTED BY: David Carson

GUEST STARS: Malcolm Stewart (Dr. Otis Ford), Jerry Wasserman (Dr. Scanlan), Samantha Ferris (Warden Anita Stone), Lindsay Bourne (Moira Sullivan)

A LuthorCorp experiment releases toxins into the air that give the residents of Smallville horribly realistic nightmares that embody their worst fears. Jason is one of the toxin's first victims, vividly dreaming that Lana leaves him for Clark. Inside prison, a born-again Lionel tries to inspire his fellow inmates to live honestly. His mission is interrupted when he learns that a mysterious benefactor has arranged for his release.

Clark learns from Chloe that Jason had a meeting at LuthorCorp earlier that day, so the two go on a mission to search for answers. The toxin outbreak spreads, inducing many nightmares. Chloe "sees" her mother, who was institutionalized when she was very young, chanting that she cannot escape. Lana imagines that everyone who was ever close to her has died. Clark hallucinates a new meteor shower hitting Smallville, rendering him powerless to save anyone. Clark also dreams that Lana learns his secret and angrily rejects him. An antidote is created, but the experience leaves Clark believing that there may not be anyone who he can truly trust with his secret.

CLARK: It's funny, because lately I've been thinking I've gotten closer to telling someone the truth about me. Now I'm convinced more than ever that I can't tell anyone. Especially not Lana.

'Scare' is particularly notable for two things: one, it offered, in its own way, a teaser of things to come later in the season; two, it gave the opportunity to show off some of the characters' greatest fears. Previous episodes had established Lana's fear of being alone, Lex's fear of falling into Lionel's evil footsteps, and Clark's insecurities about Lana's reaction to his secret; but no episode had combined all of these elements into one complete package. Furthermore, this episode revealed a new facet of Chloe Sullivan's background — the revelation that her mother had been institutionalized for a mental condition that frequently plagues the women of her family.

"It's not good," Allison Mack said of her character's estrangement from her mother. "I think a big part of why Chloe is as ambitious and tenacious as she is, is so that she doesn't have to focus on the pain that she feels every day because she doesn't have any sort of relationship with her mother. I mean, her mother essentially abandoned her when she was old enough to realize what was going on. I think that it affects her constantly."

The storyline involving Chloe's mother was not followed up again on *Smallville* until the later season five and six episodes 'Tomb' and 'Progeny'. With this storyline involving her mother and Gabe Sullivan nowhere to be seen, would Allison have liked to have seen

Opposite: What scares Lana Lang?

Above: Lana's worst fear is revealed as everyone she cares about lies dead.

more exploration into the lives of the Sullivan family? "Selfishly, of course," Mack admitted. "Because it could flesh my character out beautifully, but if I look at the show realistically, it's not about each individual character, it's about Smallville, and it's Clark Kent's story. If there was a way that we could involve Clark in those storylines, then it would be a great episode, but ultimately the show is about Clark and his journey, and how we play into that. I don't know how interesting it would be for the fans to see just a story about Chloe and her family."

CHLOE: I mean, if you can't tell your best friend, who can you tell? Right, Clark?

Lex's dream sequence of an apocalyptic future that hearkened back to the season one episode 'Hourglass' was not what was originally scripted and filmed. Initially, the sequence had Lex getting married, only to have the bride's face revealed as that of his disapproving mother. The scene can be found on the *Smallville* season four DVD box set. "Basically, it was something that Miles and I never liked, but the writers sort of pursued," Al Gough revealed. "[Lex's nightmare of marrying his mother] just had no climax, [especially] when you look at the other scares. The change was last minute. We were down the road with shooting, and the final scene was completely constructed in post."

Many of the nightmares in 'Scare' reflected things we would see later on in the fourth season and beyond. "Clark's nightmare of the meteor shower, we intended for that to pay off," writer Brian Peterson said. "I don't know that we knew it would be in the finale, but later in the season we wanted it to pay off." ■

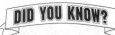

DID YOU KNOW?

Lindsay Bourne portrayed Chloe Sullivan's mother for brief moments in this episode, but when we meet her properly in season six, she is played by the one-time Wonder Woman herself, Lynda Carter!

SMALLVILLE TORCH

SMALLVILLE RESIDENTS STILL JITTERY ABOUT METEORS

Memories Of Devastating 1989 Shower Remain Fresh For Many

News stories about a meteor shower that surprised many people in New England last Sunday reopened some old wounds here in Smallville. Officials at the Federal Aviation Administration fielded hundreds of calls that night from worried residents ranging from Portland, Maine, to Long Island, New York, speculating about a possible crashing aircraft and, of course, making the usual UFO claims as well.

Reading the national papers at the Talon yesterday, fifty-eight-year-old Jason Dick took a decidedly sarcastic stance. "Freaked 'em out back East, huh? I feel bad for those folks. Must have been quite a scare seeing those little lights moving in the sky." Dick was forty-two years old when the Smallville meteor shower rained huge flaming rocks on our town, leaving scars and traumatic memories that persist today. Returning from a big Crows' victory at the school with his kids, he recalls the explosion that threw his pickup twenty-five feet into the air with no warning, destroying it and sending its three occupants to the Smallville Medical Center with major lacerations and broken bones. "They call that a meteor shower? I got your meteor shower right here," he scoffs.

Indeed, even sixteen years later, reminders of the 1989 event are everywhere on the streets of Smallville. While even those who didn't directly experience the incident will never forget it, scientists from the Kansas Emergency Management Association (KEMA) insist that there is no need to worry about another destructive shower hitting the area anytime soon.

"On a geological scale, you might have small meteorites landing every couple of hundred years. But for a large-scale meteorite event to cause significant damage to the same place twice? The odds are enormous," assures Dr. Drake Todd of KEMA. "That shower in New England was nothing more than the annual passing of the Earth through the Lyrids, which produces visible streaks in the sky during April. We can predict these things fairly accurately now."

Local historians remember that Ezra Small wrote about the meteor shower. As Chris Beppo reported in a special *Ledger* issue a few years ago, Ezra witnessed the famous 1833 occurrence first hand: "In the cloudless sky above him, hundreds of bright streaks slashed the night, as if multitudes of stars had escaped their moorings and were fleeing west in a brilliant mass."

To us, this is known as the Great Leonid Meteor Storm of 1833, caused by Comet Tempel-Tuttle crossing Earth's path. To the eyewitnesses of the day, it was a rain of fire that signified the coming of a great being. Ezra Small recalls: "The shower increased in magnitude until almost the entire sky was in brilliant motion, shifting in great waves of luminosity. Occasionally, one fireball would shoot from the mass, leaving a bluish trail of smoke before exploding near the horizon. The meteors varied in size, some appearing as large as the full moon."

Although he is loath to admit the fallibility of his hero, Beppo acknowledges that an early Ezra "prophecy" — as Small's largely incoherent scribblings are sometimes called — may have been mistaken. Beppo says, "One of the poems I found referred to another, bigger celestial event occurring 172 years from the time of the Leonid shower Ezra lived through for eight hours in 1833. If you do the math, however, you only get 156 years between 1833 and 1989. I think we can give old Ezra a break on this one, though. Most of his predictions, particularly of tragic events, have proven eerily accurate."

by Jim Bradlee

UNSAFE

WRITTEN BY: Steven S. DeKnight
& Jeph Loeb
DIRECTED BY: Greg Beeman

GUEST STARS: Sarah Carter (Alicia Baker), John Pyper-Ferguson (Dr. William McBride), Don Mackay (Las Vegas Minister), Moneca Delain (Larissa), R. David Stephens (Doctor)

Clark's one-time love interest, the teleporting and unstable Alicia Baker, has been released from Belle Reve and returns to Smallville claiming to be cured. Clark is happy to see her, but is hesitant given that she previously tried to kill both him and Lana. Alicia gives Clark a necklace containing rocks of red kryptonite. The necklace removes Clark's inhibitions, and the two of them head to Las Vegas to get married.

Lana talks to Chloe about Jason and wonders if moving their relationship to the next level will keep Jason's interest. Chloe reveals that her "first time" was with someone she met during her internship at the *Daily Planet*. Lana tells Jason she is ready to move forward, but Jason reveals that he is afraid that his mother orchestrated their relationship all along.

In Las Vegas, the necklace comes off and as Clark returns to normal, he realizes that Alicia might not be as cured as she claimed to be. The two argue, and Alicia teleports away. When Clark returns home, Alicia's psychiatrist, Dr. William McBride, attacks him. McBride fires a gun at Clark, but Alicia teleports in between them to stop the bullet. Clark asks why she would do that, knowing he was invincible; she tells him that she promised to protect his secret. Clark and Alicia reunite...

MARTHA: Clark, there is someone out there for you.
CLARK: Who? Mom, a girl would have to be crazy to get into a relationship with me.

Alicia Baker first appeared in the season three episode 'Obsession', and fans and crew were so impressed, particularly with the on-screen chemistry between Sarah Carter and Tom Welling, that it was inevitable that the character would return. Since Lana and Clark were currently not together in the series, the midpoint of season four seemed like the perfect opportunity to bring in a seemingly rehabilitated Alicia.

"Kryptonite does drive people crazy," said writer Holly Harold, who first handled the character in that previous episode. "And we have established on the show that it's very unstable. While your powers can be amazing, it's hard to exist in this world with powers. It's hard to be that different. To have super-abilities is a double-edged sword, which Clark deals with all the time. And Alicia? Alicia kept tipping to the wrong side. When confronted with choices, she kept making the wrong ones, and she got a little carried away."

"She was so disappointed," Annette O'Toole said of Martha's reaction to Clark running off and getting married, even if it was under the influence of red kryptonite. "Martha's thing was: if you want to have sex, you don't have to run off and get married. The thing that

Opposite: Alicia Baker (Sarah Carter) pleads for sympathy from Clark.

concerned her the most was the physical act of sex, and what that means. You know, the age-old Superman question: will he kill somebody by having sex with them?"

Red kryptonite is a plot device that is often used to give Clark the opportunity to explore his wild side without negating the general goodness of the character that will eventually become Superman. "I think it's a safe device that they have to use," Annette O'Toole commented. "I think it's a bit of a cop-out, but I understand why they have to do it. And it's always fun to see Tom dress in black and blue and purple and all of those different types of darker things."

The use of red kryptonite suggests that Clark's responsibility for his actions in this episode is questionable. "It's a funny problem with *Smallville*," director Greg Beeman mused. "Was Clark culpable or not culpable? This girl basically gives him a roofie, and he gets married, but he obviously loved her."

CLARK KENT'S LOVE LIFE

Alicia Baker may have been one of the women Clark felt the closest connection to, but she is definitely not his only love interest on *Smallville*. Here's a look at a few that have made their way into Clark's heart...

KYLA WILLOWBROOK

Like Alicia, Kyla had some powers of her own, which made Clark feel safer about revealing his true powers around her. Kyla believed Clark to be 'Naman', the hero of her Native American people. Kyla had the power to turn herself into a wolf; she died from an injury caused by cutting herself on broken glass after taking a large fall.

LANA LANG

One can't talk about Clark's high school love life without discussing his feelings for Lana Lang. Unfortunately, Clark does not feel that he can be honest with Lana, which inevitably always brings the two of them conflict and angst. At the time Clark reunites with Alicia, Lana is still very much involved with Clark's one-time football coach, Jason Teague.

JESSIE BROOKS

A "bad girl" transferred to Smallville with her dad as part of the Witness Protection Program. She caught Clark's attention when he was under the influence of red kryptonite.

CHLOE SULLIVAN

Quite possibly Clark Kent's best friend—but does Clark realize the woman who is right in front of him will do anything to be with him?

LOIS LANE

No, Clark could never have a thing for Lois Lane. Or could he...?

'Unsafe' was unique in that it was a collaboration between two writers who normally write episodes without partners, at least when working on *Smallville*. "When I was on *Buffy* and *Angel*, we co-wrote a lot of scripts," revealed DeKnight, "because we would run out of time for a single person to physically be able to write an entire script before we would start to prep. With *Smallville* we usually have plenty of time to write the script, but this was one of those cases where we just decided to write a script together.

CLARK: How did you know about the red kryptonite?
ALICIA: Because I know everything about you, Clark. We were meant to be together, remember? Just like you said.

"I can't remember if it was Al and Miles who suggested it, but Jeph and I are friends, and it was a great experience," DeKnight added, although the experience was quite different from his days co-writing for *Angel* or *Buffy*. "Often when writers write a script together, especially writing partners, they will write together in the same room. I am spoiled from my *Angel* days where, when we split a script, it was like, 'I'm getting half as much money for the script, but it's going to take me half as long. All I have to do is write this half; I'm done. I'm in and out, lickety split.' It's funny, 'cause Jeph was really excited, thinking we would sit in the room and write this script! And I go, 'Whoa, whoa, wait a minute. Sit in a room? Oh, no, no. I'll write my half; you write your half and then we'll put it together.' I think he was a little disappointed, but I just couldn't do that. If you do it that way, you are spending as much time as writing a full script. And time when you're on a TV show is at such a premium." ■

SMALLVILLE MUSIC

'Beautiful Soul' by Jesse McCartney
'Laura' by Scissor Sisters
'Life For Rent' by Dido
'Welcome To My Life' by Simple Plan
'It's Now Or Never' by Elvis Presley
'Funny Little Feeling' by Rock 'n' Roll Soldiers
'Break So Easy' by Johnathan Rice

PARIAH

WRITTEN BY: Holly Harold	GUEST STARS: Erica Durance (Lois Lane), Jane Seymour
DIRECTED BY: Paul Shapiro	(Genevieve Teague), Sarah Carter (Alicia Baker), Derek
	Hamilton (Tim Westcott), Camille Mitchell (Sheriff Nancy
	Adams), Nicolas Pernisco (Jack Garner)

Clark and Alicia are now an item. When Lana and Jason are attacked, Alicia is the prime suspect. The overwhelming evidence, including the discovery of Alicia's scarf at the crime scene, causes even Clark to question Alicia's innocence. Alicia tells Clark that the only way that they can ever "be free" is if he, too, is open about his abilities. When Clark refuses, Alicia takes matters into her own hands and orchestrates a scenario in which he uses his superpowers right in front of Chloe.

Clark gives the scarf to Sheriff Adams and learns that Alicia couldn't have left it, as she was in the interrogation room at the police station at the time the second victim was attacked.

Lois meets Tim Westcott, who turns out to be a self-loathing 'meteor freak' with the ability to dissolve into a sand-like substance, and it is he who is committing these crimes and who has left Alicia to take the blame. Before Clark is able to tell Alicia that he believes in her innocence, Tim hangs her and stages it to look as if she has committed suicide.

Lois tells Clark that she believes that Tim was behind the attacks. Clark's rage leads him to nearly kill Tim before Lois intervenes. Clark visits Alicia's gravestone, where Chloe approaches and offers to be there for Clark if there is ever anything he wants to talk about.

CHLOE: It must have been so hard, being different. Having everyone judge you before they know you. Knowing that there are some people that might never accept you. I just — I want you to know that I'm here for you, if you ever need to talk.

Not only did 'Pariah' offer a serious tragedy for Clark, it also opened up a new beginning as his closest friend, Chloe Sullivan, finally learned his secret. Furthermore, the episode featured one of the season's best special effects sequences, as Clark catches a car in mid-air right in front of Chloe's eyes.

"We did ninety percent of that out in the street over by our other studio," special effects supervisor Mike Walls said of the daring stunt. "I would say a good eighty-five percent of it was Tom himself. We built a green cage that replicated the front end of the car, and we had guys swing it in. Tom would grab onto the cage and react to it

Opposite: Genevieve Teague
(Jane Seymour) meets with Lex.

'I Love Rock 'N' Roll' by Joan Jett
'To Die For' by Dan Zweben
'Deeper Water' by Minnie Driver

like that. That's how we got him actually physically catching the car, because it was too dangerous to have the car itself swing through.

"We launched the car on a pipe ramp: a guy drove it and hooked the car down the road, and it landed past the cameras," Walls added. "After that we took another car and we physically mounted it onto a crane and hung it in the air. The actual car was full-sized in midair, and it was just suspended by wires."

"That was a fantastic stunt," stunt coordinator Chris Sayour recalled. "I wouldn't allow Tom to do the very dangerous part, but he did the majority of the rest of it." For the parts where Tom needed to be doubled, Sayour performed the stunt himself. "They actually piped a car right at me. Piping means it goes off a pipe ramp," Sayour explained. "Imagine a big, thick pipe that starts at ground level and rises up like a little ramp. The car hits that on one side of the inside of its tires, and comes up on

SMALLVILLE TORCH

SECOND CHANCES

When Alicia Baker was released from Belle Reve and started telling people she was "cured", you could count me in on the side of skepticism. After all, she had tried to kill one of my best friends. What I ended up learning, though, is that everyone deserves a second chance — no matter how unstable their behavior may be.

I am not going to say that the recently deceased Alicia was the poster child for the perfect life. The girl clearly had some issues. However, with all of this talk of treatment and the knowledge that meteors do make people do strange things, it makes me think that maybe we had misjudged her. Perhaps now is as good as any time to actually apologize to Alicia Baker.

When things started going a bit crazy here in Smallville last week — "crazy" being a relative term — and people started getting attacked, all eyes immediately turned to our resident sparkly Nightcrawler wannabe. All evidence pointed to her, so it's not a surprise. I can't help but think, though, that maybe what Alicia needed and deserved was a second chance. For us to put the differences in our past and know and accept that she could and would, indeed, get better.

Unfortunately we'll never get that chance. While all of us were busy pointing fingers, the real culprit kept attacking, and kept killing. And now, Alicia Baker is just another casualty thanks to the Smallville meteors.

Where am I going with this story? I guess I want to remind everyone to keep an open mind. Even if your closest friend is a little different, it doesn't necessarily mean that they're bad. Talk to them. See if there's something redeemable within. Don't wait until it is too late.

by Chloe Sullivan

DID YOU KNOW?

Fans began requesting Alicia Baker's return within minutes of the conclusion of season three's 'Obsession' episode.

Above: Chloe pledges her support for Clark as he grieves for Alicia.

the inside of that rail, tires on one side, and turns, because there's nothing on one side, so it naturally wants to spin. It piped right at me: it flew fifty-eight feet, right to where I was standing. I stood there as long as I could, until I had to dive out of the way. It got extremely close, because the longer I stayed in there, the better the shot — they ended up with a lot of footage for that.

ALICIA: Chloe Sullivan, ace reporter. You write all these articles about the people you call freaks and you don't even realize that someone close to you is one of them. Why are you ignoring what's right in front of your face, Chloe? Don't you want to know the truth about Clark Kent?
CHLOE: Everyone knows you're crazy. Why should I believe you?
ALICIA: You don't have to. I'm going to prove it, and then you can write the story of a lifetime.

"It's all well planned out. It's not just guesswork," Sayour added. "We do test runs of timing and distance, and we figure that out to the closest fraction of a second that we can. Then it gets to Tom, where we had the car up in the air, and he does a little jig and catches it, and then turns it and runs it down. That was all Tom, and it looked great in the end." ∎

RECRUIT

WRITTEN BY: Todd Slavkin & Darren Swimmer **DIRECTED BY:** Jeannot Szwarc	**GUEST STARS:** Erica Durance (Lois Lane), Chris Carmack (Geoff Johns), John Novak (Football Coach, Metropolis University), Colby Johannson (Coop), Steve Makaj (Gary Bergen), Marcus Sim (Marcus)

When a member of a Metropolis University fraternity named Coop is found paralyzed following a drunken interaction with Lois, she is arrested for attempted murder. Clark visits Met U to check out the football program and sees all of the perks that a school athlete would enjoy. Clark learns that a former Smallville High football hero, Geoff Johns, has been using his ability to paralyze people to succeed on the field, which causes Clark to seriously question the morality of using his own powers in the game. Clark also finds out that it was Geoff who attacked Coop, after Coop had learned the truth about Geoff's power and was going to expose him.

Although Lois is cleared of the charges against her, she is kicked out of Metropolis University for her underage drinking. Clark decides to turn down Met U's scholarship offer after witnessing the consequences of Geoff's behavior and realizing the risks of exposing his abilities.

Lana learns from Lex that Genevieve Teague has been studying the Countess Thoreaux for decades, and is shown evidence that Jason has been aware of his mother's plans — and the Countess Isobel — all along.

CLARK: Why can't I have a shot at what every other high school kid dreams of?
JONATHAN: Because you're not like every other high school kid, Clark.

The events of 'Recruit' finally forced Clark to rethink his plans of using his powers for football success. "Clark realized, [to paraphrase] the words of Glenn Ford [as Jonathan Kent in *Superman: The Movie*], 'You were put here to do more than throw a football,'" Al Gough detailed, "and what Jonathan brought out was, 'You know, no matter what you're doing, Clark, you're cheating, because you're always gonna be better than everybody else. So, you know, is it a true victory?' Additionally, when he saw what happened to the other kid with powers in 'Recruit', I think Clark recognized that he's stepping into a much bigger, much more complicated world, and it's going to be harder to hide his secret. All the things that people will look the other way from in a small town, or questions they won't ask — that's not going to be the case if you're a huge college football star. So I think it was a combination of those two factors. And I think ultimately, like Superman, it was very selfless, to give up what you want, knowing your powers are to be used for more than just your own edification and glorification — and also realizing

the kind of pressure it's going to put on your family."

One sequence in this episode that was not so pleasant for Erica Durance was her character's near-drowning. "I think I scared the crew a couple of times," Erica recalled. "I have this thing: for some reason, I don't like putting my face in water, and I get real panicky about it." Fortunately the panic is only temporary. "After a few takes of going up and having a breakdown and freaking out the crew — because they don't know what this girl's doing — I kind of warmed into it a bit," Erica continued, "but it's just a very odd physical reaction I have."

CHLOE: I just have a feeling that you're destined to do a lot more in this world than just score touchdowns.
CLARK: Chloe, you've been saying a lot of weird things to me lately. What makes you think I'm destined to do anything?
CHLOE: Just a hunch.

Fans often wondered why the death of Alicia Baker, seen in the previous week's 'Pariah', was not mentioned or touched upon in this episode that took place so soon after. "Usually when we have a massive loss or a moment like that, we always have to

Smallville Ledger

FORMER CROWS TAILBACK CHARGED

Geoff Johns, the Metropolis Bulldogs' 'Teflon Tailback', has been charged with the attack and murder of fellow Met U player David 'Coop' Cooper.

Details from the Metropolis courts are pending, though informants within the Police Force claim that Johns surrendered voluntarily and confessed his responsibility for the crimes.

Cooper, twenty, was found dead in his hospital room on Friday, and hospital surveillance reveals that Mr. Johns did visit him. Cooper's death itself had been surrounded by mystery, as doctors had noticed his condition improving.

"To say we are shocked is an understatement," Bulldogs coach Clyde Calloway said in a statement released by the school. "Our prayers and thoughts are with the Johns and Cooper families at this time."

The Metropolis Bulldogs have released Johns from their line-up, and junior tailback Rich Donner is expected to take his spot on the roster.

Prior to his time in Metropolis, Johns was a star tailback for the Smallville Crows, under coaches Walt Arnold and Wayne Quigley. The Johns family could not be reached for comment at this time.

By Lacey Lee

kind of hit the reset button a little bit the next week, because otherwise every one of our characters would be in an insane asylum because of all the people they've seen die," writer Brian Peterson explained. "We always try, even if it's in the B story or the tone, to thread through some kind of an aftermath of the emotion, whether it's Lana killing somebody on a pitchfork or Clark losing Alicia. What is that person going through in the next episode? Even if it doesn't seem that they're talking about it on-screen."

"It's one of the obstacles in telling the Superman story," writer Kelly Souders added. "Every week, Clark comes across a difficult issue where people die, they go to insane asylums, it has a very dark effect. But, the truth is, he's our American hero, and we don't want to watch him wallow all the time."

Episode writer Todd Slavkin was pleased with the finished version of 'Recruit'. "Jeannot Szwarc did a great job," he said. "I'm a sports fan, and I particularly liked that show. Just the scope of the stadium and the seduction of Clark Kent in the sorority house and those moments made a really fun rite of passage show." ◾

KRYPTO

WRITTEN BY: Luke Schelhaas
DIRECTED BY: James Marshall

GUEST STARS: Erica Durance (Lois Lane), Bud the Dog (Einstein/Shelby), Jane Seymour (Genevieve Teague), Alvin Sanders (Store Owner), Alex Green (Dr. Kline), Bucks the Dog (Hercules), Nolan Funk (Zack Greenfield), Diego Klattenhoff (Josh Greenfield)

A LuthorCorp experiment has created superpowered animals. Two of these animals, dogs named Hercules and Einstein, rob the Smallville Cooperative under the command of brothers Zack and Josh Greenfield. Einstein escapes and is hit by Lois's car; she brings the wounded animal back to the Kent farm to take care of it. When Chloe comes to visit, the dog escapes its chains and wrecks half the Kent property; Clark quickly realizes that the dog has superstrength. Clark and Lois learn that the dog is far from your ordinary pup, with enhancements coming from a LuthorCorp-developed kryptonite-based serum. Clark visits Lex, who reveals that his father was conducting experiments combining steroids with meteor rocks to enhance canines, and the Greenfield brothers stole the research. Clark becomes attached to the dog, while the criminals hunt for it to use in their next heist.

Meanwhile, Lana overhears Genevieve tell Jason that she set him up with Lana, and that their ancestor Gertrude was an enemy of Isobel's — and Isobel swore vengeance on Gertrude and all her heirs.

When Lois and Clark try to stop the thieving brothers, Einstein saves Clark's life before losing his powers completely. The Kents end up adopting the dog, which they name Shelby. This doesn't go over too well with Lois, who is violently allergic to Shelby.

In the quest for the stones, Lionel confronts Jason with the knowledge that he has been doing research for Lex, and tries to get Jason to join him as an ally. With Chloe's help, Lana confirms that Genevieve Teague's ancestors have historical connections to Isobel.

LOIS: He's annoying, and I can't seem to get within ten feet of him without getting sick... I think we should call him Clarkie.

"It sounded like a really fun idea to bring Krypto on," series director Greg Beeman said. "It's the ironic thing where what sounds fun and easy and cheap ends up not being that way. At the end of the day, dogs are slow, and dogs doing superpowered stunts are kind of slow."

Casting the right dog for 'Krypto' was an adventure and a challenge. "The bottom line is, there are only so many trained dogs in Vancouver, especially on relatively short notice. There was a month to train this dog to break down doors and leap on trucks and drag people to safety," Beeman explained. "We didn't have the flexibility, and it wasn't within our abilities to bring in an animal trainer from the United States, so we had a limited pool of animals to start with, especially a limited pool of dogs that have that level

Opposite: The Kent family has a new addition.

of training.

"A guy came in, and said, 'I've got this dog, and he's fantastic,'" Beeman continued. "It was actually a white-and-black spotted sheep dog, and the trainer told us, 'In three weeks, I'll have him doing everything you want,' and so we bought into this young sheep dog. Three weeks later, after we already paid the guy a lot of money, he wanted more money, and said the dog would not be able to do everything we wanted. So at that point, we went to *Air Bud*."

CLARK: I was thinking we could call him Krypto.

LOIS: Why, because he's so cryptic like you? I don't think so.

CLARK: Why not?

LOIS: Because I think it's dumb. You can call your next dog Krypto.

The search to cast the Kent family dog now seemed to be over, thanks to a canine star of several movies. "They've done all of the *Air Bud* movies in Vancouver, and there are a lot of good, trained golden retrievers who have been doing *Air Bud* movies for ten solid years," Beeman noted. "So the Shelby we got was old, but trained. It was like

Below: Clark seems to like Shelby more than he likes Lois!

SUPER-PETS!

Super-animals have been a part of the Superman mythos for decades before we met the two super-dogs in 'Krypto'. In the classic Superman comics, prior to 1985's *Crisis on Infinite Earths*, there were Kryptonian animals of almost every sort who survived their planet's explosion. Here are a few of them:

KRYPTO THE SUPER-DOG

Possibly the most famous of the 'super-pets' and recently the star of his own animated TV series. In the original comic books, Krypto belonged to baby Kal-El prior to the destruction of their planet. The dog was sent away as a test by Jor-El and reunited with Clark when he was a teen. In current comic book continuity, Krypto was found on a fake Krypton that Superman ventured to. The present-day Krypto from the comic books has many super-abilities but maintains the intellect of a regular dog.

STREAKY THE SUPER-CAT

Streaky was Supergirl's pet feline in the classic comic books. She got her powers from exposure to kryptonite. Interestingly, her origin is the most like what happened in *Smallville*'s 'Krypto' episode!

BEPPO THE SUPER-MONKEY

Another animal sent by Jor-El as a test subject, who has not been seen in DC Comics since the 1980s.

COMET THE SUPER-HORSE

This super-pet was actually not Kryptonian, but a character created by magic. The original Comet had the ability to turn himself into human form as Supergirl's boyfriend Bill Starr. In modern comics, Comet's alter-ego is a woman named Andrea.

---

bringing in Johnny Unitas off the bench. Old and creaky but could jump, could run, could drag... could do all the tricks."

There were certain requirements put on the *Smallville* production team if they were to bring a dog onto the show. For one, the dog could not resemble the comic book Krypto or have that name.

"I think that they specifically wanted it to not conflict and compete with the Krypto cartoon series, which is on the Cartoon Network," Beeman said. "At the end of the show, we had to be completely clear that it was not Krypto and it was not a superpowered dog from Krypton. It was, in fact, an ordinary dog that had had a kryptonite injection, and it was superpowered only briefly."

To get around the name change, "Lois says at the end of the episode, something like 'Krypto will be the name of your next dog'," Beeman recalled. And with this episode, the Kents now had a new addition to their family... ∎

SMALLVILLE MUSIC

'Anodyne' by Speechwriters LLC
'Give A Little Bit' by Goo Goo Dolls

SACRED

WRITTEN BY: Kelly Souders & Brian Peterson DIRECTED BY: Brad Turner	GUEST STARS: Terence Stamp (Voice of Jor-El), Michelle Goh (Professor Sen), Kai Xu (Chinese Soldier), Mike Wu (Chinese Soldier), Byron Mann (Chinese Officer)

The silver octagonal key that disappeared a year earlier is sent to Clark following the death of Dr. Swann. In a note, Dr. Swann indicates that the key will lead Clark to his destiny. Clark speaks to Jor-El, who explains that it is essential he obtain the three elements.

Jason heads to Shanghai to search for one of the stones, and finds that Lex is following him. Lionel tells Lana where Jason is and gives her a copy of the map to help her locate the stone. When Lana tells Clark that she is heading to China he decides to go with her. In a sacred temple in Shanghai, containing a secret chamber holding the air element, Lex and Jason are captured and tortured by Chinese authorities, while Clark battles an Isobel-possessed Lana. The final keeper of the sacred stone is unknown to all... except Jason, who has managed to procure the element, and shares his discovery with Lana.

In an email he sent to Clark before he died, Dr. Swann informed him that he sent Bridgette Crosby to deliver one of the stones. However, when Clark tries to contact her, all phone numbers and evidence of her existence are gone...

JOR-EL: You must find the other two stones. The fate of your world lies in your hands, Kal-El.

"I was very involved in that episode, and it was a big project," director Greg Beeman said of the task of turning British Columbia into Shanghai. "David Willson [production designer] really did an amazing job. We shot in this gigantic space, which was essentially a deserted warehouse with big columns. He did drawings and a model, and said to me, 'Here's what I want it to be.' We knew that we were going to China, and that Lana was going to do *Crouching Tiger, Hidden Dragon* stuff — but that is where David Willson is a great asset, because he had a vision, not just of how we're going to make it look, but how the look is going to integrate into the show."

Even though the final result of the Clark/Isobel fight looked really good on-screen, it was actually one of the season's easier sequences for the show's effects team. "We got lucky with Kristin," Mike Walls said. "She is incredibly agile and has a gymnastics background, so it was really easy to teach her to fly. She did ninety percent of that work better than the stunt people. She picked up all the moves in about eight hours. She was fantastic. That was one of the most fun things we've ever done."

"We pulled Kristin on a wire at forty feet with no double and turned her 180 degrees in the air and landed her about three feet from camera," explained Chris Sayour, "which was

Opposite: Another one of the elements is discovered.

DID YOU KNOW?

This is the only *Smallville* episode to date where a majority of the action takes place in another country.

an amazing stunt to do with a stunt performer, and great to do with Kristin, because she physically made it work perfectly. She looked great in the air. It's one of the cooler shots in that episode, her flying across the room, spinning in the air and right into the camera. It wasn't green screen; it wasn't a stunt double; it was one hundred percent her."

LEX: Even though getting pistol-whipped wasn't exactly my idea of fun, I have to admit, it's good to have the old Dad back.

Greg Beeman was very impressed with director Brad Turner. "He had been recommended to me, and he had done some episodes of *24* that were really impressive. I thought he did a fantastic job on this episode. I tried to go after him to do many more, but he got snapped up as a producer of *24*. Brad Turner just got it. I think he got the show, and he really shot it well."

Earlier drafts of the 'Sacred' script had the sad news of Virgil Swann's passing being delivered by Margot Kidder's Bridgette Crosby. Scheduling and financial issues prevented Kidder's return, and Kidder said in interviews at the time that she didn't feel it was appropriate being brought back just to announce the news of Swann's death. In the end the character died off-screen, her body eventually being found in 'Spirit'. ∎

Below: Lana and Clark are reunited in a faraway place. Are they about to grow close again?

Smallville ✦ Ledger

* * * * * * * * * * * * * *

BELOVED SCIENTIST WILL BE MISSED

In honor of Dr. Virgil Swann's contributions to our world, the *Ledger* is reprinting this 1977 Man Of The Year article.

1977's MAN OF THE YEAR — VIRGIL SWANN
By Perry White

"Only through communication will people live in peace." — Dr. Virgil Swann

Gazing out his office window high atop the Manhattan skyline, Dr. Virgil Swann speculates on the future of global communications. Coming from the man who practically coined the term, his musings conjure a feeling of wonder more often found in science fiction. But Dr. Swann is wildly serious. This is a man focused on propelling the human race into an era of communication unmatched in history. Not since the invention of Gutenberg's printing press has such a revolution been so poised to impact our world. A modern Renaissance could be upon us — and there will be one man to thank when it arrives.

Undoubtedly, this year has seen its share of notable events. In the Middle East, Anwar Sadat made the first steps toward a miracle: a peace treaty between Israel and Egypt. Jimmy Carter was sworn in as the thirty-nineth President of the United States of America. NASA's space shuttle *Enterprise* took its maiden flight from the top of a 747. And the king of rock and roll, Elvis Presley, passed away.

While all of these events had a dramatic effect on our world this year, Dr. Virgil Swann's advancements in satellite technology promise to resonate for generations to come. *Scientific American* proclaimed him "The Man of Tomorrow", and this magazine now names him 1977's Man Of The Year.

At the early age of nineteen, wunderkind Virgil Swann graduated *summa cum laude* from MIT with doctorates in mathematics and applied physics. Shortly thereafter, he founded Swann Communications in dedication to his life's pursuit: advancing technology focused on global communication.

In early 1976, Swann Communications launched the first of its SWANNSTAR series of satellites, which dramatically reduced the cost of delivering data to millions of people the world over.

This year, Swann Communications became the largest producer of satellites after sending its thirty-sixth SWANNSTAR unit into orbit. Through Swann's innovations, today's science fiction can become tomorrow's reality.

"The paradigm of three television networks will soon be a thing of the past," comments a station owner from Atlanta who asked not to be named. "Virgil has laid the foundations for what we might call a global village. It's not inconceivable that we'll someday have networks devoted solely to sports or news or finance — networks that could have a global reach twenty-four hours a day. Anyone on the planet who wants it will have access to the latest events as they happen."

Clearly it will take years to comprehend the sociological impact of Swann's work. But it has taken very little time to see the financial effects on Swann Communications. With contracts in hand from over ninety percent of the world's television networks, Swann's privately held company is valued in the tens of billions of dollars.

However, Swann is that rare businessman who would continue his work even if there were no financial gain involved. "I do this because I believe that only through communication will people live in peace."

Swann downplays his role in the predicted revolution. "Communication is simply the transmission and reception of a message. What I do is no different from what a postal worker does. I deliver the message. It's what the recipient does with that message that is really important."

LUCY

WRITTEN BY: Neil Sadhu &
Daniel Sulzberg (teleplay);
Neil Sadhu (story)
DIRECTED BY: David Barrett

GUEST STARS: Erica Durance (Lois Lane), Bud the Dog
(Shelby), Peyton List (Lucy Lane), Peter Wingfield (Marcus
Becker), Kaleena Kiff (Lex's Aide)

Lois Lane's younger sister Lucy comes to Smallville on a break from boarding school in Switzerland. Much to Lois's disappointment, Lucy and Clark hit it off. Jason and Lana return to her apartment to find it has been robbed and the knowledge element is missing.

Clark catches Lucy stealing money from the Talon and she weaves a tale about owing a serious amount of money to a dangerous European loan shark named Marcus Becker. Clark goes to Lex for financial assistance for Lucy. Lex puts up bearers bonds and takes them to Becker with Lois and Lucy. En route the girls are captured by Becker, who is trying to get hold of Lex's money. Clark and Lois discover that Lucy's debt is an elaborate ploy to steal money from Lex Luthor, arranged between herself and Becker. In the end, Lucy speeds off in one of Lex's cars to parts unknown with fifty thousand dollars of Luthor money. Meanwhile, at her apartment, Lana has hidden the stone herself without telling Jason or anyone else…

LOIS: You're amazing, Smallville. You always look for the best in people even when they walk all over you.
CLARK: I guess that explains why we're friends.
LOIS: Oh, we're friends now?
CLARK: Well, I won't tell anyone if you don't.

"I really, really enjoyed that episode," Erica Durance said of one of the first stories that gave Lois Lane the spotlight. "Of course, it was in my first year, so I was still running on nerves. It was fantastic, because it was a chance to explore a little bit more of where Lois came from, and hopefully be able to show people why she has some of her idiosyncrasies and really delve more into her history."

Erica saw 'Lucy' as an opportunity to help people understand a little more why Lois is so gruff and full of defense mechanisms. "She's come from a home life where she never really had a childhood," she explained. "She had to be an adult from a very young age, and so it was nice to be able to work on that aspect of her character."

One of the most fantastic special effects sequences in the episode occured when Clark took a giant leap from an overpass onto Becker's truck. From season five on, the shot has been immortalized in *Smallville*'s opening credits. "There were a lot of different pieces to make that happen," detailed special effects supervisor Mike Walls. "Out on the

Opposite: Lex is impressed with
Lucy's skill at playing the violin.

'Club Foot' by Kasabian
'Spaghetti Streetwalker' by Speechwriters LLC
'Hold On' by Newcomers Home
'Fly' by Mark Joseph

location, we had a stunt guy climbing up on the rail and making it look like he was getting ready to jump. We cheated by using this bridge that we found so we could actually go over the rail, and he was only jumping about ten feet onto some pads.

"Then we had this mechanical contraption we built called a parallelogram, which we use for all of our flying," Walls continued. "It basically keeps everybody in a constant plane where you can lift them up and down like a big arm. We had Tom on that, and we'd just create the path that they wanted him to fly; then for the sliding part we had Tom run across the stage and jump onto a piece of Teflon. As he hit the Teflon, we pulled it along so it looked like he was skidding down the length of the trailer, kind of out of control."

SMALLVILLE TORCH

HURRICANE LUCY PASSES THROUGH SMALLVILLE

Visitor Leaves Questions About Her Future And A Lesson From Her Past.

When my cousin, Lucy Lane, fled town yesterday behind the wheel of Lex Luthor's six-figure sports car, she left behind more questions than answers. Most notably, will she ever come back? And, if she does, will she do so as a prisoner?

Lex Luthor has done his part to answer the latter question by refusing to press charges against Lucy for both the elaborate scam she tried to pull on him and for the theft of his car. Incidentally, Lex VI or VII or VIII (I can't keep up anymore) was found in the parking lot of Metropolis's Central Train Station five hours after we last saw her. The car was unmolested.

No doubt, Lex's own notoriously rebellious childhood played a part in his charitable decision to let Lucy flee *sans* police pursuit. No doubt, Lucy is anywhere but in the United States by now.

Lucy left behind a hastily scribbled, remorseful apology note to her sister Lois in Lex's car. Here's what it said:

Lo,
The General always said, "If you want inner peace, prepare for mental war." Well, my emotional troops are about to give up the fight, so I'm off to search for the lesson to be learned from all of this on my own. I hope you can forgive me.
I do love you. And I am sorry.
Lucy

Lucy will get a second chance, and as her family member I can only hope she figures out that not keeping up with the Joneses of the private Euro school elite is far less painful than getting your legs broken by the debt collector.

by Chloe Sullivan

"We liked the idea that Lois had a sister that, even in the comic books, had a troubled past, so that's really where that came from," Al Gough said about the introduction of Lois Lane's younger sister to the series.

Above: This is the first time in *Smallville*'s history that Lois Lane and Lex Luthor share a scene together!

CLARK: I guess no matter how bad you want to, you just can't save everyone.

Despite the appearance of what should have been an exciting new character, the episode didn't resonate too well in fans' minds. "It's so hard for people to get emotionally tied to a character that's just in one episode, who has just shown up to do a guest spot," series writer Kelly Souders said. "I think you remember, 'Oh, yeah, Lois's sister came to town,' but you are really going to cling to the moments in the episode that were between our main cast. We always try to center everything around them. Every once in a while we veer out, but we really care about our main cast, and that's what the audience tunes in for."

'Lucy' ended with Lucy Lane going off to parts unknown. General Lane charged Lois with the job of finding her, though she has yet to resurface on the show. ∎

DID YOU KNOW?

The first live-action Lucy Lane was Maureen Teefy in the 1984 film *Supergirl*, directed by *Smallville*'s very own Jeannot Szwarc!

ONYX

WRITTEN BY: Steven S. DeKnight
DIRECTED BY: Terrence O'Hara

GUEST STARS: Rekha Sharma (Dr. Harden), Malcolm Stewart (Dr. Sinclair), Carra Maureen (Fencing Instructor)

A LuthorCorp experiment involving heated black kryptonite accidentally splits Lex into two beings: a benevolent Lex, who represents his good side, and Alexander, who embodies his repressed dark side. Alexander locks away the good Lex, forcing him to wear an iron mask (like in Alexandre Dumas's novel, *The Man in the Iron Mask*) and wreaks havoc as he taunts Lionel, tries to kill Chloe and Clark, and attempts to coerce Lana into becoming his lover. When Clark resists Alexander's pursuit to recruit him as an ally in evil, he uses a green kryptonite ring to overpower Clark. Seeing the ring as an opportunity, Clark uses his heat vision to turn it into black kryptonite, thereby fusing the two Lexes together. Lex tries to apologize to Lionel for his behavior as Alexander, but Lionel in fact thanks him for "the wake-up call". Lionel ceases his charitable endeavors, and the true Lionel Luthor returns...

ALEXANDER: I am the villain of the story!

"We really wanted to play with the idea of a glimpse into the future with your classic Superman Lex Luthor, where the gloves are off, and, literally, the kryptonite ring comes on," writer Steve DeKnight said about the conception of 'Onyx'. "I remember when we were breaking that story in the room, we were thinking: 'Okay, so he splits. Where do we go from here? I mean, he's evil and it's missing something!' And I said, 'Oh! The kryptonite ring! He puts on the kryptonite ring and beats the hell out of Clark!' We even reached in and borrowed something from the final fight between Superman and Batman in Frank Miller's *The Dark Knight Returns*."

"Michael Rosenbaum, in a good way, gets sort of freaked out when he's challenged," Greg Beeman revealed. "For whatever reason, he's just pretty good at playing regular Lex, and he steps into it very easily and very fluidly. 'Onyx' was a challenge that really got him anxious, and he worked really hard on Alexander, and who Alexander was going to be. He's a hard worker. And so, when it came down to filming, he had a lot of ideas that were different from what he was being told. I think some people — not necessarily Miles and Al but other powers — thought that it was important that Alexander would be much darker and much straighter. I think people in the *Smallville* team wanted to stay away from the comedic Gene Hackman version of Lex," Beeman continued. "There was a lot of discouragement of him finding any comedy in that character, but I think Michael found a really good balance of making Alexander funny and dark and more menacing than the regular Michael Rosenbaum Lex, and in clearly differentiating the two. I know he also worked really hard with Terrence O'Hara, but he did a lot of work on his own and really brought that to the table. It's a pretty cool episode. We did some nice split screen work to put him in the same shots with himself, and some of the

Opposite: Alexander taunts Lionel, challenging him to a fencing match.

Above: The two sides of Lex, both in one frame!

stunts were very successful."

In one of the episode's major scenes, Alexander approaches Clark in his barn and tells him that he knows of his powers. He then speculates that with Clark's powers, and his own intellect, together they would be unstoppable. "There was a little Darth Vader-Luke Skywalker in there when he was saying, 'Join forces with me, and we can control the world,'" DeKnight commented, remembering his *Star Wars* influences.

CLARK: You're not him. The real Lex would never try to kill me or Chloe.

ALEXANDER: No, you're probably right. But he's thought about it! All the times you've meddled in his plans, derailed his ambitions. He's thought about killing all of you. He just never had the guts to go through with it.

DID YOU KNOW?

Lex putting the moves on Lana may have foreshadowed their relationship in later seasons.

Mike Walls revealed that a lot of the double-Lex effects were actually achieved by body doubles and photo doubles. "I think you only ever saw them together in two scenes," Walls noted. "When they fought, we got pretty involved with the body double

Smallville ✶ Ledger

LEX LUTHOR LOOKS TO FUTURE
LuthorCorp powers through explosion and death

Lex Luthor, CEO of LuthorCorp, remains optimistic about the future, despite recent setbacks.

Quarterly profit margins are up once again for LuthorCorp, as stocks continue to rise.

Lex Luthor, CEO of LuthorCorp, was recently featured in *Forbes* magazine, discussing his theories on the future of American business. "I firmly believe we must reach out to related companies in other countries," Luthor was quoted as saying. "We cannot survive in the current business world, let alone the future one, if we do not embrace our many sides. LuthorCorp continues to remain one of only a handful of international corporations dedicated to promoting fair market trading and renewable resources, and the message from both the general public and our investors is clear. We pledge to not only continue making use of the Earth-friendly technologies available today, but we are also committed to further research and development aimed at the betterment of everyday life.

"In keeping with our growing company, we are expanding and building new, state-of-the-art facilities for our scientists and researchers. There were already plans for renovations in the pipeline, but minor damage caused during a recent experiment has pushed the construction start date."

"It was actually very fortuitous," said Graeme Levinson, Chief Construction Supervisor, in an interview following the explosion. He intends to break ground on the new Sinclair Research Center soon.

The center will be named after one of LuthorCorp's brightest and most promising scientists, who tragically died of heart failure. "We are obviously deeply affected by the loss of Dr. Sinclair," Amy Sanderson, assistant to LuthorCorp's Director of Public Relations, said in a statement after Sinclair's death. "Our sympathies are with his family, as well as our sincere appreciation for all of his contributions to the scientific community. He did what every scientist dreams of doing. He showed us the future."

By Ainsley O'Carroll

there, but most of the time it was pretty straightforward and easy to do. There were a couple of tricky shots where we wrap around from one guy to the other, but we've always got to add a little twist to it, to make it that much more incredible." ■

SPIRIT

WRITTEN BY: Luke Schelhaas
DIRECTED BY: Whitney Ransick

GUEST STARS: Erica Durance (Lois Lane), Beatrice Rosen (Dawn Stiles), Camille Mitchell (Sheriff Nancy Adams), Lifehouse (special musical guests), Jesse Hutch (Billy Durden), Bud the Dog (Shelby)

DID YOU KNOW?

Jesse Hutch also played Troy Turner in the early *Smallville* episodes 'Shimmer' and 'Redux'. In 'Redux', he was killed, but that didn't stop him from coming back as a new character here!

Popularity-obsessed high school senior Dawn Stiles desperately wants to be Smallville High's prom queen. When she is accidentally killed after distractedly driving off a cliff, her car lands near a bed of meteor rocks, which allows her spirit to take over the body of the nearby Martha Kent. Her spirit then transfers to the body of Lana, and later at Smallville Medical Center she takes over Lois's body. Dawn-in-Lois appears wearing a pink prom gown and demands that Clark attend the dance with her.

The students elect Chloe as prom queen, and as Chloe hugs Lois, Dawn enters her body and gives an odd acceptance speech. Dawn then attacks Jonathan and Clark. Her spirit jumps to Clark, and it's up to Jonathan to stop 'Clark' with a rock of kryptonite. Dawn's spirit leaves Clark's body and dissipates, and the prom is safe to continue. Clark then shares an intimate dance with Lana.

Meanwhile, Bridgette Crosby is found dead on the Luthor mansion grounds. Jason reports the body to Sheriff Adams, but when the authorities arrive, no sign of Dr. Crosby — or even any proof that she ever existed — can be found. However, Lex's expected cover-up was just a part of Jason and his mother's elaborate plan — they have now finally found a way to get hold of one of the elements.

CHLOE: Well, we *are* in Smallville. And what would the senior prom be without a body-snatching prom queen?

"One of the things that the show does well is what we call these sort of 'personality changer' *doppelgänger* episodes," said executive producer Al Gough. "Quite frankly, we may have gone into that well a few too many times in season four; but in its defense, I think they're all quite good episodes.

"I think what we wanted to do with Dawn Stiles was to have a character where we could have a bunch of different people [portray her]. It's kind of like the Nicodemus flower. We liked the idea of a spirit who couldn't stay in one body, or could jump from body to body, and the idea of Clark Kent grabbing the crown and saying 'The crown's mine, bitch' was just too much fun to pass up! That's really how it came about," Gough continued. "Then it was about finding a very specific actress to [play the part], which I think we did."

In the end, Annette O'Toole, Allison Mack, Erica Durance, Tom Welling, and Kristin Kreuk all got to have their own turn at playing 'Dawn' during the episode. "It was fabulous. It was a great opportunity to be someone totally different," Allison enthused.

Below: Clark finds an unlikely prom date in Lois.

"It was really great because it was an opportunity to play a character totally opposite from me," Erica Durance said of the experience. "Being on the set and watching the different actors on the show become possessed by this little drama queen was really, really fun. I think that was one of the first times that you get to see Lois possessed, but I got to play a character who is this crazy girly girl in love with Clark, so that was a little treat. I enjoyed it."

CLARK: When I was a freshman, I remember standing outside and watching the seniors going into prom. The guys in their tuxes and the girls in their dresses. I guess I always thought that that would be Lana and me.

Below: Clark and Lana share the prom dance fans waited four seasons for.

"Everybody had a really good time with it," Al Gough recalled. "Annette O'Toole is especially hysterical and great. They all just really went for it. I think that's the nice thing about those personality change episodes: for the actors who are doing this, week in and week out for years and years, when they get to bust out and do something different, they all really rise to the challenge."

"I absolutely loved that," Annette O'Toole said of her first *Smallville* behavior-change experience. "The only bad thing was having to listen to that Ashlee Simpson song and trying to learn it! Anything that's out of character like that is always really, really fun to do, to dance around and be stupid — it was great."

'Spirit' was another time in which the show's writers hoped to bring back Pete Ross, this time as Chloe's date to the prom. Unfortunately, as he was shooting a film in New Orleans, Sam Jones III was again unavailable, and so Pete's storyline was written out. Al Gough still doesn't rule out the possibility of Pete's return. "I think there's a chance you could see Pete come back, even if it's just for one episode."

Clark's dance with Lana at the prom was a callback to *Smallville*'s very first episode. "It was a payoff to the homecoming dance, where she's dancing and Clark's sort of left alone," Miles Millar revealed. "We wanted Clark to actually make it to his prom this time, and actually get to dance with the girl."

John Schneider enjoyed getting to chaperone the prom with his TV wife. "It was great. I felt like a dad

SMALLVILLE TORCH

POST-PROM REBUTTAL

I have to admit, it was only prom eve and I had already formatted the *Torch*'s front page for the surprise-surprise victory story of Dawn Stiles as this year's prom queen. The article (prewritten for immediate publication) was rife with sarcastic shock and I-told-you-so annoyance. There was even a box for Dawn's photo, with a caption that said, "Dawn Stiles, Prom Queen: Wow, was that a short reach for the stars." And then, roll-eyes, I won.

It was probably best that, while onstage, my body was inhabited by Dawn Stiles (in case you missed it — Dawn Stiles had body-jumped her way into mine). Had I actually been able to address my fellow classmates, I would not have known what to say. This opinion-packed-and-not-scared-to-voice-it *Torch* editor would have been too shocked to formulate a compound phrase such as "thank you".

I'd like to use this free press opportunity to hand in my one-time-foot-in-the-mouth article retraction notice. As Dawn would have said, I'm a hippercrat. And, Dawn, you would have been right.

We all know I didn't win prom queen for my ability to tell a Marc Jacobs from a Calvin Klein. And I certainly didn't win because I posted Chloe Sullivan headshots around school accompanied by catch phrases like "OMG! Rock the Vote!" I won because a student body, whose views on prom I totally underestimated, proved to me why I've spent the last four years trying, with this publication, to represent them.

So here is my prom speech, granted a buck short and a day late:

I was so disgusted by the whole Miss America pageant angle that I overlooked the majority vote, and the majority vote considers fairness, allegiance, and an active participation. Chloe Sullivan didn't win prom queen. Smallville High was the noble victor in this one, and I am honored to represent my class in accepting the title. I've learned through this experience that the tiara doesn't represent the Best or the Coolest or the Hottest. The tiara — this shiny, prickly, ornamental crown — represents unity. And Class, thank you for reminding me that, even in a town with the capacity to shrug off a body-jumping episode, we are still united. Thank you.

by Chloe Sullivan

attending the prom with my lovely bride by my side, looking at all the young Smallvillain folks. It felt terrific," he remembered. "When you're an actor, you forget at times that you don't have an opportunity to feel like an adult all that often when you're acting, because you're having a great time on the set, and you're with your best buddies for the moment. It's a rare feeling to have an adult moment on the set of a television show, and it felt great." ∎

BLANK

WRITTEN BY: Kelly Souders &
Brian Peterson
DIRECTED BY: Jeannot Szwarc

GUEST STARS: Erica Durance (Lois Lane), Camille Mitchell
(Sheriff Nancy Adams), Jonathan Bennett (Kevin Grady),
Tom Butler (Lawrence Grady), Heather Doerksen
(Receptionist), Ryan King (Dillon Grady)

A boy named Kevin, who has the power to erase portions of people's memories, robs the Talon. He uses his ability on Lois after getting caught swiping money from the register, and Clark is his next victim when he tries to apprehend him. Suddenly the world becomes a confusing blur to Clark, and he no longer remembers or recognizes anything. With Chloe's help, Clark learns that he can bend steel with his bare hands. Lex tries to take advantage of Clark's memory loss: he pretends that he and Clark have been working on studying the Kawatche caves together, in order to pump Clark for what he knows. Unaware of their complicated past, Clark approaches Lana and tries to capture her interest.

Chloe breaks into Summerholt to gather information and is captured. Clark and Lois discover that Kevin's memories were erased by his father. Together Clark and Kevin break into Summerholt, where they find Chloe tied to a large mechanical contraption. When they rescue her, the machine breaks and Clark's memories are restored.

Lana grows increasingly concerned that her relationship with Jason is mired in deceit. Meanwhile, with his memories intact, Clark vows to Lana that he's not going to let her go and make the same mistakes again…

CHLOE: You've sort of taken it upon yourself to be Smallville's self-appointed hero. And if you ask me, I think that that is amazing.

Clark's dramatic memory loss in 'Blank' gave the writers a chance to have Chloe discover the full extent of Clark's powers, even as he was rediscovering the powers that he had forgotten himself. Thanks to Alicia Baker, Chloe had first learned that Clark was more than an ordinary teen eight episodes earlier in 'Pariah', but this was the first time that she really learned the full extent of what he could do as she helped him piece his identity back together following Kevin's attack.

Up to this point, Chloe had kept her knowledge of Clark's abilities to herself. "Chloe wanted Clark to tell her," executive producer Al Gough said. "She knew but wanted Clark to feel comfortable with it, which is why if you look at the latter part of that season she's dropping hints the whole time. She really is his best friend, and she'll protect him, and she'll make sure that he's not compromised."

The show also gave a rare, early opportunity to show that despite their bickering, Lois Lane really does care about Clark Kent in a friendly way — that despite driving one another crazy, Lois and Clark will be there for one another when needed. "It's been fun to be able to play those moments," Erica Durance commented.

Opposite: With Clark's help Kevin
pieces together his lost memories.

Above: Chloe tries to jog Clark's memory.

'24' by Jem
'Let Me Go' by 3 Doors Down
'Satie' by Paco
'This Is Your Life' by Switchfoot

Lex Luthor used Clark's meteor freak-inflicted amnesia to his own advantage to try and discover what knowledge Clark possessed regarding the caves and the crystals. "Again we see Lex being manipulative," explained executive producer Al Gough, "playing the cards that are dealt in front of him to his own advantage."

CLARK: What did I do?
CHLOE: You trusted me.

One particularly memorable sequence in 'Blank' comes as Kevin takes away Clark's memories, and features a montage of clips, moving backward all the way through to the *Smallville* series pilot, and even beyond that point to shots of baby Kal-El from the season three finale episode 'Memoria'. This fast unraveling sequence gave fans brief glimpses of popular characters from the show's past, including Alicia Baker, Pete Ross, and Dr. Virgil Swann.

'Blank' also stands out as one of the last regular episodes of *Smallville*, aside from the season finale 'Commencement', to prominently feature the Kawatche caves. Once the three elements were combined at the end of season four, the Arctic Fortress of Solitude became Clark's new haven of knowledge and seclusion. ∎

Smallville ⬤ Ledger

MEMORY LOSS A YOUTHFUL CONCERN
Short-term lapses result in turmoil and injury

Memory loss is often listed as one of the main concerns for those of us growing older, but rarely is it fretted about by high schoolers. After recent events, however, some Smallville High students may change their tune.

A series of bizarre and inexplicable occurrences of short-term memory loss plagued Smallville High Seniors this week, bringing much confusion, and even harm, to others. Billy Durden, one of Smallville's star athletes, was hospitalized for injuries caused by electrocution. In a police statement, Durden explained that he was shocked in the school locker room but could not identify his assailant. With no leads, authorities are currently speculating that Durden was attacked by a student now suffering memory loss.

Clark Kent, resident hero and another Smallville High student, found Durden lying on the floor, unconscious. When asked in an interview about the assault, Kent could not shed any further light on the mysterious attacker. "Everything, and everyone, seemed a little different. Maybe it had to do with prom," said Kent, cryptically. "Let's just say people weren't acting like themselves."

Chloe Sullivan, editor of the school newspaper, went on record saying that she believed the spirit of another student, Dawn Stiles, had inhabited her body. "I know it sounds crazy. But, then again, this is Smallville," Sullivan told the authorities. Stiles was reported missing a day before the first incidence of memory loss was reported. She was later found at the bottom of Carlton Gorge, her car having crashed into the ravine. Stiles died at the Smallville Medical Center shortly after being admitted.

Sullivan insists that Stiles was responsible for her unusual behavior at the high school prom. "One second I was me, and then the next thing I know, Dawn and I went *Freaky Friday*. Without the knowing part. I can't remember a thing. It's a terrible feeling," Sullivan said. She then added, a grimace twisting her bright face, "And I only lost ten minutes. Just imagine if the entire slate got wiped clean."

By Ainsley O'Carroll

AGELESS

WRITTEN BY: Steven S. DeKnight
DIRECTED BY: Steven S. DeKnight

GUEST STARS: Jane Seymour (Genevieve Teague), Camille Mitchell (Sheriff Nancy Adams), Colin Ford (Evan, 'age 7'), Jeff Ballard (Evan, 'age 16'), Matt Ellis (Tanner Sutherland), Pascale Hutton (Karen Gallagher), Owen Stewart (Evan as 'baby'), Elizabeth Stewart (Evan as 'baby'), John Shaw (LuthorCorp Scientist), Frank C. Turner (Mechanic), Marshall Kaplan (Lex's Aide)

Mirroring a situation faced by Jonathan and Martha Kent fifteen years earlier, Clark and Lana find a baby abandoned in a field. Clark convinces his parents to let the infant stay with them until Child Services can claim the baby.

Lionel and Genevieve play a game of cat and mouse, both denying that their sons each possess one of the stones. Lana and Clark name the child Evan. Soon after Clark places Evan in a crib, an explosion of light occurs and the baby matures into a seven year-old boy. Lex's scientific team determines that a bone marrow transplant from Evan's parents may be the only solution to Evan's abnormal energy and cell growth. With Chloe's help, Clark locates Evan's biological father, Tanner Sutherland, who denies even having a child, and refuses to help. Lex informs Clark that Evan's next rapid growth may come with enough energy release to kill himself as well as anyone within a square-mile radius.

An angry Evan accidentally kills Tanner, and all hope of recovery is lost, as there will now be no bone marrow. At the windmill Evan undergoes another burst of rapid aging and finally explodes in a brilliant burst of light. Despite their loss, Lana and Clark enjoy a renewed connection with each other, possibly heralding a new beginning...

CHLOE: I found an arrowhead in Evan's Field once, but never a baby in a crater.

Every season on every TV show has some high points and some low points. For *Smallville* season four, the low-water mark may have been 'Ageless', known ever since as "the exploding baby episode".

"I blame, once again, myself," writer and director Steve DeKnight admitted. "This was my first year on the show, and the first time I was directing for *Smallville*, and I was very much following the party line, like 'Oh, okay. Let's get in there and make it work.'

"We were breaking that story while we were still working on 'Onyx'," DeKnight continued, "and we were talking about kryptonite zombies — a story that I still love — with a LuthorCorp chemical spill, a graveyard — the classic thing. Kryptonite zombies attack, and it's *Night of the Living Dead* on the farm, and Clark's weakened because they're radiating kryptonite. But that didn't [work out].

"I left to work on 'Onyx', and then I came back and got told, 'Hey, we've got a great story

Opposite: Clark and Lana enjoy their new find.

for you: Clark and Lana find a baby.' And then Jeph Loeb and I just started making things worse. 'What if every time he age shifts, he expends more and more energy, so he's basically a human bomb?' It just went downhill from there, really," DeKnight said, laughing. "Everybody did their best on the show, but because I was up in a van in the Canadian wilderness for six days location scouting, I couldn't rewrite the script."

LANA: We think we have all the time in the world, that we're going to live forever, but it's not true. I guess we should make the most of the time we have, before it's too late.

Executive producer Al Gough also admits that 'Ageless' was not everything that it could have been, citing it as one of his least favorite episodes of the season. "It's another one of those things where, when you set out to do these stories, you intend for them to be good, but when you get to the exploding baby point, that's hard. You think, on paper, 'good idea', but that one just got a little out of hand."

One of the things 'Ageless' is remembered for in a positive way, is that it featured several scenes where Clark and Lana take care of baby Evan together and gradually start rebuilding their friendship. This is one of the initial steps the writers would start to take to finally reunite the characters. "Slowly, we continually played up the attraction," DeKnight said. "Finding the baby did allow them to have a couple of romantic scenes together without being one hundred percent romantic, which was nice. It really set up where things were headed." ∎

Right: Little Evan is growing up... and quickly!

SMALLVILLE TORCH

YEAR IN REVIEW

We've had our prom and ordered the yearbooks, and now all that remains is for the senior class to take that walk in two weeks. It's been a crazy four years for me, and we've had some amazing times together. As we look ahead to the future, let's pause and look back at the top ten most important events at Smallville High this school year.

10. Rumors of Her Death Were Greatly Exaggerated: *Torch* editor Chloe Sullivan had quite a year. When we kicked off school, she was presumed dead. Happily, she reappeared and continued her investigative endeavors — uncovering stories and having experiences she'd never imagined.

9. Mysterious Dog Attacks: Two SHS students were involved in a series of burglaries involving dogs. By most accounts these dogs appeared to be extra violent and strong. Zack and Josh Greenfield were arrested in connection with these robberies, but they denied the dogs were anything super. In any case, they are both awaiting trial.

8. Met U Student Becomes SHS Student: Metropolis University freshman (and cousin to our own Chloe Sullivan) Lois Lane joined the SHS party part-time this year. Met U required she make up some credits, so SHS and the *Torch* welcomed a super-senior.

7. Coronation of a Crow: Despite the fact that she railed against the archaic tradition of crowning a prom queen, our very own Chloe Sullivan received the honor at this year's prom. We're proud of you, Chief!

6. Flashy Visitors: In a small town, you pretty much know every face. That's why it was interesting to see Bart Allen and Lucy Lane show up in our leafy little hamlet. Even though their time in Smallville came and went quickly, they sure charmed a lot of students. It was a good reminder that there are always new people out there to meet.

5. Former SHS Football Star Involved in Murder Mystery: We all remember Geoff Johns' powerful play on the SHS football field. He made us proud playing college ball for Metropolis University. But the legend may have died when he was charged in connection with a murder at Met U.

4. Remember That One Time?: A rash of temporary amnesia ran through SHS recently. Even though teachers didn't buy it as an excuse, LuthorCorp and the Smallville Medical Center released a statement confirming several occurrences. Too bad we don't really remember...

3. State Championship Crows: It was a great year for the gridiron Crows. Led by a seemingly superpowered quarterback, Clark Kent, the team went on to take the state championship. The win was all but overshadowed, however, by several off-field incidents: cheerleaders were accused of spiking the team's sports drinks, an underground gambling ring was broken up, and assistant coach Jason Teague was fired for inappropriate relations with a student.

2. Graduation: I know it's still two weeks away, but this is a big deal for the seniors — the real world awaits. So whether you're going to Metropolis University, Central Kansas A&M or Kohlen Beauty School — wherever your life is taking you — good luck!

1. In Memoriam: We lost some friends this year. As we begin our new lives after high school, we'll never forget those who lost theirs. We pay special tribute to scientist Dr. Virgil Swann. He wasn't a member of the SHS community, but regardless, he was a legend. He led us forward into unknown scientific frontiers. The world was struck by his courage, touched by his power. He became a heroic icon on par with legends. As we commemorate his life at his passing, it is with tender poignancy that we look up in the sky and see what can be.

by Jake Black

FOREVER

WRITTEN BY: Kelly Souders & Brian Peterson
DIRECTED BY: James Marshall

GUEST STARS: Erica Durance (Lois Lane), Jane Seymour (Genevieve Teague), Steven Grayhm (Brendan Nash), Veena Sood (Schoolteacher), Chad Krowchuk (Wendell Johnson)

DID YOU KNOW?

Guest star Jane Seymour (Genevieve Teague) and John Schneider (Jonathan Kent) appeared together on several episodes of *Dr. Quinn, Medicine Woman.*

The end of high school is near, and the *Torch*'s resident photographer, Brendan Nash, is having a lot of trouble letting go. To keep his high school life going forever, Brendan kidnaps several of his peers and holds them in a replicated Smallville High. Those who don't play by his rules are petrified into statues of wax. One of his first victims is Chloe, who was named 'Most Likely To Succeed'. Afterward, Brendan approaches the student 'Most Likely To Be A Cover Girl', and Lana becomes the latest addition to his wax collection.

Jason and Genevieve abduct Lex and Lionel and hold them hostage with hopes of obtaining one of the elements. Lionel claims he has given the element to Lana, because she is "the chosen one". The Luthors escape to the woods, and Jason chases after them. Just as Jason is about to reveal the secret of Clark Kent to Lex, Lionel shoots him and Jason falls off a cliff, supposedly to his death.

Clark and Lois discover the faux Smallville High inside a warehouse and rescue Chloe and Lana. Brendan Nash accidentally petrifies himself before falling over and shattering.

As their real high school time is about to end, Chloe takes down the Wall of Weird for the very last time. She, Lana, and Clark walk away from the school, about to begin the next era in their lives...

JONATHAN: Clark, your destiny lies far beyond those corn fields out there, and I'm not about to let you turn your back on that just because of us.

"We all talked about our own experiences leaving high school," writer Kelly Souders said about this episode's planning process. "What are the issues you came across when it was your final day? You're never going to go back again. The first four years of the show were so centered around Smallville High, it was a question of, 'What are we losing by the fact that everybody is moving on?' We also just talked about, emotionally, what happens to a person in that time, in their senior year.

"The real thing that came up was that your life is never the same again," Souders continued. "Maybe it's better, maybe it's worse, but it's never the same. A lot of people want to hold on to that small world that they were in. 'Forever' really came out of that psychology of leaving high school, asking what you are leaving behind, and whether or not you're able to move on."

Full wax body casts were made of the cast members who were "frozen" by Brendan; though on set, as their characters were in the process of being frozen or unfrozen, the actors had to keep themselves in very rigid positions. "I had to hold a kicking position for a really

Opposite: Jason Teague is having a very, very bad day...

FOREVER

long time at a specific angle, and I was within inches of doing it incorrectly," explained Erica Durance. "It was a really great workout for the body, I'll tell you that."

CLARK: Suddenly, all those tests and teachers we hated seem a lot less scary than the big question mark that's hanging out there.

One of the most memorable sequences in 'Forever' is when Lex and Lionel are being chased by Jason Teague in the woods. "This is what [episode director] James Marshall does the best," series director Greg Beeman said. "James is a dog to a bone. He will not let go of something he wants to do, no matter how many times he is told not to do it, and no matter how many times you tell him: 'We're not making a big deal out of that.' He was told repeatedly by numerous people, starting with Miles and Al, and working their way down, past me and [producer] Bob Hargrove and the studio, that that sequence was not going to be elaborate and not going to be complicated. But he knew what he wanted

Below: Smallville High's most likely to succeed.

Smallville ⊕ Ledger

* * * * * * * * * * * * *

Jason Teague Presumed Dead
Sheriff: "Next to No Hope" Missing Coach is Alive

'Anywhere With You' by Split Habit
'Down' by Tim Cullen
'Around The Way' by Wonderlife

Former SHS football coach had been fired for having improper relations with a student.

Central Kansas A&M sophomore and former SHS football coach Jason Teague is missing and presumed dead, according to Lowell County Sheriff Nancy Adams.

Teague was last seen buying a quadruple latte and some English breakfast tea yesterday morning at the Talon coffeehouse in downtown Smallville. Teague reportedly frequented the establishment, which until recently was managed by SHS senior Lana Lang, who also lives in the upstairs apartment.

Teague moved to Smallville from Paris late last summer and was hired to assist Head Coach Wayne Quigley with the Crows football team. Teague had been the starting quarterback for the Metropolis University Bulldogs before his career was ended by a knee injury.

Quigley was forced to fire Teague this fall when school officials learned of Teague's relationship with Lang. Quigley has since publicly regretted the firing, saying "Jason was a large part of why we won the State Championship this season. He's an upstanding guy, and [Lang] was not even a minor when they began their relationship. There were some politics involved, let's just say."

Sheriff's Department officials retrieved Teague's wallet after a fisherman found it in the Elbow River. Sheriff Adams was unwilling to discuss details of the situation, but she strongly advised townspeople not to get their hopes up. "Usually we would insist on calling the operation a search-and-rescue at this point, but I'm not going to string Jason's family and friends along for no good reason. We've got next to no hope that we will recover Mr. Teague alive."

Teague was the son of famed international attorney Edward Teague. His mother, Genevieve Teague, is one of the country's most active philanthropists, with a particular interest in the preservation of ancient artifacts.

By George 'The Streak' Talmer

out of it, and he made a meal of it. They're running, and chasing, and the angles are incredibly dramatic, and it's very tense. And when Jason gets shot, he was told not to do a high fall. How do you get told by the studio you're not doing something and still do it? So, that's why I love James."

"It was a bit strange," Allison Mack said about Chloe and the rest of the cast and crew saying goodbye to high school, and more specifically, the *Torch*. "I mean, I was ready to move on. I was ready to not carry the backpack anymore. And I was ready for a new set. I'd spent a lot of time on the *Torch*," she said, though the final goodbye to the *Torch* was still an emotional one. "I got a little choked up when we did that last shot of me turning off the light and closing the door forever." ∎

COMMENCEMENT

WRITTEN BY: Todd Slavkin & Darren Swimmer DIRECTED BY: Greg Beeman	GUEST STARS: Erica Durance (Lois Lane), Jane Seymour (Genevieve Teague), Terence Stamp (Voice of Jor-El), Bud the Dog (Shelby)

Genevieve pulls a gun on Lana, demanding to know where the stone is. They fight, and Isobel possesses Lana one last time. Isobel stabs Genevieve with the element, killing her. With Genevieve gone, Isobel departs Lana's body for good as Genevieve's blood is spilled on the element. Lex walks in and finds a cowering, bloody Lana. Clark has a chaotic dream in which he opens the door and finds the sky is bathed in blue, red, and yellow flashing lights. Clark is awakened by his parents, who tell him that he kept yelling "It's coming." Meanwhile, Lex wants Lana to stay with him under his protection, and promises he will not take the element from her. At the graduation processional, Clark and Chloe get their diplomas, but Lana is nowhere to be seen. The graduation is quickly interrupted by the military, who announce that a massive meteor shower is on its way and that everyone is in danger...

JASON: When my mother came to Smallville, she thought the Luthors would lead her to the stones. But she was wrong. It was a farm boy. The one who has no record of ever being born. He's more connected to those stones than any of us.

"In so many of these shows, they graduate their characters after two or even three years, and we decided to do it after four years," Al Gough said. "For us, at that point in the series, it was time to move on, too. It was great to be able to have that senior year play out in those sort of stories, then end it with a huge high school graduation you'll never forget; and then be able to move them on into young adulthood, which I think has been fantastic."

"I think it was good for all of us," director Greg Beeman shared. "I think we were all really looking forward to getting out of high school and exploring more mature relationships. Like Al [Gough] always says, everyone would be legal, so certainly we could fulfill some relationships that had been dangling the whole time. One of the things I really liked about *Smallville*, overall, was that we progressed through high school in a good way. The series serviced how the characters had matured in the four years of high school; especially Clark, who starts to deal with more responsibility and mature issues in season four."

The finale featured many effects, big and small. In addition to spaceships, helicopters swerving in the air, and the merging of the crystals, the show's special effects team had the task of hitting Smallville with another meteor shower.

"We were trying not to make it so much about the meteor shower as it was about Clark being heroic," Mike Walls recalled. "The first time you didn't really get to see anything

Opposite: Clark Kent graduates!

Above: The combined elements will soon take Clark somewhere he could never have imagined!

other than the meteor shower. This time, the meteor shower was background, it was never focused on — it was all about what Clark was doing to be a heroic person."

CHLOE: Lightning does not strike twice in the same place without some kind of lightning rod, right? I just wonder what that is...

Clark's heroism actually changed one planned sequence: "Originally, the truck that was on fire got hit and flew off the road — it was supposed to be bearing down on the kid, and Clark was supposed to superspeed past it and pull him out of the way," Walls explained. However, "We wanted to have something personal," said writer Darren Swimmer.

The sequences in what appeared to be the Arctic, where miles of snow surrounded Clark, were actually filmed in Whistler, an area outside of Vancouver. "The whole crew drove to Whistler, and then we helicoptered in to this glacier," Greg Beeman recalled. "Tom and I flew in the first helicopter, and we stood out on this glacier which is just ice as far as you can see. We watched these helicopters coming in, dropping in the crew and the equipment. We were laughing, because it's just not like a regular TV show.

"And then I went up in the helicopter with Tom, because he's supposed to appear in the middle of nowhere. He gave me his video camera to film it, and jumped out of the helicopter into the snow. I started in a close-up, and then the helicopter went up, and in five seconds he was a dot. When we went back to the base camp, you couldn't see him; he was gone. It was him and a walkie-talkie in the snow, in the middle of nowhere.

"I will always have the warmest spot in my heart for *Smallville*. I had some of the most amazing experiences with people who I truly care about, and the day that we filmed on the glacier at the end of the season was one of the most amazing days ever." ■

Smallville 🐔 Ledger

METEORS STRIKE AGAIN
Ledger Building Destroyed; Devastation Widespread

As I type these words, an eerie, unsettling silence envelops me as thickly as the night's darkness. The sirens have faded now. The spotlights of rescue choppers can still be seen piercing the horizon, but the shouts of rescuers and rumble of emergency machinery are faint this far out on the edge of town.

It is now eight hours since the unthinkable occurred — again — with almost no warning. Today, Smallville fell victim to its second devastating meteor shower in sixteen years.

Thankfully, my dingy abode above the Wild Coyote was spared, as was the bottle of Jameson's that has been my faithful companion for the evening. The same cannot be said for the building that contained the *Smallville Ledger*. My house is still here; my home is obliterated.

Through a combination of denial and obsession, I made the long walk home this afternoon, swimming upstream past hundreds of fleeing residents. More than a few of my friends grabbed my arm and begged me to join the creeping caravan trying vainly to get out of Smallville before destruction rained from the skies. But where would I go, given three hours notice of Armageddon? How far could I get? Would it be better to meet my end out on Highway 54 than within my own four walls?

Thanks to the small generator that has gathered dust in my closet for years, I've got some precious time to impart a few observations via my laptop.

Reporting today's events is pointless. We were there. Anyone reading this doesn't need me to repeat the cold, hard facts that are surely already blaring from CNN.

Throngs of seniors at Smallville High were celebrating their greatest achievements to date, looking forward to even brighter futures in their bulky caps and gowns. Those not in attendance were engrossed in their workdays, tending farm animals, brewing cappuccinos, proofreading copy for an issue that no one knew would be the last.

We could hear the bullhorns, urging everyone to remain calm and, oh yeah, to immediately evacuate a fifty-mile radius because giant flaming space rocks were about to wipe out the area.

My friend George Talmer — not quite 'the Streak' he used to be, but still able to hold his own in a footrace — was the first down the stairs. Gena McGuiness followed, no doubt rushing home to collect her infirm husband, John, the financial editor of the *Ledger* until his retirement three years ago. Ever the pragmatist, Angie Perez persuaded Kathy Romita to drop her society page and vacate the premises. And with the rest of the afternoon crew either out or on their way out, I took a last look around and exited for the last time myself, joining the growing crowds as panic gradually began to set in.

No time for hugs and good-byes. No time to gather much from our desks. No time to sing 'Tipperary' and shut out the lights with a sad smile and a sentimental tear. My memories of the modest rooms where we tried to uphold Silas Kent's legacy will remain populated by the people with whom I was fortunate to work all these years, not by the empty, shadowed chamber I left behind today.

And with the news of the building's destruction, along with large swatches of downtown and the surrounding properties, those memories will be all I have. Farmhouses that have stood for more than a century are nothing but smoldering rubble. The Kawatche caves may never reveal their tantalizing secrets, given their already fragile state before this tragedy. Even the glowering, fortress-like Luthor mansion, a relatively recent addition to our community, is likely to have sustained major damage.

My generator's battery meter is playing editor and warning me to wrap up this indulgent farewell piece or risk having it cut from the issue. It's just as well; I'm below the label on that bottle now, with a long, haunted night ahead of me. Forgive me, dear readers, for any editing gaffes I commit herein —looks like this one's going up raw.

Will the *Ledger* return? Should I even be so selfish as to entertain such a mundane thought when so many of my friends and loved ones are grappling with much larger troubles tonight? Call me an idealist (the preceding 800 words notwithstanding), but I suspect that we will survive in some form or other. Word will be passed to you where to find us if and when we rise again. For now, I humbly speak on behalf of everyone who put their hearts into this endeavor. Thank you for reading. Goodnight.

by Christopher James Beppo

CLARK KENT

"I spend so much time trying to hide who I really am, I'm starting to feel like two separate people."

A relatively dark turn for *Smallville*'s third season took the show away from its original "Superman in high school" premise, and one of the goals of the series' producers was to bring Clark back to that environment for the fourth season. To further incorporate the school element into the show, the writers decided to let Clark have some fun, and made him a part of the Smallville Crows football team.

"I really liked that run," series creator Al Gough said about the first half of *Smallville*'s fourth season, when Clark would finally achieve some popularity and football stardom. "I know there were criticisms about it, but I sort of like that, because again it's a teenage thing to do. Let him have some fun, use his powers, you know, he was able to win the big game and stop Mxyzptlk, but then, ultimately he realizes that there's more to life than this, and this really isn't what he was put here to do."

"It's a callback to an episode in season one, 'Hothead', where Jonathan forbade Clark from joining the football team," writer Darren Swimmer explained. "Now we can see how that father-son relationship had, at that point in the show, grown to where he could trust Clark."

The assistant coach for the football team was Jason Teague; who, unbeknownst to Clark, was having a relationship with Lana. When Teague was fired from the team because the relationship had been discovered, Lana blamed Clark, even though Lex Luthor was the one who reported them. This accusation would provide more conflict between Lana and Clark until she could fully realize her feelings for Jason.

Before Clark started playing football, however, Clark Kent, totally embracing his Kryptonian heritage as Kal-El, took flight for the first time. "I would have been foolish to think that it would not happen at some point," Welling said in an interview with Paul Simpson in the *Official Smallville Magazine*. "It would be insane to think that you could play this character and not get into that eventually. What I think you have to do is look at how it affects the greater story arc, and still maintain the integrity of what we first signed on to do, which is Clark Kent in high school."

This decision fueled conflict between Jonathan and Clark that would resonate through most of the first half of season four, and marked the first time that Clark would truly defy his adoptive father. "I think season four signifies the coming out of Clark Kent from under his father's shadow," writer Todd Slavkin said.

Jonathan and Clark did get to share some father-son moments in season four, including a trip to Metropolis, where Bart Allen stole Jonathan's wallet. Having interaction between the characters away from the farm was enjoyable for John Schneider. "I enjoyed any time where Jonathan and Clark did anything together, just as father and son. Be it a heartfelt conversation, a piece of advice, or just having a good time. I enjoyed that show especially, because those moments were very few and far between in season four. I really appreciated

Above: Clark faces challenges both with magic and with working on the Kent farm.

those moments."

The episode 'Run' also introduced Clark to another comic book character — Bart Allen, the fastest boy alive, who someday would be known as Impulse. "Working with Kyle when he came in to do Impulse was a lot of fun," Welling said in his *Smallville Magazine* interview. "It's another character who has these abilities, and he and Clark can see a lot of themselves in each other, who they want to be and what they might have been, and questions they have. The whole idea of 'we don't know where this is going, but we're going to try to use our abilities for good rather than bad' is a very comic book hero theme. I enjoy those themes."

A vision of his own nightmares changed Clark's opinions about revealing his secret to anyone else, but the ability to be completely open with Alicia Baker showed him that being completely open could be something of a relief.

Being an invincible hero from another planet makes it a tough notion for Clark to even have a relationship. "Everybody Clark loves is going to die; he's going to outlive everybody," Annette O'Toole reflected, contemplating the burden her screen son has to endure. "Martha thinks about stuff like that all the time. He's doomed to be lonely, so she wants him to grab whatever love he can.

"When I go online," O'Toole continued, "and I read about this whole Clark and Lana thing, and how people don't understand why Martha's advocating for Lana or whatever, it's not about Lana; it's [about] love. Martha wants Clark to love and be loved when he can be. And he genuinely, whatever viewers feel about it, loves her. And of course that's first love. That's your innocent first love. But at the time, there were moments where Martha thought this might be his only chance."

Season four of *Smallville* brought Clark Kent closer to being a man, but putting on the tights and flying regularly is still not part of the agenda for Tom Welling. "I will never allow this character at this time to be Superman on the show," Welling said in an interview with *Smallville Magazine*. "I don't believe in that. That's not what I signed on for. I signed on to help show the evolution of this character, which will potentially lead to him becoming that."

Smallville's fourth year concluded with another meteor shower, for which Clark again felt some blame. Clark had finally been reunited with Lana Lang, but it may have been too late, because the second meteor shower could have killed them all. As Clark found himself transported to the middle of the Arctic after the three elements were combined, the next step of his journey was about to begin. ∎

Below: The arrival of Lois Lane introduced someone quite different into Clark's life.

LANA LANG

"I had to come back to these caves. I had to find out why I was missing twelve hours of my life. But all I found were more questions."

After several years of secretive behavior from Clark Kent, Lana Lang decided she needed a fresh start, so she moved to Paris to attend art school. While there she soon became acquainted with a visiting fellow American named Jason Teague. Lana and Jason enjoyed a brief romance in France until a mysterious occurrence at the tomb of the Countess Margaret Isobel Thoreaux. Lana woke with an unexplained tattoo on her back — a tattoo that looked exactly like a Kryptonian symbol found in the Kawatche caves back in Smallville.

Lana felt compelled to return home to Smallville, despite her lingering feelings concerning Clark — the mystery of the symbol was just too pressing. Lana had also taken on a mature look, both in her fashion sense, as well as in her new-found confidence.

Soon after Lana returned to Smallville, she was greeted with a surprise — her Paris boyfriend, Jason, had relocated to Kansas to be with her and would soon be taking over as the assistant football coach at Smallville High. Because of the small age disparity between them, and the fact that he was a member of the Smallville High faculty, their relationship was kept a secret — that is, until the truth about what was going on was uncovered by Lex.

"I think Lana did love Jason, I really do," Kristin Kreuk said to interviewer Richard Matthews in the *Official Smallville Magazine*. "He was a wonderful guy, and how that all unfolded was a little strange. I think she did love him, but there's a part of her that will always love Clark — he's her first love, and she hasn't had the opportunity to explore that first love in any way, so she still has those feelings. She doesn't know what that would be like if they were together — she doesn't know what that relationship would be. So even though I'm still sure that in Lana's lifetime she will fall in love with other people and have successful relationships, I feel like this thing with Clark is such an intense connection between these two people that she needs to know what that's like before she can want anything else."

Jensen Ackles also felt his character was truly in love with Lana. "I think he sees innocence and purity — he's probably grown up with very jaded people in that upper crust, high society stratum who either a) don't know how well they have it or b) know too well how well they have it. He sees Lana as a breath of fresh air, something that is real, something that is honest, that is pure. He grew up with a mother whose motives he was probably always questioning. I think he sees that Lana is someone he doesn't have to do that with," Ackles told *Smallville Magazine*'s Paul Simpson.

After Lana purchased a spell book once owned by the Countess Margaret Isobel Thoreaux, the witch's spirit took over Lana's body. This happened most spectacularly in

Above: Though Clark thought Lana was coming to football practice to cheer him on, she really had eyes for Smallville High's assistant coach, Jason Teague.

two episodes, 'Spell' and 'Sacred'.

"That was a lot of fun; I thought it was funny as well," Kristin said in her *Smallville Magazine* interview. "The beginning of the season, when Lana got her tattoo and all that, we didn't know what was going on, so it was such a strange season for me. It really was wonderful to be able to stretch and play this driven woman who has a goal and is going to reach it, and in the meantime she's going to be sexy doing it. That was a lot of fun for me because the show [sometimes] isn't realistic so, as actors, we get to play with different types of things. If it makes sense or not really doesn't matter; we just do it and have a lot of fun.

"For me as an actor, just having fun with Isobel was really a breath of fresh air," she continues, "also because I made a fool of myself and, honestly, working with Jensen Ackles was wonderful — we got along really, really well. He's an excellent actor."

The Isobel storyline also allowed Kristin Kreuk to do more physical work than she usually would take on as Lana. Many of the action sequences in the episode

'Sacred', where Isobel fights Clark, were performed by Kreuk herself, as Kristin is a natural gymnast.

For most of the fourth season, the show took a break from the relationship angst that often plagued both Lana and Clark. As things progressed, however, Clark and Lana grew closer again. Many fans wanted to see this happen, but Allison Mack felt that the characters should have been a bit more honest with one another before proceeding. "There's no honesty in their relationship, and there's no way that they could have a healthy relationship without that honesty. I know the 'Clana' fans are going to hate me for saying that, but it's — it's realistic. It's not a healthy relationship. You can't be with someone if you're not honest with them."

Kristin Kreuk, in her *Smallville Magazine* interview, agreed. "In any relationship, the most important thing is that you have to be honest and truthful and share things with the person that you're partners with," Kristin said. "If Clark can't do that... well, Lana's not stupid."

It would be almost a year after season four's conclusion before we'd find out what would happen if Clark did give Lana the honesty she had been craving. But first, there was the matter of a crashed helicopter, a meteor shower, and a spaceship opening before Lana's eyes... ◼

Below: The prom gave Lana and Clark a chance to put their differences aside and enjoy a dance together at last.

LEX LUTHOR

"You shouldn't wound what you can't kill, Dad."

When season three of *Smallville* ended, Lex Luthor had fallen to the ground, poisoned by his father in revenge for finally being put behind bars. Lex quickly recovered and began his quest for the three stones of power. It was this quest for the stones that would drive Lex for most of the show's fourth year.

In addition, Clark Kent and others like him scrutinized every decision Lex made that season, even if those decisions were for altruistic purposes. When Lex hid the truth about Chloe Sullivan's location from Clark and it was discovered anyway, Clark found he could trust Lex even less than he thought.

Tension between Lex Luthor and his father, Lionel, had also come to a head with his father's imprisonment. According to Michael Rosenbaum, there was just so much his character could take. "If you ask John Glover he'll say 'Lionel is innocent; I would only assume that he's trying to teach Lex; he loves him' and I just think that's [not true]. I do — there's a threshold to the abuse," Michael said to interviewer Paul Simpson in the *Official Smallville Magazine*. "Lionel pushes that every day. I think he's just pushing and pushing. Lex keeps fighting back, but he is being pushed further and further. Lex is resisting because he doesn't want to go there, to go to that one place that he knows ultimately he can't come back from. He's fighting it."

"Lex probably does have some ulterior motives, because there are a lot of ulterior motives in the Luthor family," Rosenbaum said about his character's true intentions for allowing his father to be imprisoned. "Perhaps by putting his father away, he thinks people will see him in a different light. People will say 'He put this monster away. Maybe Lex isn't that bad...' but at the same time, they're thinking, 'Wow, what a monster. What kind of monster puts his father away?' There's a *double entendre* to everything."

When Lionel switched bodies with Clark in the episode 'Transference', he tried killing Lex while in Clark's body — but once Lionel emerged from that situation, he claimed to have turned over a new leaf. This "born again" Lionel even found a way out of prison, thanks to Genevieve Teague. "Even if you believe Lionel, even if the audience believes Lionel, it doesn't matter," Rosenbaum said in the *Smallville Magazine* interview. "It's Lex who has to believe. How could he believe Lionel Luthor after what he's done? In Lex's eyes you have to wonder why he's done it — maybe it's to keep a closer eye on Lionel, or maybe he's thinking 'Dad, I feel bad for you... You're not that good an actor. You can stay here.' Ultimately, Lex can only be pushed so far, and I think if Clark saw this, he'd understand Lex a little more."

While filming season four, Rosenbaum felt that only he, as the actor playing Lex,

Above: Lex or Genevieve — who is the better manipulator?

could truly know where the character was coming from. "It's hard to understand when you're on the outside looking in; you're not on the inside looking out. No one else is inside Lex, inside his mind. You haven't been put down your whole life, ridiculed your whole life — the bald-headed freak growing up. You haven't had women come in and out of your life and screw you over, team up with your father, or try to kill you repeatedly. You haven't had your mother pass away because of your father, and your brother killed. This is a horrible life that he's lived, and I feel for the guy — whatever he does, I'm with him."

Lex Luthor's adventures in the show's fourth year predominantly involved the quest for the three stones. "Season four was very much about those crystals," Al Gough said. "Obviously Lionel had been looking into them, but the idea was Lex wanted to take up this mantle because of the legend that these crystals would lead to ultimate knowledge, which eventually they did, [in the form of] the Fortress of Solitude. That's really what he was up to." Lex's quest for the stones would take him all over the world, from Egypt to Shanghai, and put him into contact with new characters such as Bart Allen and Genevieve Teague. The elder Teague even flirted with Lex to try to get him to ally himself with her. "She was trying to seduce him, and he was very aware of it and played along just long enough to say, 'Okay, what do you really want?'" writer Holly Harold revealed.

Furthermore, season four offered some of the first hints that Lex Luthor had eyes for Lana Lang... even though that plotline had its genesis many years earlier. "From episode two, where they first meet, you can tell he's interested in her," Gough pointed out. "In season four Jason was somebody that in a way Lex was protecting Lana from, and also trying to get out of the picture at the same time. I think Lex has always had feelings for Lana."

"You have to ask yourself, in the words of Lex Luthor himself: Why would some billionaire want to be bailing out this girl and buying her a coffee house to begin with? What's that all about?" Darren Swimmer noted.

Swimmer's writing partner Todd Slavkin described how this new relationship fit into Lex's ultimate scheme. "In season four, obviously his motives are mainly the stones, but protecting Lana plays a big part in Lex's emotional state by the end of that season. I think that that marks the beginning of the true seeds of the Lex-Lana relationship." ∎

Below: Who would have thought that Lex Luthor was a dog person?

JASON TEAGUE

"I don't think we met by accident. I think that my mother arranged it. My mother was the one who convinced me to go to Paris in the first place. She said that I would meet someone special, and I did."

"Jason Teague was interesting," *Smallville* co-creator Al Gough says of the character's incorporation into the show's roster. "It was actually an idea that the network had. They wanted a boyfriend character for Lana who was different than Clark, and Miles and I were initially kind of resistant to it because we were [already] introducing Lois Lane this season, and the idea of trying to service two new characters wasn't greatly appealing.

"Then we realized the dynamic of Clark and Lana after season three — he kind of turned his back on her, and she needed to at least move on, and we needed to create a new triangle. As we started thinking about it, we thought that maybe it could be a good idea to bring him in, so Lana's having a secret fling with this guy who's the assistant coach," Gough said, "and then we decided to bring him into these bigger story arcs for the season," he added, referring to the ongoing storylines involving the crystals.

"Jensen Ackles was really our only choice," Miles Millar added. "He was the runner up to getting Tom's role for the pilot, and we always liked him and knew he was available, so we went after him." Jensen had recently filmed several episodes of a series titled *Still Life* for FOX that never aired on U.S. television, so Ackles was in the market to appear in a new series. "We told him that he was ultimately going to [become involved in] the big story of the season and have interactions with the Luthors, as well as Lana and Clark," Millar said.

Jason Teague gave the writers an opportunity to bring in someone with the opposite qualities to those Clark possesses, especially when relating to Lana. "Clark brings depth and angst, and we wanted somebody who could bring into her life some fun, some joy, some levity, that Clark clearly could not," writer Brian Peterson explained. As the season progressed, Jason's role in the series evolved, though contrary to fan rumors, most of Jason's arc was planned in advance, and Jensen Ackles' casting in the TV series *Supernatural* did not change the overall plan. "He was always envisioned as a one-season character," Al Gough confirmed.

Despite having some misgivings about having a character seemingly forced on to them by the network, director Greg Beeman had very positive things to say about working with Jensen Ackles: "He's a dynamic actor who has a lot of integrity, and he's a really nice guy, and a leader.

"Right away, he integrated with the rest of the cast. It's hard to come in in the fourth season and suddenly be a new series regular and fit in, and he did all of that really well." ∎

CHLOE SULLIVAN

"If you're watching this, it means I am probably dead. You were always the one good thing in my life. If I didn't tell you enough, I care about you more than you'll ever know. Please find out who did this, Clark. You're the only one who can."

When *Smallville* entered its fourth year it looked like one of Clark's closest friends, Chloe Sullivan, would not be continuing on in the series. In one of the dramatic cliffhangers that ended season three, a safe house exploded just as Chloe and her father, Gabe, entered; this, combined with the conspicuous absence of Allison Mack in the opening credits of 'Crusade', made fans think that this was one death that may have been real.

Fortunately, the video message from Chloe that started the season was not the last we'd see of her. In truth, Chloe and her father were in hiding until Lionel Luthor's trial and when she emerged, it was to experience one of her most exciting years on the show thus far. Thanks to a clever ploy by Alicia Baker, the ever-inquisitive Chloe finally learned the truth behind Clark's secrets and his coincidental ability to be in all the right places at all the right times. Later, when Clark lost his memory, it was up to Chloe to help him remember — and in doing so, Chloe learned even more truths about her friend.

The decision to let Chloe in on Clark's secret was an exciting one for Allison Mack. "I think I knew that they wanted to have someone in the cast find out before the end of the season," she said. "I guess I was the one who had the least baggage. You couldn't tell Lana. You couldn't tell Lex. I guess I was the only option at that point.

"My character in the last two years, since that episode [when Chloe learned Clark's secret], has become so much more interesting and exciting and fun," Allison enthused, "because I am one of the only three people in his life that he can fully rely on and trust or tell anything to. I'm in his life so much more, which just gives me the opportunity to explore *my* character that much more, and it's been great. It's been so much fun. It's given me a whole new identity on the show. She's so loyal and trustworthy and such a fabulous, strong female character. If it wasn't for that element, she wouldn't have the opportunity to prove all of those things to the audience, and to Clark."

Annette O'Toole agrees that letting Chloe in on the secret has been advantageous. "I think it's great, and I think it adds richness and a lot of great stuff to the series," she noted. "She's such a buddy. She's Robin, basically."

"Once Pete Ross left the show, we always knew we needed someone else, and it always felt like Chloe would be that person, because without those old-style scenes of Clark and Pete breaking in, and Pete being able to rib Clark about his powers, there's an emptiness, since Clark has no one to talk to," writer Todd Slavkin said

about the decision to have Chloe learn the truth.

"You need him to be able to talk to somebody, frankly, who is not either of his parents, who isn't constantly trying to give him advice and look out for his safety," writer Darren Swimmer added. "[Having her know the secret] turned out to be so successful."

Even though Chloe learned Clark's secrets in midseason, she did not immediately come to Clark with that knowledge. "I think she needed to figure out why he didn't tell her in the first place, so that she would know how to approach the situation. Because there was a reason why he kept that from her, and I think that she needed to understand what that reason was before she plowed him down with the information," Allison said.

Season four also included the introduction to the series of Erica Durance as Chloe's cousin, Lois Lane. Adding Lois to the *Smallville* cast put a crimp in the long-lasting fan theory that Chloe Sullivan would change her hairstyle and adopt the name of comics' most popular journalist at series' end. "I'm not Lois Lane — Erica is. She's fabulous and embodies her beautifully," Allison said in response to the long-standing 'Chlois theory'. "I think that Chloe is a much softer version of Lois. She has had a much softer, gentler upbringing, and that's allowed her to be much less jaded. I think her closeness to Clark also allows her to have that sort of soft, gentle side because she doesn't have to look out for herself all the time. She has someone there doing that alongside her.

"I think that Lois is more shortsighted," Allison continues. "Chloe has a tendency to look at the bigger picture and look further into the future, whereas I think Lois is much more immediate and kind of wants it now, and doesn't really have an idea as to what she wants for the future, so she never really pays that much attention to it; whereas I think Chloe is very deliberate in the steps that she takes in her life." While Chloe Sullivan plugs away at the Smallville High *Torch* newspaper, perfectly aware of her destiny, her cousin Lois hasn't caught that journalism bug and isn't quite the "mad dog" seen later in the comic books.

Ever protective of her friend, Chloe even tried to protect his secret in the chaotic midst of the second meteor shower. The last we see of Chloe, she is face to face with a very bright light coming from a secret room in the caves... ■

Above: Romantic notions are put aside as Chloe firmly earns her place as Clark's Girl Friday.

Opposite above: Chloe Sullivan — prom queen? Or is that Dawn Stiles in action?

Opposite below: Boy trouble: Mikail Mxyzplk tries to get Chloe on his side.

LIONEL LUTHOR

"You'll never know when it will happen, but it will happen. Each swallow of wine you take, every key you turn, every friend you make. You'll never have another moment's peace."

At the end of *Smallville*'s third season, Lionel was finally arrested for many of his catalog of crimes, including the decades-old murder of his parents. The most damning testimony hinged on the participation of Chloe Sullivan — a witness who, it appeared, had died in a safe house explosion. If his son's betrayal wasn't enough to drive Lionel mad, he also had to contend with the knowledge that he was dying of an incurable liver disease and had only months to live.

Without the presence of his star witness, it seemed that Lionel might be able to escape prison yet again. However, when it was revealed that Chloe was indeed alive, hidden away thanks to Lex Luthor and General Sam Lane, it was inevitable that Lionel would be spending the rest of his days in prison. It seemed that Lex would finally be the victor in their neverending game of cat and mouse.

Once imprisoned, Lionel was attacked, bullied, and blackmailed by other inmates. He knew he needed a way to get back at his son. Lionel eventually met a fellow prisoner named Edgar Cole, who would help him escape with the assistance of the water element. The element gave Lionel the ability to switch bodies with someone else. Initially, his plan was to lure Lex in and switch with his young, vital son, so it would ultimately be Lex who would rot in jail until his death.

The body switch had an unforeseen effect, however. Instead of trading places with Lex in the episode 'Transference', Lionel found himself in the body of Clark Kent. Suddenly, Clark Kent's secrets were laid out on the table for Lionel. 'Transference' quickly became a fan favorite thanks to the performances of Tom Welling and John Glover in their "dual" roles.

"John was really generous in that he would go on the set when Tom was doing his scenes, and would act it out, and Tom would mimic what John was doing," 'Transference' co-writer Todd Slavkin said. "And I think Tom's performance is legendary in that show."

The episode also gave Lionel Luthor the opportunity to spend time with different characters. "We wanted to make sure that the Lionel-as-Clark character could interact with each one of our cast members, so we could see how they would respond to each other. It was great," Slavkin's co-writer Darren Swimmer said. Most of the other characters didn't react so well, as Chloe, Lana, Lex, and even to some extent Martha had unexpected altercations with the young man they believed to be Clark.

After the body switch, Lionel had no explicit memories of what had happened. However, his body had gone through an unexpected change — it appeared that his liver disease was gone. This second lease on life made Lionel decide to change his ways. The

Above: Clark (trapped inside Lionel's body) tries to convince his mother it's really him.

Opposite above: Clark and Lionel meet in prison.

Opposite below: The aftermath of the body switch gives Lionel new understanding — and a second chance.

once-malevolent elder Luthor started serving as an advisor to others within the Metropolis Penitentiary, encouraging them to do better with their lives and avoid the mistakes he had made in his own past.

Director Greg Beeman sees Lionel Luthor's redemption as an experiment in the show's fourth season that ultimately failed. "I was very interested in it at first, but then as it started to unravel, it was sort of like 'enh'. So we had to turn him evil again. The problem with drama, is that television is drama, and drama is conflict, and when somebody who's essentially been the main source of conflict for a number of characters suddenly turns nice, then there's no conflict, so what are you going to do? I don't think that that experiment succeeded, although John gave it his college-best try."

Did John Glover believe that Lionel had truly turned over a new leaf? "I kept trying to," Glover said. "I mean, I've tried to play everything truthful. That's what I was attempting to play, but he was pretty boring." Fortunately, by season's end Lionel was back to his dastardly ways, concocting schemes and manipulating people to obtain the three stones of power for his own gain. After getting an early release from prison (thanks to Genevieve Teague), and following an encounter with his son's dark side, Lionel's true colors were shown again, and the full-on "magnificent" antagonist that fans knew and loved had returned.

As Lionel Luthor came back to power, his trademark mane of hair that was shorn in the season three finale slowly grew back. Lionel had storylines in which he embarked on his own quest to obtain the stones of power. Some of these storylines gave Glover the opportunity to work with Jane Seymour, the actress who played Genevieve Teague. "We had a good time," Glover said of the experience. "She was a Bond girl, you know. Lionel likes beauty."

Glover had an interesting way of looking at the relationship between Lionel and his son during *Smallville*'s fourth season. "It's complicated with Lex," he said, voicing his opinion as if it was coming from Lionel Luthor himself. "The poor boy is so weak. I think if they hadn't been blood, Lionel would have destroyed him by now; but, because he is blood, there is a responsibility, too. He's Lionel's heir. But Lex is a bit spineless in Lionel's eyes, so he can't trust him. It's not that he's meant to be a foe, it's just that the poor boy's weak, so he's got to mold him. Lionel is continually trying to strengthen his son, to teach him. [Lex is] just a hard student."

As season four met its conclusion, Lionel Luthor was completely involved in the quest for the stones. This journey left Lionel in a catatonic state at season's end, although when he awakes, he will have much Kryptonian knowledge coursing through his brain. The next step in Lionel Luthor's journey will take the man who grew up in the slums of Metropolis on a journey connected to the stars... ∎

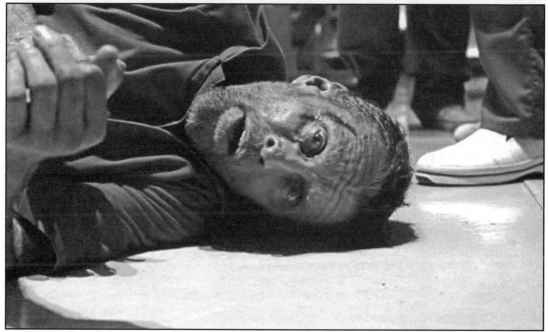

JONATHAN KENT

"All the years that your mother and I spent raising you, from a wide-eyed toddler running around on this farm to the man who is standing in front of me right now, was for this moment. You do this, son. You make us proud."

The fourth year of *Smallville* began with Jonathan Kent in the hospital, struck down after a confrontation with Jor-El in the Kawatche caves. Though he soon recovered, Clark Kent's father faced some difficult challenges at home. John Schneider feels that Jonathan's constant protection of his son was something that is expected of any father, regardless of what planet their offspring comes from. "In my mind, that's what fathers do," he said. "Requirement number one when you sign up to be a parent, you sign up for protecting your kids regardless of the situation, regardless of what the outcome may be for yourself." It was this sense of responsibility that always drove Jonathan Kent to do the right thing.

Clark's senior year found him taking on a spot as a Smallville High quarterback, and this development made Jonathan a little uneasy, even though he knew it could teach Clark some valuable life lessons. "That was a very legitimate place for Clark and Jonathan to butt heads, so I liked the friction that father and son had at that point," Schneider said. "It made wonderful sense. Jonathan got to not only protect Clark's secret, but protect the people that Clark would be playing against."

Back at home, the Kents had some tension as Jonathan, with his weak heart, insisted on continuing to do his chores on the farm. This exertion particularly caused worry in Martha. "She worried about him because she loved him," Schneider said. "Running the farm was much of what Jonathan Kent was. He was a provider. I think Martha knew that, and she really didn't want to take that away from him, but she was worried about his health. It's a wonderful story of her protecting her husband against himself."

Despite this, Schneider didn't feel that Jonathan was threatened when Clark tried to take on his father's chores for him. "Just because you're strong doesn't mean you're good at it," Schneider laughed. "John Schneider as Jonathan Kent actually thought it was pretty funny when Clark wanted to do all the chores. He couldn't. He couldn't fix a tractor. How could he fix a tractor? He could lift it up, but then what was he going to do?"

The dangers that come with raising a superpowered son thankfully also came with positive times for Clark and the Kents, including the Smallville High prom, which Jonathan and Martha Kent attended as chaperones. "It was terrific. I sent my daughter off to her prom, so I had that experience personally," he enthused. Schneider also greatly enjoyed sharing in the moment of Clark Kent's graduation. "I loved it. It was one of the few times I got to dress up."

Jonathan Kent's greatest advice for Clark would prove to be especially poignant later: to "do the right thing at all costs, even if the costs are yours." Jonathan's ultimate sacrifice would occur halfway into season five... ■

MARTHA KENT

"My future is lying in that bed. I will not give up on him."

The fourth season of *Smallville* began for Martha Kent with a giant leap and ended with a blast from the sky. In the course of one year, she became the first — and only — person to witness Clark fly, nearly lost her husband, took a part-time job at the Talon, and saw her boy begin his journey toward his ultimate destiny.

Staying at Jonathan's bedside for several long months at the beginning of the season was something that Martha Kent wouldn't have thought twice about. "She was dearly in love with this guy and was totally committed to him and would have done anything to stay in the hospital all night, reading to him," Annette O'Toole said of her character's devotion to her husband. "That's just Martha."

Later in the season, the Kents' marriage hit some shaky ground as the headstrong Jonathan insisted on maintaining the farm despite his heart condition. To raise more money for the family, Martha took a job working at the Talon for Lex Luthor, an idea which had its genesis in a summer 2004 meeting between O'Toole and the show's executive producers, Al Gough and Miles Millar. "I loved the whole thing before, having worked for Lionel in season two." Annette revealed. "I was sorry when that went out the window, because I felt like there was so much we could have done with that, in terms of my being a bit of a spy. So I said, 'Why don't I go to work for Lex?' I really wanted to have more scenes with Michael [Rosenbaum]." The producers seemed to like the idea, and soon the season saw Martha working at the Talon. "Anything where I could get out of the house and away from the oven and doing something more was always a good idea to me," O'Toole said of Martha's new job. She enjoyed the opportunity for Martha to interact with the other people who came into Clark's life.

Annette believes that, unlike Jonathan, Martha prefers to trust in Clark's independence and his ability to figure things out for himself. "I think Jonathan's thing was more like, 'Let me show you the way, son. Let me guide you in this direction,'" Annette said, "and I think she is much more forgiving and understanding about a lot of things. I think it's the combination of the two of them that makes Clark who he is."

Even though she made her first Superman-related appearance as the movies' first Lana Lang in *Superman III*, Annette is happy to have been a part of the reimagined mythos in *Smallville*. "It's such a different take on these characters," she said. "It's a different time in Clark's life. It's a different focus on the relationship with him and Lana, and of course Lex now being his childhood friend. None of that existed [on TV or in the movies], and all of these wonderful new characters, like Chloe and Lionel, and the Kents being young, vital people... that was a big reason to do it. It's just so different and wonderful and exciting." ∎

LOIS LANE

"Even if I could spell, the last thing I'd want to do is spend my time in a newsroom."

"**B**ringing in Lois Lane was always the plan," Al Gough said. "Season four felt like the right time to do it because she had a real reason to come to town: it seemed that Chloe was dead and Lois was investigating her alleged murder."

Casting the right actress was essential to the success of the character. According to director and executive producer Greg Beeman, dozens of actresses were seen and considered, but the right Lois Lane had yet to come through the door. Then a tape came in from a young actress named Erica Durance, and the rest is *Smallville* history.

"I thought that right away Erica was Lois," Beeman said. "She had a toughness about her. She was tough and sexy and direct. Originally she was a brunette, like Lana, so we talked about lightening her hair and turning her more into the Lois of today. The other good news came when Tom first met her. Just before episode one, she came in and worked with Tom for an afternoon, and he obviously really responded to her. They had a really good chemistry together right away — a really strong friendship formed. It was almost like a brother-sister, punch each other in the arm type of thing."

The show's writers also reacted well to the newly-cast Lois. "We all responded to her right away in the writers' room," said Kelly Souders. "She was tough, and we felt that she was not going to compete personality-wise with Lana and Chloe, who both had such distinctive roles in the show. It was a character that, if you cast wrong, I think it could have really thrown off the balance."

"In the *Smallville* pilot, Al and Miles established Lex and Clark as best friends, which is, to me, one of the best aspects of the show," Brian Peterson said. "So when you're introducing his future love interest, why not introduce her, not as an enemy, but as the one who is constantly going to butt heads with him, where they're not gonna like each other at all at first? I think that because we chose such a different take on her, it wasn't that intimidating. She could grow into the person that everybody sees on-screen later."

Because it took so long to cast Lois Lane, Erica Durance had very little time to prepare for the new role. "I got cast on a Friday and started on that Monday, so I didn't have much time to do tons of research. I just had to throw myself into it. It was somewhat surreal," she added. "I had done guest star bits before, so it seemed like any other role when you first go in to do it. But of course, there was the added pressure of playing the [famous] Lois Lane."

Initially the Warner Bros. feature division had only allowed *Smallville* to use Lois Lane for four episodes. "In 'Devoted', you see her leaving, like she's going to leave permanently, and that's because that's all we thought we had her for," Al Gough revealed. The creators, however, were hoping for more. "Through some orchestrating with Peter Roth at the studio, and explaining how the character was going to work, and

how she and Clark were not going to have a romance and instead be more like sparring partners, the feature division then said we would be able to [use] her for more episodes."

When Lois made her return to the show, the decision was made to have her move into the Kents' home. "We wanted to have a situation where there was somebody in that house who didn't know the secret, and who was kind of annoying, and could get into Clark's space," Al Gough revealed. Lois moving in with the Kents also provided the writers with an easier reason to have the characters interact.

Although sometimes controversial with fans online, the producers also wanted to give Lois more of a wild side. "Here was this character that came from the outside world, so to speak, and had this sophisticated, worldly experience," writer Todd Slavkin explained. "We felt like she was much more of an adult than the rest of our cast."

This worldly experience took inspiration from other mediums and legendary leading ladies in cinematic history. "There's a scene in *Raiders of the Lost Ark* where Karen Allen [as Marion] is drinking with these [burly Tibetan] guys, and drinks them under the table," Slavkin continued. "It was an image that Al and Miles thought would be fun with Lois, and we could really picture her in that situation."

"She'd grown up on army bases, and she'd hung out with guys much older than her her entire life," Darren Swimmer added.

Erica feels that every actress who has

played Lois Lane to date has brought something unique and different to the role. "I think that my tendency is to make a lot of jokes, and I have a sense of humor where I'm the type of person that will laugh when somebody wipes out, because I'm really clumsy myself, as long as they're not hurt," Erica said. "I think that what they were looking for in the role of Lois in *Smallville* was a girl that's trying to find herself, and she's got all this nervous energy as a result; and I think I have some of that, where I feed into it with my own nervous energy. There are certain sides of Lois that are really me: I am incredibly independent, and I am pretty sassy; but on the other side of things, I'm also very introverted. Lois will jump into a situation. I tend to be a little bit more analytical, and I step back unless I feel really safe. Unlike Lois, I'm a little bit more the kind of girl that could sit in a room with people and let everybody else talk."

One of the biggest fans of Erica Durance's portrayal of the character was a former Lois

Lane herself, whom Erica met at a convention appearance. "I was busy talking to someone in front of me, and then somebody covered my face with their hands and hugged me from behind," Erica revealed. "I turned around, and it was Margot Kidder. I didn't know what to say. I had my moment, right, because I grew up thinking that she *is* Lois Lane to me. She was so awesome, and she said to me, 'You hit it out of the ballpark, kid.' It meant so much, because to me, that's the lady that should know, right? If she thinks I've done all right with it, then I feel pretty good." ■

Opposite: Usually Lois Lane wouldn't be caught dead in this prom outfit!

Above: Lois quickly learns that people in Smallville are just a little on the weird side.

BART ALLEN

"A couple of years ago, there was, like, this accident, right, and there was this huge flash of light... and my body went into overdrive."

I t took over three full seasons of *Smallville* before Clark Kent finally encountered another hero from the DC Comics universe. When that happened, the character he met was Bart Allen, one of comicdom's fastest men alive — as it turns out, faster than Clark Kent himself.

"My agent told me that there was going to be a part coming up for a super hero on the show, and she couldn't really give me more information until word got out about who it was," actor Kyle Gallner said about the start of the audition process. "When she told me that it was going to be Impulse, I said to myself, 'I'm going to get this part.'" While Kyle felt good about his first audition, he was disappointed about his performance the second time around. He remembers how he felt, "I was bummed out and pretty upset, but it actually ended up that I got the part, so it was all good [in the end]."

The majority of Kyle's time as Bart in his first *Smallville* appearance was spent working alongside Tom Welling, as Clark tries to teach him the error of his thieving ways. "Tom's a really nice guy. He made me feel very comfortable," Kyle said. "There was almost an older brother/little brother dynamic where he took care of me, but I tried to show him a good time, and I think he kind of liked having another guy around."

While Clark is focused on the power and responsibility of his abilities and feels that he must keep them secret, in contrast Bart looks at things in a very different way. "Bart doesn't really hide the fact that he has powers," Kyle explained. "He accepts them. He uses them. He may even abuse them a little bit. But he's not ashamed of who he is. He's not scared of being who he is, and he kind of lets the world know that he's there."

The popularity of Bart's appearance on *Smallville* left fans hoping and wondering if there were any plans to spin the character off into his own series. "I heard rumors, but until something is official, you never hold your breath," Kyle revealed. "At the time, it could have been interesting. But I'm kind of glad they just kept him on *Smallville* and ended up doing the future Justice League thing, bringing everybody together."

When Clark first met Bart, the younger hero was at a dark time in his life. Gallner explained his views on the troubled juvenile hero: "I think he was a very confused kid, because he had these powers and I think his parents didn't accept him. They may have kicked him out of the house. He had to live on his own and take care of himself, so I think thieving was pretty much the only thing he could do to get money. He probably stole anything and everything he could to get by and survive." ■

ALICIA BAKER

"All I want is a chance to prove to you who I really am."

Alicia Baker, the teleporting girl famously played by Sarah Carter, made her first appearance in season three's 'Obsession'. Her character and the on-screen attraction between her and Tom Welling inspired a great deal of fan demand for Alicia to return. With the mid-season two-parter of 'Unsafe' and 'Pariah', the creators of *Smallville* had the chance to bring her back to the show.

"I'm a charter member of the Alicia Baker/Sarah Carter fan club," writer Todd Slavkin explained. "I think she was fantastic on the show. Totally lit up the screen with Tom."

Alicia's return brought out suspicion in everyone, especially considering she had tried to kill both Clark and Lana during her last visit to *Smallville*. The incident in 'Unsafe' where Alicia convinces Clark to run off and get married in Vegas, using red kryptonite to bring out his bad side, made some of the others trust her even less.

"I don't think Chloe liked Alicia very much, because she was manipulative and destructive, and she snuck red kryptonite into Clark's shirt so he would do what she wanted. I don't think Chloe was much of a fan," Allison Mack said about her character's approach to Alicia.

Being around Alicia brought out a side of Clark rarely seen in the series. "It's the first time we really saw Clark with somebody that he thinks he can be an equal to, that he can be honest with; and it's the first time that we brought out the issue of how much him basically 'coming out' as an alien would make the lives of all the krypto-freaks around him better," noted writer Brian Peterson. It is Clark's reluctance to reveal his powers to everyone that convinces Alicia to try and expose his secret to Chloe.

Special effects supervisor Mike Walls credits Greg Beeman with the appearance of Alicia's teleportation. "We wanted to do something completely different from anything else we had ever done to show that she was able to move around the world, or move around whatever environment she wanted to, in her own unique way," Walls explained. "So it started out being a shrinking world; shrinking her one way, and sort of flipping everything around so you can do it another way, and backward again. That was the general idea at the beginning, and then it evolved from there."

Sadly, Alicia Baker did not survive past her second visit to *Smallville*, as Clark discovered her hanged in her stable, a victim of krypto-freak Tim Westcott. Although Alicia didn't make it, Sarah Carter was obviously not injured in the process. "We have special harnesses that we use, so we can make it look like someone is hanging, but they're actually supported in other places; through their feet and in their hips," Mike Walls explained.

"She wasn't a bad person; just really misunderstood," writer Holly Harold said of Alicia. "She just wanted love, like we all do. True, she went about it in the wrong way, but at the end of 'Unsafe' she found her honest self; and I think in 'Pariah', she and Clark almost had a shot." ■

MEET THE CREW

"The crew, top to bottom, is really first-rate. It's a hard show to produce. It is like doing a movie every week, and they do it so well, season in and season out. We're just really lucky to have them and glad that they're here." — Al Gough

T he writers, producers, and editors working on *Smallville* are primarily based in southern California, but the actual physical production of the series happens up in Vancouver, British Columbia. Hundreds of people work on the behind-the-scenes crew that brings the show to life; these are but a few of them.

Stunt coordinator and occasional stunt double for Tom Welling, **Chris Sayour** has been with the series since the very first episode. As the years have progressed, he has developed an incredibly capable team of stunt performers. By the time the show had reached its fourth year, Sayour had begun to see some of the cast members performing their own stunts. Can that be scary for a stunt supervisor? "Always," he said. "It's 'always' in the sense that if a cool head does not prevail, little accidents can happen when you're doing a fight scene. If in a fight, the choreography is such that the actors just step out at that moment when a punch is coming, and the stunt double steps in, then those little accidents can happen. It's obviously not life-threatening, but it can shut down production if the actor is hurt, as it has on many other shows in L.A. and Vancouver."

Working on a stunt-heavy series such as *Smallville* can often be a challenging task. "I think a lot of it is daunting because we're doing episodic television and we're trying to do feature-sized stunts," Sayour said. "Not many television shows take on as many big stunts as *Smallville* does on a constant basis. We usually don't have just one big stunt per episode; we have five or six. Sometimes the daunting part is figuring out how it will work in terms of time constraints and budget constraints, but still be as grand as *Smallville* deserves. That's one of the most daunting tasks I have."

Without the right crew in place, things might not go so smoothly. "It's a

Below: The two Clark Kents: stunt/body double Chris Sayour with Tom Welling.

team effort, and if all the teammates, the editors, the producers, the director, the DP [director of photography], everybody is in line, you're going to come up with an amazing sequence. It's going to look beautiful. I love it when the editors do a great job, they can just make it look phenomenal."

Sayour works with a standard team of six stunt personnel, though the number changes depending on the requirements of the episode. For the prison riot scene in 'Transference', there were over thirty stunt performers.

Sayour is proud of the time he has spent working on *Smallville*. "It's an extremely rewarding show in that it's so stunt-orientated. We get to bring a lot of amazing things from birth to finish, and create stuff on such exciting levels – because we create the boundaries. There are no boundaries in a comic book world – other than the ones we set, and the producers and writers set. I think it's fantastic. I feel very lucky, because not very often in a stunt performer's career do you get to be a part of a show that is so filled with excitement, challenges, and adventure."

Christine O'Connor has been doing hair on *Smallville* since the first year, and her title as of season four was Key Hairstylist. The fourth season of *Smallville* brought new characters and new challenges for the New Zealand-born O'Connor.

First on the agenda was to create a 'look' for newcomer Lois Lane. Christine explains her approach: "Erica has a totally different type of hair to the other girls anyway, and they wanted her to be a little bit more blond than her natural color," she said. "So when we did the camera testing for her we put in a few little blond extensions, and once everything was approved, we gave her some highlights. Because her hair has quite a curl to it, we could do lots of different things, and it does look different than Chloe or Lana's."

The other new addition to *Smallville*, Jensen Ackles, also took on a different look from his male counterparts on the series. "I sort of sun-touched it a bit," O'Connor explained. "I

Above: One of the season's most spectacular stunts: Clark catches a car in midair!

Below: Even assistant coach Jason Teague would be impressed with the stunt team's plays on the field.

Above: Jane Seymour's appearances gave Christine O'Connor the chance to work on the hair of one of Hollywood's most glamorous stars.

put a little bit of color in it, just so it had a bit more *oomph*. He has naturally dark-blond hair and I combed in some color, so it looked a little bit lighter."

Jane Seymour, who played Jason Teague's mother Genevieve, is widely considered to be one of the most glamorous women in the business, so was this intimidating? "We were all prepared to have a lot of time, and they gave me an hour-and-a-half to meet her and find out what she'd like. I had a few ideas of how I would like her to look, seeing as she was sort of regal, and she was going to be the evil lady that showed up as Jensen's mom, who had a lot of money," she said. "We got along famously. I just started to do her hair, and that was it, she was pleased right away. I guess they can tell that you know what you're doing. She was very relaxed and we had a good time. She was loads of fun."

The final major difference in O'Connor's duties for the fourth season came with the shortening of John Glover's hair: Lionel Luthor no longer had as much hair to manage. "It was kind of frightening when we had to shave it off at the end of season three. But as it grew out, I thought he looked quite nice with his hair shortish."

While a lot of *Smallville*'s visual wizardry is created at the Santa Monica-based EntityFX, things begin first in Vancouver with all the physical aspects brought to life by special effects supervisor **Mike Walls** and his crack team of special effects experts.

Planning for physical effects begins well before an episode starts shooting. "When we get the outline for each episode, I start thinking about the big pieces," he said. "I can be thinking about it a month ahead of time, but I really get into the specifics of it after the concept meetings. We get the concept idea through the earliest meetings, and then we start getting into the technical side of things. Last comes the budgeting and scheduling."

Although the cast had been working with effects for four years, it was still a difficult aspect of the show for them. "Most of the time they have to be put in positions that are fairly uncomfortable, especially with all of the flying work," Walls said. "And when

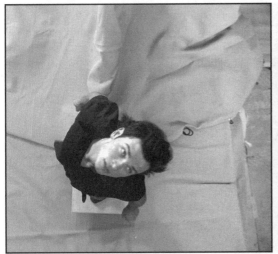

we're having Tom leap, run, whatever, we've tried to take his comfort into account with the rigs that we have built; but it's not easy to do, to achieve what they want to achieve for the shot. So the actors put up with us, but they're not really fond of it."

Walls can often have up to five crews working at once in order to create the show's magic. He revealed that although all the shots are challenging in their own way, one of the most difficult season-four shots was the car in 'Pariah': "It took a lot of time and energy to get that to happen."

Season four also gave the show what may have been one of the most memorable moments in the entire series — when Clark, as Kal-El, took a giant leap into flight. "We all agreed that the one thing we wanted to put out there was a better, more natural-looking flight than what has been done before for Superman. I have always thought that the flying [effects for] Superman has been the weakest part of the whole legacy," Walls noted. "Greg Beeman had very specific ideas in his head of what he thought Superman was and what he should be. He started talking about having a vortex of wind, and it's like all of the energy around Clark is being consumed at that moment of takeoff. Then we went one step further with, 'Well, you know what? Let's have him really look like he's using every ounce of strength that he's got, let's indent the ground and then let's have Kal-El just rocket away as fast as we can.'

"I think we just get better at everything as we go along. We know what works and what doesn't after watching it. We're always trying to come up with a new way of doing superspeed, or a new way of doing heat vision. We don't like to repeat ourselves. We try and always improve. That's the motto of everybody around here."

Costume designer **Caroline Cranstoun** joined the *Smallville* crew in its first season and has remained a vital part of the series ever since. One of the most frequent questions Cranstoun receives from fans is where to get the famous red jacket worn by

Clark in almost every episode of the series. "The original red jacket came from The Gap, and it wasn't red, because they don't really sell red jackets; it was tan. We did a lot of work on them, including having them all dyed. We probably had about twenty-five to start with," she said. "As Clark's gotten shot or blown up, a lot of those jackets have gotten destroyed, so we now have custom made a whole bunch of red jackets."

The location of a scene is a very important element when deciding which costumes are used. "The Talon has golden-colored walls; although there are a lot of different colors in the Talon. When Clark had a tan coat, he would never wear it in the Talon. We have to be aware of that," she revealed, pointing out that there are very few rooms with red walls to clash with Clark's most famous jacket.

One of Cranstoun's most successful costume designs for the show's fourth season was the clothing worn by Bart Allen, a.k.a. Impulse. Not only did it have to resemble a

comic book costume in some ways, Cranstoun also worked to make it look contemporary. "It was very specific, right from the time they gave us that script," she said. "We pretty much knew that he'd be in yellow cargo pants, because cargo pants were the thing then." Little touches were added to Bart's design to make him look unique and offer subtle winks to his Flash heritage. "He had little lightning bolts," Cranstoun revealed. "He had one on his cuff, on his sleeve, and he had one on his backpack." This 'look' for Bart proved to be very popular with the show's fanbase.

Though she enjoys designing clothing for the entire cast, Cranstoun does have some preferences: "I think the girls are more fun to dress than the guys, because there's more of a fashion element to it," she said. She particularly pointed to 'Spell' as being a fun episode to design for. "That was one of the first times, I think, that we'd had the three girls together, and they were really sexy and got to get out of their regular characters [for a while]. We got to take it quite far with the whole look.

"But the guys are fun to dress, too," she added. "The guys — Clark, Lex, Lionel — they wear a bit of a uniform, so it's fun developing that uniform and getting it to a point where it's an identifiable look. But then once it's there, it's fun to get them out of it, too."

Smallville's fourth year brought graduation, and that meant that Cranstoun would no longer be creating costumes for high schoolers. Does she miss it? "We did it for quite a long time," she said. "You run out of things to do. There were all the cheerleader costumes, the football uniforms, and then the letterman jackets — there's more that we can do now that they're out of high school."

Since she has spent so much time designing clothing for the young Clark Kent, would she ever like to see him wearing his most famous uniform? "I would," she said, smiling. "I don't know if we should, though..." ∎

THE PHENOMENON

"I love *Smallville* and won't miss an episode, and it's every bit as influential as the rest of Superman's grand history." — *Superman: Birthright* writer Mark Waid

As *Smallville*'s fourth year approached, fans waited in anticipation for the creators' promise of a "lighter" season than the one that had come before. Promotion for the new season kicked off with an appearance at Comic-Con International in San Diego, California. In attendance were series creators Al Gough and Miles Millar, supervising producer Jeph Loeb, and actors John Glover, Allison Mack, and Erica Durance. This event was the first opportunity for fans to get a personal glimpse of Ms. Durance as Lois Lane.

Thanks to the *Smallville* season three cliffhanger, Allison Mack had the tough task of convincing her fans that Chloe had died in the season finale, and thus would not be returning for the fourth year. However, this didn't damage the experience for her. "It was pretty amazing walking out on stage and having that huge room full of people cheering for you and your show," Allison said of the experience. "It was an incredible feeling."

Also coinciding with the beginning of the fourth season was the release of the first issue of the *Official Smallville Magazine* from Titan Publishing. Starting off monthly before going bi-monthly, the magazine featured interviews, scoops, and the latest news from the world of *Smallville*. The first regular issue sported a Tom Welling and Kristin Kreuk cover on newsstands, and an exclusive Tom Welling cover from Diamond Distribution was released to comic book specialty stores.

Continuing in its US timeslot of Wednesdays at 8 p.m., *Smallville* faced some tough new competition with the coming of ABC's *Lost*. Even with this added challenge, the season première achieved very healthy numbers, beating out competitors such as *That '70s Show* and *America's Next Top Model*.

In October, John Glover participated in the annual Memory Walk in Salisbury, Maryland, benefiting the Alzheimer's Association, Greater Maryland Chapter. The walk was held in memory of his father, Jack, who suffered from the disease. The walk was accompanied by an auction of *Smallville* items that raised over $25,000. Unique items included a red kryptonite replica ring and 'kryptonite keys' containing genuine locks of Lionel's hair. Also in support of Alzheimer's research, Glover and Allison Mack appeared at a Delmarva Shorebirds baseball game in May. "That was actually a really special experience for me, just because I got to go home with John and that was lovely, because he's a really close, close friend of mine. I consider him family. So getting to see where he grew up, and meet a lot of the people that are really important to him, was really cool," said Mack.

Fans also felt a great deal of excitement when they learned that the season's fifth episode would guest star DC Comics hero Impulse. Similar excitement cropped up when word leaked that Clark's friend Chloe would learn his secret in the episode 'Pariah'. All the while, many websites and fan communities continued to thrive in their *Smallville* discussions,

from locations ranging from Television Without Pity (www.television-withoutpity.com) to Sweet (www.geocities.com/lana_n_clark/), a community of Clark and Lana fans who still wanted their favorite pairing to have their day in the sun.

Smallville's season four promotion kicked off with a poster campaign telling fans to 'Look Up' on September 22, 2004. The poster featured a flying Tom Welling from the episode 'Crusade'. Erica Durance appeared on the WB11 *Daily News* and the Howard Stern radio show, and The WB *Insider* special provided fans with a first look at a football playing Clark using behind-the-scenes footage from the filming of 'Devoted'.

The complete third season of *Smallville* on DVD hit US stores in November, and it was an instant bestseller. The season three set included audio commentaries from the show's producers Al Gough and Miles Millar, as well as cast members Michael Rosenbaum, Allison Mack, and John Glover. The second series of *Chloe Chronicles* webisodes were also included on the set, as were deleted scenes and a gag reel.

For those fans who didn't want to spring for the DVD box set, daily doses of *Smallville* surfaced in the form of repeats on the ABC Family cable channel in October 2004. ABC Family's *Smallville* promotion began with a Backstage Special hosted by Brooke Burke, with appearances by Tom Welling, Kristin Kreuk, Annette O'Toole, John Schneider, John Glover, and Allison Mack.

Allison Mack and Erica Durance joined series creators Al Gough and Miles Millar in April 2005 for a special '*Smallville* Night' at the Jules Verne Festival in Paris, France. Several season four episodes were screened, and the show was honored with a special award. "It's amazing. The reason we do the show is to entertain people, and to know that it's being embraced so widely and people love it so much, just makes what you do so much more valid and exciting," Allison said of her experience with fans. For the fandom, and the *Smallville* phenomenon in general, 2004-2005 was a very good year indeed. ∎

THE RELATIONSHIPS

"The best ones always start that way." — Lana Lang

With the infusion of new characters into *Smallville*, relationships began to change. The rift between Clark and Lex continued to grow; Lana and Clark had called things off — seemingly for good; and several new pairings began to form. These "ships" as fans like to call them, fueled a good amount of the drama for season four.

The season four première, 'Crusade', set up many new situations for the characters. For starters, Lana Lang had a new beau, Jason Teague, whom she met in Paris. "Lana falling for the football coach who [happened to be] Clark's mentor was really fun," writer Holly Harold said of this new development. "Clark was not a good guy to her. As much as I adore Clark Kent, as a boyfriend? Not so good. He's got his own burdens and his own demons, but he was not a stand-up guy with Lana, and Jason Teague was — at least he was at the beginning. He was there for her, he supported her, he traveled across the world to be with her. That's pretty great, you know?"

"It was so hard for Clark to see that," writer Todd Slavkin noted. "Probably one of the toughest things Clark's ever had to deal with since Whitney. But on the other hand, he couldn't get angry at Jason Teague. What a great guy he was: he was an assistant coach; he was helping Clark get into Met U; he was treating Clark with the utmost respect. It was like, you're upset to see your girlfriend with another guy, but if she's got to be with someone else, Jason Teague's not a bad guy [to be with]."

However, the Jason-Lana relationship quickly began to disintegrate when Jason's mother, Genevieve Teague, appeared to Lana in a dream. As Lana learned more about Jason's familial history, and their connection to the witch Isobel, the relationship began to fracture.

Meanwhile, Clark's return to *Smallville* collided with the revelation that one of his closest friends, Chloe Sullivan, had passed away — or had she? Her 'death' brought a new face to town in the form of her cousin, Lois Lane. Sparks between Clark and Lois immediately flew.

"It's one of those relationships where at the very beginning, you've got two people that are completely different," Erica

Below: Jason Teague's job as assistant coach at Smallville High meant that his relationship with Lana Lang had to remain a secret.

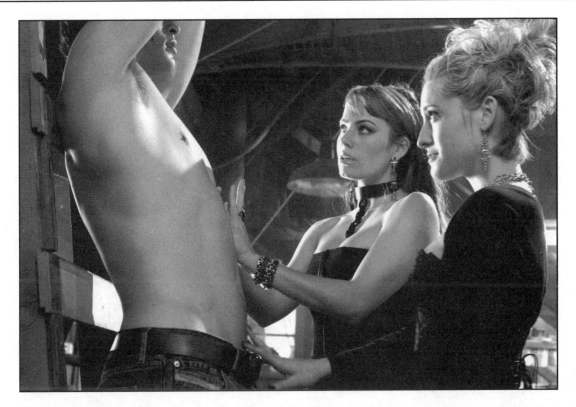

Durance said of her character's relationship with Clark. "Their relationship is very different to those he has with the other women in his life: his mother is so gracious and polite; Lana, who is wonderful; and Chloe who is so sweet; and then this Lois character comes in and she's abrasive, rude, and gives him what for. She's also clumsy and headstrong, and I think for him that's something very new. I think they both have really strong personalities, and they get stuck together [often], and there's that whole chemistry [thing] going on. I think they enjoy getting under each other's skin a little bit."

The return of Chloe Sullivan to the mix brought back some relationship issues between her and Clark, even before Chloe learned Clark's secret.

"I think Chloe holds a candle for Clark Kent, and that will never go away," Todd Slavkin mused. "Clark Kent is truly her Superman."

"They are two people that will always love each other, but in a way that is different from the way that Clark and Lana love each other," Darren Swimmer added.

An old flame of Clark's returned in the episodes 'Unsafe' and 'Pariah'. Alicia Baker caused some trouble with her obsessive behavior, but had she truly managed to turn over a new leaf? Clark would never find out for sure, as Alicia was killed by a fellow 'meteor freak'. "Here's this girl that knows the secret," Todd Slavkin said. "It's perfect. Well, of

THE RELATIONSHIPS

Above: Clark's relationships with Alicia and Lana offer two very different possibilities.

course, I mean, she's got to die, because any human relationship [right now] is going to end tragically for Clark. That's just the plight of being Superman."

The adults of *Smallville* had their own relationship problems. Martha and Jonathan Kent persevered despite health scares and Martha's new job at the Talon. "Martha is this amazing, strong character," writer Holly Harold explained, "and I think as a female being married to a man who has strong values and strong beliefs — Jonathan Kent was very strong — in order to match up to that type of man, you have to be strong enough in yourself, but also willing to let him be everything he needs to be. I thought Martha was a really good partner and could say to Jonathan 'I'm worried about your health,' but not completely make him a eunuch, even though there were times when she knew he shouldn't be doing things. But she's not his mother; she's his partner, so she has to let him do what he needs to do."

Also adding a wrench to the on-screen dynamics was the addition of the scheming Genevieve Teague, who wanted the Kryptonian elements for herself. However, writer

Todd Slavkin insists that Lionel Luthor never truly had feelings for Genevieve. "Lionel Luthor used and abused Genevieve Teague and never, never loved her. He was using her as a puppet for his own master plan. Genevieve, on the other hand, I think would have loved to have been the next Mrs. Luthor."

Slavkin suspects Lionel's interests lay elsewhere, even though the two characters didn't interact much during the fourth year. "Genevieve Teague? Genevieve Schmeague. He's always loved Martha Kent," he opined.

Even after Lana's relationship with Jason, the return of Alicia, and Chloe's discovery of Clark Kent's secret, it was inevitable that Clark and Lana would end the season together. "The main love story of the series is Clark and Lana, for better or worse, however people feel about it, and that was set up in the pilot," creator Al Gough said. "She had Jason, but ultimately it came back to Clark." But with Lex's insistence on protecting Lana — regardless of whether it was purely for his own benefit in securing the elements — someone else may be moving in on Clark's territory during the following year... ∎

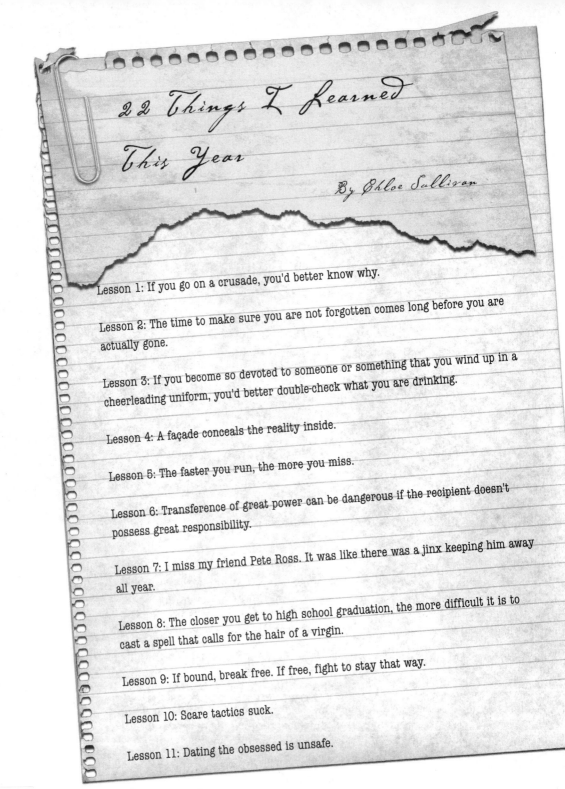

22 Things I Learned This Year

By Chloe Sullivan

Lesson 1: If you go on a crusade, you'd better know why.

Lesson 2: The time to make sure you are not forgotten comes long before you are actually gone.

Lesson 3: If you become so devoted to someone or something that you wind up in a cheerleading uniform, you'd better double-check what you are drinking.

Lesson 4: A façade conceals the reality inside.

Lesson 5: The faster you run, the more you miss.

Lesson 6: Transference of great power can be dangerous if the recipient doesn't possess great responsibility.

Lesson 7: I miss my friend Pete Ross. It was like there was a jinx keeping him away all year.

Lesson 8: The closer you get to high school graduation, the more difficult it is to cast a spell that calls for the hair of a virgin.

Lesson 9: If bound, break free. If free, fight to stay that way.

Lesson 10: Scare tactics suck.

Lesson 11: Dating the obsessed is unsafe.

Lesson 12: Getting to know the pariah can be revealing.

Lesson 13: If you are a potential college recruit, visit the school before you make any decisions.

Lesson 14: When keeping a friend's secret, you'd better not go krypto on everyone else or you could lose that friend.

Lesson 15: Love is sacred. Good friends are sacred. Family is sacred.

Lesson 16: My cousin Lucy taught me to never trust a pretty face.

Lesson 17: Even in the darkest onyx, you can glimpse genius.

Lesson 18: If you have good school spirit, you can win prom queen. If you have a good spirit in general, you can accomplish anything.

Lesson 19: If you draw a blank, it's good to have a trustworthy friend to fill you in.

Lesson 20: There is something ageless about Smallville — I'll miss it next year.

Lesson 21: Memories of our four years together will remain with me forever.

Lesson 22: And the biggest lesson of commencement? None of this would mean a thing without all of you.

HOB HOLE

HOB HOLE

'A man with faith can move mountains…'

S A Catterall

Published by Skid Publishing

A CIP catalogue record for this book is available from the British Library.

 Find us on Facebook

ISBN 978-0-9933431-0-0 (Paperback)
ISBN 978-0-9933431-1-7 (epub)
ISBN 978-0-9933431-2-4 (mobi)

Book layout and cover design by Clare Brayshaw

Prepared and printed by:

York Publishing Services Ltd
64 Hallfield Road
Layerthorpe
York YO31 7ZQ

Tel: 01904 431213

Website: www.yps-publishing.co.uk

ACKNOWLEDGEMENTS

I would like to thank David Chadwick, Deborah Gilbert and Tim Catterall for their proof reading and advice, everyone at YPS for their management and professionalism, Lucy, without whose encouragement I would still be talking about one day writing a novel and finally, you, the reader, for taking the time and trouble to share my tale.

ABOUT THE AUTHOR

S A Catterall is a solicitor from North Yorkshire. *Hob Hole* is his debut novel.

He can be contacted on hobholecat@btinternet.com

CHAPTER ONE

I have to begin this account with the silent memories that creep up and stab me when I'm lying awake. You'll know the feeling I'm sure; you're so tired and it's so late but sleep passes you over and the mind wanders strangely. Old friends and lovers. The sins and the regrets. The ghosts on your shoulder. The draining penance of staring at luminous hands as they crawl through the digits. If the clock would just lie flat for a moment we could clear up the mistakes at the back instead of having to live with them. If only, hey?

Cursed sleep. How do you break the spell? I've asked many people this question and it seems we all have our different ways. There's the obvious, of course, and tallying sheep over a farm gate is popular although my brother imagines he's up on the old railway line at Sandsend counting breakers as they rush over the slate flats at the turn of tide. Tom has a quite novel approach. He says when it happens to him, he uses the *length x breadth x height* formula to try and work out the number of blocks in Hadrian's Wall until slain by the mental arithmetic. Each to their own I guess. If we were all the same it would be a very boring world.

When I can't sleep I scramble the pillows in search of cool linen, like you do, and then flopping back into the covers I start tracing the contours of my own little life. It usually begins with that first memory on my father's shoulders in the unsaddling enclosure at Thirsk, marvelling at the steam rising off the washed down horses, either that or I drift fondly to endless blue summers digging holes in Scarborough beach. I'll recall my first impressions of Ampleforth, the distress of small boys abandoned by their parents, the strange looking Benedictines in their cassocks and above all the beautiful canticles that used to drift through the corridors and tell me that somehow, everything would be all right in the end.

These moonlit hours sketching my youth have diminished with the years and nowadays, I'm usually asleep long before a virtual stroll carries me from the college chapel and into the lecture theatre. However, if I go on to take my old seat in there, I might as well start counting waves or Roman blocks myself because if I don't, I know I'll go back to that muggy autumn afternoon when my life changed forever. There is a delicious irony it should all have begun in the lecture theatre, a place of learning. It was to be an education for sure and with the rest of my life so inextricably tied to that dreadful afternoon, I do not see how I could begin this narrative at any other interval.

It was late in the fall of 1914 and I was boarding an extra term to sit the Oxbridge exams. It remains with me now, the smell of burning leaves floating through the window together with the shouts and whistles from a distant rugby match and the Angelus chime of St Lawrence's. To my left we are walled in by layer upon layer of books stacked up to the medieval beams, the musty rows criss crossed by a pair of

2

sliding staircases giving the whole the appearance of a giant *Snakes and Ladders* board. On the other side of the theatre an enormous pair of curtains hold back the Scorpion sun although a few tiny shafts burst through the moth holes to skewer a billion particles of dust. Then down there in the middle, beyond the creaking benches and their fresh faced occupants, right in the bowl of the auditorium, just there behind the black marble island stands the hapless figure of Brother Wallace wrestling with a city of bottles and tripods as he endeavours to illustrate the combustion of ethanol.

'Now pay attention class: this is a weally important expewiment and in the final examination you will be expected to wemember how it is conducted.'

Wallace was not a young man and should have been retired long before he ever scrutinised one of my equations. He was the ultimate academic but he'd been Head of Science since at least the second Boer conflict and maybe even the first. No one seemed to know. It wouldn't have surprised me if he had been teaching chemistry since the Crimea for there was something quite timeless about him. I often studied the crablike way he used to slide his thin, humid form around the theatre with that signature sprinkling of dandruff upon the shoulders of his dark gown. I swear he'd been doing it for so long his tracks were worn in the flags.

'Now, first we place the thermometer in this beaker of water then we light the ethanol spiwit burner…'

'This is boring. How long until tea?' sighed a voice to my left with such an exaggerated yawn that everyone in the seminar appeared to hear it apart from the old monk in the pit. Tommy Brentnall was also sitting Oxbridge although it was common knowledge he spent more time boxing and

3

pursuing women from the village than he did in his books. I gave him a sharp elbow.

'Tom, don't, you'll get us turfed out.'

'What if we are? Mother Earth is burning around us Edmund, burning I tell you. We are living through the most incredible passage of world history with civilization itself ablaze, and yet you and I are destined to loiter on the sidelines, trapped in this time warp of cassocks and Latin.'

'Do you two mind? I've just about had it with your endless commentary Brentnall. Some of us are trying to pay attention to this'.

So spoke Conway, the head boy who unfortunately for us was seated in the next row down. *One-way Conway* as he was better known because he did everything by the book, fawning and crawling to the staff on his way up. He actually came from my home town too where his family ran a transport business but the bloke was a stiff and there were poles between us.

At Tom's exchange with the head boy Brother Wallace looked up and glowered in our general direction before returning to the array of implements before him.

'Now we give the spiwit burner half a minute or so to settle then using gloves on both hands we lower the beaker of water onto the appawatus so it sits diwectly on top of the flame…'

'Psst- Edmund, *Blue*' mumbles Tom. 'I've fixed up a session of *Three Old Maids* behind the 1st XI pavilion tomorrow after supper. I've persuaded big Hilda and two of her friends from the kitchens to come along – you up for it?'

Someone snorted at the end of our row. I gritted my teeth and carried on taking notes.

4

'If you two don't button it I'll be filing a report with the headmaster and I mean that' snapped Conway.

'Hey, don't look at me,' I retorted. 'I didn't say anything.'

Wallace broke away from his experiment and glared at the back row where we were sitting, a little longer and more deliberately this time before returning to his spiel.

'Note please that the mass of ethanol in the spiwit burner and the tempwiture of water must be measured before and after the expewiment. In theowee, the heat generated by the combustion of the ethanol should be twansferred to the water…'

'Surely you remember big Hilda don't you *Blue*?' quipped Tom. 'You should do having salivated over the size of her hooters these last twelve months.'

Several students burst out laughing and it was too much for Wallace who immediately stopped what he was doing and placing hands on hips, turned to the class.

'Would the young man at the back pwactising his elocution please make himself known. Come come, don't be shy, who is it?

Conway, unable to pass any occasion to advance his stock didn't even turn but merely stuck an arm out in our direction, not that there was any need for Tom was already on his feet.

'You boy, what's your name?'

'It's Brentnall sir'

'Bwentnall you say? Well then, Bwentnall, I deduce the only weason you have time for tittle tattle in lectures is because you know all about this expewiment.'

'I really wouldn't go so far as to say that …'

'No, no Bwentnall don't be coy,' interrupted Wallace before adding darkly 'we are all quite *intweeged* to ascertain if your knowledge of the syllabus is diwectly pwoportionate to your capacity to excite disorderly tittle tattle. Down here now if you would Bwentnall, come come, that's wight, to the fwont of the class'

All eyes were fixed on Tom as he shuffled his stocky frame to the end of the bench and down the steps to join Wallace in the bowl of the hall.

'That's wight, come this way. Good. Now Bwentnall, since you alweddy know so much about this expewiment you will doubtless be able to complete it for the benefit of the class. And be sure to acquit yourself Bwentnall for if you fail, you will answer for this most wecent exhibition of diswuptive behaviour to the headmaster, who might take a gweat deal of persuading that you should not be sent down from college stwait away.'

Tom shuffled round the island where to sarcastic jeers he inspected various bottles holding some to the light and sniffing the contents of others before carefully replacing the stoppers and setting them down again.

'Well Bwentnall? We are all on the edge of our seats.'

Tom cleared his throat then selecting a piece of yellow chalk turned to the blackboard and began to scribble enthusiastically.

'First of all we need to weigh the spirit burner and various fluids and record the information in a table. Next, we ignite the alcohol then using the glass rod to stir the water, we wait until the temperature rises to 40°C at which point we immediately replace the cap on the spirit burner to extinguish the flame. We then record the final temperature of the water using the thermometer.'

Wallace looked surprised. We all were.

'Yes, yes, that's all well and good Bwentnall, but what is the *purpose* of the expewiment?'

Tom twisted to the board and continued in that familiar, easy manner.

'Well sir, that's easy because from the information provided, we can establish the amount of energy transferred from the burning alcohol to the water using the equation $q = mc\Delta T$ where q is the energy transferred, m represents the mass of water and c is its specific heat capacity.'

Wallace furred his brow while Tom continued, fluent and assured, occasionally tapping the board with his chalk as he underlined various sections of the equation.

'…and so it is through the application of *this* formula that we can identify which alcohol – or rather which *fuel* – provides the most energy per ounce of liquid burned, which when considered on a commercial scale has obvious implications for the industrial consumer. Tarra! I thank myself!' at which my friend gave a small bow and tossed the chalk into the box leaving the assembly focussed back on our tutor who was still glaring at the board. After what seemed like an age, but was probably no more than a few seconds, Wallace turned back to the class.

'Well, well, Bwentnall' said he with a heavy sigh. 'Quite contwawee to my expectations it appears you shall live to fight another day. You may weturn to your seat.'

'Thank you very much sir,' beamed Tom who was already striding back up the causeway, chopping the air in acknowledgement of the raucous applause that had broken out upon Wallace's capitulation.

'That will do class. That will do!' bayed Wallace waiting for the clamour to die down before continuing. 'Bwentnall is wight, the purpose of this expewiment is not only to assess the combustion of various fuels but also to measure their *efficiency* against one another…'

Tom settled back in his place.

'Where on *earth* did you learn to do that?' I whispered.

'Piece of cake. My grandparents are chemists in York. Here now, watch closely, this should be a good laugh...'

'Watch what?'

Conway span round again. 'That's it Brentnall, I shall report your behaviour to the headmaster at the next captain's meeting.' Tom screwed his face at Conway then dipped his head to the front where I followed the cue back to Wallace still beavering away over his city of tripods and burners.

'Now class, I want you to note the manner diffewent alcohols burn at diffewent wates, let us take this second example of methylated spiwit...'

Wallace picked up a large green bottle and pouring the contents into a fresh flask, carefully balanced the combination over the tripod where it began to simmer on the indigo spike of a Bunsen burner. Within seconds one or two students at the front began to splutter, followed by others behind them, and then still others as if some invisible force was scaling the bank of desks.

'Dear me! That's ab-so-lute-ly dreadful! Who was *that*?' wailed a voice from below.

'Who was what?' thought I until a revolting smell of rotten eggs hit the back row. Tom's face was deadpan.

'Switched a few bottles when I was down there didn't I?'

Within seconds the cries and accusations multiplied, some students amplifying their distress with contorted faces and theatrically clenched throats. As he frantically dismantled the apparatus Wallace shouted to a bucktoothed lad in the front row to open the window.

'Who me sir?' replied the youth as if butter wouldn't melt in his mouth.

'Yes you boy, open that window, in fact open all the windows! Quickly man, get on with it.'

The lad did as he was told and with a roar like gravel sliding down corrugated iron, the curtains tore open filling the hall with sunlight.

'What do you mean it's stuck? Lift it up boy, don't pull! Lift! Lift! Here, move over!' at which Wallace and a couple of others puffed and heaved at the base until with an appalling shriek the window finally gave way. All the while the coughing and spluttering rose to a crescendo as even the meeker scholars made hay in the unexpected crisis.

All of a sudden, the air was cut by the rattle of the latch as the towering profile of Father Mathews appeared in the doorway. Immediately, the coughing ceased and everyone jumped to their feet as the headmaster scowled at the assembly before turning his attention to Wallace shuffling anxiously by the window.

'Good grief Brother Wallace, what the devil is going on in here? And what's that *dreadful* smell?'

Wallace looked crestfallen.

'G-good afternoon Father Headmaster. The students are conducting an ethanol expewiment but there appears to be a pwoblem with some of the labelling.'

Mathews picked up a few bottles then turned and raked the bank of students as if daring anyone to even blink. No one of course did and the tension was only broken when having murmured something in Wallace's ear to make the latter nod like a penguin, he looked up and fixed his steely gaze on the rest of the class.

'I would like to speak with Edmund Bullick in my office please.' A sea of faces turned and stared in my direction. What, *me*? What could the head possibly want with *me*? I exchanged a nervous glance with Tom then disregarding Conway's gesture of cutting his throat, edged to the walkway. I sensed the worried stare of the assembly. Something was horribly wrong. Mathews addressed the remainder of the class.

'I formed the impression on my way in here that some students are suffering from a respiratory ailment, the condition no doubt triggered by a lack of fresh air. I therefore intend to get the whole of sixth form including the Oxbridge scholars out of bed at 6.00am tomorrow for a cross country to Byland Abbey and back. That's 6.00am tomorrow morning and I shall expect everybody to be up, dressed in sports kit and assembled in the courtyard before the clock chimes. Carry on please Brother Wallace.' Without another word Mathews turned and with a swish of his gown, he was off leaving the theatre in stunned silence and me to trail anxiously in his wake.

We fell into step under the gaze of a thousand eyes from the old team photographs that lined the corridor. There was real purpose in the headmaster's stride but other than to admonish some juniors for slouching with their hands in their pockets he remained silent, and it was only when we reached his office and he was jangling for his keys that the icicle was plunged into my breast.

'Bullick, you must prepare yourself for some bad news. Your father has been killed in an accident and you are needed at home.'

He'd no sooner spoken when I heard footsteps and turned to meet the distressed gaze of my younger brother Alfie and Spangle, his line master. Alfie and I looked at one another in disbelief as the head marched to the far side of his desk and reached for the top draw.

'Gentlemen, I received a telegram this afternoon from Mr Barnaby, chief steward of the Craven estate. It would appear that yesterday afternoon, Lord William and your father were involved in an accident while riding out on the moors. I am sorry to tell you your father was killed while Lord William remains in a critical condition. I am afraid I have no further details other than you are both to return home immediately. Please accept my profound condolences.'

For a while Mathews remained quite still, eyes peering up at us over his half-moon glasses as he allowed the dreadful news to sink in. Alfie began to tremble and sob uncontrollably. I was too shocked to say anything. The headmaster closed the draw and picked up the threads of his matter of fact address.

'It's too late to set off this afternoon so Mr Spangle here will take you to the village station first thing tomorrow. I would like you to pack all your things before you depart but take with you only what you require for the immediate journey, as your books and trunks will follow in due course. Edmund, I shall expect you to return for your Oxbridge examinations in ten days' time. Alfie, as it is near the end of November we shall not expect you back until after the Christmas holidays. Please go now and make your arrangements. Look after them will you Mr Spangle'.

Mathews picked up a Latin text book and began to thumb through the pages. Was that it? Was there anything more to say? It appeared not. We waited for a second then Spangle nodded and the three of us turned to go and pack. I screwed my eyes in disbelief. Had I really just heard Mathews tell me my father was dead? Spangle's grim expression and the tears running down my brother's cheeks told me it must be so.

Alfie was billeted with the other new boys and it was to his dormitory in Bolton House that our sad little party trudged first. When we reached the top of the creaking staircase Spangle paused by the washbasins and surveyed the line of crisply made beds.

'Edmund, I'm going to leave you to help your brother gather his belongings. Let me know when you're done and I'll arrange for everything to be taken down to the stables where Robinson can send them on later. In view of what has occurred, you are obviously both excused from attending late study and benediction.'

We stood in silence for a moment before Spangle added in a low voice 'I will go now. The milk train passes through the village at six forty so I'll come and wake you both at quarter to. I'll wire Mr Barnaby to ensure there is someone to meet you when you get into Durham tomorrow. The Principal has arranged for High Mass on Sunday to be offered for the soul of your father but otherwise I don't think there is anything else I can usefully say at the present time – only that I am so terribly sorry boys about what has happened.'

I muttered some garbled appreciation. Spangle nodded and slipped away leaving Alfie and I alone in the dormitory. A flock of pigeons clattered on a nearby roof while somewhere in the distance a hand bell generated a rush of footsteps across the courtyard. Alfie began to cry, warm tears falling from his little face onto the bedspread as he manfully tried to dab them away with the back of his cuff.

'Edmund, what are we going to do? Please tell me this isn't happening and we are in the middle of a terrible dream?'

The six years that separated us had never appeared more of a gulf than at that moment. I folded a comforting arm around him.

'I'm afraid neither of us is dreaming. There can be no mistake about something so dreadful.'

'I don't want to go home. Not anymore. Not ever. If father has died I feel like I just want to die as well'

'Alfie, look at me. Look at me. Now listen. When Mum died I made a promise that I would always take care of you. And haven't I always looked after you?'

My brother spluttered in agreement.

'That's right. I always have and I always will. Now while we don't know what's happened at Craven – at least not yet – whatever it is we shall go home tomorrow and face it together. Right?'

Alfie nodded at the floor.

'Good lad. Now come on, wipe those eyes and let's get started with this packing. Which locker over there is yours?'

CHAPTER TWO

I barely slept that night, my sorrow tossed and mangled through each quarterly chime of St Lawrence's, and even when I finally succumbed, it was to emerge in a troubling dream where my father was calling out to me from the clock tower at Craven Castle. I woke with a start and believing in my confusion that the voice was emanating from the courtyard, I leaped out of bed and raced to the window. The abbey church stood graceful in the moonlight but other than a trickle of water from the broken pump in the corner, there was no sound at all.

I lay awake for a long time anticipating the trials of the next few days. I was at a loss to understand how the two of them could have been riding on the moors when they spent so little time together. Dad took care of Lord William's horses, but their relationship was strictly master and servant and apart from racedays and when his Lordship inspected the yard, they barely saw each other.

The hours passed. Midnight. One o clock. My thoughts turned to Lady Alanna and the household as I tried to picture what sort of an evening they would be having in the wake of the accident. No doubt this depended upon the extent of the master's injuries but with the telegram describing them as 'critical', I perceived the castle would be in turmoil and that word of events would have already reached Oxford from where, no doubt, Lord William's heir would also be making plans to return.

Although I was two years younger than Julian, we had grown up with the other children on the Craven estate and I have fond memories of us building tree houses in the park, and playing in the quarries or down on the banks of the Wear. As we grew older we would pick up the threads in the holidays and help Barnaby around the estate or ride the novices out with the *Braes* where we were often accompanied by Julian's sister, Jane, and Alfie when he was old enough. These were such happy times which made the cracks that began to appear in Julian's character later on all the more perplexing. Oh, the changes were barely noticeable at first like he would inexplicably turn sharp in conversation or peer rudely over your shoulder as you were talking to him, but when he returned from his first term at Oxford equipped with a cane and speaking with an unbearably contrived twang, I obviously asked him if there was anything the matter. I mean he sounded so ridiculous what else was I supposed to do? Julian, of course, promptly dismissed the notion that he had changed but if any confirmation were needed, it arrived at Craven that summer in the form of his university friend Lord Johnny Clifford.

I had grown up with most of Julian's friends who were from the Durham area but Clifford was something quite different making it obvious when we were introduced that the son of a horse trainer was not a suitable companion for the heir of the estate. *Horse Boy* he had called me, not that I needed a snub to keep out of his way because the fellow was trouble and having spent barely a minute in his company, I was under no illusions from where Julian had been taking his cue.

Lord Johnny Clifford appeared to have it all. At least, at first sight he did. His father was an hereditary peer, the family seemed to own half of Maidstone and apart from being as rich as Croesus with a dash of blue blood in his veins, Julian's friend was a handsome, powerful man with a deep booming voice and it wasn't difficult to see how he cast his spell. However what Julian failed to notice, or more likely chose to overlook, was that Clifford was proud and needlessly unpleasant and if after our first meeting I had any reservations that I might have misjudged his character, these were swiftly dissipated over the following months.

When Clifford's party first appeared at Craven that autumn, everyone understood it was a brief call to look up Julian on their way to the Percy shoot. Perhaps that was the original intention although as soon it was discovered that Lord William and Lady Alanna were in Brighton for the season, the guests promptly weighed anchor and started eating and drinking the family out of house and home. On their last night the party bestowed their patronage upon the *Black Horse* from where, having caused a large amount of damage, they went on to gate-crash a stable lads' boxing tournament that was taking place in the village hall. Needless to say their appearance was not welcomed and in the fracas that followed, Clifford proceeded to knock the front teeth out of an apprentice jockey half his size. If the incident had not already alienated the community to breaking point, the situation was compounded the following morning when the guests departed for Northumberland crowing about 'grockles' and the appalling excesses of the night before. Neither did there appear to be the faintest trace of remorse from the heir to Craven. At least at first there wasn't. It was all 'high spirits' wasn't it? The villagers, however, thought very differently and in the end it was left for Barnaby to persuade Julian that with his friends off the scene, he should compensate the lad and while he was at it cram in enough humble pie that the incident could yet be swept under the carpet before Lord William returned.

After the brawl with the jockeys I resolved to speak to Julian about the kind of company he was keeping, and a few days later when we ran into each other outside the village post office I tackled him. We had been friends for a long time so I cut straight to the quick suggesting that *the Merton crowd* (as they were known on the estate) were a bunch of spongers and that Clifford, in particular, was seriously bad news. Julian, though, was having none of it stating blandly that these were his companions now and that my comments were spawned by jealousy on account that they were all wealthy and titled, and that being of humbler stock, I could not be expected to understand their ways.

'Oh come off it Julian there's nothing *elite* or even remotely admirable about Johnny Clifford. The fellow is a complete arse.'

'You don't understand him as I do Edmund. Just know that he is my closest friend and I will not hear a word spoken against him.'

'Your friend? The only friends these people have are themselves. Look at the mayhem he brought the village the other night? The fellow is nothing more than a self-centred, stuck-up, loud mouthed thug.'

Julian coloured at these words and to my surprise began to tremble as if fighting to master his emotions.

'You should be wary what you say about my friends in future Edmund. It is not your place to try and lecture me.'

'Oh come off it man, there's no need to be so defensive. I'm just trying to give you the kind of advice which I would expect to hear from you if our positions were reversed.'

Julian turned the colour of beetroot.

'Reversed? Reversed you say? You dare to talk to me in this manner? Our positions could never be reversed. There is a gulf between our respective stations in society or hadn't you noticed?'

'Julian, can't you see what's happening? These people are *using* you and you need to ditch them'

Julian drew a sharp breath before spitting out his response. 'You dare to lecture me on how I should lead my life? Do you know something Edmund? I could never understand what induced my father to provide the Bullicks with such a generous living, when at the drop of a hat he could secure his pick of trainers from Malton or Middleham. Yes, that's right. Calvert, Elsey, Budgett, Kent; any one of them would jump at the opportunity to manage Craven but oh no, father won't hear of it, he has to persevere with a family of bogtrotters he met all those years ago. Your old man hasn't achieved anything like the level of success that would even begin to justify the estate's investment in him. Yes, that's the reality of the situation Edmund, my father has been carrying your father for years, it's a standing joke in racing circles and I'm not the only one who's been urging him to place the horses with someone who can make a better fist of their potential. Alec Birch for one would leap at the prospect of taking the string to Sherriff Hutton. You would do well to remember this because one day the inexplicably good fortune that reposes with your family will be dependent upon my goodwill, which I can tell you at this precise moment is in extremely short measure.'

I felt a surge of anger and rounded on him. 'How can you talk like that? My father is the best trainer in the region. It's only because of Dad's sheer hard work Lord William has been among the top northern owners for the last decade....'

He cut me short.

'Enough! No, I said enough! I will not hear another word from you on the subject. How dare you answer me back?'

'What do you expect when you insult my father? You should listen to yourself. You're talking bollocks.'

'I tell you now Edmund, it is you who forgets his place. You ought to remember I am the heir to Craven while you are nothing more than the son of an estate employee. First you try to lecture me about the company I keep and then you have the gall to tell *me* that I don't know what I am talking about when I bring home a few truths about your father? Consistently one of the top owners you say? I suggest that with all the investment that has been poured into the yard Lord William should be head and shoulders above any other owner north of Doncaster. Yes, that's right, head and shoulders. The best trainer in the region you say? I don't think so. Your father is a show pony Edmund. He fawns and makes all the right noises but when it comes to cutting the mustard at the highest level anyone can see he is near enough useless. *Useless!*'

Julian's face was right up against my own. At the final insult I struck him as hard as I could and we wrestled to the ground, clutching and clawing at one another. Julian was stronger and I felt his nails go down the side of my face but I was so incensed that I managed to hold my own until a giant hand suddenly grabbed his collar pulled him away. I sprang to my feet and was about to charge in when the huge figure of Harry Sample, the village blacksmith, stepped between us.

'Lads, what the fuck d'ye think you're doing scrapping in the street like a couple of yobs? Come on; enough's enough, shake hands.'

I wiped away the blood trickling down the side of my face. Sample was right. What were we thinking of? I held out my hand but Julian would not take it.

'No be still' he cried wiping his brow. 'You have greatly insulted me Bullick and from this moment on I consider any association that previously existed between us to be at an end.'

His voice was raised and half the village must have heard it. 'Julian, please, don't be like this…'

'Don't you 'oh please Julian' me. You *dare* to strike me? You can keep your 'pleases'; keep them and save them for the gods that they postpone the hour that the lot of your family should fall from my father's gift into my own.'

Julian spat on the ground then ignoring my further entreaties turned on his heel. At Sample's behest the small crowd of spectators quickly dispersed although I knew that tales of what they had witnessed would spread like wildfire.

'You all right son?'

I assured him I was and tried to play down the disagreement but Sample had seen it for what it was.

'He's not like his father young 'un. I blame those so-called friends he brought back with him from Oxford. You only told him what everyone in the village thinks, much good it will do you because he doesn't want to listen.'

Sample was right. I would have been far better holding my tongue. I left for the stables where I didn't dare confide in my father but put the injury to my face down to play fighting with one of Lord William's lurchers. Whether he suspected the truth I never knew although the incident greatly troubled me. Julian's acid dialogue had come so easily it was as if he had long since chosen his words waiting only for the kind of opportunity that was presented by our disagreement. It also left me at a loss how someone I considered as my oldest friend could turn so quickly. It was almost as if the prospect of his inheritance was starting to corrupt him.

Our quarrel had taken place in August, since which time we had not spoken. The holidays were concluded without further episode and Julian returned to Merton College and my brother and I to Ampleforth. However as I lay there in my room that night listening to the broken pump and staring at the ceiling, the manner in which Julian would respond to the events that had overtaken our respective fathers was not the least of my concerns.

CHAPTER THREE

I woke to the crashing of a hand making its way down the corridor. It was still pitch dark and flapping for the top of the locker I found my wristwatch and squinted at its' luminous face. 5:40 am. I opened the door on Spangle who from the look of the rain twinkling on the shoulders of his coat had been up for some time.

'Ah, good morning Edmund, I see you're already out of bed'.

'Out of bed?' I replied through a muzzle of mint before turning to spit in the basin. 'I know Father Mathews promised to get everyone up at crack of dawn, but that bell of his would wake the bloomin' dead.'

Spangle laughed. 'Quite so, quite so. I don't doubt the whole College is in turmoil wondering if the Germans have landed! Alas I bring you the less dramatic news that I have just loaded your cases and will bring the trap to the front in twenty minutes.'

'Where's Alfie?'

'Your brother is in the refectory tucking into one of Mrs Parson's cooked breakfasts. If you're quick you might just catch her.'

Our attention was diverted by some tuneless wailing in the corridor as Tom trotted by in his crumpled vest and shorts. 'Good grief Brentnall you look as if you have been dragged through a hedge backwards and the trip hasn't even started yet!'

Tom began running up and down on the spot.

'Indeed Mr Spangle, indeed, although a man in pursuit of excellence should not be judged on appearance alone. Wait until we get going. None of the others will see me for dust. Hoo! Ha! Hoo! Ha!'

Spangle surveyed my friend's peculiar karate-type stance.

'Dust? I think you mean mud, don't you Brentnall, or have you not seen the weather outside?'

Tom performed a few star jumps.

'Dust or mud, it makes no difference to the human arrow! Is it a bird? Is it an aeroplane? No it's Thomas Brentnall, the Rosedale Express; blink and you'll miss it! Choo! Choo!'

'Brentnall, the only time you resemble an express is in the rush to get to the front of the queue at mealtimes'.

'I shall ignore the slight Mr Spangle. This is the day where through the sheer power of my engine, I shall roar to the Abbey and back with my opponents trailing far behind! Choo Choo!'

Spangle shook his head as he set off down the corridor before calling back over his shoulder. 'Twenty minutes Edmund, twenty minutes.'

The words had scarcely left his lips before Tom was in my room pressing his substantial frame against the closed door. 'Edmund my dear fellow, I'm so sorry to hear about your father. This is dreadful. We were only given the news late last night otherwise I'd have been along sooner. Everyone is devastated. What happened?'

23

'That's the thing, I don't know. The telegram from the estate was brief merely confirming that father and Lord William had been involved in an accident and that my father had died from his injuries. If the headmaster was told any more, which I doubt, then he's not letting on. At the moment my only concern is to look after Alfie and get back home as quickly as possible.'

Tom remained silent for a while, deep in thought before replying.

'How long do you think you'll be away?'

'I'm not sure yet. I'll obviously stay for my father's funeral and make some kind of start with his affairs, but after that I don't know. At some point I'm going to have to discuss the future with Lord William and Lady Alanna and hope they'll stand by us because as you know, my last meeting with Julian was not a happy one.'

Tom frowned. 'Yes, I remember you telling me, but surely Lord William isn't going to throw you out? From what you say he appears to be a man of honour and hardly the type to abandon you in your hour of need.'

'I hope you're right because Craven is everything to me; Alfie and I were born on the estate, the stable lodge has always been our home and I cannot imagine living anywhere else. Lord William *is* a good man but I shudder when I recall my quarrel with Julian and his threat to evict us. I can only pray that his fathers' injuries are not severe enough to accelerate the promised day of reckoning, for at the time it was given I have no doubt that Julian meant every word.'

I went to the window. The cross-country runners were beginning to assemble in the courtyard and some of them were stamping around to keep warm. We walked into the corridor, Tom's gaze following the last of the stragglers as they were swallowed up by the staircase.

'Look Blue, I have to go. We'll talk again when you get back. Watch out for yourself and if you need me at any time, remember you only have to say the word.'

We shook hands at which Tom galloped off in the direction of the others, bellowing some weird chant about being mowed down by the Brentnall Express. I gathered my belongings and passing through the kitchens to pick up my brother and a handful of Mrs Parson's egg sandwiches, made it round to the front just as Spangle was drawing up in the school trap.

CHAPTER FOUR

The tiny village station was almost deserted with just the three of us and a farmer with a couple of cattle at the far end of the platform. It was a bitterly cold morning and as I spared a thought for Tom and the others bobbing up and down Jerry Carr Bank, I wondered what they would have given for a minute by the coal fire in the waiting room. A tell-tale column of steam suddenly pierced the trees and I stepped from the warmth to see the cold murky face of the engine round the corner and slowly grind to a halt in front of us. A ramp on one of the trucks at the back crashed down as the cows we had seen earlier clattered aboard. Spangle raised his voice over the hiss of the engine.

'Right lads, good luck. I'll wire Mr Barnaby to expect you at Durham sometime after midday. You've just the one change at York but it's frantic on the railways at the moment so keep your wits about you and be careful you don't leave anything behind.'

'I'll do my best sir' I replied 'and thank you very much for the lift.'

'Not a bit of it' yelled Spangle tossing his head towards the village. 'I'd far sooner do this than take the cross country' then adding with a thin smile 'seriously though boys, take care and be brave.'

An unscheduled stop at Tollerton to pick up some sheep meant it was after nine when we shuffled into York and our progress wasn't helped when even before the train stopped, an enormous wall of people closed in and began pulling at the smoky bronze handles of the doors. I could see that if we didn't act quickly we would be trapped in the carriage so I yelled to Alfie to hang on behind as I battered our way to the exit. At the far end of the coach a guard blew his whistle and shouted for order but no one was taking any notice and neither did I as the scrum carried us closer to the door until we burst out onto the platform.

The station was absolutely heaving. It had been our intention to pick up a northern connection but there were so many people milling about that morning we couldn't even see the track. It reminded me of the streets around Roker Park on Boxing Day, only instead of an ocean of red and white, we were in a sea of khaki with hundreds and hundreds of soldiers swarming around like ants, climbing in and out of the carriages, hanging onto the walls, some running alongside the trains as they swept in and out while others wandered around aimlessly or gathered in large mounds next to their packs. There must have been battalions from all over the country present, hordes and hordes of Scots and Irish Guards while up on the walkway a detachment of Welsh Fusiliers were giving an impromptu choral recital. On the platforms the mothers and fathers, the brothers and sisters and the sweethearts swayed and wept against a backdrop of magazine sellers, porters and trolleys, a Salvation Army soup kitchen and at the far end of the station a solitary porter desperately trying to clear a path through the mayhem for a small horse and trap. Above everything there was the ear-splitting discord of noise; the squealing and screeching of locomotives, the heavy sigh of steam, the slamming of doors and whistles of guards constantly mingling with the shouts of the paperboys, the calls and songs from the khaki multitude and the soft cries of women. Spangle had been a master of understatement when he predicted the terminal might be busy; every nook and cranny, every delve and covert in and around those sooty brick walls was the roost of mankind in rapture or distress and while I had expected the war to have impacted upon the rail network, I was totally unprepared for the Tower of Babel that greeted us at York station that morning.

It was quickly apparent that all of the trains were heading south and as we washed about in that rudderless mass I began to despair that we would ever find something travelling in the other direction. When a harried looking porter confirmed there was a points failure at Selby and the wait was going to be a long one, I looked to the skies suddenly noticing the unusual moon and star holes punched into the girders supporting the roof. Moon and stars! Would we ever get out of this place?

It occurred to me that news of my father's death might have made the papers so I grabbed a copy of *The York Press* from one of boys howling next to a sandwich board that Britain was now at war with Turkey as well as the German empire. I scanned the first few pages but other than casualty lists and reports of a battle somewhere near the Marne there was little domestic news and nothing at all about Craven. I quartered the paper and tucked it away in my pocket just as we were approached by a young lieutenant from the Durham Light Infantry.

'Hello, it's Edmund Bullick isn't it? *Blue* Bullick?'

I looked into a familiar countenance I couldn't quite place.

'It's me, Fergus Vaughan, I was two years ahead of you at college and played front row just when you broke into the first team. I saw the uniform from the other side of the platform and had to come over and investigate.'

'Vaughan! Of course, Fergus I remember you well, I didn't recognise you with the moustache! How's life treating you?'

'How's life treating me?' he replied twiddling the thin blades of his whiskers. 'Without a word of a lie I'm in absolute heaven! When I left Ampleforth in the summer of '12 the old man put me to work in the accounts department of the family mill, and I was half way through my training when the war broke out. I said to him 'father, I want to be released from my pupillage so I can join the army'. He tried to convince me that I was doing just as much for the country where I was, but I couldn't see myself catching the 7.40 into Newcastle every morning while my friends were fighting and probably dying somewhere so I told him that I was awfully sorry, but I had made up my mind and must go. When he realised I meant what I said there were tears in his eyes but he embraced me just the same and gave me his blessing. The next day myself and a few others went down to the Market Place and signed up for the 18th *Pals* and lo and behold here we are! How about you? It can't be the end of term yet so what are you doing in York?'

I introduced him to Alfie and explained the reason for our journey and the problems we were having getting back home. Vaughan listened grim faced then clasped his hands together.

'Well d'ye know I think I might just be able to help you there. Our battalion has just completed six weeks training in the Brecon Beacons and we're actually on our way to Chester-Le-Street at the moment. The train is drawing water in one of the sidings but we should be leaving within the half hour. What say I have a word with the CO and see if we can give you a lift? It's not quite the Pullman but we can get you there in a couple of hours if you don't mind a bit of a squash'.

I had always liked Vaughan but never more so than when for the last time that day, I stood on my tiptoes and squinted down the line. Nothing. I turned to our rescuer.

'That would be brilliant. Thank you so much.'

'Excellent. Come on Alfie, you too. Follow me' and with that Vaughan led the way over the east-west footbridge where we slipped through the Welsh chorus and dropped down onto the far platform.

The CO turned out to be a larger than life colonel from Bishop Auckland called Rowley who was surprisingly engaging as he chattered away, pipe bobbing up and down in the corner of his mouth.

'My subaltern here has told me about your pickle, boys, and I'm glad to be of help *heh heh*. I have fond memories of Durham. I was at University there and rowed up as far as the Craven estate many times, God's own country so it is *heh heh*'.

'There is no more beautiful city in the whole of England' piped Alfie before Rowley cut him short through a cloud of tobacco. 'Indeed young man, indeed. Well, well, giving lifts to civilians is probably against the rules *heh heh* most irregular of course but there is a war on and we have to help one another so we won't say anything about it if you don't *heh heh* – carry on Vaughan' and with that he wheeled away and started *heh hehing* at some junior officers gathered round the salvation army cafe.

Alfie and I followed Vaughan and his batman to the end of the north bound platform. The line was empty so we jumped down and crossed the tracks to a far siding where two scruffy black locomotives were drawing water from an enormous iron tank. I felt for the solitary operative who had to scale the ladder and swing round the hose because it looked as if the slightest gust of wind would bring the whole lot crashing down, operative, hose and all. I was watching the fellow beavering away when at three sharp blasts from Vaughan's whistle, scores of soldiers poured off the platform and scrambled towards a long line of carriages parked up further down the siding. I say 'carriages' but when Vaughan first pointed them out they looked more like the stubby boxcars we used at the stable for transporting horses. Each was about 20 feet by 10, there were no benches or furniture, the boards were covered in straw and the trucks were fully enclosed, except for a small window at each end latticed with barbed wire. As we drew nearer I noticed that stencilled in large white letters on the side of each wagon were the words *8 horses 40 men.* I didn't know whether this meant eight horses *or* forty men or eight horses *and* forty men but I assumed it was the former, at least I hoped so because when Alfie and I were hauled into the second wagon reserved for junior officers and batmen, there wasn't enough room left for one horse let alone eight.

31

The clanging of buffers announced the two dirty black engines had recoupled and we were ready to go. I made my way to the door and peered down the carriages. A real sense of excitement was in the air as a pair of NCO's ran along the track slamming the doors and sealing protruding heads and arms that right to the last were gesticulating obscenities down the long curved wall of the train. It was hard to believe the two engines could cope with such a huge load but movement began with an abrupt jolt on the front buffers that whipped along the wagons, followed by another brief jar forwards, a stop, a longer jolt, another stop and then, with a piercing groan of iron, we began to shudder forward. I looked at Alfie who smiled and gave me the thumbs up. At last we were on our way.

The train gathered momentum surprisingly quickly and very soon we had left the pale blocks of the city behind and were steaming through open countryside. From my vantage point at the door I surveyed the patched landscape of North Yorkshire as the lengthening shadows of the wagons chopped alongside the track. It was late autumn; the trees were stripped and in the charred meadows clouds of gulls trailed lonely teams of oxen as they strove to turn the soil before the first frosts of winter. In the distance the sloping chalk horse of Kilburn stole into view, its usual white profile turned salmon pink as the evening light fell on Sutton ridge. It would be dark by the time we reached Durham. I only hoped that whoever had been sent to meet us would still be there when we arrived.

A tap on my shoulder brought me back to the present and I turned to meet the friendly eye of a lean young corporal with cropped hair and glasses who had a kitbag on his shoulders that was so disproportionately large for his frame that it gave him the appearance of a human snail.

'Edmund isn't it? The name's Alix Liddle from Darlington. I just wanted to say how sorry we all were to hear about your father. I did some riding out at Catterick before the war and always followed your father's horses, especially the two-year-old *Stornoway*. Please accept my profound condolences.'

The man had been a jockey all right. His grip was like iron.

"Ah *Stornoway*' I sighed. 'Now there's a name to brighten any miserable day. That horse is, or rather he was the apple of my father's eye. When he won the *Gimcrack* last August it was the most wonderful day ever. The war seemed such a long way off then.'

'I remember it well' replied Liddle drawing on his pipe. 'I remember it well because I was there. We all backed Captain Elsey's *Nightingale* of whom there were high hopes but she didn't stay the six furlongs. It was such a different world: now there is talk of racing being suspended for the duration of the conflict. I hope it doesn't happen but if hostilities extend into 1915 there'll likely be a call on horses for the war effort. When the fighting is over, racing will need people like your father to get it back on its feet. Do you have any plans of your own in that direction?'

'Dad's accident is such a shock that I still haven't taken it in. As for plans, well we don't have any yet; my mother died when I was little and apart from some distant relatives in Ireland, who I hardly know, there is only Alfie and me left.'

Liddle struck a match and catching a ripple of discomfort across his face I berated myself for sounding so full of self-pity.

'Oh, I apologise Alix, it must appear as if I'm fishing for sympathy, but really I'm not. It's just the shock and uncertainty over the future.'

The train rattled through Northallerton. Alix drew on his pipe and I followed the smoke from his nostrils as it was snatched up by the draught and pulled out the door. Presently he spoke.

'Life can be such a sod. I'm so very sorry'

'The thing that gets me most is I know so little. The telegram to college simply notified us of father's death and gave no other information – no details whatsoever which is why I'm desperate to get back to the estate and find out what happened.'

Liddle's eyes narrowed and he pulled out his pipe.

'Have you not seen today's papers? The accident is in the press; at least there were a couple of lines in *The Yorkshire Chronicle*. I assumed you'd seen it.'

I pulled out the newspaper I'd bought at the station and shook my head up and down the pages. Nothing.

'Try the sports section'.

I jumped to the back cover and there it was, a small paragraph tucked away below the racing results.

Horse trainer perishes in freak accident

James 'Jimmy' Bullick the well-known Durham
trainer has died following an accident on the moors
while riding with the Derwent of Braes Hunt. It is
reported that Mr Bullick, 47, was killed after his horse
took fright in a thunderstorm and he was thrown.
Mr Bullick, originally from County Cork Ireland,
has been one of the leading trainers on the northern

circuit, his notable horses including Dinsdale Boy,
Three Swans and the unbeaten 2-y-o Stornoway
winner of the 1913 York Gimcrack Stakes. Mr. Lewis
Priestman, Master of the Hunt, said it was a freak
accident and they had never known a death caused in
this manner. Unconfirmed reports suggest that at the
time of the accident the trainer was accompanied by
leading owner Lord William Cavendish who has been
injured although the extent of these are unknown
and at going to press no one from the estate has been
available to comment.

I read the passage several times before instinctively looking back at Alix who was chewing away on his pipe watching for my reaction.

'This doesn't make sense. My father never went hunting.' 'According to the Master of the Braes it seems he did' replied Liddle as he cupped his hands and relit the bowl. I looked around for my brother who was talking to a few NCO's on the other side of the carriage. As if he sensed something was up Alfie turned and meeting my eye excused himself and crossed over to join us.

'Alfie, this is Corporal Alix Liddle who used to do some riding out in Civvy Street. Alix was on the Knavesmire last August when *Stornoway* won the Gimcrack.'

The two of them shook hands.

'So you were there at York to see *Stornoway*? You have to admit there was only one horse in it; he won so easily don't you think?' Alix nodded. 'He certainly did. It was an awesome performance'.

'Alfie, Corporal Liddle has uncovered some information about father's accident.'

My brother tilted his head quizzically.

'What information?'

I quartered the newspaper to the racing section and passed it over. My brother read the passage several times then looked at me blankly.

'I don't understand – it says here Dad was killed while out with the *Braes* but he never went hunting. As for being thrown from his mount in a storm he was always meticulous about the weather and would never saddle up if there was a risk of thunder. This cannot be right'

'My thoughts exactly' I replied. 'And out on the moors? What on earth were they doing up there? Father would never go out on the moors in the rain. There must be more to it.'

'Here's my take' said Alix blowing out a match. 'When you consider the unusual nature of what happened this is a very small paragraph which suggests it was cobbled together quickly to meet the print deadline. No doubt a more detailed account will make the papers later in the week'.

I kicked the wall in frustration.

'You're probably right but that's sod-all comfort to Alfie and me. It's tomorrow's news today that we want.'

A thunderstorm raged over the industrial landscape of Durham as we spent the remainder of the journey discussing the conflict. It appeared the *18th Pals* were bound for more training in Otterburn although some of them were being held back for coastal defence in case the Kaiser decided to invade across the North Sea. I was so wrapped up in our conversation that I hadn't noticed the miles slipping by and it was only when the train began to slow that I realised we must be approaching our destination. I strained my eyes into the deluge. Sure enough, beneath the railway viaduct the jagged contours of Durham city ghosted into view, the old stones a tangle of shadow in the smog and the rain while up on the hill the castle and cathedral silently looked down. Vaughan slapped a meaty paw on my shoulder.

'Well my friends, this is where you get off. I don't suppose we'll meet again during the war so God be with you and please pass my regards to Spangle and anyone else at college who remembers me.'

'I'll second that' said Alix pumping my hand 'and when you get to Craven remember to tell the stable lads we ran into each other and that I shall look forward to us all meeting again on the Knavesmire very soon.'

'You can count on it. Thank you both for your wishes and most of all, thank you for the lift home.'

CHAPTER FIVE

The tall, unmistakable figure of Barnaby waited silently on the footbridge. Alfie jumped down from the carriage and raced up the steps.

'Mr Barnaby, are we pleased to see you? York station was totally gridlocked and we only made it out because Edmund scrounged a lift from a mate of his on that troop train.'

Barnaby surveyed the engine as it slowly pulled away.

'I knew it would only be a matter of time although your resourcefulness is to be congratulated. Edmund, how are you?'

I took his outstretched hand and peered into that familiar, wrinkled face. Barnaby was soaked; the downpour had trodden his curly, black hair and darkened the shoulders of his long, felt coat. I traced his features for a window into what lay ahead. It was the eyes that gave him away. They were so sad I could only guess what hostages he was keeping behind them.

'I'm well. Thank you for waiting. Did you send the horses back?'

'No, the carriage is at Craven. I travelled here in Lord William's new automobile. It only arrived last week but it's the most wonderful machine. Jordan has it parked up round the corner and he's waiting so come on, let's not stand about in this awful weather.'

We rushed across the footbridge and out to the front where among an assortment of cabs and carts stood a white Rolls Royce. Alfie stopped in his tracks.

'I don't believe it! Is that a *Silver Ghost*?'

'The very same' replied Barnaby. 'She's a beauty and believe me with everything that's happened these last few days, she's been an absolute godsend.'

We jumped into the back bouncing up and down on the seats to get settled while Jordan cranked the engine into gear and turned down Station Approach. The weather was now closing in, the rain hammering onto the canvas roof completely drowning out the purr of the engine and splashing of tyres. Barnaby twisted round to break the silence.

'Lads, I'm glad you're home.'

'What on earth happened?'

'I'm sorry *Blue*, but I'm under instructions from Lady Alanna not to discuss your father's accident as she intends to speak to you herself when we reach the castle, although what I will say is how sorry and shocked we all are at his passing. Your father was enormously liked and respected.'

'Is there nothing at all you can tell us? The paper claims father was thrown from his horse while out with the *Braes*. Dad never went hunting. What was he doing on the moors?'

'I wish I could say but the truth is I don't know, none of us do. What I can tell you is that as soon as he was discovered by the huntsmen he was carried down from the moor and taken in a horsebox to Dryburn Hospital, where he died shortly afterwards. Once the dreadful news reached Craven, Lady Alanna arranged for the body to be given over to Seaton Maley in whose custody it will be retained pending the funeral. Mr Seaton is coming to the castle tomorrow morning to discuss the arrangements. I put back the appointment until then because I knew yourself and Alfie would wish to be involved.'

'Thank you for that although the meeting is not one I shall relish. Who else was there when the accident happened? Have you spoken to any of the huntsmen yet?'

'No. I'm as much in the dark as you are although the Coroner's Office has become involved and the police are taking statements.'

'Are you telling me they don't think it was an accident?'

'Not at all; the police interest is probably routine, just as it is routine for the Coroner to be notified where there is an unexplained death. It is believed your father was unhorsed in a thunderstorm but as I say I wasn't there and I haven't been able to speak to anyone yet who was.'

'What about Lord William? What's he had to say about the accident?'

'His Lordship has not been in a position to say anything. He was carried from the moor with serious head injuries and remains at the castle where he has yet to regain consciousness. Dr Addison thinks he's fractured his skull. A specialist neurosurgeon has been sent for from Edinburgh but the signs are not good and we are all extremely worried.'

'Good grief this is dreadful. What of Julian? I assume he knows of the situation?'

'I sent a telegram to Merton College at the same time I contacted Father Mathews. Julian was apparently in London with Lord Clifford and will not have received word of events until a few hours ago. I anticipate he'll leave Oxford first thing in the morning and we can expect him at Craven tomorrow night. Lady Alanna may have received further information in our absence. We will know soon enough because as I say, I am instructed to take you to her when we get back.'

We left the cobbles of Durham behind and picked up the old Howden road. The night was as black as coal while all the time the rain lashed down pitilessly, choking the tiny brooks and drenching the livestock in their flooded fields. I focussed on the *Spirit of Ecstasy* perched at the end of the bonnet like Boudicca, defiant to the elements as the front lamps cut a path through the night. I suddenly remembered Jane and realised that with the shock of what had just been imparted by Barnaby, I had completely overlooked Julian's sister.

'And Jane? How is she coping with the situation?'

'In a word, badly. She sits hour after hour wiping her father's brow constantly talking to him in the hope that somewhere deep inside his broken body, Lord William can still hear her. Alas, these efforts and everyone else's have been in vain, there's not the slightest flicker of recognition and we must face the possibility that he may not recover at all. It's that serious.'

At the northern entrance to the estate a few blasts on the horn brought old Jefferson out of the lodge.

'Welcome back Mr Barnaby sir' he shouted through the driver's window. 'I'd given up and assumed you had decided to remain in Durham.'

'We nearly did Amos. I don't believe I've seen a worse storm in all my years at Craven. Lock up when we're through will you? There'll not be anyone else on the roads tonight'.

Amos loosened the enormous chain and slowly lugged the gates open. Jordan cranked the Rolls into gear and with a light touch of the throttle we slipped beneath the old sandstone arch and into the grounds of the estate. The castle was another mile; we had to pass through some woods first where with each twist of the lane, the *Ghost* headlights swept eerily across the face of those once familiar thickets. In the shifting shadows a line of rhododendrons stood silent guard to acknowledge our arrival. Julian and I used to play hide and seek amongst these bushes when we were children and I thought how much smaller they looked now. We emerged from the trees into open parkland where the rain lashed us with a fresh vengeance and I felt no little sympathy for all the deer that would be huddled in clumps under the sparsely dotted oaks. Every autumn the horses were turned out onto this plain for a few weeks although none were visible in the darkness. I supposed they would have been taken into the stables at the end of October, they usually were and I fought a pang of grief as it dawned upon me that my father was no longer caring for them.

At the edge of the park Barnaby fell silent as the road suddenly dropped and threaded between two large kidney shaped lakes. They had a mixed history. When we were little we spent many happy afternoons swimming and picnicking at this spot and it was on these ornamental tarns that my father taught me to fly-fish. However, six years ago Barnaby's wife had drowned here in mysterious circumstances. Lord William had engaged a top London KC to represent the family's interests and the Coroner was steered to a bathing accident, but no one believed it for a moment. We just didn't know why.

The old tower was the first part of the castle to peek over the brow as if its medieval stones had sensed our approach. There were few lights burning in welcome. The hall and library were clearly engaged but above the neatly clipped yews the upper rooms merged into the night, all, that is, except for one window high over the entrance where a solitary candle flickered behind the diamond panes. Alfie stirred as the rattle of a grid under the wheels heralded our approach. Outside the storm was nearing its zenith with the rain hammering down at near right angles thrashing the rose beds and weathering the curved blocks of the boundary walls. Jordan swung across the gravel and halted at the steps leading up to the giant oak door.

'Main house or stables sir?'

'The boys and I are going into the library. Take their bags down to the trainer's house would you and then see if you can find anyone in the kitchens to make them some dinner? Oh, and while you're down at the house can you make sure the fires are lit in their rooms and the beds have been made up. Either myself or Monmouth will bring them down later.'

Jordan nodded in salutation while high overhead, unseen gargoyles spewed out torrents of black water that crashed onto the flags around us. Barnaby twisted in his seat.

'Looks like it's time to get wet lads. One, two....'

CHAPTER SIX

The heavy nailed door swung open on the unflappable figure of Monmouth who waited until everyone was stamping around in the foyer before bolting the storm behind us.

'Good evening gentlemen, her ladyship is waiting in the library. If you would care to hang your coats and follow me?'

We shook off the rain and followed Monmouth across the chequered tiles of the Great Hall, our footsteps ringing around the hunting trophies and suits of armour while high on the whitewashed walls the previous occupants of the castle exchanged their knowing glances. In the library we were met by a wave of heat and I instinctively looked to the hearth where three leather armchairs formed a semi-circle around an enormous log fire. A large Irish wolfhound stretched out on the carpet briefly raised its head while the occupant of the closest chair, Lady Alanna herself, now rose and crossed the room to greet us.

'You're here boys, thank goodness for that. I won't ask if you had a good journey because the foul weather speaks for itself and I can only imagine what you must have gone through on the roads this evening. Mr Barnaby have they eaten yet? I wonder if you would be good enough to go to the kitchens and see if Mrs Pearce can fix them some supper?'

'Jordan is already taking care of it ma'am'.

'Very good, very good. I wonder if you might go down there anyway and hurry her along. You may want to grab a hot drink yourself, you look as though you could do with a rest and anyway, I'd like to speak alone with the boys. Monmouth, can you go with him? I'll ring when I need you'

'As you wish ma'am' replied the butler at which he and Barnaby left the room, their footsteps echoing through the Hall before fading away down a distant corridor.

Lady Alanna must have been about forty and although her hands and neck were creased and her fine strawberry hair was beginning to wane, she was tall and slender with high cheekbones and long pale arms that protruded regally from her velvet gown. It was said she hailed from a clan of Irish landlords where she was considered the beauty of her generation and even if shiftless whispers about her true origins had been circulating the stables for years, there was no question that in her youth she must have been an extremely attractive woman. Lord William had certainly thought so because he proposed to her at a ball in Tralee on the first evening they were introduced. Lady Alanna was only eighteen and her Catholic family were utterly opposed to the match but she went ahead anyway and it was said they married in secret before she followed Lord William back across the Irish Sea. The absence of a society wedding and the faint whiff of scandal was fertile ground for gossip, and almost from the day Alanna arrived at Craven, rumours about the couple caught fire in the county drawing rooms.

Some said there had been no marriage at all and that Alanna had appeared unaccompanied and penniless on a Liverpool steamer, disowned by her family and disgraced by the obvious conception of Julian. Others claimed stories about her blue blood were a myth and that she had been taken in from a family of itinerant horse dealers. One Irish apprentice holding court in the *Black Horse* swore blind that Alanna had been given her looks by the devil himself, and that when she refused Lord William, he had resorted to the occult to win her over. This was too much for Barnaby and my father who were in the pub at the time, but while the jockey was promptly sent packing, the tale he left behind duly sprouted wings only adding to the conjecture.

In the end I heard so many conflicting accounts about the lady of the house that it was impossible to know what to believe. The subject had cropped up but once in conversation with my father and I always remembered his reaction because it was one of the few occasions he was ever short with me. I was about fourteen at the time and had asked him if it was true that Lady Alanna was descended from Irish gypsies to which my father responded that I was playing with fire involving myself in scandalous tittle tattle, and would do well to remember that our family depended upon Lord William for our livelihood. It was a severe dressing down but I had deserved it and from that day on, while I could not steer completely away from the gossip, I brought no more of it to his ears. We *did* rely upon Lord William for our livelihood quite apart from which the lady of the house had always treated our family with kindness and respect, and for this alone she deserved our loyalty. It was also true that irrespective of the intrigue that surrounded her, Lady Alanna was palpably well educated with the kind of elegance and style that made her a most worthy mistress of Craven. She and Lord William were an illustrious couple and in their early years very much favoured by society where no fashionable ball or house party was complete without them. Even when the seasons passed and her beauty began to fade, Alanna was never short of admirers, the irony being that many of these were the husbands of the gossipmongers whose brittle industry had only enhanced her allure.

As I grew older I, too, had observed her from a distance and in the dreamy meadows of youth would sometimes imagine what it must be like to be master of the castle with Lady Alanna at my side. It wouldn't have bothered me that she hailed from a family of drifters, any more than in my salad way I could see no obstacle in the seasons that lay between us, believing that the love of this woman could have held any man forever. In the real world though my father was right. Whatever people said or thought of Lady Alanna behind closed doors, only a fool would talk about her in public because Lord William had sharp eyes and ears and he was ruthless when it came to protecting the reputation of his family. Not that his wife's Achilles heel lay in the circumstances of her birth, although society was not to know it. Lady Alanna's weakness was that she drank to excess, particularly when Lord William was absent from the estate. Neither had she succumbed to intemperance overnight, the illness having a long gestation with the seeds of youthful excess not flowering until lonely middle age.

Boarding at Ampleforth I was oblivious to the condition creeping up on her but by the time Julian left for Oxford, alcoholism had taken a hold and the servants were already becoming adept at covering it up. Lord William, having failed to recognise the early signs, now sought to manage the problem by restricting his wife's access to funds and keeping all liquor in the castle under lock and key, but Lady Alanna was nothing if not resourceful and employing all the deceit that serves the condition invariably found a way round the embargo. When I first learned she was an alcoholic I used to study her closely for some tell-tale sign of distress, but Lady Alanna's demeanour gave very little away, and as she seldom left Craven these days it was unlikely that anyone beyond her immediate society was aware of the addiction. However an addiction there certainly was and the unpredictability of her routine together with inexplicable confinements only underlined the helplessness and misery of it. And now, as I stood in Lord William's library and measured those fine features that had once so captivated me, I saw only grief and wondered if she had been drinking on this particular evening. She could scarce be faulted if it were so.

I was brought back to reality by Dr Addison climbing from the farthest armchair to acknowledge us with all the bonhomie of a Shetland undertaker. A tall, thin man about sixty, Addison was regarded as the foremost practitioner in Durham but the grim expression told me all I needed to know about the condition of the patient upstairs. Lady Alanna seemed to pick up on this too and after a brief exchange about Lord William's treatment, Addison was despatched to check on his well-being leaving the three of us standing alone by the fireplace. Lady Alanna waited until Addison was out of earshot then addressed us in that beautiful soft Irish voice.

'Please boys, come and sit down and let us talk for a while. We have a hectic few days ahead and there are some things I have to say to you.'

Alfie and I exchanged a nervous glance but did as we were asked and settled in the two empty chairs as the mistress of the house stood for a while longer holding the palms of her hands to the fire. I had never been alone or virtually alone with Lady Alanna before, our only previous conversations being very matter-of-fact and always in passing, and yet here we were, just Alfie, me and the mistress of the house among the flickering shadows of Lord William's library. The scene about to play out before me would have been unthinkable when I was home a few weeks ago yet as Lady Alanna threw another log on the flames and sat down in her chair, her vulnerability was real enough.

'The first thing I want to say to you both is how dreadfully sorry I am about what has happened to your father. He was not only a most trustworthy servant to the estate but also a much valued friend of Lord William and myself and I offer my sincerest condolences. I realise the news about his accident will have come as the most frightful shock, and I am so sorry it had to be communicated by telegram, but information travels so quickly these days and I did not want you finding out from any other source.'

Alfie and I listened in silence as Lady Alanna drew her hands from the sides of the chair so they were resting on her lap and then looking first to the door and then straight at us continued in a low whisper.

'The second thing I want you to know is that whatever changes follow in the yard as a result of your father's death, there will always, always be a place for you both here at

Craven. It may not be in the stables because I cannot say at the moment what we are going to do with the horses, but if it is not in the stables we will find you somewhere else on the estate. However all that is in the future, for the time being it is my wish that we carry on as before and that you continue to live in your father's house.'

Although I hadn't expected to be turned out I thanked Lady Alanna just the same. Alfie also piped up appreciatively. With so much else in the air it was one burden off my mind.

'Please, there's no need to thank me, it is in my gift and the least I can do. What becomes of the horses is going to depend upon his lordship when he recovers, or in the event that he does not…in the event that he fails to recover at all…' at this point Lady Alanna drew her hands to her face and began sobbing uncontrollably. It was a most awkward moment and for a while Alfie and I sat looking helplessly at each other not knowing what to do. The wolfhound sensing her distress pricked its ears and began to whimper and it crossed my mind to reach out and console her until I remembered this was the mistress of the house in her husband's library and abruptly dismissed the idea. Instead, I motioned to Alfie that we should leave but just as we stood up and made our excuses, Lady Alanna regained sufficient composure to carry on albeit her words came and went in small tracks.

'No, please, don't go, I am fine, or I shall be in a minute. I just ask that you bear with me for I do not know when I will get the opportunity to speak with you again on these matters.'

I exchanged another uneasy look with Alfie but we duly sat, apprehensively, while Lady Alanna retrieved a small lace handkerchief from her cuff and began to wipe her eyes. It was a most embarrassing interlude for us all but particularly for her and I cursed my inability to find something to say that would ease the tension but what *could* I say? Nothing. Words were inappropriate and all Alfie and I could do was sit it out until Lady Alanna felt able to continue which after an interval that seemed much longer than it probably was, she finally did.

'I'm so sorry you bear witness to my grief boys. It shames me to break down before you but there are some things I have to say before we are overtaken by events. The decision whether we keep the horses and appoint a new trainer or dispose of the string altogether will be made by my husband once he recovers. You will know Lord William has been seriously injured and we have sent for a specialist neurosurgeon from Edinburgh, but until I am advised differently I must work on the basis he is going to pull through. In the event that my husband is permanently incapacitated or dies, and I appreciate I must face that possibility, then the future of the training establishment will be decided by Julian. Nevertheless, I am acutely aware that Craven has always been your home and as long as it is mine, I give you my word now that whatever happens there will always be a place here for you.'

We sat through another silence while Lady Alanna blew her nose. Her grief was distressing and when a spark suddenly jumped out of the fire, Alfie and I followed it across the hearth thankful that we did not have to meet her gaze. I stared into the flames and wondered if the promise she had just made was beyond her power? I had to know.

'I must ask you something ma'am and it is this: do you consider it likely that Julian will agree to Alfie and me remaining in the stable house?'

At first Lady Alanna said nothing as if thinking the question through in her mind before making a response. At length she brushed down the arms of her chair then looked straight at me, her long curls and soft skin glowing in the firelight.

'Julian has views on many matters and they do not always accord with my own. I know from talk in the village that the two of you do not see eye to eye, but whatever his sentiments on this particular issue, my son will bow to the will of his parents and there will be an end to it.'

'You are not misinformed. Julian and I quarrelled in the summer, it was over nothing really, but we haven't spoken since and I don't know how he will to react in the current crisis. When do you expect his return?'

Lady Alanna leaned forward and stretched her hands out towards the fire. She was still an attractive woman but I suddenly noticed how thin she had become.

'I received a telegram this afternoon from the principal of Merton College and so long as the weather holds, Julian will arrive on the Pullman tomorrow evening. However you should not fret at his homecoming. My son might be impulsive but he will not wish to see you displaced.'

'I am relieved to hear it; after all we grew up together on the estate and were friends for many years.'

That much of course was true. We *had* been close once although Julian's dark promises were real enough when he made them, and I found myself hoping rather than believing his mother was right.

Lady Alanna stopped crying and slipping her handkerchief into her sleeve reached for the cut glass tumbler on a small hexagon table to the side of her chair. In the firelight the contents looked like rosewater, but whatever was in there it appeared to fortify her and I took my chance.

'I have to ask you Lady Alanna, do you know anything at all about our father's accident? The newspapers claim he was hunting with the *Braes* but father disliked the sport and I am at a loss to understand what was he doing up on the moors with them?'

Lady Alanna held her glass up to the light before taking another sip and replacing it back on the table.

'You ask me what he was doing on the moors? I honestly cannot say. That your father had little time for hunting was common knowledge but the *Braes* were on the fells that afternoon and it appears that for whatever reason, he decided to go up there. I only spoke briefly to the huntsmen when they carried Lord William in and as you will appreciate, our conversation did not extend beyond my husband's immediate condition.'

'I apologise ma'am, it was an insensitive question but you will know that I am most anxious to find out how our father died.'

Lady Alanna leaned forward, gathered the poker and stabbed at the flames.

'I do understand Edmund, believe me I do and if I was sitting in your place I would ask the same. Alas, I can tell you very little other than I don't believe your father was riding with the hunt because he saddled up some time after Lord William and the others left, and I can only assume their meeting was either a coincidence or because your father went to look for them. I don't doubt he will have had his reasons for being on the moor and knowing your father, I expect they were sound, but more than that I cannot say. The

Coroner has instructed the police to look into the accident so I expect they will get to the bottom of it soon enough.'

With that Lady Alanna rose out of her chair and pressed a small button on the wall by the side of the hearth. At the same time the wolfhound which had been stretched out at her feet sprang up and waited expectantly beside her.

'Now it's been a long day and I expect you are both very tired. I am certainly near the end of my tether; these last few hours have been utterly exhausting and I must beg to be excused. Mr Seaton is attending the castle at ten tomorrow morning to discuss your father's funeral arrangements so I recommend you both go and have something to eat and then get a good night's sleep, and we shall meet in the library then.'

I turned to the sound of footsteps entering the room.

'Ah, Monmouth?' said her Ladyship 'what news from the kitchens?'

'Mrs Pearce has made up some dinner and taken it down to the house as you ordered ma'am.'

'In that case gentlemen I will take my leave and bid you good evening. Monmouth, please be good enough to see the boys down to the house and then lock up the castle on your return. I will not be requiring you again this evening'

'Very good ma'am."

'Thank you. Gentlemen, again I bid you good evening' and with that Lady Alanna picked up her glass and clacked her tongue at the wolfhound which followed her dutifully into the hall and up the magnificent Jacobean staircase.

My father's house lay next to the stables about two hundred yards to the rear of the castle. It was a modest building of sandstone block constructed in the early 1800's by Lord William's grandfather to house the then resident trainer, a purpose it had served ever since. My family were its most recent tenants; my father moving in some twenty-five years previously after Lord William brought him back from Ireland to look after the horses. Three seasons later he was joined by my mother, Derina, a young vetinerary assistant he'd met in the steward's room at York races. It seems one of Lord William's horses had interfered with the runner up and Derina who was on duty that day gave testimony to the stewards that led to its disqualification. My father was absolutely livid but love must have blossomed because by the *Gimcrack* the following year they were married and settled on the estate. Alfie and I had been born at this place but our mother had died in childbirth here and as we raced home in the pouring rain, I knew only too well how those walls must have held bitter-sweet memories for him.

Monmouth turned the key and we entered the hall to the familiar smell of saddlery and an enthusiastic welcome from Domino, my father's old black lab. The dog was actually mine; he had been given to me as a Christmas present many years before although Dad looked after him when I was away at College. Domino hobbled around whimpering softly, tail thrashing. That's the great thing about owning a dog. They never forget and are always pleased to see you.

'Now then old fella, how are you doing? Get down now, down, there there, good boy.'

Domino fell obediently to heel as I made my way through the hall where the scattered boots, general clutter and pegs groaning with coats testified to the lack of order in my father's house. In the kitchen Monmouth had laid two places on the table together with some cold meats and a loaf of bread, while a bright copper pan simmered away on top of the stove. Monmouth ladled out the soup then announced he would leave us. I saw him to the porch then slid the bolts on the storm. On the way back to the kitchen I poked my head into the sitting room where the crackling fire and my father's print in the cushion of his favourite chair tricked me into thinking he was somewhere in the house, and for a moment I half expected to hear him call down the stairs. This spooked me and pulling myself together, I quickly joined Alfie in the kitchen where we started on our supper, glad to be home but unsettled by the circumstances that had brought us here together with the unspoken presence of our father. Alfie cut a slice of bread and dipped it in his soup.

'Lady Alanna promised she would look after us but in truth, how long do you suppose we can remain here?'

'I wish I knew. I would like to think as long as we want but the horses need looking after and the house has always gone with the job. There are enough lads to keep the yard ticking over but I expect the family will engage another trainer and you and I will be relocated somewhere else. I would it was different but we are in their hands because we don't have anywhere else to go.'

'Well if father was alive, I'm certain he would want us to stay here. Is there no way you can ask Lord William if you can take over the string?'

'It's a grand idea but I can't Alfie. I'm in the middle of my studies and anyhow, I don't have enough experience. In a few years maybe but it's out of the question at the moment. Look, it's been a long day, let's go to bed and get a good night's sleep like Lady Alanna suggested. It might seem like the end of the world right now but take heart, things can only improve and whatever lies in store we'll face it together. Okay?'

Alfie put down his spoon and looked at me

'If only Dad was here, he'd know what to do. I can't believe he's gone and never coming back.'

I walked round the table and held out my arms. Alfie stood up and gave me an enormous hug at which we both burst into tears.

'I'll take care of you, I promise it.'

It was after midnight when we grabbed a candle each and went upstairs. The door to my father's bedroom was closed and for a moment I thought to look in but instead, Alfie and I parted on the landing and I went into my own room and lay on the bed staring at the ceiling. Outside the rain still pattered on the windows but the rolls of thunder were becoming fewer and more distant. I thought about what Lady Alanna had said in the library and hoped she was right about Julian not wishing to see us displaced. In retrospect I thought she had spoken surprisingly freely about his being headstrong. It was true enough of course – Julian was worse than that – but for his mother to acknowledge any weakness in his character was something of a revelation. As I mused on this I suddenly felt very tired and without changing into my pyjamas I rolled over and snuffed out the candle.

CHAPTER SEVEN

I hadn't been asleep very long when I was woken by Domino howling at the foot of the stairs. It was still pitch black and at first I didn't know where I was until collecting my wits, I felt my way onto the landing where I met Alfie coming out of his room with an oil lamp. There were shouts in the yard and someone was hammering on the door. I told Alfie to stay where he was and grabbing a poker from my room, raced down into the hall and called through the letterbox.

'Who's there?'

'Master Edmund, Master Edmund you must come at once, you are needed at the castle'

'Who is this?'

'It's me, Monmouth. I've been sent by Mr Barnaby. Quickly, you must hurry. You have to come with me at once.'

I drew back the bolts and opened the door on the butler who stood awkwardly in his dressing gown seemingly oblivious to the drenching he had sustained on the way over.

'Monmouth, what on earth is going on? What time is it?'

'You have to come with me now Master Edmund. I have instructions to bring you to the castle at once.'

'To the castle? What on earth for?'

'There's no time to explain Mr Edmund, you are to come over at once'.

There was a resolve in his voice that unnerved me.

'Wait there' I said and ran back upstairs to Alfie who was leaning over the banister trying to figure out what was going on.

'Alfie, I have to go to the castle. Heavens knows what this is about but when I leave the house, I want you to bolt the door after me and let no one, absolutely no one, pass until I return. Do you understand?'

Alfie nodded firmly. I handed him the poker then, grabbing one of my father's coats, raced after Monmouth who was already half way down the flag path that led to the servants' wing of the castle. We were met at the door by Barnaby who ushered us into the kitchen.

'What on earth is going on?' I cried.

'It's Lord William. He's regained consciousness and insists on speaking to you.'

'To me? Lord William wants to speak to *me*? Whatever for? Can't this wait until morning?'

'No it cannot' replied Barnaby abruptly. 'His Lordship is half delirious, he's making no sense at all and we are unable to calm him down. What's more, he is refusing any further treatment until you are brought to him and Doctor Addison fears if you do not go directly it may not just be Lord William's sanity at stake but his very life'.

Barnaby was leaning forward as he said this, the palms of his hands spread over the table, his eyes burning. Monmouth, usually so unflappable was prowling around the kitchen like an expectant father. My mind was racing but the panic written across the faces of them both left me in no doubt as to the gravity of the situation.

'I don't understand what this has to do with me but if you think it will help, then I'd better go. Where is he?'

Monmouth gathered a candelabrum from the sideboard and shielding the flame from the draught, led the way as we chased our shadows through the narrow corridors. The Great Hall was empty but the fire still blazed away, its light dancing on the richly polished panelling and spindles of the staircase. I was suddenly aware of raised voices coming from the next floor including that of a young woman and, realising this was Julian's sister, I forged ahead of the others and sprinted to the top. I had not previously ventured into this part of the castle and on the landing I was forced to check and gauge my surroundings. The staircase had met a long, east west passageway and there was a labyrinth of doors to either side. Ahead of me was another, shorter corridor and at the end of that another staircase. Which way? I spun to the left but could see nothing other than Lady Alanna's wolfhound which growled at me from outside one of the rooms at the bottom. Monmouth and Barnaby reached the top of the stairs.

'Quickly, Edmund. Follow me.'

I trailed them down the eastern corridor where Jane emerged from one of the rooms at the end with her head in her hands. She looked up at our approach and ran straight to me.

'Oh Edmund, thank goodness you're here. I knew you would come.'

'What on earth's the matter?'

'It's father, he's wild with fever. We don't recognise him.'

Monmouth and Barnaby went into the bedroom while I stood with Jane, her little body trembling with grief as she wept on my shoulder. We had always been close, she was the younger sister I'd never had and while her brother scoffed at our friendship, he had never been able to turn her kind heart.

'It's alright, it's alright. Really it is. Now tell me, what's happened and what can I do to help?'

We were joined on the landing by Addison who had his sleeves rolled up and was drying his hands on a rusty-stained towel. He spoke quietly so as not to be heard in the bedroom.

'Thank you for coming so promptly. I regret bringing you here but Lord William has asked to see you. It seems his injury has unhinged his mind because though half mad with pain, he refuses to be sedated and fights us with the strength of a bull whenever we try and get near him.'

Addison was short of breath. He was perspiring profusely and I could see the panic in his eyes.

'So long as he was unconscious we could at least stabilize him while we waited for Sir Marcus Beattie to come down and remove what we suspect is a blood clot under his skull. Unfortunately, about an hour ago, His Lordship suddenly regained consciousness and began lashing out wildly and screaming at everyone. It's mostly drivel but the one recurring theme appears to be an urgent desire to speak with you. We've repeatedly told him that you're not here but he won't listen and having tried everything else to calm him down, I felt we had no choice but to send for you. I'm sorry young man, it was a last resort.'

'No, that's fine doctor, I'll obviously help in any way that I can. What do you want me to do?'

Addison pulled down his sleeves and replaced his cufflinks before draining a glass of water handed to him by Monmouth.

'The first priority is to get him settled before he aggravates his injuries further. Hopefully your presence will achieve this and we can take it from there.'

'I'll do what I can. Shall I go in and see him now?'

I felt Addison's hand on my sleeve.

'A word of caution before you do; Lord William may appear lucid but he doesn't know his mind and speaks of strange and outrageous things. You should be prepared for this.'

I stepped into the dimly lit chamber hardly knowing what to expect. The first thing that struck me was the closeness of the air together with a disgusting odour of sour vomit that stopped me in my tracks, and it was all I could do not to wretch myself. On the table by the bed a solitary candle illuminated a large jug of water, a silver kidney dish and an assortment of glass medicine bottles. Over on the far side of the room a second candle lit the wall near the window and I wondered if this was the light I had noticed when we drove into the courtyard earlier that evening. I made my way forward to where the master of the house was propped up in the fold of a large four poster bed swatting away at a nurse who was trying to dab his brow. Lord William was always such an impeccably well-presented man and as I stared at the dribbling wreck before me I was taken aback, even on this night of shocks. The first thing that hit my eye was a massive jagged cut that ran down the forehead to the bridge of his nose. The wound was freshly sewn and still weeping and while the patient appeared oblivious to its existence, I grimaced to think of the scar that would be its legacy. As I moved closer I saw how under the mask of stubble, one side of the face was covered by a shocking purple and yellow bruise, the sight only exacerbated by a gory orange stain on the pillow next to his ear. I then saw how Lord William's fine silver hair had become tangled in a braid of sweat and bile. I deduced his lack of condition was indeed because the attendants had been unable to get close enough like Barnaby said. Certainly the Lord William of old would never have allowed himself to get in this state let alone admit people to his presence who could see it. Perhaps he didn't know or care anymore because he had taken leave of his senses like Addison had said. I reasoned I would find out soon enough.

Jane spoke first.

'Father, Edmund is here to see you.'

At the sound of her voice Lord William pushed the nurse away and struggled to sit upright.

'Edmund? Edmund? Where are you boy? Come into the light so I can take a closer look at you.'

I slowly approached the bed as the nurse gathered up her things and hurried out of the door.

'Hello sir, it's me, Edmund Bullick. I heard about your accident and thought I would drop by to see if you needed anything.'

It was a ludicrous remark but I had to start somewhere.

'Edmund? Is it really you my boy? Come and pull up a chair and talk with me for a while. I've waited so long for you to arrive. Everyone else out – I want you to leave now.'

'I don't think that would be wise my Lord' said Addison. 'I should remain in case…'

'Did you not hear what I said?' interrupted Lord William.

'Out now the lot of you! Jane my dear, I would like you to leave as well.'

Barnaby approached the bed.

'My lord, I can ask one of the servants to remain and tend to you if you wish?'

At this Lord William began to yell at them waving his arms about as he emphasised every word.

'Did you not hear what I said? I want you all to leave now. Get out. Get out, out of my sight. I said out! GET OUT!'

The others looked uneasily at each other but did as they were told, the men muttering to themselves while Jane gesticulated that she would be in the corridor if I needed her. When they had left, Lord William crumpled back in his bed and screwed up his eyes.

'They think I am mad Edmund, but I tell you I am not, I have never seen things so clearly.'

'Mr Barnaby said you wished to speak to me sir.'

'And so I do Edmund, and so I do. They told me you were away at college but I knew they were lying. I could sense your presence in the castle from the moment you arrived. It woke me from my dreams and I would not be denied this interview.'

Lord William sounded confused and I thought he misunderstood who he was addressing.

'It's me Edmund, Jim the trainer's son my Lord. Julian your own son is still in Oxford but will be home to see you tomorrow.'

'Julian? Julian?' he whispered. 'Julian is no son of mine. He never was and to think I raised him from nothing, nothing at all to be my successor. I gave that boy the finest education, wealth in abundance and a position in society;

I gave him my name, the revered title that comes with this estate and see how he repays his mother and me …'

At this Lord William began to gasp horribly and I instinctively leaned over and placed an arm around his shoulder and settled him back onto the pillow. His eyes were streaming and a trickle of mucous seeped from the corner of his mouth.

'My Lord, you must not exert yourself in this way. Please, let me go and fetch some help.'

'No. No I do not…' said he coughing again and seizing both of my wrists '…I do not want you to bring anyone, I do not need them, there may not be enough time. I have no interest in any of the others except Jane. Now tell me you will stay here and listen to what I have to say. Promise me. You have to promise me this.'

I looked down at the haggard face on the bed, gaunt, pale and sickly except the eyes which were burning and pleading with me.

'I promise sir' I whispered at length. 'Please don't vex yourself in this manner. I will remain if it is your wish.'

The tension in Lord William eased. I picked up a towel and dabbed the slime from his chin. The contorted face looked up appreciatively and I thought how its owner seemed to have aged twenty years since August when we had all been together in the paddock at York.

'Thank you, thank you my boy. You always had a kind heart and you are right, I am sick, yes lad, sick, but confused I am not. You speak to me of Lord Julian? That quarrelsome youth is no son of mine, he never was, he was dropped into this estate like a cuckoo at the nest and being the blinded fool that I was, I allowed him in. You look surprised? Why are you surprised? Did you never wonder that the apple had fallen so far from the tree?'

'I hadn't given it any thought my lord. Julian and I grew up together, he is my oldest friend.'

'Your attempt to cloak the truth is to your credit Edmund, but you well know what kind of man Julian is, or rather what he has become. That boy was brought up to aspire to the finest values: respect, decency, compassion and yet now on the verge of his majority I find the devil himself is my heir…' at this Lord William broke off into another bought of coughing.

'My lord, you are ill, I cannot believe you know what you are saying. You must rest for a while.'

'Oh I am ill, indeed I am ill, the truth has made me so, I see it only too clearly. Too clearly and too late. I am so drained but time is short and there are some things you must know. You must hear me out. Will you promise it lad?'

Lord William was fraught with emotion as he said this, his little grey eyes burning into me as every muscle in his body tensed up waiting on my response.

'Will you promise it lad?' he repeated.

I wondered if I should call for help but I was burning to hear more. Perhaps he would tell me something about my father's accident.

'You have my word.'

Lord William heaved a sigh and relaxing his grip on my wrists motioned to the entrance to make sure no one was listening. I crept to the door. Monmouth and Addison were dawdling in the passage and when they saw me moved as if to enter the room but I waved them away.

'How do you find him?' whispered Addison.

'Confused, as you say, but he is settled and I expect he will shortly be asleep.'

'I am thankful to hear it. I will wait in the library but I wish to be notified the moment there is any change in his condition.'

'Of course' I replied before turning to Jane.

'Where's Lady Alanna?'

'My mother is indisposed. I've not been able to rouse her since Lord William regained consciousness and I fear I shall not get a response until the morning. Why does my father wish to speak to you?'

'I honestly don't know. He's talking nonsense but has asked that I sit with him a while longer and as he appears calmer than before, I am happy to do so. I'll call if I need anything but in the meantime can you go back to your mother and see if you can wake her? Your father is very ill and your mother will want to be with him.'

Jane nodded and headed off in the direction of the wolfhound at the other end of the corridor. Barnaby sent Monmouth to make cocoa for everyone then threw his hands in the air and slumped across a chaise lounge.

'I'm going to get my head down for a while. This could be a long night. Call me if you need me. I'm not going anywhere.'

I nodded, and then closing the door behind me, pulled a stool up to the bed and took Lord William's outstretched hand. He spoke to me with the urgency of a child.

'Have they gone?' he whispered.

'They have. Everyone is about their business and we are unlikely to be disturbed.'

'Are you quite certain?'

I assured him it was so.

'Very well then lad. What I have to tell you goes back to the autumn of '91 not long before my own father died and I came into the estate. I was a young man in those days and having inherited the family passion for racing, I accepted an invitation from my father's cousin Lord Derrymore to travel to Ireland and purchase some yearlings at the sales. I found the society over there agreeable and quickly embraced the way of life; everyone was so informal and with Derrymore parading me as the future Lord Craven we were lionised wherever we went. In the end I remained in Ireland several weeks longer than I had intended until realising I was neglecting my responsibilities in Durham, I told Derrymore I had to leave. On our last evening we attended a ball in Tralee where I first set eyes on Lady Alanna. I had heard talk about her beauty and wit before but without wishing to appear conceited, that fact is many handsome women were placed in my path and I'd always had their measure. It was not so with Alanna. When I first saw her it was love at first sight and from the moment Derrymore introduced us I was totally captivated. I was twenty seven at the time, she was but eighteen.'

Now this much even I knew, because for all the uncertainty circulating about Lady Alanna, the setting of her introduction to Lord William was not one of them.

'We danced together for the rest of the evening and I found I came alive in her company while she for her own part teased and played me with a skill that was astonishing for one so young, not that I could see it at the time. By the end of the night I was utterly enchanted and when we parted I asked her if she would marry me. I expect this will seem bewildering to you in view of the length of time I had known her but Alanna appeared to be everything a young woman should be, and from the first touch of her hand I was so consumed with desire that nothing else mattered other than I should make her mine. Edmund, my throat is burning. Will you pass me some water?'

I reached for the jug and poured a glass. Lord William sat forward and took a sip then continued.

'She would not have me. She said she would give her answer on the 'morrow then sent a note to say that she was betrothed to another. As you can imagine I was devastated. I went immediately to her father's estate but I was informed she would not see me and eventually I had no choice but to return to England alone and disconsolate. I wrote to her repeatedly from Durham telling her I would never give up and beseeching her to allow me at least to have hope, but she ignored all of my letters. In the end, the more she rejected and rebuffed me, the more I wanted her until I was driven half mad. Have you ever felt this way about a woman Edmund?'

I confessed I had not. My understanding of the power of unrequited love was limited to what I had glimpsed between the lines of Shakespeare's sonnets, and with the interpretation coming from middle-aged monks, the impact was more than diluted.

'Not yet hey lad? Well one day Edmund it will happen to you, and when it does you will not know what has hit you and you will recall this conversation. Can you pass the water again please?'

Lord William took several large gulps then banged the glass on the bedside cabinet cracking it. I looked to the door and wondered if they heard the noise outside. I half expected someone to come and investigate but nobody did. I turned back to the patient. He had been perspiring heavily as he spoke and his nightshirt was drenched. I reached for the towel and wiped his brow.

'You say she would not have you but you must have won her over in the end.'

'I did, but I blench at the means I used. I was so obsessed with the girl to the extent that nothing else, nothing at all mattered and I was prepared to do anything to have her. My opportunity arrived most unexpectedly when I was riding out one day with the *Braes*.'

'With the *Braes*? You mean the hunt?' I repeated incredulously.

'Please, please do not interrupt. You said you would hear me out lad and I must hold you to your word. I am so weary and already feel my time ebbing away.'

I raised a hand in acknowledgment. Lord William continued.

'A few weeks after I returned to Durham I was out hunting with the *Braes*. We were drawing cover on top of Hammsterley Fell when my horse went lame and rather than hold the others up, I decided to dismount and walk him back to the road. The path led me by the ruined monastery and I remember I had to take care to keep clear of the old mine workings there. I had just stopped by the brook to water the horse when suddenly this figure climbed out of the boulders and began walking towards me. I tell you Edmund, I almost died with fright because it was starting to get dark and I remembered all the tales about the fell being haunted by monks. Foolish of me really. In the end it transpired that my companion wasn't a ghost at all but merely an old vagrant who used to drift around up there. He seemed harmless enough and when he asked if I had any liquor, I felt sorry for him and readily shared my hipflask, glad of the company to be honest. For all his misfortune this tramp turned out to be an educated man and we quickly fell into conversation in the course of which I confided in him about Alanna. Ah! I see what you are thinking. You are asking yourself how it was that I allowed myself to share such intimacies with a stranger, and yet life itself is blessed with such riches if only we recognised them when they came along. His response, surprisingly unequivocal in the circumstances, was that if I was certain she was what I wanted I should take my burden to the Galilee chapel and pray to the holy man of Jarrow. Well what do you say to that? I had never been a religious man and thought the tale was drivel – beautiful drivel mind – and told the old tramp as much. He said I was entitled to my opinion but as I had nothing to lose I should at least try.'

Lord William paused for a moment and reached for the jug.

'I never saw the old vagrant again and at first I didn't give much thought to what he had said, but as the weeks slipped by with no word from Ireland I became more and more desperate. One day, when a matter of business took me into the city I decided I would seek out the holy man of Jarrow and do you know what I did Edmund? I recalled what the old tramp had told me and I fell down on my knees and I prayed. That's what I did. I prayed. I prayed that afternoon like I had never prayed before, pleading with him to make this girl love me, to ask the Lord to change her heart so she would sail from Ireland and bring an end to my misery. Of course deep inside I didn't believe it would make the slightest bit of difference, but even as I strolled back to my horse I felt lighter. The following week a cable arrived from Derrymore to say Alanna had broken her engagement and then shortly afterwards, I received a letter from the girl herself begging me to return to Ireland. As you can imagine I required no second invitation and the following week she and I were reunited at Derrymore's at which interview I learned she was in child to a former lover, a young officer in the Irish Guards who had died in India. As you can imagine it was a shattering discovery but I was so consumed with desire that the child and disapproval of her family were nothing if she would only consent to be mine. The following Sunday we were married at St John's in Tralee with Derrymore and the church organist standing as witnesses because her kin and mine refused to attend the service. We remained in Ireland for a few weeks then returned to Craven where in the months ahead we presented the baby as our own. It was not difficult. We saw little of society in those early days and the furtive nature of the wedding together with frequent trips to the continent muddied the waters sufficiently to allay any conjecture about the child's paternity.'

Now here Lord William was wrong because the oldest rumour circulating was that Lady Alanna had come to Durham to seek him out when she discovered she was pregnant. Clearly this particular slice of gossip was misplaced but it had held a grain of truth and then suddenly everything fell into place even as Lord William fitted the last few pieces of the jigsaw.

'I expect you have already guessed that the child was Julian and that I embraced him as my own on account of the love I had for his mother. And so it was. Of course, it was our intention to have many more children but with no others arriving after Jane and with Craven rigidly entailed, Julian assumed the mantle of heir as Lady Alanna and I came to an understanding that he should succeed to the estate.'

This was such an astonishing revelation that I instinctively looked around to see if anyone else had witnessed what had just been imparted. Needless to say no one had as there were just the two of us in the room. I turned back to Lord William.

'Forgive me sir but what you are telling me is absolutely incredible. Does Julian know anything about this?'

'It was never our intention to tell him because it would have been a crushing revelation and we saw no need. However two things changed my mind. Firstly, I saw the dissolute traits Julian developed in his youth and it greatly troubled me. You will know he was given the finest possible education and that his mother and I brought him up to recognise the difference between right and wrong, yet from an early age Julian began to ascribe to values that were alien to us. I was particularly concerned at his treatment of the servants, the way he bullied and spoke to them. I pulled him up on it many times and hoped it was just a stage he was going through, but as the years passed he only became more arrogant and offensive. I hoped that Oxford would be the making of him but my fears for the future were only compounded when he fell into the company of Lord Clifford and the others. I was deeply concerned after the *Black Horse* fiasco and that dreadful incident with the stable lads but it was only when Sample told me of your own disagreement in the summer that I decided to act.'

'You knew about that? I thought the incident was closed and forgotten although I remain mortified for my part in it.'

Lord William spoke in little more than a whisper.

'There is no need to be, it was not your fault. I heard about the disdain Julian poured on your father's reputation and his threats to evict you and am surprised you managed to answer with any kind of poise. You might not know it but in addressing Julian in the terms that you did, you were speaking for most of the village.'

At this Lord William's voice cut short as he was overtaken by another ferocious bout of coughing.

'Edmund, quickly; can you pass me the bowl, under the bed lad, hurry?'

I knelt on the floor and reached for the chamber pot which was already half full and still warm. It was all I could do not to be sick myself but somehow I confined the urge and managed to position the receptacle on his lap just as Lord William leant forward spewing a mixture of blood and gastric juices. It was a terrible sight; he was so ill and distressed and the wretchedness of it all melted my heart with pity.

'Sir, you must allow me to fetch help.'

'No. No Edmund please. I do not want any help; Addison and the others would only waste what precious time is left. There is so much unsaid Edmund, please, you must permit me to finish and then by all means bring to my bedside whoever you care. Please, my boy, please you must hear me out, I beg you.'

I was at a loss what to do. I knew Addison and the others would be in like a shot if they saw how he was deteriorating yet such was the sorrow in those pale grey eyes that instead of calling for assistance, I found myself settling him back down in the crease of the pillows where I gently wiped his face and pulled the sheets forward so they covered his soiled nightshirt. For a while we sat in silence until eventually Lord William recovered his speech and continued.

'I said there were two reasons that caused me to act over the estate and so there were. The first I have already explained, the second was because I fell in love with another woman. Again you look surprised and you have every reason to be because after all I went through to secure Alanna, you might take some persuading there was capacity in my affections for anyone else, and for a time this was so. Nonetheless after a few years at Craven I found I began to tire of Alanna. I have no doubt that she loved me in the beginning as I loved her but after Jane was born, we began to drift apart and somewhere along the way I lost sight of what we had once meant to each other. To a great extent I blame myself because I allowed the business of the estate to take me away from Craven more frequently than it might have done leaving Alanna to deal with the vacuum of my absence. Craven is a beautiful home when it is ringing with voices Edmund but it can also be a cold and lonely place. Looking back, Alanna did not make friends easily and having forsaken her family in Ireland I should have realised she would become lonely but these things passed me by, and before I knew it, she had begun to drink to disguise her unhappiness. Let me tell you lad how soul destroying it is to live with an alcoholic, because having experienced it for many years with Alanna I can vouch there are few worse ailments. I would I had read the tell-tale signs at the beginning; the consumption of alcohol at dinner, an increasing lack of propriety at social gatherings together with inexplicable periods of confinement followed by startling recovery but they all passed me by. When I eventually supposed she might have a problem and could have done something about it, instead of taking action I was only too ready to accept the vehement denials which in retrospect was the biggest mistake of them all. In the end the disease gripped her like a vice and I have no one to blame but myself for the unhappiness it has brought to us both.'

I did not reply nor attempt to feign surprise at what Lord William had imparted because his wife's addiction to alcohol had been an open secret in the castle for many years.

'It was about this time another woman came into my life, or rather I should say back into my life. Unlike Lady Alanna who battered down the door to my heart this other girl crept so softly into my affections that at first I barely noticed it. You will remember me saying how, when I first went to visit Derrymore, that various attractive women were placed in my path?'

'I do' I replied 'but you said you always had their measure.'

'Indeed, and so it was. Edmund, I am not proud of the fact but before I met Alanna I was an unashamed rake and when women virtually threw themselves at me, I had no qualms in taking advantage of them. In retrospect it was an abominable manner in which to behave, using my wealth and position to entice them into bed although to be fair most of these girls were seasoned campaigners and all they were looking for was a good time and a gold necklace at the end of the affair. However there was one, a beautiful young vetinerary assistant I met at the Gorsebridge sales who was unlike the others in that she was green and showed no interest in me whatsoever until I audaciously pursued her. It was easy enough to convince her family that my attentions were honorable – although they were anything but – and to my eternal discredit I employed trickery and false promises on the road to seduction before dropping her like a stone. I knew I had broken the poor girl's heart and her reputation, not that I cared at the time because once I met Lady Alanna it was a straight forward exercise to draw a line under all my previous conquests. Nevertheless, as the years passed I found myself thinking more and more about this girl wondering what became of her and I began to regret the way I had behaved. It was her sweetness that haunted me as much as anything else, that and my wish to make amends although I knew it could never be so. Her name was Derina Colburn; she was your mother Edmund.'

I nearly fainted.

'My *mother*?'

'Your mother Edmund. I never thought we would meet again but several years later in one of those bizarre twists of fate she befriended your father at York races and the rest you know. I was shocked to see her again after all that time, it cannot have been easy for her either but we managed as best we could. I don't know if your father had knowledge of our affair, I certainly never raised it with him and unless your mother spoke of it he would not have known. Lady Alanna, though, suspected the truth from the moment Derina came onto the estate, women are very perceptive in this way, and while I dismissed the suggestion that we had been previously associated, I took great care to keep a distance between our families. It was not always easy because I loved your mother very much Edmund. I always did.'

'This is incredible' I said burning with shock. 'You loved my mother all those years?'

Lord William's voice was little more than a whisper now, and I could see every word was becoming a struggle.

'I'm not proud of the way I treated her Edmund. I loved your mother more than any other and if I could turn back the clock there are so many things I would change. Yet what was done was done and all I could do was try and put right some of the harm I had caused. When I realised the kind of person Julian had become and measured this against the inherent decency of your mother and your family, I instructed my solicitors to alter the succession. Alanna knows. She wrote to Julian last week and told him which no doubt accounted for his presence on the moor. That's right Edmund; Julian and that friend of his Clifford were up there on the moor, they confronted me during the storm. I refused to reinstate him, Edmund, and they attacked me. I ask you to try and understand, I did it for the best…'

'What? *What?* Julian was on the moor with you? Are you certain?'

He did not hear me. The tiny voice was already trailing away. I gripped his bony fingers and shook them. The glassy eyes slowly opened.

'Julian was on the *moor*? Are you certain? And my father? What happened to my father?'

Lord William tried to sit up but had not the strength and it was a while before he could say anything. When the words arrived each tortured syllable parted from his lips through bubbles of slaver.

'Your father came to warn me but was unhorsed in the storm.'

'But Julian and Lord Clifford? Are you certain it was them?'

'I am certain. They were in monks clothing but I knew their voices.'

Lord William continued in tiny whispers, his breathing heavy and intermittent between each flurry of words.

'What do you want me to do?'

'I have instructed Crake to treat with you Edmund, he knows how to act. I should have done it years ago but at least it is settled now. When you see him tell him I gave you my blessing and he…'

Lord William sank into the pillow, his eyes vacant and staring.

'Lord William? Lord William?'

Nothing. I raced into the corridor and bellowed for help. Barnaby sprang up from the settee as Monmouth tumbled down the stairs to fetch Addison. Jane rushed over to the bed and cried into her father's ear.

'Oh no, not this, not now, please speak to me'

Lord William reached for her hand.

'Jane' he whispered.

'Oh Daddy, no, please don't leave me.'

Addison cleared everyone away from the bed and placed a thermometer into Lord William's mouth.

'Quickly. Someone pass me my case, hurry man. HURRY!'

We scrambled around for his bag. Barnaby was closest and bundled it over. Addison pulled out a brass syringe and injected the contents into Lord William's neck. The patient's breathing, already light and erratic now sounded as if he was blowing through water.

Jane started to cry.

'You have to do something doctor, you must, *please*'.

'I'm trying, dammit' replied Addison as he placed both palms on Lord William's chest and pushed down violently.

'Come on man' he shouted. 'Hang on damn it, hang on.'
'Look' whispered Barnaby. 'He's changing colour.'

I looked and it was true. Lord William had turned white.

Addison ceased pumping and slowly rose to his feet shaking his head. Jane ran back to her father and wrapping herself around his neck began to wail in his ear.

'Daddy no, not this. Please don't leave me.'

Lord William did not hear her but stretching himself out, took one or two very deep breaths and then passed quietly away.

CHAPTER EIGHT

Jane invited me to stay at the castle but having left Alfie alone, I was anxious to get back which turned out to be the right decision because he was waiting up. As he unbolted the door I simply explained that sadly, Lord William had died from his injuries and that we would talk about it in the morning, although when I stuck my head round his door he was still asleep, so I dressed and went across to meet Seaton on my own.

It was a beautiful dawn. The courtyard and grounds were strewn with debris but the tempest of the previous evening was gone and as I made my way down the connecting path the air was simmering with birdsong. Mrs Pearce answered the back door in tears, she was pale and drawn and it was clear she'd had little rest. I walked through to the kitchen and sat at the table while she filled a large copper kettle and placed it on top of the stove with a hiss. Monmouth was hovering about but for once his all-encompassing gaze was vacant, and it looked as though he had been crying as well. The sound of voices in the corridor heralded the arrival of Barnaby and Dr Addison, both grim faced and still attired in the clothes of the previous evening. We exchanged a token greeting but a veil had fallen over the castle and the tea was poured in silence.

'What is there to be done?' I asked.

'A message has been sent to the cathedral for Hensley Hensen to attend and anoint Lord William's body. We are expecting him shortly although the upmost secrecy prevails around the undertaking because Lady Alanna does not wish Julian to hear of his father's death before he returns. His lordship is catching the Edinburgh Pullman and should reach Durham about eight o'clock from where Jordan will bring him straight to the castle. It's too soon to make any further arrangements and no other reports of Lord William's death will leave the estate until after Julian arrives.'

I mulled over the deceased's revelation that Julian was unofficially adopted. Could it be true? That would make Jane the rightful heir. As for being up on the moor at the time of the accident, even Julian could not be in two places at one time. Either he was in Oxford and his father had imagined his presence or Julian and Clifford had sneaked up to Durham, saddled up a couple of horses from somewhere, borne witness to the accident and then melted away. It seemed unlikely. Clifford never did anything quietly and having left such a bad taste when he was last in the area someone somewhere would have surely recognised him. Addison had warned me to be on my guard and yet Lord William had appeared quite lucid. In the end, there was so much whirling around my head that I didn't know what to believe apart from one thing: the key to it all was Crake, the solicitor. I had never heard of the fellow but I was going to seek him out. The doorbell rang. Barnaby looked at his watch.

'This will be Seaton; you're probably best discussing matters in the library. Monmouth will show him through.'

The undertaker was a short stout man about sixty who attended the castle with a teenage boy who he introduced as his grandson. Having entered a profession surrounded by constant reminders of his own mortality, I had expected someone more melancholy but Seaton was a surprisingly jocular fellow with a refreshing attitude to the job in hand.

'Ah good morning, you must be Edmund Bullick, I am honoured to meet you sir, indeed I am, notwithstanding the circumstances. My partner Mr Maley and I are fervent disciples of the turf and have always tracked the fortunes of the Craven stable. I used to ride out for his Lordship's father in my youth; indeed I would have liked to have been a professional but grew up the wrong shape. I always hoped young Nathaniel here might have more success but as you can see he's already too tall to be a jockey, isn't that right Nathaniel?'

His grandson who had been gazing up and down the walls of the library snapped to attention and began to take notes.

'I knew your father quite well' continued Seaton. 'I often ran into him at the races; excellent fellow, always found the time to stop and chat. I was so sorry to hear about his accident. Please accept my sincere condolences and those of Mr Maley and our respective families.'

Having braced myself for a difficult interview it was heartening to learn of Seaton's connection to the stable for I had not supposed horseracing would interest a funeral director.

'Why on earth not?' he replied. 'Life can be so dull sometimes, especially in this profession, and we all need a splash of excitement every now and then to cheer us up.

Some find it in science, others in the arts, I get mine at the racecourse; you cannot beat the thrill of having a wager and then waiting for the roar from the grandstand at the furlong pole, or the sight of all those beautiful ladies in their brightly coloured hats and dresses.'

He wasn't wrong but it was time to get down to business.

'If you were expecting a delegation from the family I'm afraid you will be disappointed Mr Seaton as there is only myself here to make the arrangements. Lady Alanna who summonsed you is presently indisposed while my younger brother is utterly exhausted and having a lie in. However I am ready to discuss what I believe my father would have wanted and if you are agreeable, we will determine what is to be done between us this morning.'

Seaton was surprisingly accommodating; at times his words gushed out so quickly that he tripped over them like a music hall act and while it might not have been his intention to cause mirth, his approach added a welcome lightness to the proceedings.

'An excellent idea. Like they say, life goes on or rather it doesn't, well not for the deceased it doesn't but it does for the bereaved and for we undertakers if you see what I mean? As a funeral director I always ensure I give precise attention to what the customer is asking me to do, although the relatives are not strictly speaking the customer because the deceased is the customer but then he doesn't say anything, or at least he shouldn't do unless of course he speaks from his last will and testament but this has to be at hand in the first place if you see what I mean?'

I think I understood but nodded anyhow as Seaton continued to flap his arms as his excitable little voice rose up and down the scales.

'Of course the most important thing is that whatever the instructions they must be followed to the letter and we will only ask questions if they are appropriate but without interrupting at inappropriate times. Believe me Mr Bullick, it can be a minefield keeping to these rules especially with a large number of relatives some of whom don't see eye to eye. It happens more often than it should, the frustrations and enmities of a generation coming to roost in the arrangements. On occasions these interviews have been so volatile that the families have been ready to trade blows over the slightest detail. I find it is usually the ladies who are the worst offenders. I always try and remind them of the solemnity of the occasion and invite them to take a step back and give accord to the deceased's wishes instead of their own, but it can be a thankless business, isn't that so Nathaniel?'

The boy snapped out of his notes.

'Indeed grandfather, most volatile most definitely thankless'.

'Well you will not find it so with the Bullicks' I replied.

I warmed to Seaton; he was a delightful mixture of eccentricity and down to earth humility. He talked like an old woman but his manner was most engaging and it was straightforward to do business with him. We settled upon a requiem mass at St Cuthbert's in Old Elvet the following Monday followed by internment at St Oswald's cemetery up at the top of the hill. It was not a difficult choice; my father used to worship at St Cuthbert's and often spoke of the fine view from the Oswald burial ground to the cathedral and gardens on the opposite side of the valley. Seaton would provide a hearse drawn by two black ponies to carry my father on his last journey and would see that appropriate notices went in *The Northern Echo* and *Yorkshire Post* so anyone who wished to attend the service would get to know about it. At the conclusion of our meeting it only remained to choose the hymns and readings and to source half a dozen lads from the stable to act as pall bearers. This would not be a problem as I was planning to go down there later and catch up with Fenoughty, the head lad. When we had finished I turned to Seaton and broached the one subject we had not discussed.

'I would like to see my father a final time. How might I go about this?'

The undertaker's sheen dimmed for a moment as he put his hands on his hips and slightly cocked his head.

'What is it Mr Seaton? Is there a problem?'

'I do not recommend it Mr Bullick' said he. 'Many people find the experience distressing and have told me afterwards they would they had remembered the deceased as they were in life.'

'That may be so but the police have requested a member of the family to undertake a formal identification and there is no one else. Where can I view him?'

'Your father is in the mortuary at Dryburn Hospital following a direction from the Coroner that he undergoes a post mortem. If you still feel the same tomorrow might I suggest you attend my office at noon and we will go and collect him together?'

I thanked Seaton for the offer and it was agreed; I would fix a lift into town with Jordan and meet him at the parlour. We fell into some general conversation about progress of the war, he told me his youngest son was in the BEF* and he and his wife were worried because they'd had no news. He

---

* British Expeditionary Force

then moved on to the Turkish entry on the side of the Kaiser but wary of getting caught in another loop of his ramblings, I pressed the bell for Monmouth who took Seaton and his grandson to their carriage outside the front porch. As they climbed into the cab I reached up and shook hands.

'Tomorrow at noon then Mr Seaton'

'I shall look forward to it Mr Bullick, I shall look forward to it. Well I don't mean I shall look forward to it like one tends to look forward to happy events because this is not one, but I'm sure you know what I mean Mr Bullick when I say that I shall look forward to seeing you again then.'

The fellow was as mad as a hatter.

'Of course. Good day Mr Seaton. Nathaniel.'

I watched their carriage rattle away then ambled back to the house where I found Alfie in the kitchen making breakfast. Not surprisingly he wanted to know more about Lord William's death and why I had been summoned to the castle, but I played everything down explaining they had needed a witness for a business document. Alfie appeared satisfied with this and the conversation quickly moved on to our father's funeral where after much discussion we settled on the hymns *Lord of all hopefulness* and *All things bright and beautiful*. The last choice was particularly apt because apart from caring for animals all his life my father was a keen gardener and very accomplished at growing roses. I recalled the summer evenings he spent in the walled shrubbery to the side of the house nurturing the flowers and tending the vegetable patch. Someone else would have to look after them now. The image saddened me greatly although I tried my best not to show it.

We moved on to the readings; Alfie chose the extract from St Mathew's gospel about 'many mansions' while I settled on the 'clanging bell' passage from *Corinthians*. Although I was only a boy when my mother had died, I remember my father had chosen the same reading for her funeral since when the words had always moved me.

'Alfie, I know Father Williams was happy for you to remain here until after Christmas but I think it best if you went back to school after the funeral. The next few weeks will be difficult but at least you have a routine there and your friends will be around you, to say nothing about your studies.'

Alfie looked at me unhappily over his cup.

'I thought you said we were going to stick together?'

'And so we shall, don't worry; I'll not be far behind you. It's the Oxbridge exams at the end of the month and whatever happens I won't be missing those. However I need to deal with father's affairs; I don't suppose there will be anything too complicated but I would sooner sort it out now while I'm in the mood than have to face the task in the Christmas holidays.'

'Are you sure you can manage on your own? I can catch up with my studies any time and I promise I won't get in the way.'

It was tempting because as long as Alfie remained at Craven I could keep an eye on him, however I was greatly disturbed by Lord William's revelations and having resolved to get to the heart of the matter, my instincts told me it was a road I should go down on my own.

'Look; why don't we leave it until after the funeral and then go back together on Wednesday morning? I need to speak with Father Williams and pick up a few books and it'll be good to catch up with Tom and the others while I'm there.'

'Well if you're sure you can manage on your own?'

At that moment the doorbell rang. I rose from the table still talking to Alfie over my shoulder as I started for the hall.

'Quite sure. It's only a few weeks then you'll be back home again for Christmas.'

Jane was rocking on the step in her riding clothes. We looked wretchedly at each other.

'Edmund has just told me about your father' said Alfie. 'I'm so sorry I don't know what to say. Is there anything we can do?'

'Oh Alfie, thank you but no, you and your brother have enough on your plate without shedding any tears for me. I've dropped round to see if anyone fancies a trip over to Willington because I know if I stay in the castle another minute I'll go mad. You boys up for it?'

'You can count me in' said Alfie. 'You don't mind do you *Blue*?'

'Not at all, you go ahead although I'll give it a miss as I've a few things to deal with here. When you're saddling up can you ask Fenoughty to drop into the house when he's next passing?'

''Course' said Alfie 'hang on, I'll just go and fetch my coat' at which he tore upstairs leaving Jane and me alone on the step.

'The ride out will do him a world of good. How far are you going?'

'I thought we'd cross the park to East Lodge then pick up the towpath. The rector at St Stephens is a cousin of

Monmouth's so we'll call in and see if we can scrounge a cup of tea. Edmund, why did my father insist on speaking to you last night?'

I looked into Jane's pretty freckled face, her eyebrows knitted as she waited on my response. She was as honest as the day was long, and I wish I could have told her.

'It was nothing, at least nothing I could understand. You heard Addison warn me what to expect before I went in.'

'But you sat with him for nearly an hour. You never used to lie to me so why do I get the feeling you're lying to me now? Because you are lying aren't you?'

I was rescued by my brother clattering back down the stairs.

'So be it' said Jane coldly. 'No doubt you have your reasons but this is my father we are talking about and believe me Edmund, the next time I ask you're going to tell me what he said.'

Alfie swept into the hallway. 'Tell who what who said?'

'Nothing that won't wait,' replied Jane giving me a long hard stare as she swished her crop to the side of her jodhpurs.

'Come on then, let's get going,' said Alfie eagerly, at which they gathered a saddle each from the tack room and headed off to the stables. I watched them from the door as they crossed the yard. About half way over Alfie ran on ahead at which Jane sensing my gaze on her turned around and pointed, miming the words, 'next time Edmund.'

As soon as they were gone I decided to try and get a handle on my father's affairs. He had always been a private man and the prospect of going through his possessions made me uneasy but the estate had to be tackled and with Alfie out of the way for a few hours, now seemed as good a time as any to make a start. I gathered my thoughts. I would begin with his office in the front room off the hallway. I stared at the door for a moment and hesitated. I didn't relish the idea of going in and rummaging through his things, it seemed almost as if I was going behind his back. I told myself not to be so ridiculous but the moment I touched the latch my heart jumped as I imagined my father about to swing round in his chair with that huge smile he used to give me when I was little. The image was so profound it really shook me and it was all I could do to hold myself together and step into the room. In the event my mind had been playing tricks on me. The door creaked open to a cold and soulless chamber with a cold stone floor and by the large oak desk, my father's cold and empty chair. The racing watercolours and bright rosettes still hung on the walls and the yellow eyes of the fox above the fireplace still glared into eternity but my father was not there and in that moment I understood that he was never coming back. I sank to my knees under the weight of all the memories and suddenly all the tears I had held back came at once. Oh Dad, I loved you so much and I never told you. I so wish you were here with me now.

It was a while before I felt able to put away my sorrow and make a start. It wasn't going to be easy but I would do what I could before Alfie returned. I reached into the trophy cabinet and fished for the little silver key that lived at the bottom of the Gimcrack Cup awarded to *Stornoway* the previous year. It was still there. I took it to the safe in the far corner of the office and at the first turn of the lock, its heavy door swung open to reveal a cashbox containing £23 10/4d in mixed notes and coins, a leather purse of 32 gold sovereigns, an old tattered post office savings book together with my father's last will and testament, a pile of old books and some faded photographs. Everything was in its place just as I expected. At the last count there was just over £331 in his savings account which together with his other possessions represented the sum of his estate to which Alfie and I were the sole beneficiaries. I put everything back and locked the safe then switched my attention to a pile of assorted documents scattered over the desk.

It was soon apparent that my father had been diligent and highly organised in his affairs. I discovered his systems easy to follow and was quickly able to consign the assorted race entries and Weatherby's certificates into their respective folders, setting aside the urgent correspondence and overdue invoices (including a few from Sample and the local vet) for immediate process. As I worked through the assorted ledgers I found myself agreeably distracted by the intermittent rattle of hooves on the cobbles outside, and realised that my father had arranged the furniture so he could monitor events in the yard at the same time as he dealt with the paperwork. In forty minutes I had caught up with the correspondence and reached for the journal I knew he kept in the top right hand drawer.

It was an absorbing read. Every day without fail my father had recorded information about the health and progress of the various horses, his future plans for them and any general gossip about the stable. I skipped through the pages noting the feeding schedules together with abstracts about medicines and various columns of figures I took to be weights. I peeled back the weeks, riding the highs and lows with him sometimes smiling at the comments, sometimes frowning and at one point shaking my head as he questioned the hereditary of the Ripon stewards. Neither was it lost upon me how the journal together with others that preceded it were thoroughly comprehensive manuals that would prove invaluable to my father's successor. The more I read of his methods, the more I began to understand the disciplined and dedicated approach required to flourish in the profession and wondered if the opening might not be beyond me after all? I had my university examinations in a couple of weeks but then what? Suppose I did not make it up to Cambridge? Why should I not take a post in the stable as, say, assistant trainer? I was my father's son after all and with Lady Alanna's support and the lads behind me I was sure I could make a really good fist of it. There was, of course, the small matter of Julian who had as good as made clear in the summer that when it came to appointing my father's successor, I wouldn't even make the shortlist. However for all the disappointments he would relish in bestowing upon me, I might yet prevail if Lord William had spoken the truth on his deathbed. Again, the key to it all was Crake, the Hartlepool solicitor and as soon as my brother was safely back at College, I was going to seek him out.

The entries in my father's journal ceased abruptly at the foot of the left hand page of Monday 23 November 1914, the day before he died. I leaned back in his chair surrounded by his memories and realised how comforting and indeed stirring it had been to read and learn about his work, and this in but one journal; there were another twenty or so epistles neatly arranged on the bookshelf for me to go through later. I was just about to snap the 1914 chronicle shut and place it with the others when I noticed the ribbon in the crease of the bind was slightly loose. The dislocation was so fine it was barely discernible but the date of 26 November in the top right hand corner confirmed my suspicion. It should have been the 24th which meant someone had been into the office and removed a page. I was staggered. I looked at the bind again but there was no mistake. A page was missing and the only plausible explanation was that my father had made another entry which had been removed. I looked to the fireplace and noting a curl of lilac dust on the dead embers, I would have bet a pound to a penny that these were the remnants of the missing leaf. I knelt down and inspected the residue to see if a negative image of the print had survived combustion, but at my touch the ash fragmented and the page was no more.

I returned to the desk and holding the journal up to the fading light, squinted at the surface to see if any trace of the missing 24th had imprinted below. Nothing there. I reached for the drawer where Dad kept his stamp collection and taking out a magnifying glass, held the diary up like a telescope and this time I saw it, the faintest impression of the nib had passed through to the page below which while too frail to decipher, betrayed enough in its silhouette to discount it being a cast of anything else. I stared through the curved lens until my eyes watered, the blood pounding in my ears. There was no mistake. An image of my father's last words was there, they had survived; all I needed was the time and expertise to unlock what he had written.

Suddenly there were voices in the yard and I looked out of the window to see Fenoughty barking at one of the grooms who was loitering by the horse trough smoking a cigarette. Parked on a stool next to him changing a shoe was Sample, the village smith and after the animal was led away I watched as the two fell into conversation. I had not spoken with Sample since my very public fall out with Julian in the summer, but I supposed our acquaintance was about to be renewed when Fenoughty wafted an arm towards the house and they began to make their way over. I placed a ruler in the fold to protect the imprint then carefully closing the journal, had just enough time to lock it in the safe when the bell rang. I dropped the key back into the Gimcrack Cup then went down the hall to open the door on Sample, the man mountain with his dark leather britches and dusty face towering like a Colossus over Fenoughty, the craggy old ex-jockey. For a while they swayed awkwardly on the step, Fenoughty, poker faced, with Sample switching the weight of his massive frame from one foot to the other. Fenoughty spoke first.

'Miss Jane said you needed to speak with me sir. I would have called sooner to express our condolences at what happened but my good lady figured you and your brother would prefer to be alone at the present time. If we misjudged the situation then please don't think we was being disrespectful, it's just that I'm not good with words at the best of times.'

In all the years I had known my father's head lad I don't believe I had ever heard him say so much in one go.

'Mr Fenoughty, the fact that you've taken the trouble to call round speaks volumes. Won't you come in? I'll put the kettle on'.

'That's very kind of you sir but if it's all the same to you, the string will be back shortly and I need to be there to meet 'em.'

'Of course, but tell me; how are you doing, how are things in the yard?'

'Stable is fine, the 'orses are fine and the lads are well enough too although I wish I knew for how long. Truth is Master Edmund, we're all up in the air with the accident to your father and Lord William. I overheard the lads talking about it at supper last night. Proper worried they are, worried about the future, and I can't say I blame them. Has anyone said 'owt to you about what's going to happen?'

'No, I'm afraid not' I replied truthfully. 'Julian is expected home this evening so it shouldn't be long before we discover his intentions. However, while that can wait, there is another matter that cannot. Lady Jane may have mentioned earlier.'

'She said the likes of it sir. What's the problem?'

'It's not so much a problem Fenoughty but more of a favour. My father's funeral is at St Cuthbert's on Monday and we don't have any pallbearers. I was wondering, could you muster up some of the lads?'

''Nuff said sir. Indeed, I would be honoured to be one of the bearers myself; I knew Jim Bullick better than most and don't believe he would have expected anything less of me.'

'And I too' added Sample, his booming voice chiming up for the first time.

'You're too tall 'arry' whispered Fenoughty.

'No I'm not, I can adjust my posture and we'll manage just fine.'

'You're joking aren't you?' replied Fenoughty dryly. 'How are me and the lads going to carry the boss with you tilting up one of the corners?'

There was a short silence as they looked at one another and then back at me waiting for my response.

'Well that's settled then. I'm sure I can leave you to sort the details between yourselves. '

The two of them laughed before Sample suddenly came over all serious and frowned at me.

'What about you Edmund sir? I have to be careful what I say but we're very worried what Julian will do if he ever gets the chance to succeed his father.'

It was a moot point but I batted it away.

'You don't need to concern yourself on that score. Julian can be a decent enough bloke when he wants to be.'

Sample looked around cautiously.

'I wish I could share your optimism,' he whispered 'but I believe it is misplaced. If Lord William dies Julian will succeed before his time which would be a sorry state of affairs for us all. Ever since his Lordship's accident this has been my greatest fear.'

'And mine too,' added Fenoughty shaking his head. 'I know every one of these horses inside out and I believe if we all pull together we could survive – flourish even. All we want is the chance to carry on into next season but there's a change in the wind and I dread what's coming.'

We turned at the clatter of hooves to see a line of about twenty horses file through the arch. Alfie and Jane had evidently met up with the rest of the string and were trotting their mounts in at the back. Alfie saw me and waved as he slid down from the saddle.

'Look, my brother's back so we'd best leave it. These *are* worrying times but at the moment there's not a lot we can do other than wait and see what happens. If I don't hear anything I'll meet you on Elvet Bridge Monday morning 11:45 sharp.'

Fenoughty tapped my shoulder and they headed back to the stables. In the middle of the courtyard they met my brother and the three exchanged a brief word before Alfie came and stood next to me.

'Where's Jane?'

'She's gone straight back to the castle. She said Julian was arriving this evening and she needed to get herself and Lady Alanna ready. She thinks they could be in for a long night.'

'I don't doubt it,' I replied. 'Come on then, let's go in and light the fire. You can tell me more about your trip while I bring you up to date with Dad's affairs.'

CHAPTER NINE

Seatons' premises were at the top of Allergate, the business operating from a stable and workshop that were accessed down a passage that ran to the side of one of the terraced houses. I entered the small parlour that served as a reception area and rang the bell on the counter. At first there was no response but just as I was about to shout through to the back, the door behind me swung open and Seaton himself stepped in from outside.

'Ah good morning, good morning Mr Bullick,' he said breezily 'I assume you've decided to accompany me to Dryburn after all?'

'The police have been to the castle again chasing the formal identification statement. Apparently it needs to be done today so they can release the body and I'd sooner get it over with.'

'Very good, very good. You're just in time as we'll be setting out as soon as Nathaniel brings the box wagon to the front.'

'You mean you're not going to collect my father in one of the hearses?'

The undertaker scribbled a note on his clipboard before tucking it under his arm and jamming the pencil behind his ear.

'No, not this morning. We have several pick-ups to make and we always use the wagon when there's more than one.'

I followed him to the entrance where he paused to swith the *Open* sign to *Closed*.

'Tell me Mr Seaton, are all the collections from the hospital?'

'They are indeed. The mortuary there serves as a holding room for the district and it's been a busy week even by their standards.'

'How do you mean?'

'It's the weather Mr Bullick' he replied turning the key and dropping the bunch into his suit pocket.

'The weather? What's the weather got to do with it?'

'A great deal actually. At this time of year when the nights are long, the cold starts to pick off the elderly and infirm. We had two funerals on the books even before we were contacted by Lady Alana in respect of your father. Then yesterday we received another set of instructions making four in all, hence the box wagon.'

'Who are the others?'

'I don't have the names because we've only just been notified. One is an apprentice shifter who died on Wednesday following an accident at Littleton Colliery. It seems he was crushed between two bogies, poor lad, and survived the journey to Dryburn only to perish on the operating table. Then late last evening Nathaniel was contacted by the family of a young girl who died in childbirth, and then just before you arrived we were instructed by the Coroner to look after a tramp who expired in the castle grounds. So we have four people to make ready over the next few days which is more than enough work in progress for a small business like ours. If we took the hearse it would involve several trips for which we can spare neither the time nor the horses.'

There was a jingle of harnesses as Nathaniel led the box wagon onto the road.

'Are arrangements in place for the others?'

'There are plans for them all. The funerals of the apprentice and the young girl will take place on the morning and afternoon of Thursday next week, although the tramp has no known relatives and will receive a pauper's burial.'

'A pauper's burial?'

'If someone passes away and there's no money for a burial, funds are available from the Coroner's office to provide a pauper's funeral, although this is very basic as the description infers. We supply a cheap coffin and transport to the service and churchyard but there are no frills and the deceased is buried in a communal grave with no memorial or headstone. Society regards paupers' funerals as something shameful which is why many people contribute to burial clubs so when the time comes, they have the funds for a decent send off. Pauper's funerals are such sad and lonely events, although more common than people realise. Come now. Let's be on our way.'

Dryburn Hospital was a sorry spectacle with many of the walls having subsided out of alignment with the whole blackened by railway soot. The blistered windows had not been painted in years while beneath the cracked tiles, long grey-green smears told of congealed gutters and general decline. My father told me the hospital had been built on the site of the old gallows where so many of the town's unfortunates had come to a grisly end. It was said these included a Jesuit priest who was hung, drawn and butchered there following which event the local stream expired never to flow again, thus giving rise to the name. It was a grim résumé and even before we entered the building as far as I was concerned this aspect of the day's business could not be over quickly enough.

I trailed Seaton up the fractured steps to the reception area where we were met by a short stocky man in a dusty navy coat who I took to be one of the porters. He and Seaton clearly knew one another and following a brief word, the porter went around the back and returned with a police officer who came through clasping a mug of tea.

'Morning Seaton,' said he addressing the undertaker over the rim of his drink but flicking his eyes to me. 'I take it the gentleman accompanying you is here to identify one of the deceased?'

I stepped forward and held out my hand.

'Good morning officer, my name's Edmund Bullick. We're here to collect my father who died earlier this week following an accident.'

The policeman rested his drink on the counter and looked at me oddly, as if weighing me up.

'That would be James Bullick, the racehorse trainer?'

I nodded. 'I would have come sooner but I was away at College when he died.'

The police officer leaned forward and we shook hands, his palm still warm from the mug he'd been clutching.

'The name's Tench, Sergeant Tench, first officer to the Coroner. We've been waiting days for one of the family to come forward and identify your father's remains. I'm so pleased you've decided to drop by.'

Unsure if he was being sarcastic I said nothing as Tench drained the remainder of his tea before switching his attention to the undertaker.

'Mr Seaton, if you would be good enough to wait here while I take this young man through to the back? We won't be long. If you talk nicely to Judy in the kitchens I expect she'll make you a cuppa. Mr Bullick, if you'd like to come with me please?'

I followed the policeman as he bumped through a pair of double doors into a long stone passage that served the ground floor of the infirmary. Immediately to my right were a number of treatment rooms although with enough worries of my own, I shut out the cries and quickened my step to keep up with Tench who was already bounding ahead. At the end of the corridor the policeman came to a halt and thumped on a large oak door that led off to one side.

'Tench,' he shouted.

I looked at him inquisitively as he brayed on the door.

'We're almost there but I need to get the file. Tench!'

His entreaty excited a rattle of keys and the entrance swung open on a large bespectacled nurse of middle age wearing a soiled green apron.

'Come in' she said flatly.

I followed the policeman down the steps into some kind of secure ward. A second beefy nurse joined us, and as my eyes adjusted to the light, I noticed that what little there was came from three grated windows high up in the wall. I stared down the corridor in front of us. A number of semi-secure chambers lay to either side before the passage ran into a large office at the end. It was more like a prison than a hospital. The only thing missing was the bars.

We walked through a line of patients staring out vacuously from their beds. They had been silent when we first entered but as soon as we started down the passageway a discord of tortured voices turned the atmosphere to one of menace.

'It is time. You must repent, or face eternal damnation! You must repent of your sins now!' screamed one.

'It is the soldiers, they have arrived. It can only mean death!' cried another. 'I don't want to die! I don't want to die!'

'Have you come to take me home?' came the pitiful sob of an old woman somewhere in the gloom. 'I have to go home, my mother is waiting by the fire, and she'll be worried where I am.'

In another cell a wiry youth began to twist and contort on his mattress, the springs wailing in protest as the frame of his bed jumped up and down.

'Shut your trap you vile sow,' he hissed. 'The only fire you'll ever know is when they chuck you in the oven after I've slit your fucking throat.'

I froze in my tracks.

'Good grief sergeant, who are these wretched people?'

Tench put his arm across my path to prevent me moving closer to the beds. He had to shout to make himself heard above the din.

'I'm sorry sir, I should have warned you before we came in. This is where we house the city's mental patients. We treat them in the protected environment here because they pose a threat to society and frankly, because there is nowhere else for them to go. We have to pass this way to the mortuary. It's the most secure area in the hospital which is why the files are kept in the office at the end there. Now if you don't mind sir I must ask you to remain exactly where you are while I fetch what I need from the cabinets.'

I was in a mental ward. I'd heard of such places but not in my wildest dreams had I imagined the desperate conditions in which the inmates were held captive. It was such a wretched scene, the foul air thickened with misery and the stench of decay. That the patients were unhinged was obvious, but when I listened to the pathetic entreaties of the old woman, I suggested that she at least could be as much misunderstood as ill.

'You must never let yourself be taken in by these people,' yelled Tench over his shoulder as he approached the office door, 'because you've no idea what they're really like. They might seem harmless enough at the moment, but that's because they're secured to their beds. Believe me; if the chains were undone they would fall upon you like a pack of dogs.'

'But this place is utterly dreadful' I shouted. 'Can some of them not be transferred to the asylum at Winterton?'

'I'm afraid it's impossible,' yelled the bespectacled nurse joining the conversation for the first time. 'Two of these men are killers who only escaped hanging by reason of insanity, the young man there is a cannibal and the women are lunatics who have been detained for years.'

The shouting and screaming became louder. I shook my head.

'What hope can they ever have in a place like this?'

The second nurse who had been standing next to me looked up from her clipboard.

'We do what we can for them. The patients are given drugs and subjected to moral guidance although it is more a case of managing their illnesses than anything else. Only last week some of them crammed excreta into all the locks so the soiled keys were back in our pockets before we realised what they were up to. Would you invite any of these people to come home to live with you? No, you wouldn't and nor would anyone. We are not without compassion within these walls Mr Bullick, but our first duty is to the people outside.'

Through the glass windows of the office I could see Tench rummaging among the cabinets and wished he would make haste. The screaming was approaching a level where it was impossible to hold a conversation however just as the cacophony reached its atrocious crescendo, the nurse who had been addressing me fished a tin whistle from her apron and blew the first few notes of *Twinkle, Twinkle Little Star*. The effect was extraordinary. In an instant the shrieks fell away and the unit was in silence.

'Sweety, sweety, sweety time…' she trilled to the melody.

An excited murmur rippled through the patients.

'…sweety time, sweety time,' she continued in a voice of saccharine and honey.

'Sweety time! Sweety time!' they echoed, the howls and racket nearing the previous intensity until a second toot from the whistle cut it dead.

'You must be quiet for matron,' chanted her colleague as the two of them systematically went to each patient with a small glass of medicine, one nurse to minister while the other watched over with a free hand only too ready to access the truncheon clipped to her waist. The effect on the patients was astonishing. Only a minute ago they could have been possessed by Beelzebub himself yet now they sat and waited as obedient as Spaniels.

'What on earth are you giving them?' I asked.

'It is called *Mrs Winslow's Soothing Syrup*,' replied the matron. 'Each ounce contains sixty-five milligrams of pure morphine. We try to administer it sparingly but the patients get upset when they see strangers and sometimes it is the only way we can calm them down.'

'This is terrible.'

'I'm afraid life's terrible sir,' replied Tench emerging from the office with a sheath of files. 'Terrible, terrible, terrible but that's the way it is and we have no choice but to get on with it. Your father is this way sir. Walk slowly towards me and mind you keep clear of the last few beds on your way down.'

The policeman's office was dominated by a large portrait of the king in full coronation regalia. At one end was a hefty oak desk covered in books while at the other, a large station-type wall clock marked time over a row of shelves groaning with papers and a line of battered filing cabinets. Tench reached for a thick velvet curtain behind which was a riveted iron door. I was so engrossed in the rest of the office it hadn't occurred to me there might be another way out, but there was no mistaking the notice on the cold façade:

Mortuary

Authorised persons only.

The policeman looked over his shoulder.

'Are you ready sir?'

'I think so,' I replied, but he was already turning the handle.

CHAPTER TEN

We had entered a long tunnel shaped area about eighty feet by twenty, the whole fortified by an interior wall of glazed avocado and cream bricks that met in an arch overhead, and even as my eyes adjusted to the gloom, I was struck by the coldness of the air and the unpleasant smell of what I supposed to be embalming fluid. The chamber was totally enclosed, the only natural light entering through a porthole in the middle of the ceiling, the frame of which was rotting and caked in moss and algae. I swept the walls for exits and saw one other at the far side which probably led to the yard at the back, the doors being particularly well secured with vertical bolts and a massive horizontal bar.

'This way sir.'

I followed Tench down the steps where laid out in neat order were nine granite tables, each connected to the flags by a solitary iron stalk. The unit closest to us was vacant but the remainder were all taken, the bodies concealed under green cotton sheets although the feet were visible and the measure between some of the occupants was apparent from even a cursory glance. I stared with incredulity at the line. I had never seen a dead person and shuddered at the task ahead. Tench looked up from his files.

'You all right young 'un?'

'I don't know. I've not been to a mortuary before and it's just all these, well, dead people.'

'You don't need to worry about them son,' he replied. 'I've been doing this job for over twenty years and none of them have said a word to me yet.'

I swallowed my fear.

'Which one is my father?'

'I've no idea,' he replied without looking up from his papers, 'but those who have been formerly identified have a label on the big toe. Your father will be among those that do not. Take your time. We're in no hurry.'

The feet sticking out from the three nearest tables were tagged so I made my way over to the fourth and slowly drew back the cover. It was an old man with silver hair and skin as white as marble. His eyes were closed and several days' beard grew against a number of cuts and abrasions scattered across the whiteness. There was a rupture running down the side of the head and into the ear.

The silhouette on the adjacent table was that of a child so I passed it by and drew back the cover of the next under which lay the body of a striking young woman who looked as if she was asleep. I gazed down at her china face and blue lips. Is this what people look like when they die? She seemed so peaceful I expected her to suddenly open her eyes and ask me what time it was, but then I inadvertently brushed her arm. It felt like ice.

There were two more benches. The first was occupied by a young miner who had such atrocious injuries that I supposed he must be the casualty from Littleton Colliery Seaton had mentioned earlier. As I took a closer look I noticed the scalp was partially detached from the head like the lid of a boiled egg and a dark jelly-like substance had gathered on the surface below. It was an appalling sight made all the more distressing because the poor lad couldn't have been much older than Alfie. I promptly replaced the sheet and turned to the final mound behind me, although any expectation that I was about to discover my father immediately dissolved when I pulled back the sheet on a heavily whiskered tramp with chains of matted hair that spilled over the back of the table. He couldn't have been in the morgue for long as the body was covered in tiny maggots and wreaked of unspeakable fluids that had seeped through his clothes. It was a pitiful sight, the head lying with the mouth open exposing two yellow teeth, like you sometimes see on a dead rodent. I imagined I half recognised the fellow from the stairwells in Castle Street, although there was probably little to distinguish him from the tramps of a dozen city markets. Poor man. His boots were falling apart with the flap of one so badly detached that you could see the crusted toes beneath. He had probably died of exposure all alone in the churchyard. He could have been there for days before he was discovered and someone told the police. I wondered if he had a name and whether anyone would claim him as he must have been some mother's son? I replaced the sheet and turned to Tench who was still scribbling by the door.

'He's not here'.

'Are you sure you've checked them all?'

'I'm sure. He's not here.'

Tench sighed wearily and put down his clipboard. 'You must have passed him over. You have to remember that at the moment of death the muscles in the face relax and rigor mortis often causes people to look different. Here, I'll go through them with you. Who've we got?'

'I didn't check the benches that are ticketed but as for the rest we have an old man, a young woman, a child, a miner's lad and a tramp. There are no more tables and unless there is another room somewhere my father isn't here.'

Tench heaved another sigh and crossed over to the first untagged body. I did not relish starting all over again and it probably told in my voice.

'I've already checked that bench officer; it's the remains of an old man'.

Tench ignored me and pulled back the sheet exposing the body to the cold air.

'Can I ask you to look again sir, but more carefully. Take your time.'

I measured the old gentleman with his silver hair and marble skin. There was not the faintest trace. It wasn't him. I turned to Tench and shook my head.

'Look again. Look *closely* sir. Can you see any birthmarks, any at all or any other distinguishing features?'

I twisted back to the body. My father had a semi-circular scar above his right eyebrow where he had been kicked by a horse. I stared at his forehead. There was nothing. I was about to report this to the sergeant but hang on, what's that? I leaned right down to make sure. Oh my God, the scar was there. It was there. My heart pounded wildly. I began searching for other familiar marks, many of which I remembered and some that I had not. They were all there. The tiny mole under the chin, the fine eyebrows, the small hairs growing out of the side of his ear. All there. I looked back at Tench who was scribbling away with the indifference of a reporter taking notes at a council meeting. It was all in a day's work for him but I needed to be certain. When my father was at school he had been struck in the face by a cricket ball which permanently damaged the left iris making it appear as though he had different coloured pupils. I reached down and settled my thumbs over the lids but even before I looked into those eyes for the last time I knew the answer and was asking for his forgiveness.

'It's my father.'

'Are you quite certain?'

'Yes. I'm certain. It's my father.'

There was a short pause broken by Tench turning a sheet of paper over his clipboard.

'Very well. In that case can I ask you to complete the blanks and sign this statement so the body can be released for disposal?'

I gazed at my father's broken remains.

'Mr Bullick? Did you hear me?'

'I'm sorry officer. What did you say?'

He passed his clipboard.

'Here young man, complete the blanks then sign at the bottom.'

I read through the statement. Tench must have been drawing it up as I moved from bench to bench as there were only a few breaks for me to complete.

I am Edmund James Bullick. I am 19 years of age and I live with my father James Michael Bullick and my younger brother Alfred Michael Bullick at The Stable Lodge at Craven Park County Durham.

*On Friday 18 November 1914 I attended the
mortuary at Dryburn Hospital with Sergeant Tench of
the Durham Coroner's Office where I was shown the
body of my father James Michael Bullick aged 48. I
can positively say it was my father because I was able
to recognise him from his features including the scars
and marks on his face and the distinctive colouring of
his eyes.*

*I last saw my father alive on Sunday 13 September
1914 when he accompanied my brother Alfie and me
to Durham Station to catch a train back to college.
My father had always enjoyed good health and he
appeared quite well when I had last seen him.*

Signed............................

Dated Friday 14 November 1914

I scribbled my name at the bottom and returned the
clipboard.

'Thank you young man, I'll take this through to the office
and fetch the interim death certificate so you can be on your
way. I shan't be long. If you like I can call for a mortuary
attendant to sit with you while you say your farewells, or if
you prefer you can wait in reception.'

I looked at my father. His face, once weathered by the
seasons, was like marble and as those familiar features drifted
in and out of focus I thought my mind was playing tricks on
me. His hair had never been white. It was not the same man
lying on the slab and yet there could be no doubt. Is this
what happens to people when they die? That they change
so much you have to trawl your memory to recalibrate the

senses? The opportunity to say farewell was in my grasp but for a moment. It would not return. 'If it's all the same with you Sergeant I'd like a few minutes alone.'

'So be it. I'll let Mr Seaton know you're here. He'll be along shortly anyway with the hospital porters.'

Tench gathered up his notes and disappeared into the mental wing clanging the heavy iron door behind him. I traced his progress along the corridor from the pathetic cries percolating through the wall until eventually these fell away leaving the mortuary in silence. I was alone with my father for the last time. I folded my arms and looked down at him.

What were you doing on the moor?

My father did not reply.

What were you writing about in your journal just before you rushed out? What were you trying to tell me and why would anyone wish to destroy it?

I noticed the tip of a wound just below the oesophagus. As his hands were at his side I was able to lift the shroud and trace the incision down the trunk to just above the navel where it ended. The opening was long and deep and the trough it had made was clumsily sewn back with fishing wire in the usual legacy of a post mortem.

And mother? I know you can hear everything I'm saying. Did she really court the master in Ireland all those years ago? You never told me about that. Probably because it isn't true. If it is true why did you never mention it?

The expression did not change. It never would. Cold, still, silent. I began to pace around the mortuary.

Lord William told me he had altered his will and changed the succession. Did you know anything about that? I suppose I'll learn more when I meet Mr Crake. What do you suggest I say to him?

Someone hammered on the outside door. I nearly jumped out of my skin.

'Mr Bullick, are you there? It's me Seaton; can you open the doors for us?'

I replaced the sheet over my father and crossed to the other side of the mortuary. One of the vertical bolts was jammed and I had to take off my shoe and use the heel to dislodge it, but after a couple of whacks it gave way and I shouted through that it was clear. Almost at once the heavy doors groaned open flooding the morgue with sunlight.

'Nathaniel is bringing the box wagon round now,' panted Seaton as he kicked a pair of wedging chocks in place. 'Did you identify your father?'

I confirmed it was so and that Sergeant Tench had gone to fetch the interim death certificate.

'Excellent. The porters are on their way round so we'll get started with the loading. We should be away in twenty minutes.'

Even as he spoke the jingle of harnesses announced the arrival of Nathaniel in the yard.

'Whoa, whoa there,' he cried softly as the horses were eased to a standstill and he jumped down from the plate. Seaton took the bridle and stroked the animals' while his grandson loosened the canvas cover of the hold to reveal a stack of wooden coffins. Two porters entered the yard wheeling a trolley.

'Good afternoon gentlemen. If you could bring numbers six, eight and nine in that order please,' said Nathaniel sliding out one of the coffins. 'We'll leave number five until last.'

The porters did as they were instructed and one by one the bodies were loaded up. As the second casket was slotted into position Sergeant Tench reappeared clutching the death certificate in one hand and a file and large carton in the other.

'These are the clothes your father was wearing when he was brought in. I'm afraid the hospital staff had to cut off his riding boots but they're included anyway together with the rest of his attire and the contents of his pockets.'

He passed over the carton. There wasn't much; boots, trousers, a felt shirt, tweed jacket, underclothes, belt, socks, riding crop, a pocket watch, a leather pouch containing some loose coins, his silver cross and chain and gold wedding ring.

'Is that it? Where's his coat?'

'It appears he wasn't wearing one,' replied Tench scanning down some kind of register.

'Not wearing a coat? What, in the rain? I find that hard to believe. Here, could I take a look at that please?'

'I'm sorry' replied Tench wafting the document away, 'but your father's records are government property and I'm not authorised to let you have access to them.'

'Sergeant, if you're holding an inventory of my father's belongings when he was brought into Dryburn I should like to see it please.'

'I'm afraid that's not possible. The schedule is part of the hospital file and the contents are classified.'

'Classified? What exactly have you got there sergeant?'

'These papers contain an inventory of your father's possessions together with any contemporaneous notes made by the staff when he was brought in. These include the date and time of his admission, details of witnesses in his company, records of any conversations your father had with the doctors, the notes of his initial examination together with a summary of his injuries. However the file is the property of the Coroner's office and at the present time I cannot allow you to access it.'

'For goodness sake why not? It's not as if it will be of interest to anyone else.'

'That's not the point sir. Your father's file is the property of the Coroner and I shall require his written authority before you or anyone else outside this office is allowed to inspect it.'

I couldn't believe what I was hearing and it was with some difficulty that I kept a degree of measure in my response.

'This is absurd. James Bullick was my father and as his eldest son and next of kin I insist that I am allowed to see his file.'

The policeman, however, was entrenched and brought down the portcullis by tucking the folder under his arm.

'I regret that will not be possible sir. We have strict instructions from Mr Lockwood not to let anyone have access to your father's papers. If you have a problem with this I suggest you go to his office and take the matter up with him. In the meantime until I receive instructions to the contrary, I'm afraid I cannot allow you to view the file and that is the end of the matter.'

By now I was beginning to get annoyed and had to bite my tongue before I said anything to Tench we would both regret.

'I certainly shall take the matter up with him,' I replied angrily 'in fact, I shall go and see Mr Lockwood right now. Whereabouts can I find him?'

'The Coroner's office is located in Old Elvet at the premises of Baxter, Crake and Lockwood,' replied Tench coolly. 'It's about twenty minutes' walk from here or ten on horseback, that's if he'll see you without an appointment.'

Seaton who had been listening cut in.

'Old Elvet is only a few streets from the parlour Mr Bullick. Why don't you come back with us and we can drop you off on the way?'

A squeak of trolley wheels announced the arrival of the last coffin which the porters slid into the back of the wagon so it rested on top of the others. I did not have to see the chalk scrawl to know it held the remains of my father.

'Thank you Mr Seaton, I'm most grateful' and then turning to Tench, 'You haven't heard the last of this sergeant.'

Tench shrugged his shoulders.

'I'm just following orders sir. As I say if you don't like it, take it up with the Coroner. Good day Mr Bullick,' and without another word he turned and disappeared back into the mortuary.

I kicked the ground in frustration. 'What an arse.'

'It's difficult for me to comment,' replied Seaton. 'It's not that I don't have a view Mr Bullick but we need to work with the Coroner's office, and they make far better friends than enemies.'

'Don't worry about it Mr Seaton. It's not your fault.'

We stood in silence while his grandson clambered into the back of the hold and wafted the canvass sheet over his sorry cargo. For a while the cover flapped awkwardly in the breeze until Nathaniel brought it under control as he went round the wagon tying down the ropes. Seaton drew a little closer so as not to be overheard.

'While I'm not at liberty to discuss the, er, how shall I put it? While I cannot talk about the challenges – that's it, the challenges – of my business relationship with Sergeant Tench, there's something I don't mind telling you and it is this; I've been doing this run for over twenty years and…'

His words stalled at the approach of one of the porters who required a signature to acknowledge receipt of the bodies. Seaton took the clipboard and having read it through, signed at the bottom and handed it back. The porter nodded an acknowledgement then re-joined his colleague at the empty trolley which duly squeaked away. I looked at Seaton.

'You were saying?'

'What I was saying Mr Bullick,' he whispered in a low voice, 'and I'd sooner you didn't quote me on this, but I've been doing the Dryburn pick up every week now for nigh on twenty years and this is the first time I've ever heard anything about a patient's file being classified.'

'Are you sure?'

'Oh yes, quite certain. It's never happened before.'

'Well that's extraordinary. What can be so different about my father's case?'

'I haven't the faintest idea,' replied Seaton climbing up onto the wagon. 'It's most strange because the hospital file is usually the first thing we look at when we arrive because it's our responsibility to cross reference the possessions against the inventory. It's important that we do this because items frequently go missing and it's our job to ensure that everything is passed to the next of kin. Before this afternoon I'd never known the Coroner's office reserve the task although it was clear Sergeant Tench had his instructions. Perhaps the Coroner will be able to explain.'

'I'd like to think so,' I replied as I hauled myself up on the bench, 'although, as you say, it's very strange.'

Nathaniel waited until I was settled then with a small crack of the whip we were away.

I didn't get to meet the Coroner that afternoon. Seaton

dropped me at Framwellgate Bridge from where I walked up to Lockwood's office but when I stated my name and business the receptionist made it clear that the Coroner didn't see anyone without an appointment. I asked if I could wait but having been informed he was not expected back that day, I left my details and said I would call again. It crossed my mind that Lockwood might have been in but had chosen not to see me, especially when I heard the receptionist trot up and down the back staircase before confirming his unavailability, but at the time I was prepared to give him the benefit of the doubt. I would be in Durham again soon enough and it could wait.

I walked back across the river to the undertakers where Jordan was waiting as arranged. He told me news of Lord William's death was on the streets and there had already been a flurry of visitors to the castle.

'I've been tooing and froing from town all day,' he sighed wearily. 'First the bishop then the solicitor, then you and I'm due back again in just over an hour to collect some friends of Lord Julian from the railway station.'

'The solicitor you say? Who was that?'

'There were two actually; I drove Mr Lockwood to the castle this morning then returned for his partner Mr Crake who arrived on the Hartlepool train a couple of hours ago.'

'Are they still at Craven?'

'Mr Crake is. I understand he will remain at the castle until tomorrow. I drove Mr Lockwood back to his office in Old Elvet a couple of hours ago.'

So he had been there all along. I could understand him declining to see anyone without an appointment but why instruct his staff to lie about it?

It was dusk when we arrived back at the stables. A pair of muddy boots in the hall told me Alfie had been out riding again and I could hear him splashing around in the bath.

'That you *Blue*?' he called down the stairs.

'Yes, just back from town. Scrounged a lift from Jordan.'

'How did it go?'

'Pretty much as expected,' I replied hanging up my coat. 'I met Seaton as arranged and we went to Dryburn and sorted what needed to be done.'

There was the sound of splashing water and the soft pad of feet. Alfie appeared at the top of the stairs in his dressing gown.

'Did you get to see father?' he asked quietly.

'I did. There was not a great deal to it in the end. I was able to view his body and signed a statement confirming it was him. Everyone was most helpful.'

Alfie had tears in his eyes.

'What did he look like?'

'Pretty much the same as he always did. It was extraordinary. It was almost as if he were asleep.'

'Really?'

'Really, and that's how you and I should always remember him.' The grandfather clock at the foot of the stairs struck half past the hour.

'Anyhow enough of that, the important thing is Dad has been formally identified and Seaton will be looking after him until Monday. What about you?'

'I've been at the stables most of the day. Fenoughty took the string into the park and I rode one of the new hunters. It was a bit nerve-racking and I'm absolutely exhausted. If it's all the same to you I think I'll have supper and turn in.'

'Sure. Is the water still hot?'

'Yes, I filled it to the brim. Took me absolutely ages as well, lugging buckets up and down from the back fire which is another reason I'm done in.'

I kicked off my boots and ran to the bathroom. I had just slipped into the water when Alfie called up the stairs.

'Oh, I meant to say a telegram came for you about an hour ago.'

'A telegram? Who's it from?'

'Haven't a clue,' came the barely audible reply from my brother as he wandered in and out of the downstairs rooms, 'but it looks like it was stamped at Ampleforth first thing this morning. Hang on, I'll bring it up.'

I closed my eyes floundering in the warmth as Alfie scurried up the stairs and dropped a coffee coloured envelope into my hand. 'I'll get the supper ready. See you in the kitchen when you come back down.'

'Cheers.'

I opened the envelope, taking care to waft the contents away from the bath to keep the print from running. When the steam cleared I saw the message was from Tom, typically brief and to the point.

Ampleforth Post Office 0830 hrs 18 November 1914
X COUNTRY GREAT NOT STOP HANG ON IN
THERE STOP TOM

I smiled wryly. The last time I'd seen my friend he was shivering in his sports kit. It was only two mornings previous but it could have been an age, so much had occurred. Tom would know exactly how to tackle Lockwood, Tench and the others however his counsel could wait until Tuesday when I took Alfie back to Ampleforth. For now though the telegram was just the tonic I needed.

We spent the remainder of the evening with chairs drawn to the kitchen stove sorting out the last details of the funeral, then, after the pots were washed and cleared, Alfie announced he was tired and went off to bed. I was planning to stay up a while and tackle some more of my father's paperwork but after a few minutes I found I couldn't keep my eyes open and also decided to call it a day. I whistled Domino for his last walk and in our usual routine we went to the far end of the orchard where I stamped about on the crown of the *ha-ha* while the dog hobbled up and down in the trough. I gazed across the park. It was a cold, clear night and the flush of a new moon spilled over the giant oaks and onto the frost covered pasture. I felt Domino nudge my leg to tell me he was ready to go back in. As we reached the door I turned to the sound of yet another horse and carriage scuttling up the drive. It was late for visitors but this was no ordinary evening and as I locked up I tried to picture the scene inside the castle library. There would be servants, lawyers and other bureaucrats milling around, Julian would no doubt be swinging the lead, his poor mother was probably drunk while Jane and Barnaby would be trying to keep the peace. I climbed into bed and having struggled though half a page of a novel reached over and pinched out the wick.

CHAPTER ELEVEN

The next two days passed surprisingly quickly not least because on the Saturday morning while we were having breakfast, a huge wad of mail arrived at the house, so much in fact that it wouldn't go through the letterbox and Sanders the postman had to ring the bell.

To my surprise, only three of the letters were addressed to my father, one of these being an invitation for us both to a ball at the castle to celebrate Julian's 21st at the end of the month. The remainder of the correspondence was addressed to myself and Alfie (or 'to the family of..' or 'to whom it may concern') and while the letters varied greatly in presentation and style, they were all from my father's friends and colleagues in the racing industry expressing shock and sorrow at what had happened. Oh, there was the usual unctuous standard from the local bank manager but the rest were written by people in the industry warmly reminiscing on times past, together with some amusing compositions from owners and punters alike including an anonymous note from an illegal betting syndicate to say they were sorry that the trainer of *Stornoway* had passed away and hoped that the animal that had been so good to them would quickly get over the bereavement and his form would not suffer. That gave us a laugh, in fact many of the letters did and it was a touching exercise ploughing through the mound because we could sense my father's spirit in the room taking everything in and enjoying the moment. The practical consequence of receiving so many letters was that they all needed to be answered before we went back to College otherwise we would never get round to it so that's how I spent the weekend, writing, writing, writing, trying to think of an original response to each one until shortage of time forced my hand into automatic twelve line mode.

There were over a hundred letters to compose but in the event it wasn't too difficult. Alfie addressed all the envelopes and on the Sunday afternoon, when Jane dropped in to see how we were getting along we were able to second her as chief envelope and stamp licker.

'How are things at home?' I asked scribbling furiously.

Jane was hammering stamps and didn't even look up. 'It's mad, absolutely mad. If you think you're rushed here, you should see how frantic it is at the castle.'

'Is there anything Alfie and I can do to help?'

'No, not at all. It's just a bit crazy with so many people coming and going. Mother and Julian are beside themselves, it's like they have twenty balls in the air and are trying to land them all at the same time. Barnaby and Jordan too, backwards and forwards to the railway station or the town on various errands. I'm so relieved to be out for a while'

'Has anything been decided about Lord William's funeral? Alfie and I would like to attend if we can.'

'Strange you should mention it as Bishop Moule was just finalising the arrangements as I came down. It's been decided father will have a private funeral and interment next Tuesday with a memorial service the following week.'

'You say lawyers have been at the castle. Would that be Mr Crake?'

'Both Mr Crake from Hartlepool and his partner have been constant visitors, Crake in his capacity as the family solicitor and his partner because he is the Coroner for the County. There's to be a reading of the Will in the library on Tuesday morning and one of the reasons I came over is because Mr Crake has requested that you delay your return to College so you can attend. Why do you suppose he wants you there when everyone else is staff or family?'

I was electrified by this information because the only plausible explanation for being invited to the reading of the Will was that I would benefit under its terms. Lord William had said as much on his deathbed. Could it be true? I suppressed my excitement.

'I expect it's a formality because I was present when your father died. I could certainly do without it because we're booked on the first York train and now we're going to have to put everything back.'

Jane held my gaze as she detached another portrait of the king from the block of penny reds.

'Edmund, are you absolutely *sure* you don't know any more than that? I mean did father say nothing at all during your interview that would account for Mr Crake wanting you there on Tuesday?'

I pressed the blotting paper over my latest composition and did my best to appear uninterested.

'Your father was terribly confused near the end as you know. When I arrived he barely spoke at all and what little he did say was nonsense. Ask Dr Addison, he'll tell you. I can only assume it's something to do with the Coroner's rules because I was with him at the end.'

I hated misleading Jane and my brother but Crake held the key to the future of us all and until he showed his hand, I had little choice but to play my own very closely.

CHAPTER TWELVE

The clock tower struck eleven as Barnaby, Jordan, Alfie and I convened in the courtyard for my father's funeral. A watery sun hung over the city but there was a snap in the air which made us embrace the warmth of the Rolls which Jordan brought round to the front once he had scraped the frost off the windows. For a while we jolted along the country roads until Barnaby broke the silence.

'I'd just like to say you look really smart lads, your father would be right proud of you.'

'It all just seems so bizarre,' said Alfie tweaking a lonely speck of dust from the shoulder of his suit, 'like none of this is really happening and we are in some kind of dream.'

'I know what you mean,' I replied. 'I haven't felt such a pit in my stomach since that first journey to prep school.'

'It'll not be an easy day for you lads but it will pass,' said Barnaby firmly. 'Just remember to keep your heads up as your father would expect and take comfort that he had many friends who will be there today to support you.'

No sooner had we drawn up in front of the parlour than Seaton scuttled out into the road to greet us, his immaculate coat and tails flapping in the breeze as he danced over the cobbles.

'Ah good morning, good morning to you Mr Bullick, and good morning to you too gentlemen,' he gushed as he hopped around the vehicle shaking everyone's hand. 'Now for goodness sake do come on in out of the cold. Nathaniel is round the back scrubbing down the horses so we have a little time and the kettle has just boiled.'

We trailed Seaton into the parlour where a petite softly spoken lady he introduced as his wife ghosted in with a tray of tea and biscuits.

'Gentlemen it is such a fine morning for a funeral,' enthused the undertaker sipping from his cup, 'just like an excellent pot of *Earl Grey*, not too warm, not too cold but just right (thank you so much my dear). The weather is so important on a day like this you know. I remember years ago managing a funeral at St Andrews at Aycliffe when there was the most terrific thunderstorm. Dreadful it was, one of the worst I had ever known, the deluge hammering down on the roof so loud you could barely hear the eulogy. When it was time to carry the deceased out everyone wanted to remain in the church until the storm had subsided but the parson, a fellow named Eade, I recall, had to be off for a shooting party and insisted the burial took place straight away. Frightful business it was but when we protested he shamelessly retorted that the weather was down to the Lord and *thy will be done* and all that. Needless to say the interment proceeded with indecent haste but everyone still ended up drenched and covered in mud.'

We all looked at each other. If I hadn't met him before I would have supposed Seaton was some kind of comedy hall act. He took another sip from his china cup and began again.

'No, I'll never forget that day,' he sighed running his fingers through his long grey mane, 'such a cold blooded fellow that Eade, evidently had to catch the Thirsk train which is why he couldn't wait to be off and down the hill but he might have said. Oh don't get me wrong, he was an excellent man I'm sure but not quite my cup of tea. My cup of tea? Do you see? Oh there, I've done it again, I'm so sorry gentlemen, I don't mean to make quips on solemn occasions like today, forgive me, I don't know what I'm saying sometimes.'

At that moment the door opened and Nathaniel stepped into the parlour looking as polished as a groom on the way to his wedding.

'The hearse and carriage are at the front. We're ready when you are grandfather.'

Seaton checked his pocket watch and drained the remainder of his tea. 'Gentlemen, the hour approaches. Follow me please.'

We filed back into the reception area where through the bulbous window panes I could discern a hive of activity on the street. Seaton halted in the doorway.

'I will drive the hearse; Nathaniel, you will follow behind in the carriage. Mr Barnaby I would like you to accompany me on the bench please, Mr Bullick, you sit in the second coach with young Alfie here and my two lads. If we need to stop for any reason I shall raise my right arm although St Cuthberts is not far and I don't propose to halt the cortege until we alight at Old Elvet. When the service is over we will resume our positions for the short drive to St Oswald's cemetery. After the interment we will proceed directly to the County Hotel. Does anyone have any questions?'

Hearing none, Seaton opened the door on the cobbles where two of his men waited at the side of a magnificent glass carriage behind which stood an open black Landau. Alfie and I stared at our father's coffin, beautifully arranged within the crystal facade. I felt my brother's touch on my arm.

'Is that him *Blue*?' was as much as he could say.

I placed a supportive arm on his shoulder.

'It's only a casket. It's just his remains. Dad's not really here, if he's not here then he must in heaven and at this moment he'll be looking down expecting us to be strong.'

'Do you really think so?' asked Alfie.

'Absolutely.'

It might have been true and I hoped it was but at that moment I felt as if I didn't really know anything.

'The horses are very smart,' said Alfie.

I measured the sleek outline of my father's coffin, the cherry wood buffed and polished like one of Lord William's drinks cabinets. I smiled inwardly wondering what Dad would have made of the comparison before quickly rebuking myself for entertaining such blithe thoughts at his funeral.

Seaton checked his watch a final time then nodded to his men. As if sensing the development, one of the horses whinnied and a jangle of buckles and brasses ran along the cortege.

'To your places everyone and good luck.'

Alfie and I moved through the silent crowd gathered on the pavement. As we climbed into the carriage the women curtsied and the men touched their hats.

'This is it Alfie,' I whispered. 'Remember, he'll be looking down expecting us to be strong.'

CHAPTER THIRTEEN

As our sad little party wound through the streets of Durham it was extraordinary how the people fell silent and shuffled to the edge of the road to let us pass, each one no doubt speculating who was in the casket before turning their gaze to Alfie and me in the second carriage. When we reached North Road, progress was in startling contrast to when Seaton and I had collected my father from Dryburn but three days previously. Transporting our precious cargo in a covered box wagon had been like wading through treacle, but today, from the manner in which the flags opened up in front of us you would have thought we were carrying the plague.

On Framwellgate Bridge we were whipped by an icy breeze coming off the river and sensing the clouds groaning with winter, I turned my collar and prayed Seaton was right and that the weather would hold. In Market Square the clatter of hooves made the traders look up from their stalls, hands on hips, while on the cobbles small children stood and pointed before rushing to their mothers' aprons. In the crescent at the top, little white faces peered down from the upstairs windows, each one wrestling with their own mortality as they hurriedly crossed themselves and drew the curtains. What is it about a funeral procession? It was the same at the fork between Saddler Street and Elvet, the great and good of the town frozen to the pavement, repelled and yet seemingly transfixed by our sad little convoy.

The cathedral bells chimed quarter to the hour as the cortege made its way onto Elvet Bridge. Seaton raised his hand.

'Whoa, boys, easy' cried Nathaniel.

'What is it?' I asked.

Nathaniel stood up on the bench craning his neck.

'It seems we have a reception party. I think you should take a look at this.'

Alfie and I jumped down so we could see beyond the horses. At the end of the bridge stalling our path stood the giant figure of Harry Sample, top hat and gloves drawn across his ample chest. Fenoughty was at his side reverently holding my father's binoculars and going-stick, the giant and the dwarf standing to attention with six stable lads in matching coat and tails. It was a most welcome sight and my brother and I ran up to greet them.

'Gentlemen, I'm lost for words. Totally overwhelmed.'

'Think nothing of it,' replied Sample. 'Your father was an excellent man and we wanted to honour his memory.'

'I wish he were here to see this,' said Alfie.

'He will have known lad,' replied Fenoughty quietly, his gentle words almost lost on the breeze.

Seaton climbed down from the hearse and joined us.

'You must be Mr Sample? How do you do Mr Sample, I received a message from the stable that you and Mr Fenoughty had sourced the pallbearers and I must say a fine sight they are too. Can I suggest that you and your men lead the way and we'll follow behind in the carriages? Edmund, perhaps you and Alfie would go back and join Nathaniel in the Landau? We don't want to be late.'

'Just a minute,' said Barnaby drawing a pewter hipflask from the inside of his jacket. 'You might want a quick nip of this. I find it helps steady the nerves.'

I didn't need a second invitation and took a deep swig of a warm fluid that tasted like a mixture of port and brandy. Whatever its constituents the effect was immediate and a delightful glow settled in the pit of my stomach.

'Here, let me have some of that,' said Alfie.

'Perhaps later,' replied Barnaby wafting the flask beyond my brother's reach before taking a quick draw himself and burying it inside his jacket. 'You have a reading to do.'

My brother frowned and moaned something about it not being fair but Nathaniel who was swigging from his own flask cut him off.

'Don't worry about it young 'un, you can have nip of mine later. Let's get the service over first.'

Alfie was still muttering as he, Nathaniel and I retraced our steps and jumped back into the carriage. Seaton, who was already astride the hearse twisted round and seeing we were in position rattled the reins and with a jolt and a jangle of harnesses, the cortege was on its way again.

A policeman held back the traffic as we swept over Elvet junction and clip clopped up the hill to St Cuthbert's where a sizeable crowd had already gathered on the green, their number stretching across to the court building.

'Looks like a full house,' said Nathaniel as we pulled up behind the hearse. I gazed down the footpath leading to the vestibule. He was right. They were queuing to get in. Scores of them. Alfie and I jumped down and stood by the railings as Nathaniel shepherded the stable lads into some kind of order.

'Right lads, I want you to form up between the carriages. That's right, three sets of two, tallest at the back with a corridor down the middle. No, not like that clothhead! Now pretend the person next to you is your girlfriend and you're at the local ceilidh stripping the willow. That's right. Now put your arms over each other's shoulders and link up. Don't be shy man. Good. Now link up'.

Eventually, when everyone was in position, Nathaniel and his assistants reached into the glass case and drawing on the experience of generations, carefully extricated my father's casket and lowered it on not a few anxious shoulders.

'Steady lads, steady,' said Nathaniel softly. 'We're in no hurry. Mr Seaton will not give the signal to move until we are certain each one of you is comfortable'.

For an anxious minute or so the coffin bobbed and wobbled as the stable lads adjusted to the unfamiliar burden and Seaton went round straightening backs and uttering words of reassurance. Eventually, when everyone appeared as steady as they were going to be, the order was given to proceed.

'Gentlemen, once the deceased has been securely positioned at the altar you will withdraw and wait by the carriages until the end of the service. I would remind you at all times to look straight to the front and remember we are in no hurry. Gentlemen, on the count of three you will place your left foot forward. One, two, three…'

Sample was first into the churchyard, the blacksmith's head bowed with top hat drawn tightly across his barrel chest. Immediately behind him shuffled the stable boys caterpillar-like with my father's remains balanced on their shoulders, then Barnaby and Fenoughty and finally Alfie and myself. As we approached the porch a solemn faced Cannon Brown hovered out to greet us but seeing we were already in step, promptly withdrew back into the vestibule leaving the rest of us to bump in after him. The organist, observing events through his mirror, immediately struck into *Nimrod* generating such a scraping of chairs I did not have to look up to see the church was packed. When we reached the top of the aisle Brown started to sprinkle holy water over the congregation, occasionally wheeling round to ensure the coffin and pallbearers received their fair share. It was a profound moment.

'Man, that is born of a woman, hath but a short time to live, and is full of misery. He cometh up, and is cut down, like a flower; he fleeth as it were a shadow, and never continueth in one stay'

A wall of uneasy faces twisted round to stare at us. I recognised a handful from the village but most of them were strangers.

'In the midst of life we are in death: of whom may we seek for succour, but of thee, O Lord, who for our sins art justly displeased? Yet, O Lord God most holy, O Lord most mighty, O holy and most merciful Saviour, deliver us not into the bitter pains of eternal death.'

When we reached the altar my father's coffin was lowered onto a brass bier and the pallbearers melted away leaving Alfie, myself, Barnaby, Sample and Fenoughty to occupy the vacant front bench. From the half empty pew immediately behind us Lady Alanna and Jane smiled nervously but we had no sooner taken our place when it was all eyes to the front as Cannon Brown started to address the congregation in that familiar rich baritone.

'A very good afternoon ladies and gentlemen. On behalf of Edmund and Alfred and their family and the ministers and parishioners I would like to extend a warm welcome to you all to St Cuthberts. There has been a church on this site for more than a thousand years and ever since Anglo-Saxon times the people of this town have gathered here to offer their prayers and thanks to Almighty God. This has been a place of joy and happiness such as weddings and baptisms, but it is also a place of reflection when on occasions like today we remember that life is only a temporary arrangement within which nothing is constant but change. This requiem mass is offered for the repose of the soul of James Michael Bullick who was a regular worshipper here and while our hearts are heavy with sorrow at his untimely passing, we can take comfort that he died, as indeed he had lived, under the careful watch of the Lord Jesus in the one true Christian faith.'

There was a short silence and a few coughs as Brown flicked through the pages of his missal before continuing.

'After the service the family would be honoured if you would join them for some refreshment at *The County Hotel* and there catch up with one another and share some memories of James and all the good times you had with him.'

There was another short pause while Brown stepped behind the altar before continuing in the semi sing-song voice that most clerics seem to adopt before a packed house.

'And so, my brothers and sisters in Christ, we will commence our offering to almighty God by singing together our first hymn, *The Day Thou Gavest* which you will find at page 204 of the green book in front of you.'

It is said that the closer one is to the business end of a wedding or funeral, the quicker the day passes and my father's requiem was no exception. Cannon Brown, clearly familiar with the contours of the occasion seemed to gallop through the liturgy and before I knew it we were filing back out into the churchyard. However there was one event that took place in St Cuthbert's that winter's afternoon which I shall never forget, and where just for a moment time stood still. It happened during my brother's reading when he suddenly began to choke with grief and it looked as though he might not make it to the end. The interval lasted no more than a few seconds but within the stillness of those walls it seemed like an age and the tension was agonizing. I was just on the point of intervening when the spell was broken by the rattle of a latch followed by some kind of commotion at the back. I instinctively turned round with everyone else to be greeted by the sight of Julian and Lord Clifford jostling through a wall of mourners hemmed in at the back. I knew Julian had returned from Oxford but assumed he'd far too much on his plate to be bothered about consoling any of us. Clifford, though, I had not expected to see and was just mulling over the significance of his appearance when I saw they were accompanied by another who was the last of the trio to squeeze through the gathering. I had no idea who this girl was but even from the other end of the church I could see she was striking. There was something about her form, the way she carried herself, indeed in her very presence that seized the attention and would not let it go. Neither was mine the only gaze resting upon her willowy form as the latecomers swept down the aisle to take their place next to Jane and Lady Alanna. I surrendered to propriety and switched my attention back to the front but that fleeting glimpse had quickened my heart and I was aching to steal another look even before I caught the whisper of her skirts as she moved in the pew behind me. The opportunity presented itself a few minutes later when I stood at the lectern and opened the pages of *Corinthians*.

Though I speak with the tongues of men and of angels, and have not love, I am become as a sounding brass, or a tinkling cymbal.

And though I have the gift of prophecy, and understand all mysteries, and all knowledge; and though I have all faith, so that I could remove mountains, and have not love, I am nothing...

The attention of the whole church was fixed upon me but as I looked up I saw only one and that my first impression of her allurement was not misplaced.

Love is patient, love is kind. It does not envy, it does not boast, it is not proud. It is not rude, it is not self-seeking, it is not easily angered, it keeps no record of wrongs...

She surveyed me with an unnerving intensity, her delicate chin rested upon gloved fingers intertwined as if in prayer.

Love does not delight in evil but rejoices with the truth. It always protects, always trusts, always hopes, always perseveres. Love never fails...

Over the top of the manuscript I caught the swirl of her long dark hair as she leaned back and whispered something into Julian's ear. The new Lord Craven tossed his head then muttered something through cupped hands that made her smile as she passed the remark on to Clifford who was seated to her other side.

When I was a child, I talked like a child, I thought like a child, I reasoned like a child. Now I know in part; then I shall know fully, even as I am fully known. And now these three remain: faith, hope and love. But the greatest of these is love...

As I reached the final line I closed the heavy cover of the bible and glanced up at the congregation. She was watching me closely, her head slightly cocked with eyes fixed upon my own as she squeezed Julian's arm and mouthed, 'the greatest of these is love'. Her beauty and poise were awesome and I could barely take my eyes away. I had not previously believed in love at first sight but this girl was the most stunning creature I had ever seen and from that moment onwards I was utterly captivated.

CHAPTER FOURTEEN

During the service snow had begun to fall over the city, silencing the pavements and muffling the hooves of the horses as the cortege whispered up the hill on my father's last journey. When we reached St Oswald's we dismounted and shuffled in silence to a far corner of the churchyard where through a swirl of blue flakes I saw the large bank of glazed soil that marked my father's final resting place.

'So this is it,' I thought as we rocked in the cold, waiting for the others to catch up. I wondered if Julian and his party would be among them but as I scanned the crescent of sombre faces there was no sign. After what seemed an age the ropes were carefully slipped beneath the coffin which was duly lowered into the waiting hole. I would never see my father again. I noticed how the old priest's white cassock stood out against the dark apparel of the mourners and screwing my eyes to a rush of tears I willed the contrast had been a sign from the Lord. Cannon Brown began the final prayers, his words hushed in the snowfall.

Forasmuch as it hath pleased Almighty God of his
great mercy to take unto himself the soul of our dear

brother James here departed, we therefore commit his
body to the ground;
earth to earth, ashes to ashes, dust to dust …

Brown reached for the pile of soil but finding it frozen could only dislodge a single lump which he threw into the hole where it crashed on the lid of the unseen casket. I felt for my brother's hand as we followed suit then watched while others stepped forward to do the same, then others after them, and then still others, each clod of earth beating it's shocking lament until the drumming gradually subsided and we peeled away. It was as grim an occasion as anything I had ever known but I took solace from Nathaniel who, sensing our misery, whispered that my brother and I would come back to this place on happier occasions, perhaps in the summer when the birds were singing and the churchyard was in flower.

The atmosphere at the *County* was in startling contrast to events at the top of the hill when in the normal way of funerals the tension gave way to release and the surge of bottled up conversation. As our party stepped in from the dusk the first thing that hit me was the surprising level of noise as old friends caught up with one another, many hailing a lost connection from across the room as they struggled to make their way over. Although it was impossible to count everyone, there must have been close on two hundred mourners packed into the ground floor of the hotel, although goodness knows who they all were. I relieved a schooner of sherry from a passing attendant and turned to Barnaby.

'This is astonishing. I never thought so many people would turn out to see father off, particularly on a day like this.'

'I agree,' replied Barnaby lighting his pipe as he scanned the room. 'I expected a fair few from the racing fraternity but not this many. I've been stood here a while tuning into the accents. Most of these folk sound like they're from York and Ripon way.'

They were certainly strangers to me or at least the majority of them were, although a surprising number appeared to know each other. I recognised a couple of the Middleham jockeys I knew vaguely, and then over by the fireplace I could see the Malton trainers Richard Lambton and Jimmy Budgett deep in conversation. I had known Budgett since I was little and he must have sensed my gaze upon him for at that moment he looked up and catching my eye, gave a strange kind of salute.

'Barnaby, did you by any chance catch the arrival of Julian and his friends in the middle my brother's reading?'

'How could I not?' he replied through a cloud of smoke. 'The whole church saw what went on. You'd think any ordinary, normal person arriving late would have slipped in quietly and stood at the back but not them.'

'I tell you Barnaby, the way they shoved through was awful, it showed a complete lack of reverence but when I looked to see that arse Clifford was with them I suppose I shouldn't have expected anything less.'

Barnaby waved to a bald heavyset man who was thrashing his way over through the crowd.

'Julian's memory is short. He doesn't realise how much his friend is loathed in these parts, or maybe he does and couldn't care less which is all the more worrying.'

'There seemed to be a girl with them who arrived at the same time. Have you any idea who she is?'

In my attempt to appear nonchalant I had left the question until last, but Barnaby saw though the ruse.

'Ah, that will be the Lady Victoria, Clifford's sister. She's quite a looker don't you think?'

'She's certainly that. To own the truth when she was sat there a few feet from the lectern I found it hard to concentrate on my reading.'

Barnaby struck another match and cupped it over the bowl of his pipe. 'It seems she has that effect on most people although according to the gossip columns she's destined for Julian in a match that would apparently enhance the stock of both families. And why not hey? Julian's brains are in his trousers – and who can blame him with someone like her – and the Cliffords could do with the cash I shouldn't wonder. Who says love is blind? Oh, don't look so downcast Edmund. If it's any consolation my sources tell me Lady Victoria is as nasty a piece of work as her brother which would make them very well suited don't you think?'

I grabbed another glass of sherry.

'If you ask me, she's far too beautiful to be with someone like Julian. Poor woman, she'll be in for a shock when she discovers what he's really like.'

The thickly set man had almost reached us and was extending his hand.

'You think her beautiful?' replied Barnaby out of the corner of his mouth.

'I do. She's one of the most stunning girls I have ever seen.'

'She's certainly that but if you want some friendly advice keep clear for your own good …. William!'

I had no idea who this William fellow was but from the manner he and Barnaby greeted each other, they obviously had some catching up to do so I left them to it and wheeled away to engage some of the other mourners. It had been my intention to try and get round everybody but there were so many I remained hemmed in by the door as those who knew my father cut across to share a few words, while others stopped to shake hands on the way out.

If a funeral could be remembered in that way I have to say that my father's turned into a most agreeable afternoon, especially when measured against what had gone before. Sustenance at the hotel was in no short measure and as the hard-core weighed anchor, off came the jackets and ties and the party like atmosphere that settled over the day was only enhanced when one of the stable lads produced a fiddle and some of the others began to jig. There was some memorable singing too, renditions of *Early One Morning* and *Widecombe Fair* stick in the mind, the latter especially because of the raucous struggle most people had trying to remember who came after *Peter Davy* and *Harry Hawk*. My brother seemed to know all the words, he must have learned the song at school although I inferred from the way he was marshalling the chorus that Nathaniel had been true to his word about the flask.

It was early evening and the ranks had noticeably thinned when I felt a tap on my shoulder and turned to face Julian. I was caught completely off guard because I hadn't seen him arrive and at the back of my mind assumed he must have gone straight back to the castle.

'Julian, I'm so pleased you could make it, we were just…'

Julian swotted away my outstretched hand.

'What did my father say to you?' he demanded.

'I'm so sorry about Lord William,' I replied. 'He was such

a good person and we're all numb over what happened. I really don't know what else to say.'

'You can start by telling me what you were doing in his room when he was dying. That's right, on his deathbed.'

'How do you mean?'

'Oh don't stand there all mealy mouthed pretending you've no idea what I'm talking about, although God knows what mother and Addison were thinking of letting you anywhere near him. What the hell did you think you were doing?'

At the sound of Julian's raised voice a number of people glanced uneasily in our direction.

'Julian,' I replied steering him to a quieter corner, 'look, now is hardly the time or place for this kind of conversation. If you like I can come to the library tomorrow morning and we'll talk about it then but not now, not here in front of everyone.'

'And why not here?' growled Julian angrily wafting his arm about the room. 'I couldn't give a stuff about any of these people, they were your father's friends not mine and most of them are only here for the free drink so don't give me your 'not here' patter. I want to know what my father said to you as he lay dying, the poor sod. Now. Here in this lounge. Do you understand what I'm saying?'

The fiddle immediately stopped playing and the room fell silent. Julian's squat face was inches from my own. He stank of booze. I don't think I had ever been so embarrassed in my life.

'Julian,' I whispered, 'for heaven's sake where's your dignity let alone the respect you owe to my father's memory? If we really must talk about this now all I can tell you is that when I saw him, your father was so poorly he barely said a word, at least not to me he didn't. That's the honest truth. If I knew any more, if he said any more I would tell you but he didn't and I can't and that's it. There's nothing else. Now can we leave it?'

Julian fixed his cold grey eyes on me as he gathered his thoughts. His expression was unforgiving, the contours of his plump face totally devoid of warmth or sincerity

'I don't believe you,' he said at length. 'You're lying. What were you doing over there in the first place?'

The fiddle cranked up again as the room slipped back into conversation.

'Look, it was in the middle of the night. I was sound asleep when I received the call. By the time I had dressed and was shown into his room your father had deteriorated and unfortunately he passed away without regaining consciousness.'

Julian was silent for a few seconds and I could almost hear the whir of cogs clicking away in his nasty mind as he tried to figure out if I was telling the truth. Eventually he spoke.

'I still don't believe you but it is of no matter, no consequence. My father will not be coming back to help you and neither will yours, more's the pity for you.'

'What do you mean?'

Julian took a deep drag on his cigarette, exhaling as he spoke.

'What I mean Edmund old man is the untimely demise of our respective fathers marks the establishment of a new era at Craven where one of the first things I'm going to do is run the estate like a proper business and address the blight that your family and others like you have been on it all these years.'

'Blight?' I repeated searing with anger. 'My father's only been in his grave a couple of hours, and you come here to his funeral and talk to me like that? Have you lost your mind? What the hell has happened to you Julian? You're supposed to be my friend.'

Julian grabbed a glass from a passing tray.

'Your friend?' he said draining the contents in one before replacing it and seizing another. 'Friends? What, as in equals? You and me? Don't make me laugh! The occasion or the drinks have gone to your head Edmund. We were never 'friends' as you put it and we certainly never shall be. Very soon when I'm in charge around here there's going to be a few changes. With the advent of war it's a tough old world and if the estate is to remain solvent I need to take drastic action. Looking through the accounts one of the biggest drains on our resources is maintaining the stables. It wouldn't be so bad if we ever won anything and rolled the cost over into the stud farm but the enterprise has been going backwards for years and I'm not prepared to bankroll what was in effect the old man's hobby. The stables and stud farm must either make a profit or we wind them up. If it were down to me I would close them both tomorrow but mother says I'm being too hasty and should give it another year.'

'I think you should listen to your mother,' I replied 'and remember if it wasn't for your parent's enterprise you wouldn't have your doll's house to play with.'

'A doll's house? Very good Edmund. A doll's house! I like it. That just about sums up the way the stables have been run, like an expensive toy. Well, not for much longer. You might as well know I've asked Jamie Budgett to take over and he'll be moving into the lodge on the first of January.'

Julian swigged the contents of his glass and watched for my reaction. So that's why Budgett had looked uneasy when our eyes met earlier. So much for my own pipedreams. The words came with a rush.

'The first of January? But that's only a few weeks away. I have to sit my Oxbridge entrance, Alfie is too young, Julian you cannot mean it, this is our home, we've more than twenty year's possessions in the house and I haven't even begun to sort out my father's affairs.'

'Oh I mean what I say Edmund. You would too if you had the bank breathing down your neck. How does the expression go 'the needs of the many' and all that? Craven is or should be a working estate that makes a profit and not some kind of charity for my father's old pals. I need to run the estate as a business, you know old lad, a bit like the days of the hunter-gatherer – those who don't go hunting don't get nothing to eat? Simple as that. Don't worry; you won't be on the street. Mother can house you in one of the cottages if she must but in a couple of weeks when I come of age, it will be with a new broom and one of the first things I'll be doing is clearing out you, your brother and that sick dog of yours.'

I was so absorbed in what I was hearing that I hadn't clocked much else in the room until suddenly she was there in front of me tucking her hand under Julian's arm.

'Now then darling, are you going to introduce me to your friend?'

Julian who was in the middle of his tirade suddenly stopped and stared at her, then looked at me for a moment and then back to the girl again before wrinkling his nose and speaking tersely out of the corner of his mouth.

'Oh there you are Victoria. This is Bullick, one of the workers from the estate. He's the son of my late father's late trainer and will shortly be moving on.'

The girl turned and in that brief moment when she set her gaze upon me I was so overwhelmed by her loveliness that I almost froze to the spot. She was utterly striking with high cheekbones and a porcelain complexion set against violet lips that parted on a row of perfect teeth when she smiled, although she wasn't smiling now as she looked me up and down.

'Moving on are we?' she said as her long dark hair caught the light. However it was the eyes that transfixed me; they were black and beautiful, I had never seen anything like them. She held my gaze but her words were addressed to Julian.

'Who did you say this was? Bullick your father's racehorse trainer? I thought we'd just been to his funeral."

Julian frowned and rolled his eyes. The girl looked up and considered him quizzically for a moment then the penny dropped.

'Oh, I see! I know who you mean now, *that* Bullick, young Bullick the son of the other one whose funeral it was?'

Julian rolled his eyes again. She threw her hands in the air with inappropriate elation.

'So *that's* why he was doing the reading. I see now. You're such a tease darling, really you are.'

Julian grinned piously and stooped while she hoisted her slim frame on tiptoes to peck his cheek before turning her attention back to me.

'So you're *Horse Boy,*' said she with a slope of the head as she looked me up and down. 'I've heard a great deal about you *Horse Boy.*'

'Nothing favourable I can assure you,' exhaled Julian wearily as he lit another cigarette and stared aimlessly about the room. I ignored the slight and bowed graciously to the girl, the manners my father taught me instinctively kicking in.

'The name's actually Edmund m'lady. Edmund Bullick. How do you do Miss? I'm honoured to make your acquaintance.'

If I thought I had gone over the top I was wrong as just for a moment her cutting manner subsided and she took my outstretched hand, all the time sweeping my face with those bewitching eyes.

'Quite the little charmer aren't we *Horse Boy*?' she said softly.

I savoured the brush of her fingers as she turned to address Julian whose back was to her shoulder.

'My brother sent me to hurry you along darling. He's waiting outside in the automobile. Don't forget we're meeting Lockwood for dinner at *The Dun Cow* at eight. If we don't make a move we're going to be late.'

'Why, what time is it?' asked Julian through a cloud of tobacco.

She withdrew her hand and checked the Cartier on her wrist. It was exquisite like its owner.

'Coming up seven fifty.'

'What, already?' replied Julian clearly irritated. 'I thought time was only supposed to pass quickly when you're enjoying yourself.'

I wondered why he had bothered coming at all although I was thankful for small mercies. At least Johnny Clifford had kept away although after his performance at the stable boxing match it would have been a brave call to show his face again among this lot.

Julian downed his drink in one then taking a final pull from his cigarette, flicked the butt in the general direction of the fireplace where it struck the log basket and bounced out onto the carpet. Julian, who was already making for the door paid no attention and it was left for one of the guests to intervene and discard it into the flames. Halfway across the floor Julian suddenly stopped and turned to address me a final time.

'Edmund, you and I can discuss the details next week but my decision about Budgett taking over is final. And as for the rest of you, take note because from now on I'll be watching you closely and if I find anyone not pulling their weight, believe me, your feet won't touch the ground on the way out.'

With these words he scanned the room as if daring any of the guests to say anything before calling to the girl.

'Come on Victoria; we've done our duty as mother requested. Now let's get out of this dump.'

Victoria switched on her smile for a last time.

'Looks like it's hail and farewell *Horse Boy*. Have a good life.'

I bowed my head but she was already away. I called after her.

'The name's Edmund ma'am and the pleasure's all mine.'

Victoria looked back over her shoulder.

'You wish,' she mouthed unpleasantly as taking leave of no other, they gathered their coats and marched out into the snowstorm, the thick oak door crashing onto a room of perplexed faces that instinctively turned towards Alfie and me.

It was Barnaby who broke the tension.

'Take no notice anybody, really, pay no attention. His lordship is in shock following the death of his father and he doesn't know what he's saying. Now come on, tomorrow will take care of itself. How about just this once we all live for the moment? Come on, let's all raise a glass to the memory of our good friend and colleague James Michael Bullick. Steward, another round of punch if you please, and have a glass yourself sir!'

Barnaby's call to arms sliced through the tension and with yet more drink circulating, Julian's extortions were put aside and the party resumed as boisterous as before. Nonetheless, I knew only too well that the following morning people would remember what was said and told Barnaby as such.

'I hate funerals,' he replied. 'They reek of my own mortality. As for Julian, I've seen this kind of thing before; people say stupid things when they're drunk and upset. I expect he'll apologise when he wakes up tomorrow, that's assuming he can remember anything.. Don't let it bother you Edmund; really. He didn't mean it'

'You surely don't believe that do you? Of course he meant it. People speak the truth when they are drunk, although whether he finds himself equipped with the capacity to carry out any of his threats is another matter entirely.'

'How's that?'

'What I mean is that for all his bluster, Julian may not be the man he thinks he is – in every sense of the word.'

Barnaby stiffened and immediately I knew I had said too much.

'You don't have to speak in riddles to me Edmund. What do you mean 'not the man he thinks he is'?'

'Nothing. Nothing at all. Look Barnaby, forget I said it. I've already spoken too freely which was not my intention. It must be the punch, that and the loss of my father. You said yourself that grief makes us say peculiar things and you're right. Please, I ask you to overlook it.'

'You *do* know something don't you? What is it? Did Lord William speak to you after all?'

I cursed my loose tongue. Fool Bullick, fool! Why couldn't you keep your trap shut?

'I can't say any more, really I cannot. I know nothing that could change anything at this time and I must ask you as my father's friend not to press me further.'

We watched some of the stable lads constructing a human pyramid by the door until it collapsed amid a tangle of limbs, profanities and beer.

Eventually he spoke.

'If that's your wish, then so be it. I'll not be raising the matter again but Edmund, you remember this: your brother and yourself have no greater friend at Craven and when the time comes you need to talk to someone about what's on your mind, and it will, you'll find my door open.'

I looked into Barnaby's weathered face. He plainly knew a great deal more than he was letting on but that much had been obvious ever since he picked us up from the station. It was so tempting to confide in him and I don't think I had ever been more in need of a friend than at that moment, but I managed to hold back.

'I'll not forget it Barnaby' I replied 'but I would warn you now that if I ever do knock on your door you'll not be the only one searching for answers.'

Barnaby was silent for a while then tapped my shoulder.

'Touché young fellah. Now where's that bowl of punch?'

CHAPTER FIFTEEN

On Tuesday morning Lord William's family and the various beneficiaries gathered in the library for the reading of the Will. Alfie and I had spent the early part of the day packing our trunks for college and, I was one of the last to arrive. I scanned the room. There were thin smiles from Jane and Mrs Pearce but everyone else was on edge and you could cut the atmosphere with a knife.

The library had been cleared for the event and in place of the usual furniture, a large wooden table had been set up by the window which was positioned in such a way that it was slightly (and I suspect deliberately) raised to give its occupants the appearance of looking down upon the assembly of wooden chairs that were facing it. The arrangements were such that were it not for the air of gravitas hanging over the proceedings, the uninformed observer could easily have mistaken the venue for some kind of recital. Certainly the room bore little semblance to the ruddy stage of Lady Alanna's distress but a few evenings before.

From my place at the end of the first row I scanned the long faces around me. Barnaby, Fenoughty, Jordan, Cannon

Brown, Bishop Moule, the elusive Lockwood – who wouldn't look me in the eye – they were all there together with the estate tenants, Mrs Pearce from the kitchens with the rest of the domestic staff lining the walls at the back. There were others present who were not known to me; foremen from the local mines, an assortment of tweeds and bowlers and others in uniform whose association with the estate was a matter of conjecture. I particularly remember one old boy with a chain of office around his neck slumped in a wheelchair near the front, listening trumpet pressed to his ear tuning into the background conversation which was growing with the tension as the hour approached. Friendly faces were thin on the ground. When I'd sat down Barnaby had come over to shake my hand and there'd been reassuring smiles from Jordan and Monmouth but the others were far too preoccupied with their own expectations to take notice of anyone else. The atmosphere, though, was simply electric; there was no other word for it; the very air in the room a bilious mixture of anticipation, suppressed excitement and dread.

As we all sat there waiting for the lawyers, I thought about the consequences if I were to be a major beneficiary of the estate as Lord William had implied. I remembered the awful scene as he lay dying, the revelation about my mother, his obvious distress, how he had been so appalled by his son's behaviour that he had instructed his solicitor to change the succession. That's if Julian was his son in the first place. This had been the most outrageous revelation of all, yet there was something so earnest, so utterly compelling in his address. 'Treat with Crake' he had said, 'he knows what to do'. His very last words; 'treat with Crake'. Over the last few days I had gone through our conversation time and time again, I had thought of precious little else. This was it then. I sensed we were in for a morning of high drama and a number of persons in the room were about to be seriously disappointed.

As soon as the clock on the mantelpiece pinged eleven, the door behind us opened and everyone rose to their feet as Monmouth entered the room with Lady Alanna, Julian and Jane and led them to the table by the window. The family were accompanied by two official looking individuals who were not known to me but as they also took their place I figured they had to be the solicitor, Crake, and one of his clerks. There was no mistaking the tall, imposing figure of Crake in his immaculate dark suit and stiff white collar. I was instantly drawn to the thick silver mane brushed back over his brow, that and a heavy gold chain that swung from his pinstriped waistcoat as he marched across the carpet. The man had an unnerving air of self-assurance, he simply oozed confidence and even before a word was spoken, it was apparent to everyone that we were dealing with a class act.

The person who trailed him in was much shorter and almost buried under a tower of documents which he promptly collapsed onto the table. He was not so much scruffy as slightly dishevelled with long oily hair combed over from the sides in a futile attempt to conceal his bald crown. He wore curious bottle-bottom spectacles of a type I had not seen before which tended to distract from the rest of his attire which was not dissimilar to his colleague's. I figured this must be Crake's clerk and when everyone was settled, it was he who opened the proceedings in a distinctive and rather irksome nasal tenor.

'Good morning ladies and gentlemen. My name is Glyder and I'm the chief probate clerk at Baxter, Crake and

Lockwood. In a few moments Mr Crake will impart the substance of the Will but first I would like to address some housekeeping rules. Each one of you has been invited this morning because the provisions of the Will concern you in some way. It is expected that at all times everyone present will conduct themselves with the decorum the occasion warrants, and refrain from talking or interrupting while the reading is in place. Secondly, to facilitate the smooth running of proceedings and to circumvent any unnecessary distraction, it is requested that until the reading is completed no one leaves the room unless this cannot be avoided. Lastly, I am instructed to thank you all for attending Craven Castle this morning, the family are aware that many of you have travelled some distance. I will now defer to Mr Crake.'

His master, who had sat motionless throughout the preliminaries reached over the table and selecting a large brown packet, carefully loosened the pink ribbon surround and unfolded the document inside. The tension was insufferable. All eyes in the room were upon him with only the anxious shuffling of feet and the creaking of chairs feathering the silence. Crake spread the document on the table in front of him and adjusting his glasses began to address the room in a deep, rich voice that was in marked contrast to the nasal ramble of Glyder who had preceded him.

'Good morning ladies and gentlemen.

This is the last will and testament of me, Lieutenant-Colonel William Surtees Fitzroy-Cavendish, 6th Marquis of Craven, CVO OBE TD CD DL of Craven Park in the country of Durham.

*I hereby revoke all former wills and testamentary
dispositions made by me...*

He'd revoked his previous Will. I knew this was a standard
clause at the beginning of every Will to eliminate the capacity
of any previous real or imagined instrument, but it already
sounded exciting. I sat forward lest I should miss a single
word. Crake swept the assembly over the rim of his glasses
then continued in that grave, gravel rhythm.

*I appoint my wife Lady Alanna Jane Fitzroy-
Cavendish and Thomas Edward Crake solicitor of the
Hartlepool practice of Baxter Crake and Lockwood to
be the executors and trustees of this my will.*

*I make the following specific cash legacies free of death
duty or associated taxes*

*To the parish of St Oswald's, Old Elvet in the city of
Durham I bequeath the sum of one thousand pounds
for the upkeep of the church building and to be
applied for continued Sunday school instruction for
the benefit of the young people of the community.*

*To the Durham Miners Association I bequeath the
sum of one thousand pounds to be applied at their
discretion to the purchase of musical instruments
for the colliery bands in the county with any sum
in remainder to be used for the maintenance and
replacement of colliery banners and the general
expenses of the annual Durham Miners' Gala.*

*To the trustees of the Union Workhouse at 37
Crossgate, Durham I bequeath the sum of one
thousand pounds for the upkeep of the building*

*and provision of books and facilities to enhance the
academic and spiritual welfare of the orphans of the
city.*

*To the members of the York Racecourse Company
I bequeath the sum of one thousand pounds to hold
in trust for the sponsorship of a two year old colt
classic trial to be held annually in the second week of
May together with the sourcing of a suitable trophy,
such race to be named in honour and memory of my
family.*

*To my esteemed friend and the estate racehorse
trainer James Michael Bullick of The Stable House
Craven Park in recognition of his service, loyalty and
friendship to my family I bequeath the sum of three
thousand pounds.*

On hearing this last disposition Julian shook his head
muttering to himself so that no one in the room was left in
any doubt what he thought of the bequest. Glyder, who was
clearly embarrassed turned and gave him a quizzical look
although I was too shocked and excited to care what either
of them thought. Three thousand pounds was an enormous
sum which would flow into my father's estate and ultimately
be at the disposal of Alfie and me. Perhaps we could use
the money to set up a business or purchase a small farm,
although there was no time to stop and think about it as
Crake bowled through the overs.

*I direct my trustees to invest the sum of three
thousand pounds in ten year Treasury stock the
interest thereof to be applied to the continued full*

*time school and university education of Edmund
Bullick and Alfie Bullick, the sons of the said James
Michael Bullick, the capital sum thereof to be divided
absolutely and equally between the said Edmund
Bullick and Alfie Bullick at the time both of them
have completed their full time education or when
the last of them has attained the age of twenty-five
whichever event first occurs.*

At this Julian brought his hands down on the table with such a crash that it bounced all the crockery and tipped over Glyder's pile of documents. I thought he was going to explode.

'What? This cannot be right! There must be some kind of a mistake!'

'Julian,' whispered his mother. '*Please!*'

'No mother. We're not having this. Father would never have left them so much money. They're not even employees of the estate!'

Crake paused for a moment and laying the will down on his lap peered at Julian over his glasses and gently shook his head.

'There can be no mistake sir,' he replied coolly. 'I personally attended your late father in this matter and drew up the will myself. The dispositions are precisely in accordance with his instructions and as to their integrity I can, if you insist, defer to the testimony of my partner Mr Lockwood and Mr Glyder here who were both present at the time.'

Julian exhaled loudly mumbling and cursing in the face of sustained entreaties from his mother and sister, although curiously no one else was taking much notice of him. Instead all eyes in the room had turned and were staring me. If I was in any doubt as to what had just been imparted its reality was confirmed by a warm smile and thumbs-up from Barnaby. I had been so worried how we were going to pay our school fees out of my father's modest legacy when all along the Craven estate had been footing the bill, and would continue to do so. I was totally and utterly astonished. Three thousand pounds and a similar sum on deposit for our education with the capital sum to be equally divided between Alfie and me at the end. There was never the slightest hint of the arrangement and yet in a few words from the grave, Lord William had confirmed it was so and made Alfie and I financially secure for the next few years. I could only sit in bewildered silence as the rumpus died down and Crake was finally able to continue.

To my estate steward Cornelius Barnaby and my head stable lad Paul Fenoughty in recognition of their loyalty and service to myself and my family I bequeath the sum of five hundred pounds each.

To the domestic, household and estate employees in the service of my family at the time of my death I bequeath to each the sum of five guineas to be paid by my executors on the first quarter day after the reading of this will, together with a further five guineas to be paid on the Christmas Eve first following my demise.

And so it went on, a long and detailed schedule of specific cash gifts to organisations and people that would be in need of them, the awards bearing testimony to the munificence of the deceased. While no one had been permitted to speak during the reading, with every charitable disposition murmurs of approval had rippled through the beneficiaries until the bequest to the staff which almost brought down the house.

'Ladies and gentlemen. Ladies and gentlemen. If you please' cried Glyder raising his little voice to try and make himself heard over the din.

'Ladies and gentlemen. Please. *Please*. I would remind you of the request for decorum that was made at the commencement of this reading. Thank you.'

The rapturous mood on the floor was in marked contrast to the disposition of the deceased's family. Julian's outburst at the bequests to the Bullick family gave way to a general surliness although his mother and sister remained dignified throughout. I felt so sorry for Lady Alanna who sat wretchedly with her hands on her lap, eyes watering as she gazed into oblivion, but a public reading of Lord William's intentions could not be avoided and there was little anyone could do to help her through it. My feelings towards Julian slouching in his chair next to Crake were quite different. It wasn't in my nature to dislike anyone but as I watched him there aloof and prickly, and recalled how he had spoken and behaved at the funeral it was difficult to resist a feeling of loathing. I switched to the end of the table where I caught Jane's eye. She smiled back thinly but looked totally worn-out which, with the events of the previous few days, was hardly a surprise. Crake's calm voice moved on to the specific donations. Lord William had been a very wealthy man. There were numerous disposals of money and specific personal possessions together with provision for local charities, all of which were greeted with enthusiasm. The Will then moved on to provisions for tax and so forth which mostly went over my head, although I picked up on the creation of substantial life trusts for Lady Alana and Jane which would see them financially secure for the remainder of their lives. Eventually, after what seemed an age but was probably no more than a few minutes, the document reached the non-fiduciary clauses dealing with the destination of the residuary estate and ultimately the succession. At this point Crake, who had been speaking virtually non-stop for over twenty minutes, paused and taking off his glasses reached over the table and decanted himself a tumbler of water. The unexpected recess made Julian shuffle irritably in his chair and he whispered something to his mother which I couldn't make out, but supposed it was caustic because Lady Alanna grimaced. Thomas Mathias Crake, the consummate professional, appeared to ignore the remark but as he took another sip of his water, he flashed Julian a quick look before replacing his spectacles and once more picking up the threads of the document.

Clause thirty six. I direct that the administration of the Craven Racing Stables and Equine Stud Company will be managed after my death by the said James Michael Bullick or in the event that he shall predecease me or otherwise be unable to accept the appointment then I direct that the day to day management of the said Company shall vest in such person, persons or organisation as my trustees in their absolute discretion shall direct.

Clause thirty seven. The remainder of my estate including all land, livestock, buildings, shares and all other investments in the United Kingdom and overseas, and all other property, possessions and personal chattels, whatsoever and wheresoever together with the hereditary seat and grounds of Craven Castle, and title of Marquis I devise and bequeath to my son Julian Dacre Fitzroy-Cavendish upon trust in the event of any minority but otherwise to take the bequest absolutely.

IN WITNESS WHEREOF, I have hereunto set my hand this 16th day of April in the year of our Lord nineteen hundred and five signed William Surtees Fitzroy-Cavendish, 6th Marquis of Craven.

Ladies and gentlemen, there ends the last will and testimony of the late Marquis. The instrument merely concludes with the standard clause of attestation by the two prescribed witnesses, these being my partner William Lockwood and myself. I shall now defer you to my clerk Mr Glyder who will remain in the building to verify your personal details and answer any enquiries. Ladies and gentlemen, thank you again for attending. I bid you good day.'

At this Crake folded up the Will and replacing it in the brown package, carefully retied the ribbon and promptly left the room with Lady Alana, Jane and a clearly distressed Julian trailing behind. I remember hearing raised voices as they disappeared into the hall but I was too stunned to take much notice. The reality was that Alfie and I were financially comfortable and in a position to complete our studies. Several of the assembly came over to congratulate me on my good fortune but I was in too much of a daze to take in what they were saying. The legacy was simply astonishing, a huge amount of money and yet at the same time it wasn't so much what had been said but what had not. The Will was written nine years ago which meant Lord William hadn't changed the essentials after all, and yet on his deathbed he had been adamant it was otherwise. I exchanged a few words with Barnaby and one or two of the others but there wasn't time to hang around. Our train was leaving within the hour and I was restless to find Alfie and tell him the news before he heard it from someone else.

CHAPTER SIXTEEN

'Lord William said *what?*'

'I know it sounds farfetched but he was absolutely adamant he'd disinherited Julian -who wasn't his natural son in the first place- and changed the whole Craven succession. He also insisted Julian and his friend Clifford had confronted him on the moor to try and talk him out of it, and that he wanted justice.'

Tom paced up and down staring at the floor, shaking his head.

'This is incredible, are you quite certain?'

'Regarding the exact words he used no, but as to the substance of what was imparted, absolutely. The poor bloke may have been on his deathbed but in those last few moments there was an intensity about him that left me in no doubt as to the truth of what he was telling me.'

Tom stopped pacing about and looked up for a moment.

'I assume you didn't get to speak to Crake after the reading?'

'No. He left straight away but in any event Alfie and I had to rush for the train back here.'

'That was unfortunate although from Crake's point of view, I don't suppose it was the time or place either.'

'How do you mean?'

'I mean your Mr Crake sounds like a bit of a show-off, the kind who revels in the drama and solemnity of these occasions. Many lawyers are like that you know, they forget all humility and what they're actually there for fancying themselves as lead actors playing out some Greek tragedy. Your man Crake is obviously one. I expect he was in his element this morning, no doubt seeing his own performance rather than Lord William's intentions as the focus of the occasion. It's as well you didn't speak to him. Any suggestion that the Will had been superseded by another instrument would have been met with very short shrift.'

'Perhaps you're right. It wasn't the time or place. It points to a disturbing inference though. If Lord William was speaking the truth, and I've no doubt in my own mind that he was, then Crake must be holding something back. You don't suppose he's bent do you?'

Tom lit a cigarette and waved out the match.

'I certainly do. Crooked as a barrel of hooks.'

I bit my lip trying to think a way round the obvious conclusion.

'That's one heck of a call, you know. It would explain the paradox but you should see the fellow, he's awesome and frankly, he just doesn't look the type. There's another thing. If Crake is dishonest, Julian would have to be in on it, in which case how do you explain him kicking off at some of the legacies? I tell you he went mad over the trust for Alfie and me and it took the others some time to calm him down. He couldn't have put that on.'

'On the contrary, I suggest that's exactly what he did. I would also venture the whole reading was little more than a carefully scripted performance in which the two main actors played their part. Look Edmund, it's a question of logic. Either Lord William was telling you the truth or he wasn't. Think about it. He calls you to his deathbed – which in itself is incredible considering the gulf between your positions – he sends everyone else away and then uses his last breath to tell you he's changed his Will. You were there my friend, I wasn't, but you seem to have no doubt he was speaking the truth.'

'None whatsoever. I didn't doubt it then and I don't doubt it now.'

Tom moved over to the window where he pressed his forehead and hands to the glass. I watched in silence until he drew away again leaving tiny shivers of frost melting down the pane where his hair and breath had been. Presently he turned.

'Then it's simple,' he said. 'Our default position is that Lord William was speaking the truth, which means Crake is a villain and we plan our next move accordingly.'

I recalled the way Lord William looked at me as he was dying. Tom was right. There was something up and Crake was in on it.

'It's the only sensible conclusion but where do we go from here? Do we report what we know to the authorities and leave it to them? I have to say I'm reluctant. I don't want to appear neurotic but after the carry on I had with the police at the mortuary and the way Lockwood blanked me at his office, I wouldn't be surprised if they were all in cahoots.'

Tom twisted from the window and blew into his cupped hands.

'No, we must keep the law out of it for now. We can't accuse anybody of anything without evidence. Instead you're going to have to seek Crake out, let him know you're on to him and measure his reaction. I'll come along as well if you like. If there's an innocent explanation to all this no doubt he'll tell us although I can't imagine what it might be.'

'I'll wire his office tomorrow,' I replied, 'and as soon as the Oxbridge exams are over we'll go down to Hartlepool together. I've good enough reason to make an appointment. I was supposed to wait in the library this morning to discuss the mechanics of the fees trust with Glyder, so they'll be half expecting me.'

'Right, it's decided then; we'll confront the wolf in his den and see what he has to say. In the meantime what else can you tell me about this other fellow, what's he called, that policeman at the hospital?'

'His name's Tench, Sergeant Tench of Durham Constabulary and as he was at constant pains to remind me, he's the first officer to William Lockwood MBE, his majesty's Coroner.'

'I take it this is the same Lockwood who pretended he wasn't in the office that afternoon?'

'The very same who also happens to be the partner of Thomas Mathias Crake who drew up Lord William's Will.'

As we sat there in my room I went on to describe everything else that had occurred since I left Ampleforth on the morning of the cross country. The fractious journey home, Lady Alanna's firelight misery, the revelation about my mother, the tramp in the stones, the jovial Seaton, the wretched wing of mental patients, discovering my father's body in the mortuary, the behaviour of Julian and his party at the funeral, the riddle of Barnaby, I related it all, everything exactly as it had happened. Tom, who was slumped in the other armchair with his feet across the table, threw in the occasional question but otherwise listened intently and it was late into the night when the rush of words finally ebbed away and I realised I was done.

Tom exhaled a slow whistle.

'Sheesh Edmund, what have you got yourself into?'

'I would I knew. When I listen to myself setting everything out like that it makes me question my own sanity, but that's exactly how it happened. Oh, and there's another thing. When I arrived home I discovered someone had been into my father's office and removed a page from his journal.'

'What journal?'

'Dad used to keep a diary in which he recorded day-to-day events at the stables. There was nothing especially exciting about it, just training programs for the horses, medicines, section times that sort of thing. I'd often seen him at his desk scribbling away and the volumes were one of the first things I came across when I started going through his papers. It seems he was making an entry on the day he died when he was suddenly called away. I've brought it back with me. Hang on; I'll get it out of my case.'

I retrieved the 1914 chronicle and magnifying glass from my luggage and opened the cover at the missing page. Tom looked at it for a moment then skimmed over the last few entries before bringing the final leaf close up to the oil lamp where he slowly floated the book to and from the light.

'You're right. There's a whole page missing. You have to look closely but you can just make out where the bind has been undone and retied. I suspect whoever did this was no novice.'

'Maybe,' I replied, 'but novice or not, they can't have been that competent because they've overlooked the impression my father's last words made on the next page. Look…'

I pointed to where the words had traced through. Tom ran a forefinger over the leaf.

'It's not exactly braille but there's definitely something,' he replied, 'which is perfectly logical if you think about it. When writing is fashioned on a sheet of paper resting upon other pages, which is what we have here, the surface indentations or impressions are automatically transferred to those below. This appears to be the case with your father's last entry and, if I'm not mistaken, we should be able to uncover his words with a bit of iodine fuming.'

'Never heard of it.'

'Yes you have. Brother Wallace mentioned the procedure at the end of last year, it's not complicated. All we need are a few iodine crystals and a round-bottom flask or tube and then to blow on the contents in such a way that the breath moisture generates iodine fumes. When the fumes hit the surface area of the page, *voila,* the hidden message will hopefully appear. I've actually got some crystals in a chemistry set back in my room. Hang on; I'll go and get them.'

Tom clattered down the corridor and promptly returned with a small test tube of purple crystals in one hand and an empty lab beaker in the other.

'Now when I say the word I want you to lightly blow into the flask, do it like a soft whistle,' he said, 'but be careful you only blow and don't inhale, this stuff's toxic.'

Tom unscrewed the test tube lid and having emptied out the crystals slowly tilted the flask above the blank page at an angle that would have dispersed the contents had they been fluid.

'Now keep it soft and be careful you don't breathe anything in.'

I crouched down to the table while my friend held the flask in position with one hand and brought the flame of the oil lamp beneath the bowl with the other. At the same time I leaned forward and began to blow in the spout.

'Slowly, slowly. You're doing great. Now, take a few paces back, fill your lungs again as much as you can and repeat and remember whatever you do don't breathe any of this stuff in.'

I did exactly as he asked; carefully blowing out again, slowly, softly and steadily until there was nothing left inside and I span away gulping for air. Tom held the flask in position for another minute or so then having vanquished the contents in the sink dried his hands and came back to the table.

'That should be enough,' he said. 'All we do now is wait.'

An unpleasant odour filled the room, like a kind of mixture of burning metal, nail varnish and pear drops all rolled into one. It settled in the throat and made our eyes water so I moved to the window and unfastened the top segment until an icy blast reminded me how cold it was outside and I promptly slammed it shut again.

'Look,' said Tom, 'look, it's working.'

'What? Here, move back a bit, let me see.'

I crouched by the table and stared at the blank page only it wasn't blank like before as slowly but surely a few letters began to materialise, then a few words until a small paragraph of about a half a dozen lines ghosted into view.

It reminded me of when we were children and played with invisible ink. I reached for the magnifying glass and raised it up and down over the page until the twinkling message came into focus. Tom and I stared at the page utterly transfixed.

Edmund, there's no time to explain but Lord William is in terrible danger. Julian and his friends know he's changed the succession and even now are riding out to confront him. I am setting off for the moor to try and head them off. You will only see this note if I fail to return in which case I pray God he will lead you to it.

With my love as always. You and your brother were always the source of my greatest joy.

Dad

I read the lines again, and then again and finally once more barely taking in the words. Oh my God. Lord William had changed his Will like he said and Julian had ridden up to the moor to challenge him about it. But then what happened?

'This is incredible,' whispered Tom.

'It's not only incredible,' I replied, 'it's rock hard evidence that the Will was changed and Julian was on the moor when my father died. No wonder the original page was destroyed. Thing is, I don't trust the authorities. I can't help it. If I took this to the police what's the betting the whole journal wouldn't go the same way as the top copy?'

Tom climbed to his feet and lit another cigarette.

'You're right. It's much too risky. We need to hang on to the diary while we gather more evidence and then take the whole lot to someone we can trust out of the area.'

I moved over to the window. It was deathly quiet outside; even the drip on the pump was silenced in the cold.

'If we're looking for more evidence the starting place has to be Dryburn after the carry on with my father's papers. Like the undertaker said, a patient's admission notes are hardly the stuff of official secrets so why hold them back unless there's something in there they don't want anyone to see? We need to get our hands on that file.'

'I agree,' replied Tom. 'I've been racking my brains to think of a way to do it ever since you told me about your argument with Tench; thing is how? There's no point going through official channels and I don't suppose you know anyone at the hospital who might be willing to help?'

'No, I don't. Everyone I met was miserable, the lot of them, besides which the place is forbidding, more like a jail than a hospital.'

Tom joined me at the window and spoke into the glass.

'Could we not gain access on the pretext of visiting a sick relative and then slink off and have a good rummage through the cabinets? Or how about disguising ourselves as doctors or clergymen and get in that way?'

'It would never work,' I replied. 'The office where the files are kept is at the end of the mental ward and the whole wing is locked down like a jail.'

'There has to be a way. Suppose I feign lunacy and get myself detained in the ward and then have a snoop around?'

'Tom, until you see and hear these patients and the conditions in which they're kept you have no idea just how wretched they are. We're not talking about a few cranks here; these people are dangerous, many are possessed or believe they are possessed by demons and some of them are killers. I can see where you're coming from but take it from me; anyone volunteering to join them would have no need to feign madness.'

Tom took a long drag from his cigarette and flopped back into the armchair.

'Then we're left with no choice,' he said. 'We're going to have to break in.'

'What? Break in as do a burglary?'

'If you choose to put it that way, then, yes.'

'You're joking. We'd never pull it off. The mental wing is in the heart of the building, the patients are closely supervised, all the windows are barred and the only access is through a locked steel door.'

Tom climbed out of his chair and began to pace up and down. 'There must be a way in. There has to be. What about the foundations? Did you see any trapdoors or stairs in the floor? What about the roof? Were there any skylights?'

'No. The wing is built into a kind of semi basement, the floor is solid flag and the ceiling props up another two storeys of the hospital. The only skylight was in the mortuary.'

Tom mulled things over for a while then gave me a look.

'Where's the mortuary in relation to the mental ward?'

'Oh no you don't. Oh no. You have to be kidding me.'

'Where is it in relation to the ward?' he repeated.

I recalled the layout of Tench's dusty office at the end of the wing.

'It's actually next door. There's an entrance behind a curtain that leads straight through but Tom, it's the bloody mortuary, you know, as in dead bodies, ghosties and goulies and all that. The place freaked me out in the daylight and I had Tench with me then. There's no way I'm going back.'

'Do you want to see what's in that file or not?'

'Of course I do but there has to be another way.'

Tom took a drag from his cigarette and blew a perfect smoke ring which rolled steadily towards the window until he exhaled again and shot it down.

'There is no other way. You're going to have to go back, only this time I'll be with you. And as for ghosts and ghouls, there's no such thing, its people who are haunted not places. Oh come on Edmund don't look so horrified, you know we can pull it off, they'd never dream anyone would burgle the place, let alone break in through the morgue.'

'I don't like it.'

'I don't particularly like it either but that's not the point. Think about it Edmund. We can do this. You know we can'

I did think about it. The whole concept was totally outrageous but once I discarded images of the undead and focused on the hard mechanics, I realised it was not without prospects. I remembered the mortuary skylight had moss growing around the edges and how water leaked down the sides. The frame was also rotten and probably less than secure. The arched ceiling wasn't very high either which meant a soft landing and reasonably straight forward exit assuming we could get that far. The only fly in the ointment was the iron dividing door which I knew was fitted with a bolt on the other side. It hadn't been drawn when Tench took me through the previous week but if the hospital locked it at night, our adventure would end right there on the wrong side of the office wall.

'It's a risk we have to take,' said Tom, 'because this is the only way we'll get our hands on your father's file and what's more, if we don't go in now, the information could soon be lost forever.'

Tom was looking at me intently, he was clearly excited at the prospect and his enthusiasm was infectious.

'It pains me to say it but you're right. It *is* the only way although I shudder at the prospect. I don't like it. All those dead people, the very thought gives me the creeps.'

'Oh, never mind all that supernatural nonsense. You're just afraid of fear itself. It's the spirits in this world we have to look out for. I suggest we go in as soon as possible and at night, preferably when there's no moon. Agreed?'

'I can't vouch for the moon,' I replied, 'but I think I know just the time'.

'Go on'.

'It's Julian's coming of age ball at the castle a week Saturday and there'll be hundreds there. I was invited with my father but I don't suppose anyone would mind or even notice if you went along with me instead. It would be the perfect opportunity with the perfect alibi; we could go to the party, sneak away, do the deed and be back again before anyone misses us. It'll be a cracking bash too. The County set will be out in force and with Julian keen to impress there'll be no expense spared. What do you reckon?'

'I think it's a brilliant idea,' replied Tom. 'I've always dreamed of going to a society thrash. The champagne, the orchestra and the girls! Oh, the girls! Come on Edmund; let's take a twirl around the floor. Oh if you were the only girl in the world, and I was the only boy…'

'Whaaa…'

Tom drew a forefinger up to his lips and pointed to the door. There was someone on the other side. He ghosted across the room. For a large man he was surprisingly light on his feet.

'… nothing else would matter in the world today… come on *Blue*, you must know the words…'

'… nothing else would matter in the world today, we would go on loving in the same old way…'

Tom lunged at the handle and wrenched back the door. The solitary figure on the other side didn't stand a chance and promptly crumpled in a heap before us.

'Bloody hell Conway, what do you think you're doing?'

The head boy jumped to his feet as Tom and I scowled over him.

'What do I think *I'm* doing?' he said, colouring as he brushed down the arms of his jacket. 'That's a good one Brentnall. What do you think *you're* doing more like? Organising some kind of break in by the sound of it. Have you two taken leave of your senses? I've a good mind to report this to the headmaster and ordinarily would do so only I didn't come down here to eavesdrop.'

'Oh really? Then what were you doing with your ear against my door?' I demanded. 'Checking for woodworm?'

'Actually Bullick, Edmund, I came down because I heard you were back at College and wanted you to know how sorry I am about your father. Truly I am. Having lost my mother a few years ago I know something of what you must be going through and I wanted to see if there's anything I could do to help.'

Tom was unimpressed.

'That's all very well but it doesn't explain why you were glued to the keyhole listening to our conversation,' he snarled.

'Look Brentnall, I didn't come here to spy on you and certainly not to argue. I just wanted to express my condolences to Edmund. It was only when I entered the corridor and heard these excited voices that I was curious to discover what all the fuss was about.'

'And now you know or think you know our business, are you disappointed? You bloody creep,' growled Tom.

Conway ignored the insult.

'Please believe me *Blue*. When the Head called you out that afternoon I'd no idea what it was for and I've felt awful about my gesture ever since. I'm truly sorry. As for anything I might have heard just now, well I didn't catch that much and whatever you're getting yourselves involved in, it's your business, I really don't want to know and I swear what little I heard won't go any further.'

'How can you expect me to believe that?' I replied. 'You're always slinking off for cups of tea and hob knobbing with the masters.'

'I promise you, your secret is safe with me. I give you my word.'

A look of candour washed over Conway's face as he spoke. He certainly sounded as if he meant it. Thing is, could we take the chance?

'What do you reckon Tommy? Can we trust him?'

Tom circled Conway like a farmer inspecting a bull at the market.

'It seems we have little choice in the matter and must take him at his word. But I tell you this *One-Way*, if the slightest hint of what we were just discussing leaves these four walls, I'll personally remove your testicles and feed them to the hamsters in the junior's pet club. Do you understand?'

'As I said I give you both my word and I do. I promise I'll not tell a soul,' then turning to me, 'will you shake on it Edmund?'

I looked at Conway with his small brown eyes strangely magnified behind the bulbous lenses of his glasses. He'd always been too standoffish to make friends and he'd never been one of mine but I appreciated the gesture and was prepared to give him the benefit of the doubt. I took his outstretched hand.

'Guess all's well that ends well then,' whispered Tom cynically 'although if you ask me it's a damn shame.'

'What do you mean?' replied Conway.

'I mean it's a shame about you not wanting to know what we're getting ourselves into, that is. We could just do with a getaway driver Conway, and you'd fit the bill perfectly.'

'Tom, let it go. I'm happy to take him at his word not that we have much choice. Just ignore him Conway.'

'No, no that's fine; I brought it upon myself by listening at the door. Mind you, if you want my opinion, it's not a getaway driver you need at the hospital but rather a chauffeur, or better still a taxi.'

'A taxi?' I repeated.

'A taxi.'

'How's that then?' asked Tom suddenly interested.

'Look at it this way,' said Conway lowering his voice. 'Somehow the two of you have to get from the castle to Dryburn and back again before anyone notices you've gone. Have you given any thought how you're going to manage it? How far is the trip? About six miles each way I'll bet. You could just about make it on horseback but it's asking for trouble on the lanes that time of night, plus the fact you'd need someone to mind them while you go in. You'd also have a bit of a problem explaining yourselves at the stables.'

'So what's your point?' I asked.

'Well if horseback's out of the question, and it's clearly too far to walk, there's only one thing left. You're going to need some proper transport are you not gentlemen?'

'And I suppose you're about to tell us this is where you come in?'

'Ah, I see you're ahead of me,' replied Conway dryly.

'What?' cried Tom astonished. 'Are you going to get your old man to lend us an automobile?'

'No, we won't be lending you anything, but I'm happy to drive for you. Not so much of a car though, I was thinking more of a taxi. You see there'll be that many of them coming and going from the party one more isn't going to attract any attention and I know from the office diary that most of ours are already booked up. I frequently drive for my father when I'm at home and could easily arrange to be working that night. What do you think? Are you interested?'

Tom and I exchanged glances.

'I think it's a brilliant plan and it could work,' I replied.

Tom was silent.

'Tom?'

'Forgive me for being wary Conway but in situations like this I tend to rely upon my instincts because they don't often let me down. Edmund's right, it's a sound plan and I agree it could work. The thing I don't get though is why you should be willing to put yourself at risk by helping us, because if anyone gets caught in there, we're all in deep shit. It would involve the police; we'd almost certainly be expelled from college and could even go to jail. I'm standing by Edmund because he's my closest friend and we've always looked after one another, but what's in it for you?'

'What's in it for me?' repeated Conway, shrugging his

shoulders, 'the short answer is 'nothing at all' but then I'd not be risking anything would I?'

'How do you figure that out?' I asked. 'Just driving the vehicle makes you part of the enterprise.'

'Not at all. Look gentlemen, let me make it clear at the outset I want no part of any burglary or break in. Not a bar of it. As far as I'm concerned you'd just be another couple of punters I'm dropping off in town. What you do when you get out of the cab is your own business. I'll happily take you there and when you're through I might accidentally-on-purpose be passing along the road outside, but as far as anything else is concerned, well I don't know and I don't want to know anything about anything else if you get my drift?'

I saw his drift very clearly.

'What, so if we get caught it's nothing to do with you?'

'Precisely. You must promise to leave me out completely'.

There was a brief silence while we considered the proposition.

'Seems fair enough to me,' said Tom eventually. 'Looks like we're going to have to trust each other.'

'I agree,' I replied. 'You're a star Conway. I don't know how to thank you'.

'Nor me' said Tom 'although I still don't understand why you're prepared to stick your neck out. It's just so unlike you.'

'Please, you don't have to say anything,' he replied. 'Although I haven't a clue what this is about I know you both well enough to suspect there must be good reason for this initiative which is why I'm prepared to try and help you. It's the sort of thing my father would have done when he was younger, and he didn't get where he is today following all of the rules all of the time. There's something else.'

'What's that?' I asked.

'Well contrary to what you two might think, I'm not a complete prick and a spot of adventure rather appeals to me.'

It was settled. We discussed the strategy late into the night, everything falling into place with surprising ease. Tom and I would go to the party as intended, make sure we were seen by as many people as possible then at a prearranged time we would slip away and meet Conway's taxi in the courtyard. He'd take us straight to the hospital, cruise around the area until the deed had been done and then pick us up again on the North Road. Like all the best plans it was simple and we believed it could succeed. The only drawback was the agonising wait for the party and trying not to let the anxiety distract us from our studies. We managed it though. After ten days furious study the Oxbridge exams were behind us and having said farewell to my brother until the holidays, the three of us caught the train to Durham.

CHAPTER SEVENTEEN

The castle looked magnificent on the night of Julian's twenty-first party and no expense was spared. Neither was it a small affair. It seemed that anyone who was anyone in the County and beyond had been invited while in expectation of the numbers, a host of trucks and carts had spent days tooing and froing from the city with provisions.

It was the first ever society party for Tom and me and notwithstanding the grim business of the later evening, we were determined to make the most of it. Half the enjoyment of course was getting dressed up and with the invitation specifying white tie, we raced into Durham to secure the necessary garb which my father's outfitter assured us was tails, formal striped trousers with white waistcoat and a piqué stiff fronted shirt with detachable wing collar. I'd never worn anything like it and having returned with arms full of boxes, we spent an absolute age getting ready in the way that young men do, bathing and shaving in the early afternoon before spending an inordinate amount of time meticulously pressing shirts, brushing down jackets and polishing our shoes. Eventually when all studs and cufflinks were in place and our hair was combed for the umpteenth time, we stood in front of my father's tall dressing mirror.

'Ha! This is just brilliant!' said Tom twisting from side to side. 'I look like one of those society models in *Men's Fashion Magazine.*'

'Society rake more like!'

Tom picked a speck of fluff from his collar.

'There's nothing wrong with being a rake, at least that's what my father told me, 'just mind you don't fornicate with friends of the family' he used to say.'

We burst out laughing. He was right though. He did look great. We both did. It was wonderful how simply dressing up transformed the mood even before we stepped out of the house. For the first time since my father's funeral I began to feel alive again, not only alive but strangely self-confident and positive about the future. I studied myself in the glass and thought of Victoria Clifford. I wondered if she'd be at the party. Of course she'd be there. I wondered if she'd remember who I was or even care. Or even notice. I recalled our conversation at the hotel and those beautiful black eyes boring into me. My heart skipped a beat as I imagined what it must be like to hold her body against me. 'You wish' she had said. How the words haunted me. Little did she know, or maybe she knew all too well which was why she said it. She probably said the same to all her admirers like it was her default response. Tom snapped a finger to my ear.

'Wake up Narcissus and don't look so anxious. There'll be enough girls for us both.'

I sprang out of my daydream. It was nearly time to go across.

'Right amigo, better check watches. What do you make it?'

Tom rolled up his sleeve.

'By mine it'll be exactly eight seventeen in... ten seconds... four, three, two and one. Agreed?'

'Agreed.'

It had stopped snowing. We gathered our silk scarves and locking the door behind us made our way through the yard and into the castle grounds. At the centre of the complex where all the gravel paths converged, the Lion's Fountain was strangely silent, the familiar plane of water reduced to an ugly blob of ice that hung like mucus from the creature's stone muzzle. We lit up in the safety of its shadow as I went through the itinery a final time.

'Now I've arranged for Conway to meet us outside the tradesman's entrance at eleven forty so we've a few hours yet. Let's try and stick together but if for any reason we get separated, I'll see you in the Great Hall at half past.'

'Eleven thirty rendezvous it is' replied Tom waving out a match. 'The important thing is we get round as many people as possible and establish the alibi. Also better watch the booze. A bloke can only get drunk once in a day and there'll be time enough when we get back.'

'That's assuming we get back at all' I laughed nervously.

Tom cupped a hand and took a deep drag, his face briefly lit up in the glow.

'Indeed,' he exhaled 'assuming we get back at all. But seriously Edmund, failure aint an option here because if we get caught we've absolutely had it – we're history. The only thing that stops me from wetting myself is to look at the task like a military operation, namely we go in and grab what we came for as quickly as possible, and then get the hell out and back to the party before anyone notices we've gone.'

We continued to fine-tune our strategy as we crunched over the snow. In the distance the drop off area was churning with traffic like Elvet Bridge on market day. Tom bent down and scooped up a handful of snow.

'Are you sure you've got everything?'

'It's all in the bag' I replied.

Tom lobbed his snowball into the air and booted it to smithereens.

'Excellent. Let the party commence.'

We passed from the gardens and joined the long queue of guests snaking their way under the keep. I have to say even before we reached the courtyard the setting was awesome. Although the night was as black as pitch, down in the valley dozens of torches flared on either side of the driveway, their auburn light spilling out onto the snow and fashioning strange shadows that raced across the virgin swells of the surrounding parkland. The castle itself looked magnificent, the ancient blocks illuminated by a further line of torches that crackled all along the ridge of the dried up moat. These must have been tar or sulphur based because their angry glow seared right the way up and over the parapets, turning the windows into molten gold and bringing life to the wicked faces of the gargoyles as they scowled down from the battlements. In the courtyard, it was like York races as we shuffled forward in a hullabaloo of flush and anticipation, the gentlemen in their mess jackets and tails, the ladies oscillating in a sea of colour and fur coats, everybody hollering and laughing, everyone happy and excited.

Just inside the doorway I caught sight of the reception line, Lady Alanna at the front, then Julian, then Jane, the three of them bobbing and pecking like a row of pullets.

At the top of the steps we were challenged by the master of ceremonies, an ex-military type about forty who looked resplendent and not a little self-satisfied with his bright red coat and medal ribbons. There were another two doormen standing quietly in the shadows, hard as nails and more than ready to deal with any gate-crashes or troublemakers. I stole a quick glance at Tom whose expression confirmed he was thinking on the same lines. Not the type to cross.

'Good evening gentleman, my name is Captain Sparks and my colleagues and I are looking after security this evening. May I see your invitations please?'

I passed him mine and explained that Tom had been invited in place of my late father. Sparks raised an eyebrow and flashed a quick glance towards Lady Alanna who was engrossed in conversation with the local vicar. Fortunately Jane had been watching from the door and gave a little wave at which Sparks nodded and cleared his throat.

'Mr Edmund Bullick and Mr Thomas Brentnall.'

Lady Alanna immediately turned to greet us. She wore a long navy velvet dress with full length white arm gloves and looked positively radiant as she smiled and held out her hand. It was a surprise and a pleasure to see her looking so well because she must have had a great deal on her mind, but then I supposed irrespective of the alcohol, an attractive woman who was the centre of attention at her own party could be expected to light up like a beacon.

'Edmund, I'm so pleased you made it back in time. You look quite wonderful, your father would have been so proud. How did the examinations go?'

'Very well thank you ma'am. Lady Alanna with your leave may I introduce my friend and fellow scholar, Thomas Brentnall.'

Tom took a step forward and bowed. Lady Alanna shook his hand warmly.

'Welcome to Craven Castle Mr Brentnall. We've heard a great deal about you from Edmund and are delighted you could join us. Please now, go on in, both of you and have a wonderful evening.'

Julian's welcome was predictably cooler although it was satisfying to note we were all wearing the same attire. At least we'd called that much right.

'Edmund' he said curtly. 'Who's this?'

'Julian, may I introduce Thomas Brentnall, a friend of mine from College.'

Tom bowed as he shook Julian's hand.

'How d'ye do Lord Craven. Thank you so much for including me among your guests. It's an honour to be here.'

Julian seemed pleased to be addressed as 'Lord Craven' although his response was typically caustic.

'It's not me you have to thank Brentnall but my mother. I assure you I had nothing to do with it. However, since you're here I suppose you'd better come in.'

All the while Jane had been standing at the end of the line hopping up and down, waiting her turn. I scarcely recognised her. She looked so grown up I had to do a double take. She was wearing a bright red gown with ermine trim and with her hair tied up at the back in the French style, she could have been Marie Antoinette herself. It was a remarkable transformation for someone who spent half her time shifting muck in the stables.

'Edmund, *Blue* I'm so pleased you've come home, I've really missed you' she said excitedly. 'Tell me, how were the Oxbridge exams? Do you think you've done enough to get in?'

'I hope so' I replied. 'If not, then it certainly won't be for want of trying. But never mind me, what about you? Where did you get that dress? You look stunning Jane.'

'Oh, do you like it?' she replied with a little flourish. 'It's one of Mama's, it didn't fit me at first but I had Mrs Johnson take in the seam. She's such a sweetie. She said she had to do the same for Mama when she first wore it and it was no trouble. Mind you I had to stand still for ages with all these beastly pins holding it together but I'm so pleased we made the effort. I feel like one of those London debutantes at her coming out ball…'

Her voice trailed away as she suddenly noticed Tom.

'Oh Jane, I'm so sorry, please may I introduce Mr Brentnall, my best friend from College.'

Tom smiled and gave a small bow.

'How do you do Lady Jane. Thomas Brentnall. Edmund has told me all about you and I'm delighted to finally make your acquaintance.'

Jane gave a shy curtsy.

'Pleased to meet you Mr Brentnall'.

'Please, call me Tom.'

Jane held out her hand.

'How do you do then Tom' she replied softly. 'I'm Jane, Lord Craven's sister'

They looked at each other for a moment until the spell was broken by the Master of Ceremonies hollering down from the doorway.

'Ladies and gentlemen, please, move on down, you're holding up the queue, at the end there, move along please…'

I gave Tom a nudge.

'Look, we'd better do as the man says. Jane, come and find us when you can get away'.

'You can count on it' she cried after me. 'I shall insist on at least three dances so you'd better get loosened up.'

A magnificent Christmas tree stood in the centre of the Great Hall, every branch groaning with clusters of sweetmeats, almonds and raisins in papers. Tom eyed the silver star the top as he addressed me from the side of his mouth.

'She's gorgeous.'

'Who is?'

We peered back at the line where Jane was laughing and joking with a group of young officers who had just arrived.

'I thought you said she was just a kid.'

'But she is.'

'You're nuts' said Tom.

I turned again and realised where he was coming from.

'Look, never mind all that, we've got an alibi to sort. What say we have a nosey around?'

The party was well organised and considerable care had been taken to ensure everyone was spread over the ground floor. To avoid congestion in the Great Hall, the guests were quickly relieved of their coats and shown through to the drawing room where three large trestle tables had been set up in the middle, each supporting an enormous pyramid of crystal glasses. Alongside the first pyramid was a large pair of stepladders at the top of which Johnny Clifford was wrestling with a gigantic flagon of champagne. The bottle was so big he had to grip it in a headlock and as he leaned forwards to pour, the steps were wobbling so much it looked as if the whole lot would come crashing down, yet somehow he managed to prevail. It was an exact and skilful process and for sheer audacity, a performance well worthy of all the roars of encouragement and acclaim.

'Methuselah!' shouted Tom.

'What?' I assumed he was referring to Clifford. I'd not heard anyone call him that before.

'Methuselah. The champagne, it's a *Methuselah* Edmund. Eight bottles in one named after the biblical patriarch who supposedly lived to the age of 969. Who's the show off?'

'Who do you think?'

'Really? The big bad wolf himself?'

'Yep.'

At the foot of the steps Clifford held his arms aloft to milk the acclaim. It was pure theatre and he was instantly mobbed. Two or three beaming waiters began to dismantle the pyramid and transfer the now full glasses to a range of silver trays for further distribution.

'So that's Johnny Clifford. I tell you Edmund, give the guy his due, that was some party trick.'

'Certainly was, although he has other tricks in the box that you may find less engaging.'

'How so?' replied Tom without taking his eyes away from the action.

'Well discarding for a moment his propensity to take to the moor, he's the most horrible, terrible drunk. Truly he is. In fact, if he runs to form we might even get a demonstration later on.'

'I'll look forward to it' said Tom grabbing a couple of glasses from a passing waiter 'although being a foul drunk doesn't make him a killer.'

'No, it doesn't. Mind you Lord William probably thought the same. Cheers.'

Somewhere in the distance a band was tuning up so we trailed the source into the ballroom and merged with a host of other guests lining the wall. As soon as I laid eyes on the entertainment I could see this was no ordinary turn. Instead of the usual dance-orchestra ensemble there was a combination of brass, strings, piano and drums fronted by a dapper looking male vocalist in Eton boating costume supported by three African girls in national dress. I'd always loved my music and knew about the *ragtime* craze sweeping America, however the closest I'd been to the real thing was straining my ears to a twisted gramophone record I'd borrowed off Spangle. I'd never heard a live routine and while there had been a whisper in the village we could be in for something special, it never occurred to me that one of the top ragtime bands would venture this far north. Yet here they were, *Billy Murray and the Haydn Boys* right there in front of us in the Craven ballroom thrashing out this fabulous wall of noise with it's exhilarating, infectious beat.

I'd read in the society columns that the band had docked with *RMS Olympic* for a whirlwind tour of London and Brighton and that tickets to any of their performances were like gold dust. They must have been persuaded to break off their schedule especially although goodness knows what it had cost the family to lure them all the way up to Durham. As entertainers they were simply sensational, I'd never heard or seen anything like it and it would have been worth all the dressing up and preening to be within earshot let alone have a grandstand pitch. I remember as we leaned against the wall, they suddenly struck up a rendition of *Alexandra's Ragtime Band,* a melody I had not heard before but would come to know very well later in life. The effect on the guests was simply electric; there is no other way to describe it as the room exploded from the very first bar.

'Get in! This is tremendous' shouted Tom screwing up his eyes and clicking his fingers as he started jumping up and down. Nor were we the only ones intoxicated by what we were hearing. Within seconds the floor was packed with youngsters whooping and waving, leaping and spinning round as the older generation either backed off at the noise or stood aghast at the band and some of the dance moves.

As I gazed into the melee I was suddenly aware of Victoria. She was easily the most handsome woman in the room and knew it as she leaped about with a group of young men all vying with one another for her attention. She wore a strapless black sequin dress with a daringly short hem and taut black stockings that showed off every sinew of her beautiful long legs. Her pale arms were exposed to the shoulders and she wore neither rings nor jewellery except in her hair, which was tied up at the back and sparkled with studs of diamond. All the time I watched her she was laughing and singing, her eyes mostly closed as she danced without inhibition or care, totally locked into the music. She looked so fabulously beautiful, she moved as if the devil himself was in her step and I couldn't take my eyes from her.

'That's the girl isn't it?' shouted Tom who was still bobbing up and down with his eyes screwed up.

I could barely hear myself think above the noise.

'What?'

Tom cupped his hands into my ear.

'Don't come that with me mate' he shouted. 'You know exactly what'.

Youch. His voice was so loud it hurt my eardrum. I peeled away and jumped around in the throng for a few seconds.

'The girl haunts me' I shouted.

'She does what?' he yelled.

'She HAUNTS ME!'

There was a tap on my shoulder. I turned to see Jane standing there with her hands on her hips.

'Who's hunting?' she asked.

'What?'

'Hunting. I asked who's hunting, they're out tomorrow I think…oh, look never mind. Are you going to dance with me or what Edmund Bullick?'

'I'd be delighted to. Here Tom, can you hang onto my glass?'

Tom gave me a wink as I led Jane off to the floor.

'Right young lady you asked for it. Get ready to flap those joints and stick close to the boss!'

Jane threw her hands in the air and laughed.

'Ha! Whatever you say boss'.

Now my father always told me that if you're going to dance with a girl, never mind shirking around the borders, you take them smack bang right into the middle of the action. It was always sound advice although that evening I had another reason for being particular where we surfaced.

'Tell me about your friend' shouted Jane.

'Tom? He's my best pal from College. He lives in York. His family are chemists there.'

'He's very handsome don't you think?'

'No. He's a moose.'

Jane laughed.

'Well I like the look of him very much.'

'Hey young lady' I replied spinning her around 'let me tell you something. When a gentleman is dancing with a beautiful woman he's in no frame of mind to press the suit of another, especially if it's someone like moose face over there.'

We turned to the window where Tom was laughing and joking with a group of people I didn't know. He always had that knack of making friends easily. He must have seen us out the corner of his eye because he suddenly turned and pulled a face. Jane smiled and waved back as we danced on raucously, jumping up and down with the infectious refrain.

Oh let me take you by the hand,
Up to the man, up to the man,
Who's the leader of the band!
Who's the leader of the band!

It had been my intention to try and engage Victoria at the end of the first song but I didn't get the chance as the band played through and the numbers came thick and fast. Eventually she saw us, or rather she noticed Jane and shuffled over the floor until her little group were dancing alongside.

'Darling, I love the dress. Where did you find it?' she shouted.

'It's one of Mama's' yelled Jane although she was cut off mid-sentence as the song came to an abrupt end and everyone burst into applause.

'Lord, I need a rest' she said clapping her hands. 'Edmund, do you mind if we take a break? These shoes are killing me.'

'Of course not. Go and check on moose face will you and make sure he's behaving himself.'

Jane laughed then peeled away leaving me standing next to Victoria. It was now or never.

'Miss Clifford. It appears I've been abandoned. Will you do me the honour of dancing the next number with me?'

Victoria turned and looked straight through me.

'What, with you? Now?' she said, still catching her breath.

'With me' I replied. 'Now.'

In the distance Billy Murray was introducing each member of the band. The floor was still packed, everyone coiled like springs waiting for the next song.

'You know you want to' I said quietly.

Victoria burst out laughing bringing her hand to her face as if she hadn't meant to. A few people turned and glared at her for a moment before switching their attention back to Murray.

'Well?'

Victoria gave a little sigh and scanned the room until her dark eyes rested upon my own. She turned to the others she had been dancing with.

'Would you excuse me for a moment? Would you mind awfully? This gentleman and I have some unfinished business. We shan't be long.'

Her little group didn't seem very happy but she had left them with no option but to trudge away.

'Well *Horse Boy*' said she at length. 'Looks like it's just you and me.'

'Indeed it does Miss. And the name's Edmund.'

She looked at me and slowly mouthed the words *Horse Boy*. I was struggling to think of something droll to say back when Bill Murray came to the rescue.

'Ladies and gentlemen, we're going to slow things down a little bit with a beautiful number written by my old friend Gus Edwards. If you'd take your partners please and get ready for *By the Light of the Silvery Moon*. Ok fellahs, two three and in…'

Victoria reached for my hand and suddenly I was holding her as we moved in time to the music. I felt half the eyes of the room upon us, and flushed with rapture and desire. Victoria spoke first.

'Jane tells me you're famed for your party trick of leaping onto the mantelpiece from a standing jump. Will you show me later?'

'I don't think so Miss'.

'Oh come on. Why ever not?'

'It's not my party. If you don't mind me saying so Miss, I think you are the most beautiful woman I have ever seen.'

Victoria tossed her head back and laughed.

'Oh no, not you as well'.

'Yes, me as well. Put me down if you must but you are beautiful, and if I don't say this to you now, I may never get another chance.'

We swayed for a minute or so until Victoria broke the silence.

'Look, I'll cut to the quick. You're wasting your time. I only danced with you so I could get rid of those Oxford creeps who won't leave me alone. If there's one thing I abhor, it's hangers on with two left feet. Yak!'

'Charmed, I'm sure'.

Victoria leaned forward so she could speak into my ear. I caught the scent of her perfume, it was as fragrant as May blossom.

'Charmed or not I'm just saying how it is so you know where you stand. Let me tell you something. There's a young Guards officer over there in the bright red mess suit. You'll catch him on the next turn staring at me. That's Roland, or rather the right honourable Roland, a cousin of the Earl of

Faversham and heir to half of Bilsdale. He's madly in love with me and would propose this evening if I gave him enough encouragement. There are other illustrious young men in this room and believe me I could have any one of them, any single one if I wanted to but instead, I choose to dance with you *Horse Boy*, do you want to know why?'

I looked at my partner for a moment, her beautiful black eyes mocking me in the candlelight.

'I thought it was *me* who asked *you* to dance but anyhow, let me guess' I replied, drawing her a little closer. 'Is it because you find me utterly irresistible and you cannot help yourself?'

'Hah!' she retorted pushing herself back. 'As if. The reason I say you're wasting your time is because nice lad or not, you're too poor and irrelevant for me to take seriously. Oh come on, don't look so crestfallen, you know it's the truth. You had the nerve to ask me to dance and to tell me I'm beautiful and I like that, I really do. I appreciate men who say what's on their mind which is why you will find me just as frank. No, I'm dancing with you now because I want to make the rich boys jealous. Word has it you're the finest horseman on the estate, you certainly move well and that you allow me to use you in this way is because it is *you* who finds *me* utterly irresistible and you cannot help yourself. Please, you don't need to try and answer that because we both know it's true.'

We danced for a while in silence. What a cow. She had it all worked out, or at least she had me worked out to a tee. I was stung for sure but damned if I was going to show it.

'If you ever scratched the surface you would discover more in me than movement, I assure you.'

Victoria smiled sweetly.

'Perhaps,' she said, 'but I never shall. I saw the way you looked at me in church and later in the hotel, but I'm not interested. There's a gulf between us, you must see that. Your family is poor and more to the point, I don't like you in *that* way. Now please, put aside all this wooing nonsense and let's enjoy the music while we can. Dance your very best with me *Horse Boy*, it's the only time you will find yourself ahead of the field and able to savour the distress of the rich kids as I drive them wild.'

At this she moved closer and placing her cheek against mine, slowly folded her arms around my neck. An enormous pit opened up in my stomach like reverse homesickness, and I was helpless.

'Now dance with me' she whispered. 'Come now, I won't bite, put your arms around me and let's dance.'

Looking back I should have stood her up but I was intoxicated and couldn't bring myself to break away, as well she knew. Instead I surrendered to the bitch and placing my hands around her slim waist drew her closer to me so her sweet little voice chimed into my ear.

By the light,
Of the silvery moon,
I want to spoon,
To my honey I'll croon love's tune.
Honeymoon,
Your Silvery beams will bring love dreams,
We'll be cuddling soon,
By the silvery moon.

The bitter sweetness of holding her body against my own was inexpressible as for several minutes we glided in and out of the other couples, all the while her beautiful voice singing into my ear. I didn't bother to look for the host of hungry eyes upon her because I knew they were all out there, exactly as she had predicted. I just felt nauseous with longing and frustration until the end of the dance when there was nothing for it but to disengage and politely join in the applause, even though every sinew in my body was already craving her embrace. The feeling of loss that rushed through me was overpowering; it made me want to grab her in my arms there and then and tear away her dress and ravish her and the devil with the consequences. Instead, I had to linger at her side as I struggled for something to say.

Victoria gave a mock curtsy.

'I'm much obliged to you *Horse Boy*' she supposed as if she was addressing someone from the Gas Board. 'You dance very well.'

'I think you're wonderful Miss. Will you dance with me again before the end of the evening?'

'I might but I doubt it. I'm counting on Julian or my brother to come and rescue me long before then. Have you seen them anywhere?'

'In the bar.'

'Of course' said she 'although Julian will find his way to my side. He always does for he cannot help himself either.'

I took her hand and kissed it gallantly.

'In that case it only remains for me to thank you for your company Miss Victoria. It was a great pleasure to dance with you.'

'I don't doubt it' she answered coolly.

'Your humility does you no justice Miss.'

Feversham was hovering in the distance. Victoria crooked a little finger at him as she addressed me a final time.

'A cat may look at a queen *Horse Boy* but without money or connections he should keep to chasing mice. If you don't know that, then you don't know women.'

'You mean some women.'

Victoria put a finger to her lips.

'*Horse Boy*. Love will conquer most things but the commercial aspirations of a beautiful woman is not one of them. Your family are minions or hadn't you noticed? End of, I'm afraid.'

'Up yours.'

'You wish' she replied sweetly as her gaze rested on Faversham who was already striding over.

'I do wish it' I replied. 'I desire it above all things.'

Victoria turned and switched off her smile.

'*Horse boy*, we can never be together. Goodbye.'

I felt a surge of rage welling up inside me but we were no longer alone. For a brief moment I faltered exhaling in frustration as she slipped her fingers under Faversham's arm and whispered something in his ear that caused him to look me up and down and laugh. It made me want to smack him in the teeth, the prat. Another time maybe. For now there was nothing I could do but walk away exactly as she had intended. The bitch. Bugger, bugger, bugger.

Tom and Jane were bouncing across the floorboards, both of them laughing and clearly enjoying themselves. I tried to catch his eye but they were oblivious to anyone else so I left them to it and went for a wander. In the Great Hall under the tree I found Barnaby, Sample and Fenoughty surrounded by stable lads, all of them well into their cups.

'Whoa Edmund, you look quite the dapper young man' roared Barnaby with a huge grin. 'Have you broken the hearts of any fair maidens yet?'

'Not exactly'.

'But you're working on it hey lad?' boomed Sample with a friendly cuff on my shoulder which made the others holler even more.

'You could say that'.

'Did you hear that fellahs?' said Barnaby. 'We saw you in there dancing with Lady Victoria. Do you reckon you're in?'

They howled with laughter. His words were in such startling contrast to the warning I had received at the *County* that I figured he must be drunk, and resisted the temptation to say anything.

'Actually *Blue* boy, I'm glad you've come over' said Fenoughty draining his glass 'because we're taking the string out with the *Braes* tomorrow and I need my best riders. The snow's still a bit thick, but the horses are all whinnying in their boxes and kicking at the doors and I can't keep them in any longer. You up for it lad?'

At that precise moment I didn't really feel up for anything but at least it would blow away the cobwebs.

'Sure, why not? What time do you want me?'

'We're heading out at first light so come over about eight thirty. That's if you can haul yourself out of bed by then. Hah! The young 'uns today, they don't make them like they used to hey Barnaby?'

'They don't Henry' he replied jovially. 'When you and I were bucks we worked hard and played hard and ne'er would the twain meet, unless it were after a night out with the milk maids.'

The others roared with approval.

'That's settled then' I replied. 'I'll come straight on from the party.'

Everyone burst out laughing.

'Love it, love it, he talks a good talk this one' cried Sample slapping me across the shoulder as he grabbed a mug of ale from a passing tray.

'Aw don't be so hard on him man' bawled Fenoughty as he covered everyone with spittle. 'Hey young fellah, young fellah, you enjoy yourself while you can and we'll see you if we see you.'

Good grief Fenoughty. For a man who hardly ever spoke the transition was remarkable. I wondered what they'd been giving him. I opened my arms in supplication.

'Eight bells it is then gentlemen, white tie optional.'

This provoked yet more hilarity and another shower of spittle from Fenoughty.

'He wouldn't be the first jockey heading out in coat and tails would he lads? Remember the Zetland Ball in '89 when young Willie Manners and that friend of his Edward, -what was he called- Dorkin, that's it, Eddie Dorkin, when young Willie Manners and Eddie Dorkin raced to the top of the moor and back at midnight?'

They were clearly drunk and not being on the same frequency I mumbled an excuse about getting something to eat and drifted through to the library. The room was just as we had left it, absolutely heaving with the new Lord Craven and Johnny Clifford still holding court at the champagne bar. I passed the time with one or two of the servants as they zipped about like hornets in their black and gold tunics. They were clearly enjoying the party as much as the guests and with one of them, Marley he was called, also a huge fan of ragtime, we conversed in snatches until his duties finally carried him away.

'Hello Edmund, I trust you're enjoying yourself?'

I turned to find Lady Alanna smiling behind me, her skin radiant in the firelight.

'I am indeed ma'am. This is a most excellent party. The band are superb.'

'Yes, so I gather, they're causing quite a stir by the sound of it. The only disappointing thing is no one has asked me to the floor, at least not yet, and it's my party. Well of course it's not actually *my* party, it's obviously Julian's but all his friends seem to think I'm out of bounds which is ridiculous. I do so want to take a closer look at the musicians. Would you do me a great favour and dance with me Edmund so I have an excuse to go through?'

'But of course ma'am, I'd be delighted. This way.'

'Well thank you kindly young man.'

Lady Alanna gripped my arm and we headed back to the ballroom crossing through the Great Hall where Barnaby, Fenoughty and the others were still laughing and carrying on by the tree. From the crook of my eye I fancied I caught Barnaby watching us a bit strangely although I didn't think anything of it at the time. Back inside the ballroom it was now roasting hot, the atmosphere highly charged with the slog and sweat that was ever the hallmark of a good party.

Lady Alanna was a wonderful dancer. Although she no longer moved with the vivacity of youth she was elegant and had style and I found myself enjoying our little dalliance very much. After a few numbers she began to let herself go a bit and as she laughed and crooned to the music it was not difficult to imagine the allurement that first drew in Lord William all those years ago. All the while Victoria was strutting up and down in the background, laughing and teasing. I tried my best to look away but my partner was nothing if not astute.

'She's very beautiful don't you think?'

'Who is?'

'Really? Can you not guess?' she asked then looking over to the girl in question. 'I do so wish Julian would get a move on. It's high time we secured the succession.'

So it was true. They were earmarked for one another.

'Grandchildren my lady? But you're still a young woman!'

Lady Alanna burst out laughing.

'You make my night Edmund Bullick, you really do.'

Alanna lifted her arms above her head waving at the ceiling before dropping them around my neck.

'Do you know, you're such a charmer *Blue* boy' she said with a faint slur 'the way you melt the girls and mould them to your design, and you don't even know it.'

'I wouldn't say that my lady.'

'No, really, it's true. Here, let me give you some advice.'

'What might that be my lady?' I asked frivolously. I wasn't sure where this was heading.

Lady Alanna suddenly stopped dancing and gripped my shoulders. It happened so quickly there was no time to feel uncomfortable.

'Savour your youth' she said shaking me. 'Savour it Edmund, and make use of its gifts. Don't be like me. When I look back now it's not the things I did that I regret, it's the things I didn't do. It's all the things that might have been. Don't make the same mistake.'

This was getting a bit heavy. One or two people were nudging each other and beginning to look in our direction.

'You're starting to embarrass me my lady'.

'If I was twenty years younger that would be the least of your worries, I assure you.'

Yikes. I hoped no one else heard that. She didn't look that drunk but then the wiliest drunks never do; it's only when they speak that the mask slips. I was rescued by a tap on my shoulder. I hadn't noticed Barnaby come into the room but I saw the expression on Lady Alanna's face soften and was more than happy to give way.

'Oh oh. This looks like a gentleman's excuse me' I said 'but thank you for your time my Lady, I think you're the most wonderful dancer.'

Lady Alanna beamed back as she reached for the hand of her new partner.

'Flattery will get you nowhere young man' she smiled over her shoulder 'but thank you for the compliment just the same and remember what I told you'.

I left them to it. I hadn't expected her company to be so intense and it was a relief to get away. Was *everyone* at the ball drunk? It certainly looked that way. Or perhaps I noticed it more because I was sober. Same thing really. I checked my watch. Ten to eleven. I made a beeline for the buffet. I was not hungry but I wanted to dislodge a stack of plates so people would remember me being there. I even assisted with the clearing up in the knowledge that the servants would be the first port of call if anyone started asking questions. Eleven twenty six. I excused myself and headed for the tree where I found Tom nonchalantly smoking a cigarette.

'We about set?'

'Affirmative. Conway's at the back.'

'Meet you there in five.'

Tom stubbed his cigarette into the bucket and made for the front door. I waited until he had disappeared then headed for the men's cloakroom before veering off into the staff wing. There was some shouting coming from the kitchens but the corridor leading to the back was deserted. I made my way to the end then checking there was no one about, quietly opened the door and slipped into the courtyard. A dark green hackney cab was ticking over in front of me. I recognised Tom's silhouette in the back and jumped in. Conway twisted around.

'All set?'

'Where's the holdall?' I asked.

'Under the driver's seat.'

I reached down. It was there.

'Right. Let's go.'

CHAPTER EIGHTEEN

Tom and I stooped down to keep out of sight as the taxi crunched into gear. I heard Conway squeeze the hooter and swear at some pedestrians but within a minute or so we had rumbled over the cattle grid and began picking up speed.

'All clear.'

We sprang back up. In the rear window the castle was rapidly disappearing from view. In front of us there was nothing but darkness. I tipped out the contents of the holdall. A small *Ever Ready* flashlight. Six inch nail. Two black sweaters. Two army surplus balaclavas. Tom started to remove his jacket then noticed the tin whistle.

'What on earth do you want with that?'

'Let's just call it insurance. I'm hoping we won't need it at all.'

We hit the outskirts of Durham at a quarter to midnight. The roads were empty and there were few people about. At Dryburn Conway slowed down and we made a pass of the hospital. The building was in complete darkness, the only sheen coming from the broken slates glowing eerily in the moonlight. Conway drove on for half a minute then pulled up under a large beech tree.

'Ok fellahs, we meet back here at twenty past. If you're not around I'll do a sweep every five minutes but if there's no show by twelve forty, I'll assume the worst and you're not coming. Good luck.'

We watched from the shadows as Conway trundled off into the night, the taxi climbing through the gears until the drone of the engine disappeared altogether. Suddenly we were very alone. Tom dipped into his pocket and pulled out the balaclavas, the coldness of the night riding on his breath.

'You ready?"

'If it were to be done then 'twere well it were done quickly.'

'Macbeth?'

'Aye.'

We crossed the road in single file keeping clear of the flickering street lamps. At the hospital entrance the wrought iron gates were closed but surprisingly there was no chain or lock. I flipped the latch and unfastened one side just far enough for us to slip through before quietly closing the gate behind me. We hurried through the gardens until we reached the milky stone wall that marked the boundary of the mortuary yard. Tom scrambled to the ridge and hauled me alongside. Not a soul in sight. We lowered ourselves from the coping stones and dropped silently down. Tom wiped the grime from his hands.

'Okay?' he whispered.

'Lead on.'

The mortuary building waited in darkness at the far end of the yard. When we reached the wall I gave Tom a leg up and he pulled me onto the roof where we rested for a moment to catch our breath. The asphalt was completely covered by a lake of frozen snow that sparkled like mother of pearl and crunched to the touch. In the centre of the roof was the unmistakable hump of the skylight. I looked around warily. The building was in total darkness. Shit, it was cold. I strained my ears. Somewhere far off a dog was barking but otherwise it was deathly quiet. We clambered on all fours to the skylight and wiped away the snow. The bulbous glass and frame were thick with ice and the unit looked worryingly secure. I bent down and gave it a shunt just the same but it didn't budge. I looked at Tom who was pointing to his feet. Immediately I understood and we crouched back on our haunches placing our soles against the rim as Tom held up three fingers and mouthed the countdown. When he reached the word 'two' I screwed up my eyes and pressed against the wooden frame for all I was worth. No movement. I pushed again, harder this time but again, nothing. I took my feet away and paused for breath.

'We can't stop now,' panted Tom. 'Again, come on, *harder*. We can do this. Come on. Three, two, one…'

We repeated the process, this time consumed by an urgency that harnessed every bone, every tendon and muscle to the task. Suddenly there was an earsplitting crack as the skylight flew off its mountings and jumped several feet across the roof. I almost died with fright. Crikey, that was loud. We held our breath and steeled ourselves for the inevitable commotion but there was none. I scanned the facade of the hospital and the neighbouring cottages expecting all the lights to come on, but not a curtain rippled. We were riding the devil's luck. I stared at our handiwork. A dark vortex had opened up in the roof where the skylight had been. It was no time for faint hearts. Please God, don't let my courage fail me now. I shuffled to the edge and dropped into the void.

CHAPTER NINETEEN

I landed with a crash against some kind of trolley and instinctively assumed the foetal position as several pathologists' tools and kidney dishes went flying across the floor. The noise was ear-piercing in the stillness but thankfully, it was short-lived. I reached into my pocket and fumbled for the torch as Tom landed beside me in a shower of ice crystal.

'What the hell was that?' he whispered.

I placed a finger to my lips as I fought the noxious reek of embalming fluid and decay. This godforsaken place was every bit as hideous as I had remembered it. I passed the flashlight to Tom who began to mow our surroundings. It was a harrowing spectacle, the beam cutting from one silhouette to the next, each sweep casting wicked shadows that rose and fell on the tiled walls of the chamber. We were in the company of the dead; they were laid out before us, the projecting feet confirming that all the slabs were taken, all, that is, apart from one at the far end of the chamber where the sheet was as flat as a millpond.

'The office. Where is it?' whispered Tom.

I pointed to the back wall. Tom followed with the flashlight then turned round and swept the beam over the tables.

'Now, don't go away you lot.'

How could he make a crack at a time like this?

We tiptoed to the dividing door. It was the moment of truth. If this were bolted we would go no further. I turned the handle and pushed. It held fast. Damn. I tried again this time forcing my shoulder against the iron bulkhead. I sensed a slight movement. I tried again, more weight now. The heavy door swayed open an inch or so then quickly slammed shut almost trapping my fingers.

'It's not locked but there's something on the other side holding us back,' I whispered. Tom gave it a push with the same result.

'The curtain. You said there was a curtain. This must be what's stopping it. Here, try again but do it gradually, slowly build the pressure then when I say, give it everything you've got.'

It worked. The door suddenly burst open bringing the curtain, the rail, and a large chunk of plaster crashing down on the other side.

A murmur of unease rippled down the cells.

'Who's there?'

We froze in the shadows. Outside, the Cathedral bells started to chime midnight as with a whir of cogs the clock on the wall followed suit.

'Who's there?' wailed a little voice in the darkness.

I instinctively made a soft 'shhh' noise. It dampened the appeals but not for long.

'Who's there? Who is it?'

'Have you come to take me home?'

'You out there in the dark. Show yourself.'

Suddenly the whole wing resonated with the clatter of chains and springs as the patients began to climb out of their cells. Somewhere in the darkness the tortured youth began to thrash about on his mattress.

'Kill, kill, kill, kill, kill…'

It was no time for stealth.

'Tom, quickly, get to the end of the passage and fix that bloody door while I grab the file.'

Tom raced off as I frantically began pulling at the filing cabinets. Where was it? Where? It had to be here somewhere. I flew from draw to draw ignoring a large pile of documents that fell on top of me from an overhanging shelf. Come on you bugger, where are you?

'It won't lock!' yelled Tom.

'The nail,' I shouted. 'Use the nail and wedge the keyhole.'

I clawed away furiously running the torch over the top of the files with one hand as I raced through the names with the thumb and forefinger of the other. There were six cabinets and many folders to get through but the documentation was filed chronologically and I made sharp work of it. In the top draw of the third cabinet I suddenly found what I was looking for and bellowed to Tom who was crouching by the door with his own torch.

'I've got it.'

Tom turned and raced towards me but had only covered a few feet when something tripped him and he measured his length in the corridor. Immediately, several figures leaped out of the shadows and a violent struggle ensued.

'Edmund!'

I raced down the passage and neutralised the first attacker with a boot in the stomach but as I reached for the hair of the second, someone sank their teeth into the top of my leg. I lashed out with my feet, screaming in shock and pain as Tom gripped my assailant around the neck and pulled her away. As we struggled to force our way through, other patients came out of their cells blocking the way back to the office. They must have broken the shackles in their desperation to get at us and now we were surrounded. I ran my torch over the haggard faces of the filth encrusted wretches who were screaming at us. This wasn't supposed to happen. Everyone was supposed to be secured with some type of galley chain. How did we come to be in this dreadful place? I cursed Tench. If only he'd let me see the file. But it was all too late now. The patients' obscenities rose to a crescendo as if Beelzebub himself was scoring them. Tom raised his fists as they began to close in.

'Come on then, come on!' he yelled.

In desperation I reached for my pocket and took out Alfie's tin whistle. I was no maestro but I knew where 'C' was and earlier that week I'd made a point of learning the first seven notes of *Twinkle Twinkle Little Star*. The effect was extraordinary and if I hadn't been there to see it with my own eyes I would never have believed what happened. Immediately all the screaming stopped, it didn't just die down, it ceased altogether as the patients suddenly looked to each other and then at Tom and I.

'Sweety time?' asked a young woman excitedly. A one eyed man repeated the phrase, then someone else until the chanting was embraced by all as if it was the overture of some ghastly opera.

'It is sweety time,' I said 'but only if you stop screaming and go back to your cells and wait. We have plenty of sweets. Go now and we will be round to see everyone in a minute.'

Again, if I hadn't seen it with my own eyes I would never have believed it but incredibly the patients started to go back to their cells. Not everyone at first, a few lingered for a while but gradually they too drifted away and the passage was clear.

Suddenly there were raised voices in the corridor.

'We've got company,' whispered Tom.

Even as he spoke there was the sound of a key in the lock.

'Let's get out of here!'

We tore down the corridor and back through into the morgue. As I looked over my shoulder I saw the patients crowding the far entrance as if waiting for the nurses.

'It won't hold for long' said Tom 'one good shove with the key and the spike will be out.'

The words had barely left his lips when the door swung open and three people tumbled into the wing. Two were night watchmen I had not seen before. The other was Sergeant Tench in his dressing gown.

'Run for it.'

I shut the connecting door and raced to the skylight where Tom climbed on my shoulders and hauled himself up. There was shouting and swearing coming from the passageway.

'Quickly, quick Ed, give me your hand.'

Someone was fumbling the handle of the connecting door.

'There's no time,' I whispered. 'I'm going to have to hide. Pull the skylight back. Hurry man. I'll give three flashes when it's clear.'

I dashed to the far end of the morgue desperately looking for somewhere to hide. Think Bullick think. I could hear

Tom stamping about on the roof and winced at the dreadful grating sound as the skylight was dragged back into place. The voices in the office grew more animated. Any second now they would be coming through. Think Bullick think. There was nothing else for it. I dived onto the empty slab opening a tiny crevice in the shroud so I could see out.

I was just in time. Seconds later the connecting door opened on Sergeant Tench, flashlight in one hand, truncheon in the other. Now I was for it. I dissolved into the table. Got to keep still. Tench took a few steps forward then ran his beam in a slow arc across the chamber. I pressed my cheek into the cold marble. A shiver ran down the back of my neck. Don't move Edmund. You have to keep still.

'Come on out. I know you're in here.'

I remained completely motionless, hardly daring to draw breath. The policeman's torch was powerful and as it flashed over the enamel walls, the mortuary filled with an eerie glow.

'This is your last chance. Come on out now,' he ordered.

I cursed all the bravado back in Tom's room when we decided upon such a perilous venture. If I were discovered in this awful place I would never be able to explain myself because no one would understand or believe me. Instead I would pay for my sacrilege with a prison sentence, vilified by everyone who knew me; it would destroy my Oxbridge aspirations and bring shame to the College and above all disgrace to my younger brother and the family name. No wonder Conway had been so meticulous in keeping himself out. I thought about the party back at Craven and wished to hell we'd never left it.

Tench took a pace forward, slowly probing each ghastly figure as he swept down the line. There was nothing I could do but melt under the shroud and keep as still as a church mouse. Suddenly, the beam was on the floor below and when it danced over me I swear I almost vomited with fear. Had I been seen? Silence. Was he about to charge across? It appeared not, although any sense of relief abruptly turned to dread as Tench marched to the nearest table and threw back the cover. In the half-light it was difficult to be certain but it looked as though he was standing over the body of a middle aged woman. Tench brought the torch up against the bleached face then having waited for a few seconds, suddenly raised his truncheon and slammed it down on the torso of the corpse. I was utterly appalled. What was he thinking of? Making sure they were dead? The hobnailed boots grinded over to the next table where the bone crunching process was repeated, and then on to the third and then the fourth. It would be my turn next. I couldn't even make a run for it. There was nowhere to go. Oh please God, please, please help me.

Just then a head poked through the connecting door.

'You in here Sergeant?'

Tench almost jumped out of his skin.

'Whooaahh! For fucks sake man! What d'ye think you're doing creeping up on me like that!'

'Sorry Mr Tench, I didn't mean to scare you. Just letting you know the patients are all accounted for and we're locking them back in the cells. You couldn't give us a hand could you?'

'All of them? Are you sure? I could have sworn I heard someone rattling around in here a couple of minutes ago.'

The other laughed dubiously.

'What, in the mortuary? Don't be daft man.'

Tench scratched his head.

'But I heard something. I know I did.'

'What, as in *goulies and ghosties* and things that go bump in the night? If you ask me you need a holiday.'

Tench swept the morgue a final time then switched off the torch.

'Aye, perhaps you're right. Anyhow what happened back there?'

'Looks like some of them were expecting *Mrs Winslow* and the rest kicked off in sympathy. One or two have been scrapping but there's no serious injury. Mind you, they've wrecked the office and torn the chain out the wall so we're having to lock individual grates. I'll send for the stonemason tomorrow to fix the rings…'

The voices trailed away as the heavy iron door clanged shut leaving the morgue in darkness. This time the bolt on the far side was drawn and the second it clicked into place I leaped from under the shroud and raced to the skylight. At the agreed signal the giant dome growled to one side leaving Tom peering down from the gap.

'Shit mate, I thought you were done for. Are you okay?'

'I think so. Just get me out of here before I go mad.'

I passed up the file then Tom hauled me onto the roof where I almost burst into tears with relief. The air was so fresh, so clear, I felt like the condemned man who had been reprieved on the scaffold.

We were not out of the woods but having come this far I was damned if anyone was going to catch us now. We heaved back the skylight and within a minute or so had traversed the courtyard and vaulted back over the wall. Three more and we were crouched in the shadow of the tree back where we'd started. Had we been followed? I stared anxiously down the road. A few windows in the hospital were now lit but the street between us was clear. Against all the odds it looked like we might have got away with it.

'Someone's coming,' whispered Tom.

I strained my eyes to the bottom of the hill where the goggle lamps of a motor vehicle loomed out of the mist. A Taxi! It had to be him. We walked towards the city pretending to take no notice until the vehicle ground to a halt on the other side of the road. Conway pulled back the window.

'Taxi gentlemen?'

We scampered over the road as fast as whippets and jumped into the back. Oh sanctuary, blessed sanctuary. I locked the doors as Conway chewed through the gears and Tom lit a couple of cigarettes. For a while no one said anything until our driver spoke into the mirror.

'Well chaps. How did we get on?'

Tom and I looked impishly at each other then bringing our faces together both let out a tremendous scream.

CHAPTER TWENTY

Conway wasted no time getting back and as he flew through the castle gates, Tom and I hunched down again to keep out of sight. I felt the shudder of the grid and familiar munch of gravel.

'Anyone about?'

'Loads. Somebody just tried to wave me down. He's probably my fare,' said Conway checking his watch. 'I'm late but that's too bad. Believe me, it's normally the other way round with us trying to shoehorn people out.'

Conway swung into the stables and yanked on the brake.

'You can sit up now guys; this is the end of the line. I only hope it was worth it.'

'Amen to that,' I said. 'What do we owe you?'

'Don't be ridiculous.'

'I insist. You can't drive all that way for nothing.'

'Honestly, I don't want anything. I really don't. I was just pleased to atone for that day in the theatre.'

'Well if that's how you want it, I'm not going to argue. Let me just say I can't thank you enough Conway, I really can't.'

Conway laughed.

'Glad I could help. Maybe one day you'll tell me about it although from what I saw in that bag I'm not sure if I really want to know. Anyhow can't hang about, there's an angry man at the front wanting a lift home. Goodnight lads.'

We jumped out and went into the house. As ever Domino was overjoyed to see us and while Tom took him for a quick wander in the garden, I locked the file in the safe and stuffed the bag of clothes into the kitchen stove topping the flames with a large shovel of coal. That would do the trick. I checked my watch. Twelve forty. We'd been gone just over the hour. I dropped the key into the Gimcrack Cup and after a quick conference by the Lion's fountain, Tom and I slipped back into the castle the same way as we had left.

We reconvened at the Christmas tree. The party was in full swing. A few of the older guests had retired but there were still hordes of people stumbling around with most of the gentlemen having taken off their jackets. I poked my head into the ballroom where the band were still playing like demons. Jane was nowhere in sight but Victoria was dancing as evocatively as ever, this time with Julian who was shuffling awkwardly beside her. Victoria looked incredible. Her brow was drenched and her long hair tangled from exertion but she was still amazing. Suddenly she opened her eyes and catching me staring at her, blew a sarcastic kiss. Damn it. I was about to go across and say something when I felt a paw on my shoulder and turned to see Tom pointing a finger at the ceiling.

'Drink?'

We made straight for the library where we fought our way to front of the queue and demolished a couple of mugs of ale. We then ordered a couple more and set up camp by the trestle tables where the champagne glasses had been.

Two of the towers had completely disappeared but the third was virtually intact. I checked our surroundings. The room was absolutely chock-a-block, the men, as ever, congregated by the supply of alcohol while the ladies gossiped in the background. In the far corner a mound of people were gathered around a white grand piano murdering *I'm Henery the eighth I am I am*. It was a dreadful racket, it really was but a few more drinks and I knew I'd have been straight in there. Tom removed his jacket and hung it on the back of the chair.

'You're trembling mate. Are you all right?'

'I think so. But shit Tom, when Tench was belting those corpses I nearly died. Talk about saved by the bell.'

'What would you have done if he'd pulled back your cover?'

'Filled my pants and then given up. I wasn't going to wait to be beaten. Who knows, if I'd sat up he might have run off in panic – you should have seen him jump when his mate called over from the door. It was class!'

We laughed like hyenas at the picture. When it came down to it, Tench had shown himself to be just as vulnerable as anyone else although it had been an incredibly close shave and we knew it.

'What now?'

I reached for my tankard and took a deep slug.

'We'll look at the file when we get back and take a view then. Judging by the thickness there's not a lot in there. I just hope after all we've gone through we're not about to be disappointed.'

Tom moved closer so no one could hear.

'We're going to piece this together you know. We've already recovered your father's last diary entry and of course there's your testimony about Lord William's last words.'

'True, but who's going to believe *that*?'

'You shouldn't underestimate yourself. I believe you and there's many others out there who will. The fact that he called you to his deathbed is irrefutable and while no one else heard what he said, what possible motive can you have for making the whole thing up?'

'Maybe out of spite because I detest Julian? Or perhaps because Lord William could be my real father?'

Tom nearly choked on his drink.

'What?'

A few people looked across to where we were standing. 'What?' he whispered.

'Oh, I don't know. He implied that he and my mother had been lovers. It happened back in Ireland before she met my father so the timings are wrong, or so it seems. If it's true it would certainly fit with Julian being a cuckoo and talk of changing the succession. Thing is we need more before we go to the authorities, you know we do. There has to be something else; there has to be although I don't know what, maybe a letter or document or something?'

Tom wiped some froth from his chin.

'Crake will know. In fact, Crake is the key to everything. When shall we pay him a visit?'

'I contacted his office yesterday. His clerk says he's tied up in some Admiralty case or other but is available next week. Can you stay until then?'

'Thanks for the offer but I ought to get home. I haven't seen my folks in a while and they're counting on me to lend a hand in the shop.'

'And I've still got a heap of my father's papers to sort through. How about we take a train to Hartlepool say, a week Tuesday afternoon?'

'Good idea. I can go straight from York and meet you in the town.'

'That's settled then. I'll wire his office first thing to confirm.' My eyes jumped to the door. 'Hang on; we'll talk about it later.' Jane had entered the library and was making a beeline over. Immediately behind her were Julian and Clifford.

'There you are Edmund. I'm sorry I've neglected you but mother was taken ill and I've been looking after her. She's asleep now thank goodness. I was beginning to worry I'd miss the rest of the dancing!'

There was barely time to acknowledge her before Julian cut rudely between us engulfing me in a waft of beer and cigar fumes.

'I want to know what my father said to you, you know, as he lay there dying in his bed, the poor sod.'

'Oh Julian for goodness sake not again, I've told you everything I know. I don't want to talk about it.'

I tried to walk away but Julian grabbed my lapels.

'Let me go Julian.'

The room suddenly went quiet. It was the *County* all over again.

'Not this time I won't, you lying little bumshit. What gave you the right to worm your way in there with him? I want the truth and you're either going to tell me or I'm going to drag you outside and belt the living daylights out of you.'

Tom leaped between us.

'Whoa whoa whoa. Come on now, Julian; he's already told you he doesn't know anything.'

Clifford, who had been observing proceedings stepped forward from the side-lines

'Stay out of this silly boy,' he mewed as he patted my friends' cheeks with the palms of his hands. Now I had seen someone do this to Tom before and I knew he didn't like it.

'I'd be obliged if you didn't do that,' said Tom.

Julian grabbed me by the collar and lifted me half off the ground. I began to struggle for breath.

'Come on, what did he tell you? I'm going to count to three…'

'For goodness sake' I cried hoarsely. 'Where's your dignity? You're showing yourself up in front of all your guests.'

Julian dropped me to the floor but before I could get out of the way he circled his enormous fat hands around my throat and began shaking me violently. This time I'd had enough and crashed my knee into his groin.

'Get *off* me …'

Julian released his grip, his eyes on stalks as he doubled up in pain. Some of the men started to jostle forward mumbling 'foul play' but I wasn't going to stand there and let him throttle me. Julian clambered to his feet and took a swing at me as Jane tried to pull him away.

'For goodness sake Julian, stop it, stop it.'

'You, stay out of this.'

'This is ridiculous,' said Tom. 'Come on. Enough's enough.'

Clifford leaned over and began tapping my friend's face again. 'Sonny, you're playing out of your league; be a good lad and go and sit down.'

Tom swatted Clifford's hands away.

'Look, I've asked you once as nicely as I can, don't do that; I won't be asking you again.'

'Is that right?' sneered Clifford. 'Or else what?'

The atmosphere immediately turned to menace as the ladies chewed their fingers and the men shuffled forward to get a better view. Clifford, who was in his element playing to the crowd, attempted to pat Tom again but as soon as he raised his hands, quick as lightening, Tom thumped him, once, hard in the face and Clifford crumpled to the floor. Immediately all hell broke loose. Julian attempted to head-butt Tom while myself, Jane, and others desperately tried get between them. At the same time Clifford staggered to his feet and recovering his bearings, let out a huge roar and charged into the melee whirling his arms like some kind of deranged beast. This was the cue for various factions, would-be peacemakers and screaming women to enter the fray, and it was only a matter of time before the indecorous, blaspheming tangle of humanity bumped into the trestle tables bringing down the surviving pyramid of champagne flutes.

The crash was so loud it would have been heard in Durham itself. It was certainly heard by Sparks and his men who raced through from the hall and started dragging people away. They had a job on their hands too because it was the classic free for all with men shouting, fists and furniture flying and women howling. Eventually, and with no small effort, Sparks and his colleagues restored some kind of order although even then, Clifford had to be restrained as he desperately tried to get at Tom.

'You, you're fucking dead, do you hear? I'm going to fucking kill you.'

Tom was leaning against the fireplace smoking a cigarette. His left eye was closed where someone had thumped him but

Clifford's nose was swollen and there was blood all down his front.

'You, you're fucking dead,' he shouted again, 'Do you hear?'

Tom blew a smoke ring.

'Fucking dead? Who, me old chap? Never felt better actually. Now if I were you I'd get that silk jacket of yours to the cleaners before all those nasty red marks set in.'

Clifford went purple as he struggled to break free, heaving and snorting like a rhinoceros, but Sparks and his colleagues were also strong and held him fast. Sparks turned to Julian.

'It's such a shame my lord. There's always a handful of idiots who ruin it for everyone else. What would you like us to do sir?'

'Throw them out.'

'What, this one here?'

'No, not him you fool. The one over there holding his eye and the other yob, this one here.'

'That's not fair,' said Jane, running up to her brother. 'Edmund and Tom aren't to blame. It was you and Johnny who started it.'

Julian pointed a finger at his sister.

'You, shut your mouth. I've already warned you about the company you keep.'

Jane brought her hands to her face and started to cry. 'Don't speak to her like that,' said Tom angrily.

'I'll talk to my sister and anyone else how I like. Now get out of my house before I have you thrown out.'

'Don't worry about it Jane,' I said. 'We were leaving anyway.' Julian pointed to the door.

'And don't come back in here Bullick, neither you nor that oik you brought here with you, not tonight, not ever. You'll be hearing from me later but the devil himself won't be able to rescue you from what's coming.'

'You should know all about that,' I replied.

Tom glowered at Julian. He looked set for another round until Jane cut in.

'It's all right Tom. I'll be fine. Really I will. Best if you leave like he says and I'll see you tomorrow.'

'Like hell you will,' snarled Julian.

The doormen were closing in. It was time to go. I put an arm round my friend and turned to Sparks.

'It's all right fellahs, we're leaving, we're leaving. Come on mate let's go home.'

CHAPTER TWENTY-ONE

'Are you ready?'
'Just a minute.'

Tom reached into his jacket and pulled the stopper from a litre of Croizet Grande Reserve. He took a long, deep swig then crashed the bottle on the table.

'Helped myself on the way out, didn't I?'

'Pass it over.'

I rubbed the top and wolfed a large mouthful. It felt like someone had dropped a red hot coal down my throat. When my eyes stopped watering I passed the bottle back and reached for the file.

It was a small binder with just a few sheets skewered through the top left hand corner. The first was a Medicine Log but the blank page testified only to the short time my father had been treated before he expired. I flicked over to an inventory of the patient's property. It was all there; boots, trousers, a felt shirt, tweed jacket, underclothes, a leather belt, socks, riding crop, a pocket watch, a leather pouch containing some loose change, his silver cross and gold wedding ring. There was a handwritten note in different coloured ink at the bottom confirming the nurses had to cut his boots off but otherwise nothing remarkable. I turned the page. The root document was the hospital admission sheet and this time there was plenty of information. I swept my finger down the margin. Name. Gender. Date of birth. Place of birth. Occupation. Religion. Marital Status. Address. Next of kin. It was all neatly written so he must have been conscious when they brought him in. The next section was multiple choice to record the patient's mental condition upon arrival. The options were *unconscious, semi-conscious, delirious, confused, semi-lucid, anxious* and *lucid*. The word *lucid* was circled. My father had been in control of his faculties.

In the next section a précis of his injuries recorded a severe head injury, a broken left femur and a suspected broken pelvis but that much I already knew. It was the last section titled *History* that I was looking for and I nearly fainted when I read it.

Patient claims Lord Cavendish has altered the succession and is in extreme danger. Patient rode to the moor to warn him but was challenged by monks at Friars Cross and unhorsed in the storm.

Oh my God. I fumbled for the brandy and took another draught. Tom snatched the file and scrambled through the pages.

'Holy shit,' he whispered. 'This was no accident. What does it mean though, challenged by monks? And what's Friars Cross?'

'It's a fork at the top of Hamsterley Moor. The monastery nearby was dissolved by Henry VIII but legend has it the ruins are haunted.'

'Haunted? It says here 'challenged by monks'. You say Lord William claimed Julian and Clifford were on the fell dressed as monks. Julian is many things but hardly a monk.'

'More to the point, how did they manage to be in London and Durham at the same time?'

Tom took another slug of brandy.

'How indeed? What is certain though is Lord William spoke the truth about changing the succession. He didn't just tell you, he must have told your father and this proves it. There's nothing more to be done for now except lock everything away until we see Crake next week. We have him Edmund. We have him.'

CHAPTER TWENTY TWO

I slept like a log that night. With the stress of the burglary, all the excitement of the party and the cognac I'd no sooner climbed between the sheets than it was morning again and Domino was baying in the hallway. I clambered out of bed and stumbled onto the landing.

'Hang on, hang on.'

The knocking continued louder than ever. I scuttled down the stairs and opened the door on one of the stable lads who looked me up and down with a mixture of trepidation and bewilderment.

'I'm sorry to bother you sir. Mr Fenoughty sent me to remind you the horses will be leaving in just over ten minutes.' I glanced at my watch. Quarter past eight. Damn, I'd promised I'd help with the riding out. I raced back upstairs, splashed my face with water and pulled on some clothes. Tom's sleepy voice drifted in through from the next room.

'What are you doing?'

'I promised Fenoughty I'd lend a hand with the string,' I said pulling on a shirt. 'We're taking them out with the *Braes.*'

'You must be mad. I'm going back to sleep.'

'What time's your train?'

'They run at half past the hour. I'll catch one later this morning.' I pulled on a pair of boots

'Right, I'll have to leave you to it. There's a few tradesmen kicking about who'll give you a lift into town. If you get stuck find Jordan, or if he can't take you ask Monmouth to call a cab.'

'But maybe not go too close to the castle hey?'

'Aye, maybe not too close although how much Julian and Clifford will want to remember about last night is open to debate.'

I grabbed a coat from my father's wardrobe and stuck my head round his door.

'I'll see you in Hartlepool next week. Wire me to confirm what time you're getting in.'

'Right you are,' said Tom, diving back under the blankets. 'Just make sure you keep that safe locked.'

'Don't worry, I will.'

I snatched a helmet and crop from the hall and ran over to the yard where the horses were already beginning to assemble. Fenoughty was by the trough inspecting the shoes of a large grey gelding.

'Ah, Edmund, you've decided to join us.'

'Sorry Mr Fenoughty,' I said, catching my breath, 'bit of a late one.'

'I don't doubt it young fellah, I don't doubt it. Anyhow the less said about last night the better.'

Fenoughty slapped the animal on the rump as he climbed off his stool. It seemed I wasn't the only one a bit green round the gills.

'Edmund, I'm putting you up on *Button*; he's a nine year old gelding, bit of a fruitcake but a sound jumper. Warm him up gradually in the park then when you meet the hunt, put him through his paces.'

Fenoughty gave me a leg up and I trotted off to join the others who were clattering around the yard. There were about twenty of us in all, most of the riders having been connected with the stable for years and those who were not known to me I recognised from the *County*. There were also two girls in the string. I'd been expecting Jane but not the other. Her face was turned away from me but the willowy form was the same that had first captivated me on that awful day at Saint Cuthbert's. Jane trotted over smiling broadly under her navy blue hunting cap.

'Well hello there Edmund Bullick. And how are we feeling today?'

'Fit as a fiddle,' I lied. 'What about yourself?'

Jane wheeled her charge alongside.

'I feel great although I wasn't sure after last night if you'd remember you promised to join us.'

'I didn't. Fenoughty had to send one of the lads over to fish me out of bed.'

There was a brief silence as Button dipped his head and neighed impatiently. Time to test the water.

'It was a terrific party, don't you think, notwithstanding the unfortunate little episode at the end? How's your brother?'

'I've not seen him this morning. He and Jonny didn't come to bed until a couple of hours ago although I expect they'll materialise in the pub later. Where's Tom?'

'Gone home. He's not seen his parents since we left college.'

Jane's horse stamped around for a moment, the crisp air blowing in and out of his nostrils.

'That's a shame although it's probably as well for now. They were still calling him every expletive imaginable long after you went home. Crazy when you think about it because it wasn't Tom's fault. Johnny can be a complete twit and had it coming to him so I wouldn't worry about it.'

'I'm not,' I replied.

'Can I tell you something in confidence?'

'Sure. Go ahead.'

'Your friend. I like him Edmund. Like I really *like* him if you know what I mean. I want to see him again although Julian's absolutely forbidden it and would go mad if he found out. Do you know when he's coming back?'

The lead horses were starting to move off. I flicked Button's reins.

'He's still at the house. If you hurry, you might just catch him.'

Jane said nothing but I could sense her mind working overtime as we trailed through the arch and out into the park. Somewhere behind me I could hear Victoria laughing but I conquered the temptation to look round.

'Where are we heading?' asked Jane. 'I thought everyone was going hunting.'

'Not everyone. Fenoughty wants to gallop the horses across the plain first. The snow will do them good because it offers resistance and forces them to pick up their feet. It also treats any inflammation of the joints and tendons. We'll work them for half an hour or so and then those who want to go hunting can join the Braes at the kennels while the rest can go home.'

We cut away from the drive and into the open meadows, the hooves of the animals falling strangely quiet as they left the gravel. The early morning air was wonderfully clear and for a while the only sound was the jangle of harnesses and crunching of snow beneath us. When we were well into the park Fenoughty gave the signal and broke into a canter and then a gallop, with the rest of us following on. It was a circular course of about three furlongs taking in a couple of brushwood jumps and a long downward slope towards the river which turned into a challenging uphill run on the return leg. The horses, who sensed what was coming, relished the workout, their ears were pricked and they didn't seem to notice the drifts although these were quite deep in places. The exercise also blew away my own cobwebs and as the wind rushed through my ears, I was glad I hadn't wasted the morning in bed.

After a couple of circuits Fenoughty called everybody into a large semi-circle. All the flat horses and young hurdlers were to return with him to the stables, the rest were free to join the Braes. I knew Jane had intended to go hunting but if she turned back now she would catch Tom before he left the house and sure enough, without saying anything to anyone she quietly slipped away. I was just mulling it over when Victoria suddenly drew alongside. In my resolve to ignore her that morning I'd not been keeping an eye on where she was.

'I'm off to the kennels,' she said casually. 'Are you joining us?'

I looked into those witches' eyes and without being able to help myself could only admire her splendid form. She was dressed in a close-fitting navy blue jacket with white hunting shirt and stock tie, beige chaps and jodhpurs. She wore knee length black leather boots with matching garter straps, silver spurs and in her gloved fingers she clutched a bone handled stalking whip. She was straddled across a magnificent dark steeplechaser, every inch a champion with at least two hands over Button. The animal must have been one of Lord William's last acquisitions because if it had been in the stable for any length of time I would have remembered it. I wondered how she'd managed to talk Fenoughty into putting her up. A sweep of those eyes no doubt.

'Well?' she said swishing her crop through the air a couple of times. 'Wakey, wakey *Horse Boy*. You coming along with us to the hunt?'

'What's it to you?'

Victoria patted her horse on the neck. Her complexion was surprisingly fresh. You'd never have guessed she had been up half the night.

'Still sulking from our little dance are we?'

I leaned forward and scratched Button behind the ear. My father told me horses loved the sensation and it helped to build up trust between animal and rider.

'Miss Clifford, you take great delight in teasing and mocking me. It seems it has been thus ever since we met. You behaved terribly to me last night, leading me on then insulting my family so as you ask, yes, I am still *sulking* if that's what you call it. Wouldn't you be?'

I pushed my heels into Button's midriff and trotted off to join the others. I heard Victoria click the roof of her mouth as her charge followed and moved back alongside.

'You seem to forget that it was you who came on to me; I never wanted or invited your advances. What did you expect me to do? Encourage you? Lie to you? Well?'

'Just forget it,' I said. If I could have thought of a slicker response I would have made it although deep down I knew she was right.

'No, I *won't* forget it,' she said harshly. 'It was you who came on to me with your *la-de-dahs* and when it was clear you wouldn't take no for an answer I responded in the only way I knew that would silence you.'

'And how's that? Oh, I get it, by humiliating me in front of Faversham and the others? The slow dancing and teasing, the cow eyes and sweet whispers in the ear? No doubt all part of your little game where you make up the rules as you go along. It must be so amusing messing with other people's emotions. Do you suppose I'm oblivious to your charms?'

'No, I supposed only to play you as you appeared. I would have expected at your age you would have had more experience of life which I concede was an error on my part. What do they teach you at that college of yours? Believe me *Horse Boy*; you have a great deal to learn about women.'

'I might lack understanding in the ways of *some* women I grant you, but heaven forbid any of my close acquaintance are so shallow as to live their life solely in pursuit of riches like you seem to.'

'Hah!' she replied with a toss of her head. 'Women are all the same or hadn't you noticed? They all crave money or rather they covet the freedom and security that money brings. They always have and they always will. It's certainly how things are where I come from; wealth and connections are king and from one generation to the next we forge alliances to preserve and consolidate our society. It's in the genes of us all and neither you nor I can do anything to change it.'

'It's the genes of greed and unhappiness more like.'

She did not answer and for a while we rode on in silence.

'Lady Alanna seems to think you're going to marry Julian,' I said presently. 'Are you?'

'Perhaps,' she replied tossing her head back disdainfully. 'I might, but then I might not. I'm not sure yet. He's certainly rich enough but then so are Faversham and a few of the others. I'll probably wait and see if there are any more declarations before I make up my mind.'

'Is that *all* you care about? Money? Is there no place in that shallow mind of yours for mutual respect, affection and love? What about passion and the unconditional yearning to want to look after another person and to make them happy? Is your heart so cold that you are immune to these things also?'

We had reached the kennels where the riders from the Braes were already circling round. I remember the sudden burst of colour with all the red jackets and the black and sandy coloured hounds standing out against the whiteness of the snow. Some of the riders were shouting over, urging us to hurry. A small crowd from the village had also gathered and were mingling between the horses. Victoria reached down and grabbed a drink from a passing salver.

'I'm no stranger to love and passion believe me, and, contrary to what you may think, my heart is anything but cold. However as I thought I'd made clear to you last night, I don't see *you*, I don't look at *you* in *that* way and I never shall. You're too poor for me, yes it's true but this is not just about money; it's much more fundamental. It's something neither of us can change and the reason we can never be together.'

Before I could reply the air was ripped by the blast of a hunting horn sending the hounds into a frenzy. As the bystanders rapidly dispersed, the Master turned and roared something I couldn't make out but its effect was immediate as the riders howled back in the same dialect and began to shuffle their mounts forward. Victoria tensed her grip on the reins. A look swept over her face I had not seen before, like a mixture of cruelty and wild excitement. She dug her spurs into the flank of her mount and turned scornfully.

'See you at the kill *Horse Boy*. That's if you ever get there on that pit pony of yours. Hahhh!'

I seared with rage. If I could have reached the girl I swear I would have put my hands around her neck and throttled her but she was already away. I shouted at Button and with a furious shake of the reins we tore off in pursuit.

There must be something aboriginal to account for the thrill of hunting; perhaps it's a legacy from Neanderthal times and the lionisation of those who brought home sustenance for the community, either that or the anticipation of the kill. I'd been brought up with the baying of hounds and always revelled in the chase although on this occasion more than ever, I was determined to overtake my quarry. Button was no pit pony. He may not have been as powerful as Victoria's mount but he had a decent stride and I was able to keep tabs on her as the field strung out across the park.

We would have been galloping for about a mile when over on a small hillock to the right, a fox suddenly broke cover and made a dash for the woods.

'Halloo! Halloo!' screamed the master.

The kill was on. Suddenly all hell was let loose as to a profane discord of howling and horns Victoria and the others ahead of me swung off line drawing the cruel, merciless pack in their wake.

This was my chance. I yelled at Button and pulling the reins to cut the apex, rode like fury to head the fox off before he reached the safety of the thicket. In the end it was a close run thing. I thought I was about to succeed and very nearly did but Reynard was nothing if not cute and when I reached the boundary, it was just in time to see him look over his shoulder and slip underneath the hedge. As I cursed our luck, Victoria and the others arrived on the scene hotly pursued by the hounds who thundered through the gap and into the forest.

The Master smacked his thigh in frustration.

'Damn it. The jammy rascal, I was sure we'd got him.' Victoria rode forward and inspected the hedge, her face glowing with the exercise.

'You're not going to give up are you?' she panted. 'Come on, we have to get after them if we want to be in at the kill.'

'The privet is too high miss,' said the Master.

'Nonsense,' cried Victoria wheeling her charge round. 'We can clear that surely?'

'Maybe we can miss but there's barbed wire in the hedgerow and it's too dangerous for the horses. Mr Fenoughty would not want you to risk your charge Miss. We'd best crack on. There'll be other foxes. This one's going to ground.'

'Not if we catch him first he's not. Come on. What's wrong with you all? I'm going after him. Hahhh!'

Before anyone could stop her Victoria sailed over the hedge, her gelding disappearing into the wood with a scissor kick of the hind quarters. The Master was furious.

'That bloody woman. For goodness sake someone, bring her back before she kills herself or worse still injures the horse.'

'I'll go,' I said and swung Button round. The hedge was solid blackthorn and must have been over five feet but there was no time for second thoughts as it suddenly loomed in front of us. Fenoughty had assured me my mount could jump and to my immense relief we brushed through the top of the foliage before landing heavily on the other side. I pulled Button to a standstill and leaned forward to cradle his neck.

'You're a good boy,' I whispered.

Inside the forest it was strangely quiet. Somewhere far off the hounds were baying but as I broke into a gentle trot, there was only the rustle of foliage and snapping of twigs to feather the silence. I shouted her name. Nothing. I cried again, this time at the top of my voice. Nothing. Not even the palest echo. Just silence. It was as if the very trees had closed in and were sucking away every tortious syllable. I looked to the carpet of rusty bracken. A light covering of snow had somehow made its way through the crown of evergreens and a few hoof prints were visible. I patted Button's neck and followed the tracks deeper and deeper into the plantation, all the while calling her name. Suddenly, in the distance, I saw her riderless gelding standing uneasily beside the skeleton of a fir tree. Something had clearly spooked it because the saddle was slipped and one of the stirrups was broken, although of the rider there was no sign. I jumped down and taking Button's reins in one hand started to walk forward. As I drew nearer, the gelding whinnied nervously and stamped a warning.

'Whooa. Easy boy, easy now.'

I gathered the bridle then, having tethered both horses to the dead fir, I began to comb the surrounding area, all the while calling her name. This time there was a faint answer.

'Hello? Hello? I'm over here.'

'Where?'

'Over here. Down by the brook.'

I followed the contour of the land where it fell towards a small stream. Victoria was at the bottom of the bank lying face down in a tangle of driftwood, her legs half in the water, her fine clothes splattered with mud.

'Victoria! Thank the Lord. Are you alright?'

Victoria twisted onto an elbow and wiped the mud from her face.

'Hello *Horse Boy*, what are you doing here?'

'I've been sent to find you. Didn't you hear me calling?'

'Not really. I vaguely remember someone shouting but I was desperate to keep up with the hounds.'

I crouched down and took her hand.

'It's alright, now don't move. Just keep still for a moment. Are you injured?'

'I don't think so.'

'What happened?'

'I'm not sure. I remember going flat out when a pheasant sprang up in front of us and next thing I knew I was down here.' She was smiling now, almost half laughing. She didn't appear to be injured at all. I pressed her hand and looked straight into those devil's eyes.

'Are you *insane*? The Master expressly told you not to jump the hedge and you deliberately went and ignored him. Do you think he was talking for the benefit of his health? You could have been cut to ribbons on that wire.'

A shaft of daylight poked through the trees. Victoria brought a hand up to shield her eyes.

'Pah, fiddlesticks,' she muttered sarcastically.

'Is that all you can say?'

'What do you expect? It's only a horse for goodness sake.'

'No it's not. It's someone else's horse or does that not bother you either?'

'Oh stop being so pious, it really doesn't suit you.'

I listened to the gentle trickle of water. Somewhere high up in the branches a lonely pigeon had seen enough and clattered away. I looked into that lovely face streaked in filth and without saying another word, leaned forward and grabbing the back of her head pulled her towards me and kissed her roughly. Our mouths met for a second or two, no more. I had barely time to savour the experience before she went berserk.

'How dare you!' she screamed lashing out wildly as she jumped to her feet. 'How fucking *dare* you!'

'I'm sorry Victoria, really I am; I'd never do anything to offend…'

'Get off! Get off! Take your hands off me! Just who the hell do you think you are?'

'Please, don't be like that….'

She was already striding up the bank to where the horses were tethered. I ran after her catching her arm just as we reached the broken fir.

'Please; I'm sorry. You must know I'd never do anything to hurt you.'

Victoria, who was already reaching for the saddle, span round and swatted me away.

'Take your hands off me. No! How *dare* you?'

'Look, I've said I'm sorry and I am. Truly I am. It was a mistake. I just thought…'

Victoria grabbed the cantle and vaulting herself astride the horse, glared down at me, eyes burning.

'You thought *what* exactly? Let me tell you something *Horse Boy* and you listen real good. If you ever, *ever* try and touch me again I'll make you wish you'd never been born.'

'Look, I've said I'm sorry. I can't help the way I feel. What else did you expect after the way you tease and tempt me?'

'You just don't get it do you?' she glowered, the horse twisting round as she stamped in vain for the broken stirrup. 'I don't *like* you. I don't like you in a sexual way or any other way for that matter, and I never shall. Your conduct, your manners, they disgust me. Now get out of my way. I never want to see or hear from you ever again. Ever. Hahhh!'

'Wait! Will you just *listen* for a moment you stupid woman…' but it was no use. She was already away, charging off into the distance and I might as well have been shouting at the trees.

Bugger.

Bugger Bugger *Bugger*.

CHAPTER TWENTY THREE

The memorials stood guard on Palace Green as they must have done for over a thousand years. There was no sinology in their placement or design, the weathered slabs protruding from the whiteness like broken, crooked teeth, the epitaphs lost with the memory of the people they had spoken of, people like me who had once passed this way but were no more. I spared a thought for the illustrious men of their times who would be lying in these graves and it saddened me they were no longer mourned. What was the point of it all? I remembered the words Cannon Brown had spoken at my father's funeral. *Life is a temporary arrangement within which nothing is constant but change.* He was right. Whatever else the future held, the only pathetic certainty was oblivion at the end of it all. And yet surely, there had to be more to living than dying? I kicked the frozen slush off my boots and stepped through the great North Door.

Inside the cathedral I experienced an overwhelming sensation of stillness and calm, and from the moment I stood before the magnificent East Window I was at a loss to understand why it had taken me this long to explore such riches on my doorstep. There were few people about. It was still early and as I wandered through the cloisters, the only sound keeping me company were the quarterly peel of bells from the top of the Great Tower, that and the rolling whispers from a service taking place in one of the side chapels. I took a seat at the back of the aisle and craned my neck to where the massive drum columns melted into the ribbed vault of the nave roof. How on earth did our Norman ancestors manage to do all that? I thought it an astonishing feat of construction made all the more so because it must have been accomplished using nothing but mathematics, chisels, blocks, pulleys and ropes. And faith of course. The man who has faith can move mountains. That's what it says in the bible doesn't it, not once or twice but over and over again? The man with faith, albeit the size of a mustard seed, can move mountains. I supposed the architects and masons from all those centuries ago must have been deeply religious people, for many mountains had been moved to create their monument.

Hearing footsteps I turned to catch the outline of a clergyman passing by the baptism font. I jumped out of my daydream and crossed the aisle to intercept him.

'Excuse me, I'm sorry to bother you but I'm looking for the holy man of Jarrow?'

He was an elderly priest who reminded me very much of Brother Wallace with his wisps of snow white hair and twisted gait that made him shuffle rather than walk. He carried a rosary and prayer book in one hand and a walking stick in the other and when he looked at me, I saw his eyes were partially milked over, although his voice was soft and clear.

'You are looking for the holy man of Jarrow you say? Of course. Of course. You will find his shrine in the Galilee Chapel at the back of the cathedral. The entrance is over there.'

He steered a finger in the direction of an enormous pipe organ to the side of which was a small archway. I thanked him for his assistance and crossed to the south aisle.

I discovered the resting place of Saint Bede among some other ancient graves at the foot of a small bank of stone steps. I have to say I was expecting something far more splendid, perhaps akin to the likes of Walsingham or Canterbury but instead my eyes rested on an unassuming marble sarcophagus adorned with nothing more imposing than a large wooden candlestick at each corner. I reached for the marble and ran my fingers over the Latin inscription. The letters had worn greatly through the ages but there was no mistaking the word and I knew I was gazing into history. At the foot of the tomb was a small cushion. I fell to my knees and gathered the piece of card.

Christ is the morning star, who when the night of this world is past, brings to his saints the promise of the light of life and opens everlasting day. Alleluia.

There was much to pray for. I started by asking Saint Bede to beseech God for the repose of the souls of my parents and also for Lord William who throughout his life had shown my family nothing but kindness. I then prayed for the living, for my brother in his grief and to give strength to Lady Alanna and Jane. I was not intending to pray for anyone else but awkwardly aware of Christ's teaching to be reconciled with one's adversary before making any offering, I prayed for Julian and for Clifford and then at length for all those people on Palace Green and elsewhere who had no one to pray for them. Lastly I prayed for myself.

> *Oh Saint Bede in your wisdom and through the grace of God you already know my most earnest desire yet I shall ask it. Please, I beg you, please, please help me for I am sick and I cannot go on any longer. I implore you with every part of my existence here and now on bended knee to fill her heart until it overflows with love and desire for me, that she will run into my arms and that henceforth we might always be together.*
> *Amen.*

I meant every tortured syllable of every single word. This girl had crept so deep under my skin that I could barely think of anything or anyone else, and the more she refused me, the more I wanted her to the point I was starting to go out of my mind. I hadn't had many cards in the first place and now they were all played there was nothing else but to turn to a pile of bones over a thousand years old in the vain hope the person who once lived in them could somehow hear my prayer. *The man with faith can move mountains.* According to St Mark's gospel, Jesus said that you can pray for anything at all, and so long as you have faith, it would be given to you. The notion seemed absurd but what was done was done. I had asked in faith and while only myself and Saint Bede (if he had been there at all) knew about it, for one fleeting moment I had believed. There was nothing more I could do. I left the cathedral feeling strangely positive and fortified with a resolve to make the most of every precious moment that had been given to me, and to leave no stone unturned in my quest for the truth about my heritage.

As for the rest, God knows.

CHAPTER TWENTY FOUR

About a week later I was in my father's office burning
the midnight oil over some probate documents when
Domino's ears went up and he began to growl at someone in
the courtyard. I listened for a moment expecting the footsteps
to pass but when they reached the house they suddenly fell
silent, and there was a soft knock on the door. I racked my
brains who it could be this time of night remembering only
too well that the last occasion I'd been disturbed in the early
hours, it was with the summons to Lord William's deathbed.
I knew there was no one at the castle. Jane and her mother
were staying with relatives in Bath, while Julian, Johnny
Clifford and their party had left several days previously for
a fortnight's shooting in Northumberland. It crossed my
mind it could have been an unexpected visit from Tom, but
then he'd have let me know he was coming, and anyhow we
were meeting in Hartlepool in a couple of days to confront
Crake. I couldn't think of anyone else. There was another
knock, much louder this time and Domino started to bark.

'All right boy, let's go see.'

I grabbed an oil lamp and trailing the dog through the hall, slid the bolt and opened the door on a young woman standing alone at the bottom of the step. At first I didn't know her for she was almost totally enfolded in her shawl, however when I raised the lantern to her face and saw the eyes, I could not help but cry out in astonishment.

'Victoria! Oh my God. What on earth are you doing here?'

Victoria pulled down her scarf to speak.

'Hello *Horse Boy*,' she said softly, 'are you going to show me in?' I looked over her shoulder and swept the courtyard. There was no one else about.

'Well?'

'Of course, of course, please, do come in; come in out of the cold.'

Victoria stepped into the hall and kicked the frozen snow from her shoes as I bolted the door behind her.

'Here let me take your things. It must be freezing outside.'
'I'll say. I've only walked from the castle and I'm chilled to the bone.'

Victoria passed her shawl and coat and shook her long black hair as I hung everything up in the hall.

'Please, come through the back where it's warmer and let me get you something to drink.'

We walked through the house in silence. In the kitchen she leaned against the stove while I lit an oil lamp and pulled up a couple of chairs.

'Please, take a seat and warm yourself. I'll make us a hot drink. I only have tea in at the moment, is that all right?'

Victoria nodded. I turned to fill the kettle as my unexpected visitor gathered her skirts and sank into one of the chairs. As I ran the tap my mind was racing and I almost had to pinch myself to make sure I wasn't dreaming. Here was the girl that dominated my thoughts from the moment I woke to the moment I fell asleep, here in my father's house with me, all alone in the middle of the night. I struggled to second guess why she had come round at this hour. What was she doing at Craven in the first place? She must have known she risked a scandal if anyone from the village had seen her. The flags scraped behind me as she drew closer to the stove. I lifted the cover from one of the hobs, set down the kettle then parked myself in the chair beside her. Not knowing what to say, I resolved to say nothing and for a while we listened to the ticking of the clock on the wall until Victoria broke the silence.

'How are you?'

I thought it a strange question in the circumstances but answered in similar tenure.

'I'm well, thank you. I'm surprised everyone is back so soon. I understood you were shooting with the Percy's until the end of next week?'

'Julian and the rest of the party are still in Northumberland. I left early because I must return to London to attend my mother who has been taken ill.'

'I'm sorry to hear it. Your brother, he does not choose to accompany you?'

'No, he would rather not, at least not at the present time. The sport on the estate is exceptional and he and the others are making the most of it, bagging pheasants in the day and drinking in the taverns at night. I don't care much for either activity, I never did and everyone else we know up there has been grounded by the weather. Alnwick may be beautiful when the daffodils are out but believe me, the town is no place for a young woman when its streets are choking in snow.'

I reasoned she must have journeyed back on her own and my heart quickened as I realised there was no one to disturb us. What was she playing at coming around to see me when she could be under no illusions as to my feelings for her? She had said she never wanted to see me again but now she was here. Why? I determined to say as little as possible and let her make the running. If she had an agenda it would be apparent soon enough.

Victoria swept her long black hair behind her neck then held her hands towards the stove.

'When I say I had to return to London it was more of a pretext so as not to offend our hosts. Don't misunderstand me. My mother is genuinely unwell, she has been ill for some time but to own the truth there is nothing so urgent in her condition that would command my immediate presence. The reality is, Northumberland, or rather your northern weather, does not suit me and at this time of year I would rather be at our home in Belgravia.'

I decided to cut to the quick.

'Why are you here Victoria?'

Victoria leaned back in her chair and brushed the top of her legs as if sweeping away some invisible dust.

'Alnwick to Kings Cross is too far in one trip,' she said matter-of-fact, 'and it suited me to break my journey at Craven to gather the remainder of my belongings and run some errands for Julian. I continue to London on the Pullman tomorrow afternoon.'

'That's not what I meant and I think you know it. Why have you come here to my father's house? Is your quest for amusement such that in the absence of any other you thought you would seek me out? If that's your game I would sooner you left now.'

Victoria's face softened as she drew her chair closer to mine. 'No. No, not at all. I can understand why you think that way but nothing could be further from the truth. I walked over here tonight for two reasons. Firstly I've come to see you because I owe you an apology for the way I have behaved towards you, and for some of the things I said, particularly when we were last together.'

I stared at her uneasily, barely able to believe what I was hearing. Her beauty, her very presence intoxicated me and fearful of what might follow if I said the wrong thing again I went to the stove where the kettle was humming.

'Milk and sugar?'

'Just milk, thank you.'

I passed her a mug and sat down again without another word. Victoria seemed to take this as encouragement and reaching for my hand continued in the same fashion as before.

'I want you to know that I am utterly ashamed of the way I spoke to you, especially after you demonstrated nothing but guarded admiration and a desire for friendship. I can scarcely countenance what you must think of me for I shudder when I remember some of the things I said. I didn't mean any of it, not a word, really I didn't. I thought I was being clever trying to show off to some of the others but in reality I was just making a fool of myself. I can see only too clearly that you are an honourable man, just like your father before you, and I ask from the bottom of my heart that you forgive me for being so odious and wretchedly narrow minded. I am so sorry, truly I am.'

There followed a brief silence as those dark eyes seared into my core. I could swear there were tears in them but were they real? I leant forward and brushed her cheek.

'Hey, hey don't get upset, please don't, it's all right, really it is.'

'I'm so sorry,' she whispered, 'and to think I said all those things at a time you were already grieving for your father. It was utterly selfish and I am ashamed when I think of how I behaved. Will you forgive me?'

'Of course I forgive you,' I replied adding quickly, 'believe me I've been called much worse.'

Victoria laughed, sincere and spontaneous; it was like a bird singing; beautiful, infectious.

'Thank you. Thank you so much,' she said softly. There was a short pause then she suddenly held out her hand.

'Look, I know I've done nothing to deserve it but can I ask that you overlook what happened between us before and that we can start again?'

As she spoke she looked straight at me as if reading my mind. Her words were everything and more I could have wished to hear and I felt myself starting to well up. She smiled again. It was not the switched on accessory I was used to, this time her whole face was shining as she cocked her head, all the while holding my gaze.

'Friends?' she asked again.

I slipped my fingers into her outstretched hand.

'Friends,' I replied. She reached for her mug and for a while we drank our tea.

'You said you walked over for two reasons. What was the other?' Victoria drew a tissue from her sleeve and gently blew her nose.

'I have a few hours to kill tomorrow before I catch my train. I've always wanted to explore the moors around Craven only I don't know the area well enough. I came to ask if you were not doing anything else if you would ride out with me?'

My heart leaped at the prospect as she surely knew before she asked me. It was settled in moments and we arranged to meet at the stables at nine the following morning. Victoria rose to her feet. 'Now I simply must go. It's been a long day and I'm so tired.'

I was disappointed at this although at the time I should not have expected anything else. In fact I hadn't been expecting anything at all and was still reeling at her sudden appearance. I gathered her coat and shawl from the hall and walked her to the front door. Victoria turned and held out her hand.

'Until tomorrow morning then *Horse Boy*. Goodnight.'
'Goodnight Victoria'.

For a moment we stood and looked at each other. I felt an overwhelming urge to grab her but after what happened in the forest I didn't dare and the moment passed. When she was half way across the courtyard I called after her.

'And the name's Edmund.'

Victoria smiled amiably over her shoulder then disappeared into the shadows.

CHAPTER TWENTY FIVE

Needless to say I barely slept that night and at 6.00am instead of reaching for a book I decided to get up and re-lay all the fires. While I was about it I realised the whole house was due a good clean so I scrubbed all the flags and swept and dusted upstairs and down, then, having changed all the sheets and replenished the scuttles from the coalhouse I slumped into an armchair and tried to get my head around the sudden change in Victoria. Was this really the same girl who had screamed at me in the forest? I thought of the Galilee chapel. I would take a great deal of persuading that the road to Damascus cut through the snowdrifts of Northumberland but her unexpected friendliness and anxiety to make amends was extraordinary. I fished the key out of the Gimcrack Cup and checked the contents of the safe. The purse of gold sovereigns, my father's various bank books and statements, they were all there together with his last diary note and the file Tom and I had taken from Dryburn hospital. I checked my watch. It was 8.50am. I locked the safe then dropping the key back into the trophy, pulled on some riding clothes and made my way across to the stables.

It was a grey, overcast morning and Victoria was already saddled up talking to Fenoughty who to my surprise had entrusted her with the same black gelding as before. I could only assume he didn't know about her reckless behaviour in the forest, or if he did, he chose to overlook it. Probably the latter. She had that way with men did Victoria; one smile and they would forgive her anything as I knew only too well from our conversation the previous evening. She greeted me amiably.

'Morning' said she. 'Sleep well?'

'Like the dead' I lied. 'Yourself?'

Victoria shook her long black hair as she put on her riding hat. 'No, not really. Too much on my mind.'

She looked straight at me as she said this but before I could reply Fenoughty cut over us.

'Edmund, I'm putting you up on Button again. I hope you don't mind. He's not the swiftest as you know, but he's reliable and the two of you seem to get on well.'

'Button and me, well we're like that aren't we boy?' Button gave a little whinny as he nuzzled into my open palm.

'I feel like I've been cooped up for an age,' said Victoria brightly. 'Shall we get going?'

Victoria felt for my shoulder as I instinctively cupped my hands to afford her a leg up into the saddle. For a brief moment I took the weight of her body as it stretched out in front me and I swear my heart clanged with lust. Sensing my face changing colour and knowing what must have been written there I turned and vaulted across Button before anyone would notice. Victoria tossed her head and twisted into the stirrups as Fenoughty gathered both bridles and led us out of the stable, his eyes searching the sky.

'Well Edmund, the weather looks like it'll hold but there's a low cloud and your options might be limited. Where d'ye reckon on going?'

'It'll depend on the drifts but assuming the trail's clear, I'll take Miss Clifford as far as Friars Cross then drop down the back and pick up the towpath.'

A look of unease swept across Fenoughty's brow because he knew we would pass close to where my father and Lord William had met their end. He appeared as if about to say something but then checked himself as if he understood I was resolved to make the journey and that argument would be useless. All the while Victoria was humming to herself as she adjusted her hat, my exchange with Fenoughty bypassing her completely. I shuffled Button alongside her black gelding.

'We about ready then?'

Victoria nodded although it was Fenoughty who spoke. 'I'm sure you don't need a lecture from me young 'un' he said ruefully 'but mind you take it steady up there and keep clear of the old workings.'

I knew exactly where he was coming from because the moor was a deathtrap to anyone who didn't know their way around. I assured him we'd keep to the established trails and return the horses well before dark. Fenoughty nodded then switching his eyes to Victoria then back again gave me a peculiar look before shaking his head and disappearing into the stables. I wheeled Button round and set off over the cobbles, Victoria quickly drawing alongside as we slipped under the arch and out into the Park.

'What did Fenoughty mean by old workings?'

'There's a monastery at the top of the fell about seven miles from here. The community was wiped out by Henry

VIII but a number of shafts are dotted about where the monks used to source their iron and coal.'

'A ruined monastery?' exclaimed Victoria. 'How exciting! It sounds the stuff of fairytales. Will you take me there?'

'If you like. The trail passes right by or almost right by. There's not much of the original building left but it's only a couple of hundred yards from the fork at the top. We'll be there in an hour or so.'

'Then its settled boy isn't it?' said Victoria leaning forward to address her horse. 'We can't wait can we? No we can't. Do you know I asked Mrs Pearce to pack us some lunch so maybe when we take a rest if there's an apple in the parcel you can have a piece. Yes you can, you know you can, you good boy. Da, da da.'

Her black gelding snorted in approval and I couldn't help but smile. I had not previously thought of Victoria as someone who regarded horses as anything other than a means of transportation, yet here she was all clucking and sweetness itself. Perhaps I had misjudged her. I tweaked Button's ears so he didn't feel left out as we trotted alongside a small brook that stumbled down from the top of the fell.

'Tell me, isn't this the place where your father and Lord William had their accident?'

'The very same,' I replied. 'I knew I would have to come back here some day and when you called last night, it not only gave me the incentive to get on with it but meant I wouldn't be riding out alone. It's such a beautiful view from the top you see, and I always felt it was wasted if there was no one to share it with.'

Victoria coaxed her mount a little closer.

'I used to hear so much about the beauty and solace of these fells,' she said quietly. 'Ever since I saw the landscape from my room in the castle I've wanted to ride out to this place and explore its secrets.'

We followed the track as it wound in and out the contours of the fell before disappearing into the boulders altogether. A faint breeze swept down from the top where little seahorses of mist had started to dance around the crags. Victoria hoisted herself up in the stirrups and stretched out her arms.

'It's so beautiful up here,' she cried. 'So wild and desolate and yet beautiful. Tell me what's that strange *peta peta peta* noise all around us? It sounds like someone playing the castanets.'

'They're Red Grouse. The heather up here's full of them, so much so that I'm surprised Julian and your brother went all the way to Northumberland to shoot. Their call which you can hear is very distinctive; it's as if the birds are telling us to go-back-go-back-go-back. They're extraordinary creatures. Do you know that when they sense danger, the hen will protect her chicks by scuttling across the moor dragging a wing, as if feigning injury to divert the predator? It's not just the Red Grouse that are worth watching. There's a host of other magnificent birds on the moor, Partridge, Curlew, Lapwing and Merlin to name but some. But forgive me; I don't want to bore you with anecdotes about Mother Nature when we hail from such different worlds.'

'Oh please don't say that. You're not boring me at all. Really you're not. This is fascinating.'

I dipped my head and looked into her face.

'Truly?'

Victoria smiled warmly and gave a series of nods. 'Truly.'

'Well it's not just the wild animals and birds that draw me up here. There's all kinds of rare and beautiful plants that only grow on the moor. There's the heather, obviously, but there's also rare cotton grasses, bilberry and beautiful yellow bog plants that come out in the spring. I know it might be cold and a bit miserable today but the moor changes so much throughout the seasons, all the beautiful colours, the different fragrances, I just adore it. When Alfie and I were little my father used to bring us up here and show us all the different flowers and teach us the various calls of the birds. It changed my life, it really did and a part of me has remained up here ever since.'

We reached an old wooden gate. I slid down from the saddle and walked the horses through.

'You must have loved him very much,' said Victoria. 'He sounds so different from my own father who I barely saw at all when I was growing up.'

'How was that? Did he not live with you?'

Victoria leaned forward and stroked her horse behind the ear.

'In a fashion. To the outside world it appeared we were this big happy family but in reality we were anything but. When he wasn't working at the Foreign Office, father spent most of the time at his Club and mother, Johnny and I came a poor third. Truly, he was hardly ever at home, either in the morning when I got up, or in the evening when I went to bed. He never once read me a story or asked us to ride out with him in Hyde Park although I knew he used to go there every Sunday. We never even sat down as a family, just the four of us and ate a meal together; not even at Christmas when my brother and I were consigned to a different room. Next thing I knew I was grown up and there he was, this stranger. Oh, I'm not saying I don't love him. I do love him, very much, I always did, he was always so dazzling and he looks after me but I can't say I know him in the same way you knew your own father, and it's at times like this that I would it had been otherwise.'

I closed the gate and pulled myself back aboard Button.

'And your mother? I take it you are close to her?'

'I am. I saw far more of my mother when I was little and unlike my father, she was always there for me. I didn't realise it at the time but looking back my father's long absences must have been very difficult for her.'

Her words struck a chord as I remembered what Lord William had said about Lady Alanna rattling around the castle and how it was the beginning of the slippery slope.

'You said your mother is indisposed?'

'She is. I might as well tell you this because you'll find out eventually. About six years ago my mother caught smallpox when she accompanied my father on a ministerial trip to Egypt. She became so ill she was not expected to survive and indeed for several days she lay close to death. In the event she managed to pull through but the infection left her with terrible scars and drained what was left of her youth. It was so utterly tragic for them both. My father couldn't bear to look at her once lovely face and spent less time than ever at home, while fearful to show herself in public my mother retreated into the family's home in Belgravia where she still lives like a recluse.'

'I'm so sorry,' I said and I meant it. With all the grief and uncertainty of our own situation I hadn't stopped to consider there might be other people out there suffering, particularly a family like Victoria's who seemed to have so much going for them. 'It's why I left Northumberland,' she continued. 'Yes, there were other reasons, tedium not being the least of them but I would still be at Alnwick if my mother had not sent for me. I don't expect you to understand because you have probably never been on your own, it's not something that young people think about but I've seen how loneliness afflicts my mother and when she sent for me, I didn't hesitate.'

The trail was rising sharply now and the seahorses of mist that had swept the fell all morning began to close in around us. The top of the moor was shrouded in fog and while there had been no rain, the horses were dripping and tiny globules of water were settling on our faces and clothes. All the while Victoria remained a most engaging companion without the faintest trace of her previous arrogance or self-regard. Her manner was easy, her conversation intelligent and amusing and, as time and distance slipped by, I found myself opening up to her. Oh, don't get me wrong, I didn't divulge anything regarding Lord William's death or what Tom and I had discovered in my father's papers, and I certainly wasn't going to impart anything about our excursion to Dryburn the previous week and to be fair to her, she didn't pry, far from it. Instead we just talked about this and that, sometimes seriously, other times laughing and joking, it was light and it was easy although I would be doing these pages a disservice if I did not also record how with every passing moment she only increased in my esteem.

At the top of the fell the weathered stone guarding the fork to the monastery loomed into view. I drew Button to a halt and jumped down from the saddle.

'This is it. We're on foot from here.'

Victoria's gelding snorted as she pulled him alongside.

'Where exactly are we?'

'Friars Cross. The stone here marks the track that leads off to the abbey ruins. You can't see them through the mist but they're not far.'

'It doesn't look much like a cross to me,' she said lightly, 'more like a giant gatepost.'

'Many people say the same when they first come up here but it's a cross all right, or at least it started out as one before it was battered by the seasons. Apparently it's been here for centuries, parish records testifying to its presence as far back as the Plantagenets and there were almost certainly a number of earlier wooden structures. According to legend, the cross marks the grave of one of the monks and a local farm girl who used to conduct illicit trysts here until they were discovered and put to death by the ecclesiastical courts.'

I reached for Victoria's hand as she slid down from the saddle, her leather boots splashing into the mud as she hit the ground. For a moment we looked at one another until conscious of what must be written across my face, I turned on the pretext of gathering Button lest he started to wander off. Victoria removed her hat and brushed the moisture from her sleeves.

'How awful for them yet it's a frightfully romantic notion don't you think? You know, that they still lie together after all this time?'

My heart skipped at the poignancy of her words.

'I have always thought so. It's because of the legend that the cross has always been associated with clandestine meetings, a place for secret lovers who have nowhere else to go. They say you only have to find Hob Hole to see the truth of it.'

'Hob Hole?'

'It's a cave somewhere at the back of the ruins where the monks used to store ice and provisions. I vaguely remember my father pointing the entrance out to me when I was a child although I've never had reason to go there.'

Victoria led her gelding round so we faced one another.

'Hob Hole? It sounds a bit bleak. What does it mean?'

'I suppose a literal translation would the place or the dwelling of the Hob, a short, foul, hairy creature such as a goblin or a troll. These days you only find them in children's stories but in the less informed times of our ancestors they were real enough and blamed for everything from crop failure to the disappearance of travellers.'

'I adore spooky tales and folklore. Can you take me there?'

'What, to the cave? If you like, that's if we can find it. If I remember right the hollow lies somewhere up in the rocks at the back of the ruins. It's not far but there's a bit of a ridge so stay close.'

We led the horses in single file until after a minute or so the broken stones of the monastery ghosted through the fog. Victoria gave a cry of delight and having tied her bridle to a piece of broken fence began to scale the nearest wall.

'Be careful' I said. 'You shouldn't climb on anything round here. It's not safe.'

Victoria heaved herself to the top where she lurched upright and stretched her arms to the sky.

'Woo hoo. This is amazing. If you look down from here you can still trace the outline of the chapel and what was probably the kitchen and dormitory. And over there, that dovecote, it's still got birds in.'

'Come down Victoria.'

Victoria took no notice and began to inch her way along the ledge, her slender arms reaching out as if she was treading a tightrope.

'I'm the king of the castle and you're the dirty rascal.'

I hurried to the foot of the wall and implored her to get down.

Victoria pulled a face.

'Oh I'm the queen of the castle and you're the dirty rascal.'

A rook clattered out of the stones beneath her. Victoria shrieked in fright displacing a shower of masonry as she lost her footing and ended with her midriff trussed across the rim of the wall. My heart skipped as I reached up and grabbed her ankles to prevent her falling off completely. Victoria looked down anxiously, her face as white as a sheet.

'Oh my, that was a bit close. Maybe you were right after all.'

'You're crazy,' I said irritably. 'You could have been seriously hurt.'

I eased her down from the ledge. As soon as her boots touched the ground she drew away and started to flap at the dirt and dust that was now smeared over her riding coat.

'Oh Horse Boy, you're always so reserved; don't you ever take a risk?'

'No, at least not like that I don't. There's already been one tragedy up here recently or had you forgotten? I don't believe any of us could cope with another.'

'Fiddlesticks,' she retorted. 'I was perfectly fine'.

'You wouldn't be saying that if you'd fallen and broken your neck.'

'Oh you do exaggerate,' she said brightly and then before I could respond, 'now never mind all that, tell me, where's this Hob Hole place?'

Realising that further admonishment would only shatter any real or imagined spell, I let it go and we walked through the ruins until the track came to an abrupt halt at the overhanging cliff. I was a child when my father had brought me here but I recalled him telling me the cave entrance was hidden somewhere in the face at the top of an old landslide. I looked around and sure enough the giant moss-covered rocks were still there, everything in fact exactly how I remembered it from all those years ago. I hauled Victoria onto the first boulder from where we started clambering up the fall. Near the top of the stones a small fissure no more than four feet by three opened up in front us.

'Is this the entrance?' cried Victoria drawing breath. 'It doesn't look big enough to be a hollow.'

'I can't see any other so it must be. Come on, this way.'

I crouched to my haunches and squeezed through the gap, Victoria following close behind.

My first impression of the cave was a prodigious sense of forbidding, like we had no business being in there at all. It was eerie to say the least and even after my eyes had adjusted to the darkness, there remained such a tangle of shadow that it was impossible to gauge how far it extended into the ridge. The chamber itself was as cold as the tomb, cold, musty and dank and as I stood there catching my bearings the only sound was of water dripping from the roof into some invisible pool. Victoria took my arm. She was standing so close to me I could hear her breathing.

'Can you see any goblins?' she whispered mischievously.

I called out into the blackness, my words pinging off the rock like a stone bouncing across ice. Then silence.

Victoria stood on her tiptoes and whispered in my ear. 'Perhaps they've all gone out for the day.'

'Perhaps.'

I reached into my pocket and struck a match, carefully guarding the flame in cupped hands. The cavern briefly flickered to life.

'Look!' she cried. 'By the wall!'

'Where? I can't see anything.'

'The far side, over there, something glimmered.'

I started across the jagged floor, stumbling and cursing as the match burned down and seared my fingers. I waved it away and struck another, this time looking up with the flare. In the wall ahead cut into the rock was a ledge of old drip bottles with candles of various cycle. What place was this? I made my way over and struck again, the nearest wick spitting into a flame which Victoria poured along the shelf to mate with the others. When she finished we stood for a moment and watched as the sharp contours around us melted and the chamber came alive in a ruddy cauldron of light that would have done justice to the starkest depiction of the underworld in a renaissance painting. Victoria surveyed the ever expanding vault, her voice bouncing off the rock face.

'This place is absolutely amazing. Look how huge the cavern is and I still can't tell how far back it goes. You'd never have guessed any of it from that tiny entrance.'

As the space around us filled with light I became aware of an enormous amount of graffiti scratched into the walls. The writing was everywhere; names, murals, dates; some of the script stark, much of it faint, a few segments barely visible at all but every mark the testament of others who had trodden this way before. I picked up a bottle and held it to the wall suddenly understanding the common thread.

'They were lovers.'

'Who were?'

'The people here. They were all lovers. Look at all the names woven in hearts and shields, the dates and secret messages. This is astonishing.'

Victoria picked up a bottle and went to the far side of the hollow.

'So they were. Good Lord. There's dozens of them. Dozens. Some of these go back years and years. There's a very old one here;

John and Lettice
Together forever
30 July 1825

Here's another;

Katherine and Francis
My love as always on this silent night.
24 December 1873

And here, although this one is a bit strange. It's some kind of message.'

'What does it say?'

'Hang on; I'll put the light a bit closer. Here it is. It reads

Dearest Alice
At my back I always hear
Time's winged chariot hurrying near
Percival

What does he mean *Time's winged chariot*?'

'It's a line from the poet Andrew Marvell' I replied. 'His girlfriend was shy and he wrote to her saying you have to seize the moment before it passes forever. The *winged chariot* is time itself about to cut him down.'

'It's incredibly romantic don't you think? All those trysts here, fraught with danger, the unions no doubt as swift as they were secret?'

Victoria brought her bottle over and placed it back on the shelf as I continued to explore the graffiti. It wasn't just names either. There were sketches, diagrams, lines of verse I didn't understand, strange numbers and figures, the whole a rich testimony to generations of lovers who had been hostages to this place because there had been nowhere else for them to go. I moved the candle closer raking the wall and then suddenly the word ghosted in front of me. Derina. The name of my mother. It was intertwined with the initials WFC. Obviously not her then. Not a common name mind. Must be a coincidence. WFC? Who was WFC? Abruptly the identity of the author leaped out of the rock. William Fitzroy-Cavendish. My mother and Lord William here in this place? Surely not. There must be other girls who bore the same. But Derina? No, she was the only Derina I had ever heard of. If she had been with Lord William it would explain everything. Could it be true? I was so consumed by the discovery that I barely noticed Victoria as she gathered a stone and began scrawling on the wall.

'What are you doing?'

A finger went to her lips.

I watched as her slim hand weaved and scratched over the rock. When she had finished I held up my light and stared at the trace.

Edmund and Victoria
lovers in this place
14 December 1914

I looked at the words again hardly taking in what was before me. I read it for a third time then switched back to the girl. Victoria dropped the stone and folded her arms around my neck until our foreheads touched, the candlelight dancing in her beautiful black eyes as they bored into my own.

'What I have written, it's the truth,' she whispered. 'I swear it is. I've felt that way ever since I first saw you at the church.'

I was too confused and overcome with shock and desire to say anything. Victoria drew her long willowy body against mine.

'I know you feel the same way, I know you do. I can see it when you look at me.'

I had never been in this situation with a woman before let alone someone who I craved and wanted as much as she. All the time images of my mother and Lord William flashed before me. It had to be true then. They were lovers. It was what Lord William had tried to tell me on his deathbed before guilt and time ran him through. Another thought washed over me. My God had I been conceived in this place? All of a sudden I didn't know who I was any more. Victoria traced her fingers over my lips.

'See around you. These walls do not lie.'

I looked again at what she had written and read it out loud.

Edmund and Victoria
lovers in this place
14 December 1914

'But this sudden change, the *County*, your behaviour to me at the ball, what you said in the forest. I don't understand. You told me we could never be together.'

'I said those things to put you off, and to try and chase you from my affections. Oh believe me, I knew what I wanted from the moment I first saw you but I also knew that any liaison between us would be totally repugnant to just about everyone else and it was for that reason and for that reason alone I said what I did.'

What was this? That she had liked me from the first after all? The image of Lord William and my mother fornicating here in the candlelight rushed through my mind. I read the mural again. What kind of lovers? The thought of having sex with Victoria had intoxicated me from the moment I first saw her. She wouldn't mean it like that. The girl was a tease, like a cat playing with a mouse.

'Tell me Victoria why do people live their lives in dread of what others might say or think about them? If you really felt that way then why did you let other people's aversion stop you? The names on the walls here, they are from different times when people who wanted to be together had no choice but to meet in secret. But that was then and this is now. Surely times have changed?'

'It's a spirited notion but you are not being realistic. Who is to stop us you say? How about just about everyone I can think of? Lady Alanna has thinly disguised hopes in my direction whereas Julian's more rudimentary aspirations are barely disguised at all. My father and mother have their own plans for me and while my brother has no plans for anyone but himself, I am as certain as I can be that you will not feature in any of them. If this wave of hostility wasn't enough, there's a social gulf between us, you know there is. You are without wealth or connections, it's not your fault, it's not even a fault and it's certainly not an accusation but it is a fact and from where I come from these things matter. You and I, we are as far apart as a fowl and a fish and just about everyone, certainly everyone in the orbit of my life would be totally against me having any kind of relationship with you. Surely you can see this?'

'Of course I can see it, but if it doesn't matter to you and it doesn't matter to me and we want to be together then what is to stop us?'

Victoria sighed deeply and buried her head in my shoulder.

'Oh, were it that simple. What is there to stop us you say? It is the crux that I have struggled with these last few weeks. What people will say and think, or rather what people of position and influence will say and think. It matters enormously, but then it is my life, no one else's and closing my eyes to the way I feel about you is making me ill. I am so afraid, frightened of what will happen, frightened of how my friends and family will react but most of all frightened that I don't have the courage to see this through. I knew I wanted you from the moment I first saw you. I had never felt that way about anyone before and it scared me which is why I tried to put you off by making you detest me, yet the more I tried, the more I wanted to be with you, I still do. I always will. And now it's come to this as it was always going to, that very soon I shall be forced to choose between my family and friends and what lies in my heart. I am so utterly confused between what's right and what's not that I don't know what to do.'

She was crying now, her tears wet against the side of my face. I folded my arms around her and spoke softly into her ear.

'Hey, shhh, shhh, you mustn't weep on my account, please don't for I cannot bear it.'

'You have no idea what it's like and how it's been for me. Why can't we all be free to love who we choose? I want you so much, you do not know the half of it but I'm so scared.'

I brought a finger to her lips and folded her trembling body into my own.

'Listen to me Victoria and listen well for what I am about to say is the absolute truth. At this precise moment I couldn't give a damn about anything other than what you mean to me. You are all I think about from the moment I wake up until the moment I go back to sleep. I eat, drink, walk, talk, I even think and breathe in fact I live every part of my existence dreaming and praying that I might be with you. I don't want or need anything else either in this life or the next other than your love. I have to tell you this because it is the truth. I am utterly yours forever, and I swear to you here and now that if you place your trust in me I shall never let you down. I will always take care of you, I am completely and totally mad for you. I would die for you.'

Victoria reached up with both hands and grabbed the back of my head. In a moment she had pulled her mouth to mine and we were kissing violently, the tip of her tongue penetrating my lips, her grip tightening as her body rose and melted into my own.

'I love you Victoria, God, I love you, I love you.'

'Oh Edmund, I'm so sorry for hurting you. I love you too. You know I do, you're everything to me. Oh Edmund I'm so sorry.'

It was the first time she had spoken my name. A bolt of lightning ran through me and I began to pull wildly at her clothes urgently exploring her body. Victoria winced and pushed me away.

'No. No, don't,' she sobbed.

'Forgive me,' I cried catching my breath, 'forgive me for I cannot help myself.'

'No, don't apologise, it's fine. I'll do it.'

Victoria removed her jacket and waistcoat and lifted up the front of her shirt to reveal an ugly graze stretching across her midriff just above the navel.

'It's from the fall on the abbey ledge earlier. It's why I stopped you'.

I gazed in wonder at her hourglass figure and beautiful skin, her body radiant and irresistible in the flickering candlelight. I had never seen anything so completely and utterly captivating and that first memory of it was to haunt me forever. I reached down and wetting the corner of my handkerchief in a nearby pool gently dabbed the wound. Victoria flinched and cried out.

'I'm sorry; I didn't mean to hurt you.'

Victoria raked her hands through my hair, twisting and wrenching at the curls.

'Kiss me,' she whispered. 'Kiss me there, over the gouge, where it hurts, oh Edmund.'

I sank to my knees and grabbing her hips put my mouth and tongue to the porcelain skin of her belly, stroking and exploring the ridge of the graze and in and around her navel before impulsively trailing upwards probing for her breasts. Victoria began to wail, it was a cry that I had never heard from a woman before, almost like a wounded animal.

In a moment she had wrestled her shirt over her head and was pulling at the buckle on my waist. The blood rushed through my ears as every sinew in my body tore in a million directions.

'I'm crazy about you. Oh my God I love you Victoria. I love you.'

'Hold still Edmund, just a moment longer.'

Victoria placed a hand on my shoulder and kicked off her boots. As she stepped out of her jodpers I saw her beautiful long legs and wondered if the darkest craving in my heart was about to come true. Victoria placed her soft hands on my shoulders and looked me in the eye.

'Do you want to screw me Edmund?'

In my shock and embarrassment I could only mutter something about whether she felt certain it was what she wanted.

Victoria's breath was heavy and the words came fast.

'I've never been more certain of anything in my life. I knew that we would be lovers from the first moment I saw you. It was as if our destiny was already written on these walls. I've always held myself back until now but with you there is a force inside me that I cannot suppress. I want to do this more than anything else Edmund, now, quickly, before the world out there finds us and this moment passes forever.'

There was no inhibition as I tore off my shirt and trousers, all the while staring and burning up as Victoria removed her underclothes until she stood naked before me with her arms across her breast.

'Hold me Edmund, I am cold.'

How desperately and ardently had I longed for this moment. I drew her against me, our naked bodies trembling in the dancing shadow. It was the most intoxicating, utterly exhilarating feeling I had ever known and there was nothing else in creation that could come near it. I gave silent thanks to God and Saint Bede for the impossible moment I had dreamed about and prayed for. As we kissed I fell deeper and deeper into those beautiful dark eyes while the boiling urgency that only lovers can understand rushed within me.

'You must know it Victoria. You must. I have never been with a woman.'

'Don't be afraid,' she whispered. 'We shall manage well enough.'

She motioned to the far end of the cave where a small piece of rock protruded from the wall.

'I want you to sit down on that ledge and face me.'

Without asking why I seated myself on the rock and pressed my shoulders into the cold granite. Victoria followed me across with a drip bottle which she placed on the ground to the side. In the flickering light I traced her long sleek body from her beautiful hair to the brightly painted fingers and toenails. I was so mad for her I thought I would burst.

'Place your arms behind your head Edmund, close your eyes and keep perfectly still.'

I shut my eyes and sank into the rock. I heard Victoria blow out the candle then sensed her edging towards me. After what seemed an age her knees brushed mine at which she arched her torso, threw back her head and coiled her limbs around me.

CHAPTER TWENTY SIX

Victoria didn't return to London that afternoon. Instead we wandered back down the fell, our spirits hostage to what had passed between us and where it would lead from here. In the evening she came over to the house and we took Domino for a walk around the gardens before cooking supper together in the kitchen. I found a bottle of claret in one of the cupboards and when we had eaten, we stretched out in front of the fire exchanging stories and singing songs as we toasted our future from the Gimcrack trophy. Later, when we went to bed, I opened my heart and told her everything starting from the dreadful news at college to what transpired at Lord William's bedside, sharing also the secret of my father's diary and the papers Tom and I had stolen from the mortuary. It was the longest, sweetest night of my life, each savoured contour the essence of undiluted happiness as we passed the hours making love and making plans and more love and more plans until mentally and physically exhausted I finally yielded to the bottomless sleep of the just. When I awoke it was midmorning and Victoria had already slipped away to catch the early Pullman. I reached for the note on the bedside cabinet.

You looked so peaceful I didn't want to wake you
Sweet dreams darling and see you next week
Love you

V x

I threw back the bedclothes ready to conquer the world, my body aching sweetly, my soul bursting into flower with all these emotions I never knew existed. Our lives had been joined. We were going to be together. I began to chant the song we had first danced to, the melody ringing around the house as I bathed and dressed.

By the light of the silvery moon,
I want to spoon, to my honey I'll croon love's tune

I went to the wardrobe and pulled out Dad's Sunday best in readiness for my appointment in Hartlepool that afternoon. The trousers were a bit baggy round the middle but I found a pair of braces in one of the drawers and after a few adjustments I was suited and booted and ready to go. I checked my watch. Jordan was calling round at one thirty to drive me to the station. I cleared away the dishes and had just finished making up my brother's bed when the horn sounded in the courtyard. I locked the front door and jumped into the Rolls. Two hours later I stepped off the pavement into *The Grand Hotel* where I found Tom in a corner of the restaurant pushing around a plate of mince and dumplings.

'I thought you'd never get here. The food's awful.'

I grinned uncomfortably at a waiter folding napkins at the next table and ordered a mug of chocolate.

'How was your trip?'

'Bloody dreadful. Two hours at Darlington hanging around for a connection then it was shuffle-bump, stop-start all the way to the coast. Anyone would think there was a war on. How about you? I like the suit by the way.'

I checked the waiter had gone then leaned across the table and lowered my voice.

'Tom, you'll not believe it. Everything fits. My mother and Lord William were lovers after all. Not just back in Ireland but later on in Durham after she married my father. I found their names side by side in *Hob Hole*. It's where they met in secret. You know what it means don't you? Lord William was almost certainly my father. You were right all along. It had to be the reason he called me when he was dying. It's what he was trying to tell me.'

Tom stopped eating and parked his knife and fork.

'Whoa slow down. Right, start again. What's this *Hob Hole*?'

'I told you, remember. It's a place, or rather it's a cave hidden at the top of an old rock fall on Hamsterley moor where the monks stored provisions. Lord William and my mother used to meet there in secret. I found their names on the wall with the others.'

'What others?'

'Other lovers. Dozens of them. Tom you wouldn't believe it, there are names carved into the rock there going back hundreds of years. I never knew the place existed and I've lived in Durham all my life. I still can't get over it. To think that all the time my mother and Lord William were having trysts up there behind Lady Alanna and my father's backs. Only now it seems he wasn't my father at all and all this time they were deceiving me as well. Tom, what's going on? So much has happened in the last few weeks I scarcely know who I am anymore.'

My friend who had been listening intently slumped back in his chair and closed his eyes.

'Do you believe your mother was capable of having an extra-marital affair?'

It was not a comfortable thought. I was only little when she died and her unqualified love for me had always been an incorruptible shrine.

'You mean did she cheat on my father? It's the critical question isn't it? Did they rekindle their love? Lord William claimed to have seduced her when they met in Ireland and I have no reason to doubt him. He also said he bitterly regretted the liaison on account of my mother's virtue which appears to have been a rare currency in the society in which he and Derrymore operated. There can be little doubt she was in love with him at the time.'

'I agree,' said Tom. 'The only question therefore is whether it is too far a step to believe them capable of rekindling their ardour when their paths unexpectedly met at Craven. Lady Alanna's confinements together with your father's absences at the races will have afforded them abundant opportunity but did they have the resolve? I wasn't sure about this until your discovery in the cave but now you must see it's the last piece of the jigsaw. They must have been lovers. Why else would Lord William call you to his deathbed and tell you he had altered the succession? Why else would he direct you to treat with Crake if he hadn't altered his Will in your favour? There can be no other plausible explanation. It's you Edmund. It has to be you. Lord William must have made you his heir which means he must have been your real father.'

It was the only logical conclusion and I knew it. Any lingering doubts I had previously harboured vanished the moment I saw their names gouged into the granite, and I had been reeling from the shock ever since. To discover after all these years that I was not the man I thought I had been or at least not the flesh and bones of the man was heart wrenching. Had both of my fathers known all along? That I was the true blood heir to the Craven estate? The key was Crake. Everything came back to him. Crake. Crake. Crake. I swallowed the remainder of my chocolate and banged down the mug.

'Let's see what reception we get this afternoon. Crake gave nothing away at the reading and if Lord William *had* changed the succession, you would have expected him to say so then. Perhaps he has his reasons for keeping quiet, and if so, no doubt he'll tell us. However I don't trust him even if Lord William did. We must tread carefully.'

'I agree,' replied Tom. 'It's impossible to look further but who knows? He might yet surprise us with his integrity.'

'I doubt it. However before we do battle with Crake there's something else you need to know. It happened so unexpectedly I still can't believe it myself but it's true.'

Tom reached for the water and looked at me over the rim of his glass. It was a cracking shiner.

'That exciting hey? Do tell. I hope it's worth the sanctimonious grin on your face.'

'It most certainly is.'

'Indeed?' he retorted damping his mouth. 'Hang on. No, no. Don't tell me. Let me guess. There you were lying in your pit minding your own business when suddenly there was this knock on the door and you opened it to be ravished by a voluptuous, scantily clothed Miss Clifford. Am I right?'

I didn't answer. I didn't need to. Tom raised an eyebrow then flicked a glance at the waiter who had returned from the kitchens and was hovering around the sideboard.

'Could I see the desert menu please?'

The waiter hesitated for a second then nodded and disappeared through to the back. Tom fished out a handful of change and rose to his feet.

'That should cover it. Come on we'd better get going or we'll be late.'

The offices of Baxter, Crake and Lockwood were at the end of Church Street a few minutes' walk towards the railway station. As usual Tom set off at a blistering pace.

'I don't believe you by the way.'

'I tell you it's true.'

'What, you and Lucrezia Borgia? Come off it Edmund, the girl can't stand you. Anyone could see that from the way she made a complete fool of you at the party.'

We paused outside *Woods* the opticians to comb our hair. Tom lit a couple of cigarettes and passed one across. I straightened my collar and squared up to his reflection.

'You shouldn't believe everything you see. It was only a ploy on her part. She loved me from the moment she saw me at the funeral and the unpleasantness was just a screen to try and drive me from her heart because she knew the trouble that would follow if we ever got together. Thing is it had the opposite effect.'

Tom snorted through a cloud of tobacco.

'Her heart? The woman has a *heart* you say? Pah! Tell me Edmund, are you feeling all right because the way you're talking anyone would be forgiven for thinking you've had a bump on the head.'

'It's true, honestly it is. She's not the madam we took her for at all. I know it's hard to believe but when you get to know her, she's absolutely delightful. Tom, I'm crazy in love and now I discover she felt the same way all along.'

'What? She *loves* you now does she? Come on Edmund, be serious. Spoilt, listless brats like Victoria Clifford don't love anyone but themselves. They never have. The only thing the likes of her get off on is cash, cash and more cash; they need it in abundance which is why their favours do not come cheaply.'

We peeled away from the window and continued down the hill.

'I can understand why you think that way but you're wrong.'

'Of course I'm not wrong. These people are all the same. Everyone's a walking balance sheet to them and people like you and me are far too irrelevant to feature in any ledger. Good wind up though. A different girl and I might have believed it but that stuck up cow? If she'd ever gazed into your eyes you'd be stone by now.'

'You're so funny. Not. You can mock me all you like but I promise you it's true. Victoria and I are lovers. We slept together last night. You've got to believe me. If you don't believe me no one else will.'

'Yeah, right. I tell you Edmund, the day you plough her I'll tie a string of mackerel round my neck and run stark-bollock naked down York Shambles.'

I was still trying to convince him when we reached the solicitors but Tom was having none of it and I could see I was wasting my breath. So be it. I would explain everything later but for now we had to focus on the assignment to hand. My friend twisted his cigarette into the pavement.

'Right. This is it. Remember what we agreed and don't jump in straight away. Take your time and let the bent bugger do all the talking then when he's finished hit him right between the eyes. I'll watch closely for the reaction because those first few seconds will tell us everything we need to know.'

'Come on' I replied. 'Let's get it over with.'

We stepped into the foyer, our appearance heralded by a brass bell that tripped somewhere above the doorway. I took in our surroundings. I thought it an expensively fitted room for a reception, all oak and brass with an enduring smell of leather and polish. My eyes searched out the counter where a smart middle aged woman in a tweed suit looked up from behind the sweep of an electric lamp.

'Good afternoon gentlemen, may I help you?'

'Good afternoon Miss. My name's Edmund Bullick. I have an appointment with Mr Crake.'

'Oh yes, Mr Bullick. Mr Crake is expecting you. If you'd like to hang your coats on the stand over there and I'll let him know you're here. Can I ask the name of your companion?'

'This is Thomas Brentnall ma'am, a friend of the family.'

'Thank you. Gentlemen if you would be good enough to take a seat. I shan't be a moment.'

We removed our coats and sat in an alcove. I reached for the table and had just started flicking through a copy of *John Bull* when we were hailed from the top of the stairs.

'Mr Crake will see you now gentlemen. If you'd like to follow me please.'

Crake's office was situated at the end of a narrow, curiously lopsided corridor. It was a musty, dusty chamber with a threadbare wool carpet, distorted mahogany panelling and a fake alabaster ceiling, the latter heavily discoloured from years of detritus generated by a coal fire which even at this late hour was still roaring away in the hearth. The room was illuminated by two spherical gas lights hanging down over the main desk, their effect enhanced by several reflections of the same in the windows which gave the impression of further light coming in from outside. A giant bookcase of *Halsburys* and other periodicals stood against one of the walls while a handful of college photographs and satirical prints of red judges stared down from another. The only other fittings of note were an old 'hunting theme' grandfather clock tucked away in the corner, and a large pelt clad desk and side table, both of them groaning with huge mounds of assorted documents some of which had splashed onto a floor where there were scattered so many other papers that it made you wonder how anyone knew where anything was. Such, then, was the ordered or more aptly the disordered chaos in the lair of Thomas Mathias Crake solicitor, the whole dominated by a large bay window that looked out over Church Street and from which vantage point the occupier slowly turned and stretched out his hand with unexpected affability.

'Good afternoon Edmund, I hope you don't mind me calling you Edmund. Please, please make yourself comfortable. And Mr Brentnall, Thomas I think it is? You're most welcome gentlemen, please sit down. Mrs Crane, can you bring me the Fitzroy-Cavendish trust papers and ask Mr Glyder to join us please? Thank you so much.'

The receptionist clucked an acknowledgement and disappeared into the corridor as the solicitor cleared a space on the desk in front of him and sat down. A few moments later, Glyder struggled into the room with a large metal strongbox and pulled up a chair to the side of his master.

'Edmund, you'll remember my clerk from the reading of the Will I'm sure. I've asked him to join us so he can bear witness to the trust deed I've drawn up in accordance with his lordships' wishes. Your friend Mr Brentnall here can be the second witness. However before we address the business of the day the first thing I want you to know is how sorry we all were to learn about this dreadful accident. I didn't have the honour of meeting your father but as the estate solicitor, I can tell you that he was greatly esteemed by Lord William who always spoke of him in the highest terms. I realise his untimely passing will have been a dreadful shock to your family and you must allow me to express our deepest sympathy on your loss.'

The sentiment was generous but the words decanted easily and the lack of warmth in the eyes of the orator betrayed every hallmark of insincerity.

'I appreciate your comments Mr Crake. My father was an excellent man who served the family with honour and distinction.'

'So it would seem, so it would seem,' replied the lawyer as he sieved through a heap of documents Glyder had suddenly poured onto the desk. From where we were positioned it was not possible to clock everything but the haul included title deeds, bank books and accounts together with a large bundle of railway and shipping debentures, a wad of marriage and death certificates with a sheath of old photographs and a few pieces of jewelry rolling out at the end. There followed a brief murmured exchange between principal and employee as they checked the contents against an inventory at the conclusion of which exercise the solicitor passed everything back except for a solitary document bound in crimson ribbon. Glyder returned the surplus material and snapping the lid shut placed the box on the floor by the grandfather clock and resumed his seat at the table. I switched my attention to Crake who was unfurling an exquisitely inscribed parchment over the table in front of us.

'Edmund, you see in front of you the form of assent that gives effect to Lord William's intentions regarding your future education. You will recall the Will directed the trustees to invest the sum of three thousand pounds in ten year Treasury Stock, the interest thereof to be applied to the continued full time education of your brother and yourself with the capital to vest absolutely and equally in you both when the last of you- we shall assume Alfred – completes university. If you are in agreement I suggest we make arrangements for the fund to address any fees as and when these are presented with the balance of the accumulated income to be paid each quarter day from the firm's trustee account at William and Glynns. Alfred, not being of full age, is unable to take the income in his own right but I deduce that if the sum is paid to you directly, you will manage it for the both. I regret we didn't get the opportunity to speak at the reading or I would have explained the proposals at that time and given my personal assurance then, as I do now, that we shall be administering his lordships' bequests to you as speedily and efficiently as possible.'

'The proposals seem sensible and practicable. I take it that the absolute legacy of three thousand pounds to my father will be paid forthwith so it can be processed with the remainder of his estate?'

'Of course. Lord William was a rich man and while most of his assets are tied up in property and bonds, there remains ample liquidity to meet all of his pecuniary bequests.'

'Lord William's settlement upon my brother and I is extremely generous don't you think?'

Crake looked up from his papers for a moment, his eyes razor sharp behind their thick lenses.

'Ah Mr Bullick,' he sighed, handing over a pen, 'you will appreciate we lawyers are not engaged to form opinions on such matters. Our duty is to give effect the intentions of the deceased and no more although as I have already made clear, Lord William held your father in the highest regard so the degree of his generosity might not be wholly unexpected. Now if you would care to sign the form of assent just there at the bottom of the page then I shall invite my clerk and Mr Brentnall here to witness the same and you can be on your way.'

'I'm not signing anything,' said Tom.

There was an uncomfortable silence as Crake and Glyder looked up with a mixture of surprise and incredulity. Glyder turned uneasily to his master as the latter removed his glasses and slowly placed them on the desk in front of him.

'Excuse me?'

'He said he's not signing anything Mr Crake, and neither am I.' Crake turned his cold grey eyes upon me, every trace of his previous attempt at civility dissolved in the moment. 'You won't sign? What, neither of you?'

I shook my head.

'Good grief. Why ever not? Can you not see that Lord William has been extraordinarily generous and that his bequests will make you a very wealthy young man?'

I held his gaze. Glyder stopped taking notes and began fidgeting nervously.

'I see it clearly Mr Crake but I am not persuaded that you have disclosed the whole of Lord William's instructions.'

'Oh indeed? And might I enquire the basis for this inclination? You were present at the reading, indeed as a beneficiary you are entitled to a copy of the instrument and I shall see that you have one as soon as the original and death certificate are returned by the probate office. I can assure you that this is Lord William's only Will, there is no other document and if my office is to make distribution according to his bidding I must insist upon your cooperation, indeed I suggest it is a matter of honour and duty to the deceased's memory that you render me nothing less.'

There was another awkward silence. I looked into the crumpled faces of the solicitor and his clerk and remember thinking Glyder's eyebrows badly needed a trim. A seagull hopped along the window ledge and cried a warning that brought me to my senses.

'Mr Crake, it is precisely because of my respect for Lord William's memory that I am not prepared to sign this document or any other document. I won't do it; not today or any other day and the reason I won't do it is because just before he died, Lord William called me to his deathbed and told me he had altered the succession to the estate. That's right; he confided in me that Julian had been disinherited. You seem surprised. Why do you look surprised? You know I speak the truth because only a few weeks ago Lord William himself came here to this office and gave you specific instructions regarding the matter. The document you read out with such aplomb in the library the other week, that was not the deceased's Will, or at least not his last and true Will. I know this because as he was dying, Lord William told me he had changed the succession; he also told me that you could be trusted to give effect to his revised intentions and with his very last breath he urged that I treat with you. In these circumstances I find it somewhat disingenuous that you should be lecturing me about fidelity and loyalty.'

As I spoke these words the solicitor steadily turned purple and I thought he was about to explode. However, after a moment's reflection Crake appeared to think the better of whatever he was about to say and recovering some of his earlier poise, leaned across the desk so his face was close to mine.

'You *dare* to come here into my office and accuse me of misfeasance and corruption?' he hissed. 'After all I have done for the estate over the years, after all my efforts to try and expedite the administration so you and your brother are not out on the street and you *dare* to come here and speak to me in this manner?'

It was no time for feint hearts.

'Oh, I most certainly do dare it Mr Crake,' I replied, handing back the pen. 'I dare it because I know you have another document in your possession which gives effect to the true intentions of Lord William. I know this because Lord William told me so himself and it seems to me that it would save a great deal of time and trouble for everyone concerned if you abandoned this ludicrous charade and started to address your professional obligations with the degree of integrity and transparency that Lord William expected of you.'

I wondered if I had gone too far but it needed to be said.

The reaction, though, was inevitable. Crake slammed his fist on the table and sprang to his feet, his face like thunder.

'How dare you. How *dare* you. I ought to have you arrested for criminal slander. Get out of my office, both of you, now. Get out before I call the police.'

'If that's your wish sir then of course we shall leave' said Tom coolly, 'but before you close the door on us we should tell you we have evidence.'

'Evidence? Evidence?' shouted Crake as he started across the floor. 'What, the unsubstantiated, uncorroborated ramblings of a delirious dying man? You call that evidence? The poor fellow was stark raving mad at the end. Dr Addison has already given a statement to the Coroner as to his Lordships capacity and his expert opinion is unimpeachable, or are you intending to attack the good doctor's professional integrity as well? Now get out.'

Tom and I climbed to our feet and made to leave.

'We have other evidence' I said defiantly.

Crake stood by the door and held it open.

'Oh really? Such as?'

'We have documents in our possession that substantiate Lord William's true intentions.'

'Documents? What documents? If you are referring to the file of papers you stole from the Coroner's office you can take those out of the equation straight away.'

The words didn't register at first. What did he say? How the hell did he know that? And then the scales fell from my eyes and I nearly threw up.

'That's right Mr Bullick. You're not the only one who made provision for this interview. And as for you Brentnall, you insolent whelp; do you know the penalty for burglary?'

Tom, who must have been equally shocked by this ghastly turn of events, responded with admirable calm.

'Burglary? Who, me?' he replied loftily. 'I haven't the faintest idea what you're talking about.'

'Oh, I think you do Mr Brentnall. My information is the two of you broke into the Dryburn mortuary only – when was it Mr Glyder – the week before last? Thank you, yes only the week before last. You know, right in the middle of Lord Julian's coming out party hoping no one would miss you? Surely you haven't forgotten already?'

'You can't prove a thing,' said Tom.

'Is that right? Then you've clearly never heard of fingerprint evidence, how the lines and grooves of our digits are unique personal characteristics, and that no two peoples' are the same? My contacts at Durham constabulary inform me that following recent advances in science, any impressions left on furniture and glass surfaces can now be lifted and examined through a forensic dusting process – not dissimilar in fact to establishing the trace of a nib from, say, the lower page of a diary. One word from me and they will go over Sergeant Tench's office with a toothcomb. Would you care to take that chance Mr Brentnall?'

My heart sank. Was there anything he didn't know? I stole a glance at Tom to catch an expression of utter bewilderment. We had been betrayed. It was Crake's moment of triumph and he seized it.

'Mr Bullick, I've a good mind to call the police and have you arrested here and now. What the two of you have done amounts to blatant obstruction of His Majesty's Coroner in the execution of his duty, conduct only exacerbated by the ungodly nature of the undertaking together with your total lack of remorse and impertinence to me this afternoon. Have you given any thought as to how long you'd get at the local assizes? Well, have you? Four years I'd say, maybe five with nothing to look forward to thereafter but the hopeless task of trying to rehabilitate yourself into a society that would never forgive the revolting nature of your crime. And your younger brother Alfred? In your blinkered self-serving pursuit of this crock of shit about Lord Julian being disinherited, did you ever spare a thought as to how he would manage with his only guardian and protector banged up? Well? Answer me? Did you?'

There was nothing I could say. There was no point. The game was up and all I could do was stand there and curse my own stupidity. Crake sustained his harangue, on and on he went calling us every label under the sun until after a while I ceased listening altogether. How could I have let myself fall into the trap? Damn it. Damn it. Damn it. Eventually, Crake fell silent as if gathering his thoughts before resuming in an unexpectedly conciliatory tone.

'Mr Bullick, I do not deny that Lord William came to see me a few weeks ago. It is no secret he was a regular visitor to the office although this is hardly surprising considering his substantial shipping interests in the town. You will appreciate I am bound by client confidentiality as to the substance of our discussions but you should understand here and now that there was never, *ever* the slightest suggestion of Lord Julian being disinherited or of his father altering the succession or any other aspect of his will. Absolutely none. When his Lordship died he left behind only the one Will, the contents of which have already been imparted. The instrument in question was drawn up personally by me in 1905 and that there has never been any amendment or codicil to it I can appeal to the testimony of my partners, and my clerk Mr Glyder here.'

Crake was compelling and I realised if he ever took the stand in this mode, the court would swallow every syllable. The man was a pillar of the establishment while Tommy and I were, well, nothing. I even started to doubt what Lord William had told me. I couldn't help it. Maybe he had been delirious after all? What was certain was that if Crake brought in the authorities we were done for. Damn it. Damn it. Damn it. How could I have been so blind? Regroup. We needed to regroup and recognizing there was no more to be achieved in the office, I caught Tom's eye and flicked my head that it was time to leave. We had reached the top of the stairs when the solicitor unexpectedly called after us.

'Wait. Come back in here and close the door.'

We followed his bidding and shuffled awkwardly in front of the desk as Crake resumed his seat and looked up with his chin resting on linked fingers. If the stakes hadn't been so high, it would have reminded me of a rollicking in the headmaster's study.

'Gentlemen, now that we understand each other I want you both to listen to me and listen well as though your very future depends upon what I am going to say, because believe me it does. The only thing stopping me from turning the two of you over to the police right now is my desire to avoid tainting his lordship's reputation with your outrageous conduct, if this is at all possible. So let me tell you what I am prepared to do, although believe you me it is against my better judgement. The time is now- Mr Glyder? Just approaching four thirty? Thank you – just approaching four thirty on Tuesday the fifteenth. This evening I am travelling to Newcastle on business and do not expect to return until late Thursday. Between now and then I shall leave this deed of assent open, that is until close of business the day after tomorrow. When I return Mr Bullick, I expect to find that you have signed it – and Mr Brentnall, I expect you to have witnessed it – so that the estate can be distributed in accordance with Lord William's intentions. On the understanding you will make the necessary arrangements with my clerk here and the document is attested by you both upon my return, we shall put this unsavoury episode behind us. If you decline, I shall immediately report everything I know to the authorities and the two of you can rot in hell for all I care. You have forty eight hours to decide. Do I make myself clear?'

Our position was hopeless. Crake held the aces and he knew it. 'Do we have a choice?' I replied.

'I suggest not. Mr Brentnall?'

'The expression *short and curlies* springs to mind Mr Crake.'

'Indeed it does Mr Brentnall, and you and your friend here would do well to remember it.'

Crake leaned forward and rang a hand bell on the edge of his desk.

'Well gentlemen, I believe that concludes our business for this afternoon. Thank you so much for attending. Mrs Crane will show you to the door. Now get out.'

We retraced our route along the twisted passageway and through reception before stepping into an arctic blast filleting the length of Church Street. Tom hugged the wrap of his coat and kicked the pavement.

'I can't believe it. I can't. How the *hell* does he know all that? *How?* It isn't possible.'

There was an awkward silence. Better get it out.

'It's my fault.'

'What do you mean?'

'Victoria'.

'What? Clifford? What about her?'

'I did try to tell you.'

Tom studied me for a moment then brought his hands to his head.

'Oh no. *Please* don't tell me you took that brat into your confidence? You didn't did you?'

Silence.

'You did? Oh no. You did, didn't you? Oh Ed, I thought you were having me on.'

'I wish I was'

Tom turned away and kicked the ground again

'You *idiot*. You bloody idiot.'

'I know.'

'What was the last thing, *the very last thing* I said to you before we parted the other week? Make sure you keep the safe locked I said. 'Oh yes' you said 'I'll make sure' you said and now this. For fuck's sake man how could you fall for it? What were you thinking of?'

Crake was looking down at us from his window. I lowered my voice so not to be overheard.

'It's easy for you to judge but it's not straightforward, believe me it's not; you didn't see the change in her. She was so, well, convincing and when she said she loved me and promised to help, I believed her. I don't expect you to understand, but at the time I thought I could trust her. In fact I was certain of it.'

Tom kicked the pavement again, his voice rising in frustration. 'Oh, I understand completely. She was sent in there to find out what you knew. She could see your brain was in your trousers so she told you what you wanted to hear; it's the oldest trick in the world mate and like the bloody fool that you are you fell for it. For heaven's sake man, after everything we went through, after all the risks we took to get that file and you go and chuck it away and for what? The hopeless, brainless, blinkered pursuit of an unattainable cow like that? Sheesh.'

The words seared and I began to get angry.

'All right, all right you've said your piece now give it a rest. It's not as if I've lost anything I ever had in the first place. Yes, I misjudged her. Yes, it was a hideous mistake but there's bugger all I can do about it now and believe me, I'll pay a heavier price for my folly than you could ever understand.'

'Oh, like you love her and thought she really loved you and now it breaks your heart to discover she was lying all along? Love at first sight and all that? Yeah, right. Truth is she had your measure from the first. I told you before; self-seeking, avaricious little brats like Victoria Clifford love only themselves. And money of course. Themselves and money. I still can't believe you fell for it. What were you thinking of? You're a bloody fool mate.'

'Oh piss off.'

Someone called out from the other side of the street. 'Hey Edmund! Ed Bullick? Hoi, is that you?'

I turned to see a clump of soldiers loitering outside the tobacconists.

'It's me, Alix, Alix Liddle' shouted one. 'You know, from the ammunition train last month?'

So it was. I raised a hand in acknowledgement at which Liddle jumped into a gap between a tram and a coal cart and sprinted across.

'Well this is a turn up for the books,' said he pumping my arm. 'What brings you to Hartlepool?'

'I had some business with my father's lawyers. We've literally just finished and are heading to the railway station.'

'What, you mean you're going back this minute?' he cried motioning over to his colleagues. 'Balls to that. Look, me and the lads over there, we've just knocked off and are going for a few beers. Why don't you join us?'

In any other circumstances I might have been tempted, but at that precise moment the thought of participating in any form of joviality was distinctly unappealing.

'Thanks for the offer Alix but I'd sooner not. To be honest things are not great just now and if it's all the same, I'd rather get home.'

Alix unfastened his arms in supplication.

'What, go home when you're down in the dumps? Nonsense. Come on man, a couple of drinks won't do you any harm. What else are you going to do for the rest of the day? Slide into an ever-deepening gloom? Come on, you need cheering up, you know you do and while you're at it you can tell me how you got on after we dropped you off at the station. Who's your friend by the way?'

'I'm so sorry Alix, forgive me, this is Tommy Brentnall, a mate of mine from college. Tommy, this is Alix Liddle, the jockey on the train I told you about.'

Liddle shook hands then leaned forward to speak into Tom's ear. 'Now see here Tommy Brentnall with the purple eye, never mind your friend for a moment, you look to me like a man who could just do with a drink. The Camerons brew here is the best in the north and it would be disgraceful to leave town without first oiling your neck. Also we're a couple of blokes light for the darts match at the *Albion* later. What d'ye say?'

'What do I say? I think it's an excellent idea,' cried Tom unexpectedly. 'Oh come on Ed, don't frown like that. It's been an absolutely horrendous afternoon and I need a drink. Come on man. It's still early and there's plenty of trains.'

I thought about it for a moment. There was no specific reason to hurry back. Alfie would be home later but I'd already arranged for Jordan to collect him from the station. Sod it. Why not?

'Alix, we'd be delighted, but just a couple mind then we have to go home.'

CHAPTER TWENTY SEVEN

There were six of us in our party that evening; myself, Tom, Alix, a young lad who played the piano called Spence and two others from the DLI and needless to say it wasn't a couple of beers, it was considerably more. Those of you who drink will know the form. You go out with the best intentions of being circumspect in your consumption, but unless you actually stand up and leave at some point, you inevitably cross the threshold when all bets are off and any agenda goes out of the window. In my own case, I've subsequently learned I can horse three swift pints and just about keep to previous arrangements but any more than that and I might as well jump into a time machine. Tom says it's exactly the same with him. Three drinks is okay but any more and he never knows where he'll end up. Well, that night in the company of Liddle and his friends was one such occasion.

We started out in the *Freemasons* and then moved on to the *Commercial* where it had been our intention to have a final pint and then leave for the station until someone – probably Tom thinking about it- bought a double round and before I knew it we'd put our departure back a couple of hours so we could play darts with the rest of them down at *The Albion*. Needless to say the minute we stepped in there we crossed the Rubicon and as the drink flowed, it washed away our plans. In the sober light of day it can be difficult to understand such a violent change of perspective, but that's drinking for you and in *The Albion* that night we ended so far in our cups that time didn't seem to matter at all. Mind you, it's also true to say that the beer was as good as we had been told, Alix and his colleagues were great company and with the pub heaving for the match it was a really good night out. I can still smell the sawdust and the hops now and hear the old battered piano in the corner that Spence was hijacked to play, quickly gathering a wall of soldiers around him as they trotted through the favourites including *You Made Me Love You (I didn't want to do it), Daisy Daisy* and *Oh! Oh! Antonio*. There was also the excitement of the darts match, the prize for which turned out to be a silver cup and a crate of stout for the winning team. I'd always been a handy player and quickly found my stride although whether this was down to skill or the freedom of movement that comes with alcohol I couldn't say. I also had a really interesting conversation with Alix, catching up on events since we had parted on that drenched night at Durham station. He told me he had been training in Otterburn with the rest of the 18th DLI when two companies were posted to the town's defences on the Headland.

'In a word it's tedious,' he moaned. 'Like every day is the same as the one before, three hours of square-bashing followed by eight hours sentry duty on top of Parton Rocks. I mean, look at us all now, fit as fighting cocks and straining for action and the CO tells us this morning 'sorry lads but we're here for another six months'. Six months? It'll be summer before we get to the front, assuming the war's still on of course, which the way things are going seems unlikely.'

Alix's frustration was palpable although I could think of worse places to be holed up. Mind you, we didn't just talk about the conflict. In-between the singing and the darts we swapped and shared tales about horses and famous races and contemplated the future for the local tracks with the uncertainty of war. We figured York would survive and probably Ripon and Thirsk but the smaller courses such as Stockton and Catterick might have to close for the duration. Alix knew of Lord William's death and we discussed the impact of this together with the subsequent appointment of Budgett and whether his training methods were likely to differ from my father's.

I was suddenly aware of Tom leaning over the table. We'd not spoken for a while, in fact the last time I'd looked up he was arm wrestling with one of the locals.

'Ready for another chaps?'

I downed my drink including as much foam as I could tip out from the bottom and banged the empty glass on the table.

'Certainly am.'

'Alix? Same again?'

Alix grabbed my empty glass and clambered to his feet. 'No, no, it's my shout. We've gone round once. What'll it be?' I scanned our team and did a quick bit of arithmetic. Good Lord, so we had.

'What's this stuff we're drinking anyway?' I asked.

'It's called Lion bitter,' he replied as he gathered up the empties.

Tom studied his empty glass. 'What, Zion bitter? Never heard of it. Is it foreign?'

'No, not *Zion* bitter, *Lion* bitter. As in L-i-o-n. It's the local Camerons brew I was telling you about when we met in the street. Wonderful stuff don't you think?'

'I'm not sure,' I replied. 'I reckon I need a few more before I make up my mind'

'Well I don't,' cried Tom. 'I love it although at this rate we'll all be roaring drunk by the end of the night. Hah! Roaring drunk? Get it? *Lion* bitter? *Roaring* drunk?'

Well, when Tom said this it was one of those moments in your life where you absolutely crease yourself laughing until you find you can't stop. We couldn't help it, and the more we looked at each other the more the tears fell until it was virtually impossible to say anything at all. Neither did the hilarity end at our table for as others turned to see what was so funny, the quip sprouted wings until the whole bar was a cacophony of roaring and other jungle type noises. It was tremendous craic; I don't think I'd ever seen or heard anything so comical. Even the sour faced landlady forced a smile, although as the evening went by and people continued to roar at her it probably started to wear a bit thin. Eventually when we managed to calm down, and believe me it took a while, Tom and I stumbled off to the gents where I lit a couple of Woodbines and passed him one.

'Fabulous idea this mate,' I said clutching the cistern pipe for support. 'Don't think I've had such a laugh in ages.'

Tom was swaying at an adjacent urinal, his eyes fixed on the trough where he was clearing a dam of cigarette butts.

'Agreed *Blue*, agreed. Just what the love doctor ordered.'

'Love doctor? Bah, don't remind me. I wonder what she's doing right now. Probably making cow eyes at some other poor sod. The way we left it she was supposed to come and stay with me next week. I guess I can put a red line through that.'

Tom buttoned his fly and turned to the washbasins.

'Edmund, there's more chance of a nine legged lobster jumping out of that urinal and grabbing the end of your dick than of Victoria showing her face when you get back. Mind you, I'd have said the same about your chances of sleeping with her and it seems I was wrong about that. Tell me something, what exactly happened while I was away?'

A heavy boot at the door announced the entry of a couple of squaddies. Time to change the subject.

'When's the last train?'

Tom shrugged his shoulders.

'Dunno. Guess it leaves when it leaves doesn't it?'

His apathy was infectious.

'True. It wouldn't be the first time I'd spent the night in a waiting room. We might as well ask though. Perhaps Alix or Spence can tell us.'

We returned to the bar to catch Spence, fag in mouth, weaving his way to the table with a tray full of drinks. The ale was already sloshing over the sides when someone bumped him and a glass rolled off and smashed on the floor. Spence howled a curse and immediately flung the lot to the ground – glasses, beer, tray *et al* – just like that. It was astonishing; I'd never seen anything like it. Needless to say a huge sarcastic cheer went up at which one of the barmaids – who fortunately for Spence hadn't witnessed the event – came scuttling round with a mop and shovel leaving him to go back to the counter and roar for another round.

Tom took a drag of his Woodbine and exhaled a clutch of smoke rings that passed through one another like the segments of a telescope. I watched mesmerized as the hoops slowly lolled towards the ceiling where a huge moth was orbiting the solitary light bulb. Over at the piano Spence had resumed his place and struck up *Daddy Wouldn't Buy Me a Bow Wow* generating the usual howling and barking to add to all the roars.

'Look Ed, I didn't mean to have a go at you back there outside the office, and I'm sorry if it came across that way. I was just a bit pissed off after everything we went through to get the file.'

'Hey, it's not a problem' I countered. 'I'd have said pretty much the same if it had been you. I've been racking my brains working out how she did it. She must have rifled the safe when she slipped away this morning, the cow. Thing is, what are we going to do now?'

Tom took a large gulp and wiped the froth from his mouth. 'I suppose it depends if Crake means what he says about turning us in. Do you think he'd really do it?'

'I don't see he has a choice. If we refuse to cooperate he'll have to apply to Court where everything would come out and the judge would want to know why he hadn't acted sooner. Faced with that unpalatable option plus the delay for a listing he has to go to the police now, unless he can blackmail us first which is effectively what he's doing. He knows once we sign the agreement he'll have us where he wants us and there'll never be any comeback.'

'Seems he has us where he wants us already.'

'It rather looks that way doesn't it?'

Alix appeared with a fresh tray just as the landlady called last orders. Tom grabbed a glass and having drained the contents in a few gulps raced off to the counter to get them in again before the shutter came down. Meanwhile someone shouted from the dartboard for Alix and me to take our place at the okey. I'd not been following the game but it appeared it was the deciding leg, both teams were down to the bull and the first person to get it took the match. Alix threw and missed.

'What time's the last train to Stockton?'

'If that's the bell I'm afraid you're too late. They leave at four minutes past and the last was at ten. Sorry Ed. I should have said something before.'

'No, no, don't worry about it. We were coming back tomorrow anyway.'

'Have you anywhere to stay?'

There was a tap on my shoulder. Someone passed me a set of darts.

'Not yet. We'll probably take a room at *The Havelock*.'

'What, the week before Christmas?' cried Alix. 'You'll be lucky, especially rolling up this time of night with a bellyful of beer on board. Why don't you doss down with us? I'm sure we can sneak you in and it's got to be better than roughing it.'

The person in front of me failed to hit the target and it was now my turn. I shuffled to the okey trying to focus on the board through a tunnel of oscillating humanity. The first dart was a tracer and missed by some distance. The next struck the outer bull and bounced out. Suddenly there was a hush. Last throw. I recalled the softness of Victoria's knees in Hob Hole and thought of her black heart and summing up all the bitter sweetness inside screamed her name to myself and hurled viciously at the board. A most extraordinary thing happened. The throw was so wild the flight came away leaving the featherless arrow to cartwheel through the air, until it somehow managed to lodge itself the wrong way round just inside the wire of the bull's-eye. If I hadn't been there to see it myself I would never have believed it was possible but I tell you, that's exactly what happened. We all gaped at the board in astonishment until realising the angle was perilous and the dart could drop at any moment, I leaped forward and recovered it at which our little posse went crazy while everyone else in the bar screamed foul. In the mayhem that followed there was the usual pushing and shoving until eventually, one of the old timers was dragged through from the Snug to mediate. There was nothing in the rules, he said, that dictated which way round the dart had to enter the board nor how long it should remain in the matting, only that the projectile should pierce the intended section and remain there entrenched until it was retrieved by the participant. The throw was therefore good he said, an adjudication promptly endorsed by the landlady who, conscious of the hour, had her own reasons for ratifying the decision. And that as they say was that. Fluke or not we had prevailed and as if sufficient refreshment had not already been taken, to the inebriated victors went also the spoils and it was way after eleven when we finally tumbled into the street. As the door bolted behind us I sucked in the cold air and gawked at the unfamiliar landscape. Where the hell were we? I hadn't a clue. Tom must have been of the same mind for he suddenly piped up the refrain of *How Much Is That Doggy?*

*'Can somebody show me to my quarters? (woof!
woof!)
I haven't a clue-oo where to go (woof! woof!)*

Can somebody show me to my quarters? (woof! woof!
Vic-tor-i-a I love you so (WOOF! WOOF!)'

'Very funny. The *woof woof* bit was spot on though. Bah, when I think about her now, d'ye know what I think?'

'Nope. What do you think?'

'Woof! Woof!!' I yelled.

Tom looked up at the moon.

'How-wow-wow-wow-wowllll'.

Alix and Spence locking arms on the outside hadn't the faintest idea what we were on about but joined the chorus anyway as we clanked down Brougham Terrace with our crate of stout. Spence was next to burst into song, I knew the words to this one and followed suit with the rest.

Show me the way to go home
I'm tired and I want to go to bed
I had a little drink about an hour ago and it went
right to my head,
No matter where I roam...

A couple of policemen watched us from the junction of Turnbull Street.

'Hoi you lot' barked one. 'If you don't put a sock in that caterwauling you'll be roaming the glasshouse yard in the morning d'ye ken?'

We *kenned* all right and apologised profusely, all the time sniggering and 'shushing' as our tangle of bodies sloped off towards the harbour. As soon as we were clear, a couple of the lads began dribbling an empty milk bottle until it smashed against a warehouse door forcing us into the shadows in case there were any other bobbies around.

At the quayside we paused to relieve ourselves against an old rusty winch. The water was at high tide and all the fishing boats were bobbing up and down. On the far side a couple of destroyers building up steam for the dawn patrol. I stared down at the trails of urine snaking over the concrete as they merged and felt their way to the sea. It was like a minuscule version of the Nile Delta we had studied in Geography. I reflected on the contrast and thought it bizarre how such an obvious comparison had only manifested itself in drink.

When we reached the Headland Alix cut through some damaged railings onto the Town Moor, a large area of spiky-silver pasture that glistered in the frost then turned to dust as it measured our footprints. The silhouette of the battery fortifications loomed large on the skyline while over on the point, the Heugh lighthouse tirelessly swept the old town, its beam cutting over Saint Hilda's churchyard and across a small city of bell tents flapping away on top of the dunes. We stopped to pee again, this time against a giant roller we found on the edge of the heath. I leant back and gazed up to the sky. It was a crisp, clear night and as the six of us watered the ground there must have been a billion stars gazing down from space. Alix and the others went ahead to square things with the guards leaving Tom and me in the company of an old donkey that came out of the shadows to see what was going on. I felt his muzzle searching my pockets and scratched his ears.

'Hello there fellah, what's your name then?'

The donkey gave a soft bray as he tried to draw my handkerchief with his teeth. Tom pulled out a cut of liquorish and stroked the animal's little woolly neck.

'According to Alix he was rescued from Blackhall Colliery at the end of his working days. He'd have been put down otherwise. Now he lives here on the Moor where he spends his old age giving rides to the children. The lads from the battery love him and are always coming over with apples and other treats.'

Spence returned from the garrison with a flashlight.

'We're sorted. We can't get you into the compound as it's a restricted area, but some of the NCO's are billeted round the corner and you can crash down with them.'

What a relief. The cold air had started to hit me and I was about done in. We bade a noisy farewell at the gates then Tom and I stumbled off with one of the batmen who came out to show us the way. Five minutes later we were tucked up in an attic room at the end of Bath Terrace watching the lighthouse beam sweep across the ceiling.

'Eight and a half seconds,' declared Tom.

'What is?'

'The time it takes to do a revolution.'

'Did Jane track you down after the hunt?' I asked quietly.

'She did.'

'And?'

'And what?'

'How did you get on?'

'Very well. I've invited her to my parents at New Year.'

'Julian will go mad.'

'Suppose so.'

We listened to the tide sloshing against the sea wall below. 'Tell me something Ed, how did you manage it? I mean get Victoria into bed? How did you do it?'

'You wouldn't believe me if I told you.'

314

'Try me.'

'No. You'll only laugh.'

'Like you'll laugh at me when I run naked down York Shambles?'

I snorted loudly. I'd forgotten about that.

'Let's just say I thought a man with faith could move mountains. How wrong can you be, hey?'

'Don't let your bitterness consume you. You got your heart's desire didn't you?'

'I wish I'd never met her.'

'I doubt that very much'.

'I mean it.'

'Look Ed, no one enjoys being turned over, of course they don't, but you can't tell me the hurt you feel now is anything as painful as the desire that went before.'

'It's worse. I love her Tom. I can't help it, even after what she's done. My life wasn't great before she crashed into it but at least it was my own. Now it's in tatters.'

'No it's not.'

'It's true. I'll never love anyone else.'

'Yes you will.'

I counted the revolutions, all the while agonizing who Victoria might be sleeping with right now and if her partner knew she was still warm from going to bed with me.

'You're going to sign aren't you?' said Tom yawning.

'I don't see we have a choice. Do you?'

Tom grunted an acknowledgement.

'We'll stop off at Crake's office first thing tomorrow. Might as well do it on the way to the station. What do you think? Tom?'

Tom didn't answer. He was already snoring.

CHAPTER TWENTY EIGHT

I dreamt I was lying in a field of corn being kicked by Sparks. 'Get up! Now! Quickly! You have to get up!'

I stirred to unfamiliar surroundings, the blows continuing as I struggled to remember where I was.

'You have to get up! Get up! Get up!'

I wiped my eyes to see Alix stride over to the window and tear back the curtains.

'You've got to get out of here lads. Now. Tom, you as well. Quickly!'

I swung to the edge of the bed and fumbled for my boots. 'Good heavens Alix, what on earth's the matter?'

'I don't know yet,' he cried breathlessly. 'I thought it was just another drill but we've been issued live ammunition.'

'What time is it?' asked Tom yawning.

'Seven fifty. We should have been stood down ages ago. Something's not right. You have to get out of here.'

Tom and I trailed Alex into the street where one of the orderlies ran up to him.

'*HMS Doon* reports unidentified vessels six miles off the headland sir. Colonel Robson has called action stations.'

Alix frowned. 'It's probably another drill but the CO won't take any chances. You'd better get yourselves to the railway station lads, quick as you can and I'll see you when I see you.'

Alix and the orderly ran across the moor and disappeared into a gun emplacement on top of the dunes. We would have left for the station but with Crake's office not open yet, we decided to kill some time and merged with a few of the locals who had come out of their homes and were lining the railings. I scanned the horizon to see what all the fuss was about but the light was poor with visibility further restricted by spray and a rolling mist. Someone yelling into a bullhorn turned my attention to the three giant guns guarding the estuary, the nearest just behind the lighthouse with a couple more poking out of the cliff next to Alix's emplacement. I traced their long dark barrels pointing menacingly over the North Sea and realised the defences were even more formidable than they had appeared when we tumbled home the previous evening.

Tom stamped around blowing into cupped palms. 'Well I can't see a thing mate. Come on. Let's go. Its bloody freezing and I'm as bad as a dog.'

I couldn't see anything either. I wiped my eyes but there was nothing; just an empty grey canvass spattered with a few gulls. The far off bells of St Aiden's chimed eight o clock. The sea air filled my lungs and I suddenly felt very hungry. We'd give it a couple more minutes then head into town and find a cafe.

Just then a clamour of excitement rippled along the wall.

'Ye Gods!' cried an elderly man next to me.

I turned back to the horizon where about a mile from the

shore an enormous grey warship ghosted out of the mist. It was the largest, most magnificent vessel I had ever seen in my life, sleek as a whippet but with tier upon tier of huge guns and rigging so tall it scraped the overhanging bank of fog.

'It's a white Ensign!' cried the old boy. 'Three cheers for His Majesty's navy'.

'Thank goodness for that,' answered Tom, 'because there's another two Dreadnaughts behind it.'

Even as he spoke a second battlecruiser and then a third glided out of the mist and lined up behind the first with all three facing the town. For a moment we gazed at them spellbound until without warning, a massive orange flash erupted on the stern of the first vessel followed by a large explosion that engulfed the whole in a dense cloud of smoke.

'It's blown up!' cried a woman behind me. 'It's blown up! The ship's just blown up!'

I was about to say something when the air filled with a terrific rushing noise like the sound of the wind passing through telegraph wires.

'Oh my God they're Germans!' shrieked Tom. 'They're firing on us! The bastards are firing on us! Get down! Get down!

We plunged behind the wall just as the first shell smashed on top of Alix's gun emplacement where in appalling slow motion, the occupants were lifted high into the air before tumbling back to earth like rag dolls with bloody, mangled limbs. Amid the pitiful screams of the wounded someone bellowed for stretcher bearers but just as help reached them, a second salvo crashed down next to the first blowing everyone and everything to kingdom come. I gaped in disbelief at the smoking pit where Alix and his companions had been. We had only been talking to him a few minutes earlier and now there was nothing.

At the seawall everyone started running for their lives, the parents shepherding the little ones into what they thought would be the safety of their homes while out in the estuary, all three cruisers joined the slaughter with the largest exchanging volleys with the battery while the other two began pouring shells into the unsuspecting town. The noise was absolutely and utterly deafening; I'd never heard anything like it, each earsplitting crack ringing over the terraces like thunder, rattling all the windows and scattering the gulls. I watched mesmerized as a canister skimmed off the fortifications and burst at the back of the moor where it blew away the old donkey and his little timber home. Another projectile the size of a milk churn crashed through the roof of Saint Hilda's. I screamed at Tom to make for the railway station but he was already ahead of me and as we sprinted down Cliff Terrace, I chanced a final look over my shoulder to see the sky filling with miniscule black orbs that grew bigger and bigger until they smashed into the streets around us tearing down buildings and sending debris and fragments of twisted metal fizzing through the air.

Tom and I ran like the wind not stopping for breath until we reached the junction of Northgate and Durham Street. Everywhere we looked it was the same pitiful scene of misery and confusion as in the absence of the men who had left for work, the terrified women and children started pouring into the streets, many of them only half dressed. Looking back, they would have been far safer indoors but oblivious to what was happening, their instinct was to get away at all costs, not realising they risked being blown to pieces in the open, as indeed many of them were.

We tore through the docks as fast as our legs could carry us, all the while stalked by the merciless *swee swee swee* of destruction raining down from the skies, and how we were not killed that morning like so many others is a mystery that I have never been able to comprehend. All through the town, between the Headland and the railway station, buildings were being toppled like stacks of cards while in the harbour several vessels were hit including a new steamer which was struck in the hull, the shell passing in at one side and out at the other. Bizarrely, I don't remember being so much afraid as utterly overwhelmed with a sense of excitement that had neither fear nor horror in it, because it was too full of awe.

We left the quayside behind and raced by shops, churches and houses all completely destroyed with furniture and people blown into the road and, in one case, a bloodstained bed blasted onto the roof. A tramway office between the two Hartlepools and the headquarters of the *Northern Daily Mail* were completely wrecked, a telegraph pole in front of the latter carried away in an eruption of earth and masonry as if it were matchwood. Another shell smashed into the side of the *Mill House Inn* barely seconds after we had passed, totally obliterating the frontage of the building before crashing through a party wall to bring down the house next door. Everywhere around us it was the same: nothing but destruction and misery as the westward road out of town started to choke with tearstained women and children running for their lives, many of them still in the nightclothes they were wearing when the attack began.

As we rounded the corner into Brougham Terrace we came across an upturned milk float where the still harnessed pony was struggling to get to its feet. The beautifully painted cart to which he was attached had splintered like balsa, while a shard of glass had lodged in the animal's throat from which blood was spraying over the smashed bottles and eggs. I ran across and put my fist in the wound to try and stem the flow but as I frantically looked about for a soldier or policeman who would have a revolver, the animals' eyes misted over and I could only watch helplessly and cradle him as he expired.

In Dene Street a whole section of terrace had collapsed and we could hear the most appalling cries coming from under the rubble. There was already a human chain in place and as we frantically clawed away with the others, I became aware of a small group of children standing over a bundle of rags further down the pavement. We screamed at them to get inside but they refused to move so I ran across to discover what looked like a side of butcher's meat a boy was rolling about with his foot. He could only have been about seven or eight and was holding hands with a young girl who cried over and over again it was her 'da'. I looked to the ground and realised she was pointing at the top section of a man's leg with crushed bones and tattered flesh. Her brother wailed that the rest of the body 'was blown into Middleton Road'. I swept the children up and ran into the nearest house where I passed them to the occupants who were taking cover under the kitchen table.

The explosion in Dene Street caused great execution as I discovered when I rejoined the human chain down which the limbless trunk of a young woman was brought into the street. A shell splinter had torn away the back of the poor girl's head and as we carried her out, globs of brain tissue like fish roe dripped onto our hands and clothes. There was nothing we could do for her and it was left to a passing doctor to lay his thumb and forefinger over the eyes and close them forever. Other shattered bodies swiftly followed, some of them children, each one laid out beside the first and this the yield of a single shell that did nothing but perform its function. As I surveyed the carnage around me, I realised the device had been manufactured for this very purpose, to be dispatched into crowded streets and there to burst and destroy peoples' homes and tear flesh from flesh. I'd always been brought up with splendid tales of the Boer War and patriotism and King and Country, but as I blenched at the pavement that morning, every glorious notion of combat with which I had been indoctrinated was vanquished forever.

When we reached the station it was to discover hundreds of others already converging, so much so that those at the head of the crush were tumbling through the barriers and onto the track. A train was on the point of leaving and a guard was actually running down the carriages slamming the doors when a ghostly whooshing noise sent everyone scrambling for cover. I looked to the skies to see the first missile overshoot the terminal and land in the marshalling yard where it threw a string of trucks into the air as if they were toys. A second shell headed straight for us, spinning over and over but just as I braced myself for the end, it clanged off the road and smashed through the station wall onto the platform where, incredibly, it failed to explode. I watched helplessly as through the dust and flying bricks, the terrified passengers leaped out of their carriages and ran blindly down the track. At the same time the horrified spectators outside the station turned and charged back into town, panic ensuing as amid the crashing of further shells, masonry falling and glass breaking came also the petrified screams of the men, women and children.

Several areas of the town were now on fire and with the railway out of action, escape was impossible. We didn't know how much longer the bombardment would last, or indeed if we were about to be invaded. The only certainty was that if we remained above ground, we were going to be killed and it was as we tore along Church Street looking for a basement that we came upon the wrecked offices of Baxter, Crake and Lockwood.

CHAPTER TWENTY NINE

The damage to the lawyers' premises was so severe that it was impossible to equate what was left of the building to the scene of our Waterloo but a few hours before. The striking Georgian fascia had virtually disappeared, the remnants condensed into a stew of bricks and timber completely exposing the interior, with all the furniture battered and broken like a dolls house on the wrong end of a child's temper tantrum. A fire was raging in one of the downstairs rooms and clouds of thick black smoke were spewing into the road together with hundreds and hundreds of papers, some of which were picked up by the wind and sent spiraling over the rooftops. I looked at Tom. He was absolutely caked in blood and filth but even as I motioned to the ruins, I knew he was of the same mind.

I scanned the street. Some people at the top were trying to flag down a runaway horse but there was no one else in sight. It was now or never. The opportunity would not come again. I climbed into the empty fascia, Tom following on, both of us knowing that at any moment what remained of the building could come crashing down and entomb us.

We groped our way through the dust and smoke until we reached the staircase. The planks and spindles were already smouldering in the heat; it was only a matter of time before they, too, caught fire but there was no other way up. Without pausing for breath we raced to the top hurdling a section of missing stairs on the way up. In the lopsided corridor the exterior wall was blown out and we were soaked by a deluge of water cascading down from the loft. Crake's office lay before us. I tried the handle. It was locked.

'We can't give up now' yelled Tom. 'Come on. Kick it down!'

We were greeted a scene of utter devastation. All the windows were blown in, the furniture and paneling reduced to matchwood while several beams and most of the ceiling had collapsed on top of the files and documents giving the chamber the appearance of an enormous builder's skip. Attempting to locate the Fitzroy-Cavendish trust papers among such chaos would have been impossible save that incredibly, the black metal strongbox in which they were retained was still intact by the wreckage of the grandfather clock, exactly where Glyder had left it.

A few streets away there was the most terrific explosion as the gasworks went up blowing in the remainder of the glass. All the while the crackle of flame from downstairs grew louder.

'Hurry man!' yelled Tom. 'The whole place is about to go!'

I tipped the box and plunged into the contents, pausing at a sheaf of birth and death certificates.

'Check these.'

At the bottom of the mound was the codicil I had been looking for. It was dated Tuesday 20 October 1914 and I leaped to the first amendment dealing with the stables.

Clause 1

I direct that the Craven Racing Stables and Equine Stud Company, continue to be managed after my death by the said James Michael Bullick or in the event that he shall predecease me or otherwise be unable to accept the appointment I direct that the management of the said enterprise shall first be offered to the said Edmund James Bullick or thereafter to such person, persons or organisation as my trustees in their absolute discretion shall direct.

'Tom, this is incredible! He made another Will and nominated me to succeed Dad as trainer!'

Tom was absorbed with his own pile of documents.

'You need to look at this.'

I ignored him and shot back to the text.

Clause 2

I hereby revoke clause thirty-seven of my original Will...

'Oh my God Tom, he's altered the succession...'

The remainder of my estate including all land, livestock, buildings, shares and all other investments...

'Edmund, you need to see this.'

*…in Great Britain and overseas, and all other
property, possessions and personal chattels,
whatsoever and wheresoever …*

'Ed, you have to look at this'

*…together with the hereditary seat, the castle and
grounds of Craven, and title of Marquis I devise and
bequeath to my son…*

'He changed it!' I shouted. 'He changed the succession! He's
changed it!'

Tom grabbed my shoulders and shook me violently.

'Will you shut up! Just shut up! Look at this. LOOK AT
THIS!'

I snatched a birth certificate from his outstretched hand
and jumped to the principals. William Fitzroy-Cavendish
was one. Derina Bullick was the other. I stared at the name
to the side and then back to the codicil.

Oh my God.

It was Alfie.